AFTER PRISON

AFTER PRISON

Navigating Adulthood in the Shadow of the Justice System

David J. Harding and
Heather M. Harris

Russell Sage Foundation
New York

The Russell Sage Foundation

Library of Congress Cataloging-in-Publication Data

Names: Harding, David J., 1976- author. | Harris, Heather M., author.
Title: After prison : navigating adulthood in the shadow of the justice system /
David J. Harding, UC Berkeley, Heather M. Harris, Public Policy Institute of California.
Description: New York, New York : Russell Sage Foundation, 2020. | Includes bibliographical references
and index. | Summary: "The incarceration rate in the United States is the highest of any developed
nation, with a population of approximately 2.3 million in 2016. Over 700,000 prisoners are released
each year, and they face significant educational, economic, and social disadvantages. After Prison:
Navigating Adulthood in the Shadow of the Justice System, by sociologists David J. Harding and
Heather M. Harris, focuses on the lives of 1,300 black and white youth aged 18 to 25 who were released
from Michigan prisons in 2003." — Provided by publisher.
Identifiers: LCCN 2020008904 (print) | LCCN 2020008905 (ebook) |
ISBN 9780871544490 (paperback) | ISBN 9781610448918 (ebook)
Subjects: LCSH: Criminals—Rehabilitation—Michigan. |
Ex-convicts—Rehabilitation—Michigan. |
Ex-convicts—Education—Michigan. | Social integration—Michigan. |
Prisoners—Deinstitutionalization—Michigan.
Classification: LCC HV9305.M5 H37 2020 (print) | LCC HV9305.M5 (ebook) |
DDC 364.809754—dc23
LC record available at https://lccn.loc.gov/2020008904
LC ebook record available at https://lccn.loc.gov/2020008905

RUSSELL SAGE FOUNDATION
112 East 64th Street, New York, New York 10065
10 9 8 7 6 5 4 3 2 1

Contents

List of Illustrations |

About the Authors |

DAVID J. HARDING is professor of sociology and faculty director of the Social Science Data Lab at the University of California, Berkeley.

HEATHER M. HARRIS is a research fellow at the Public Policy Institute of California.

MICHAEL MENEFEE is a doctoral candidate in sociology at the University of California, Berkeley.

VÉRONIQUE IRWIN is a doctoral candidate in sociology at the University of California, Berkeley.

JOE LABRIOLA is a doctoral candidate in sociology at the University of California, Berkeley.

KEUNBOK LEE is a postdoctoral fellow at the California Center for Population Research at the University of California, Los Angeles.

Acknowledgments |

THE MICHIGAN STUDY of Life after Prison is a long-term collaboration with Jeffrey Morenoff of the University of Michigan. We are deeply indebted to him for his intellectual and practical contributions to the larger project. This project would also not have been possible without the guidance, generosity, and commitment of the Michigan Department of Corrections (MDOC), particularly its research and evaluation unit and senior management. MDOC staff and leadership helped us to secure access to the data, educated us on the daily processes of Michigan's correctional systems and policies, and counseled us on the interpretation of the data. They may not agree with all that we have written here—the conclusions presented in this book are our own—but we have aspired to be true to the wisdom they have shared with us based on their many years of experience in public service. We especially appreciate the contributions of Doug Kosinski, Steve DeBor, Jeff Anderson, Ken Dimoff, Dennis Schrantz, and former director Patricia Caruso.

We owe a special debt of gratitude to Paulette Hatchett and Charley Chilcote. Paulette was an integral adviser to this project from the start, providing access to the administrative data and mentoring University of Michigan project staff at the MDOC headquarters in Lansing. During the project, Paulette retired from state service, but she remained an essential adviser on a regular basis for many years regarding MDOC practices and data systems. Charley provided a critical jump-start to the data collection, creating and guiding the process of coding the parole agent case notes that became the core of the administrative data on which this project relies. His commitment to producing high-quality data was central to the project's success. This project would not have been possible without the devotion and generosity of both Paulette and Charley.

Many research assistants worked on coding, cleaning, and analyzing the administrative data for the Michigan Study of Life after Prison. We thank Brenda Hurless, Bianca Espinoza, Andrea Garber, Jonah Siegal,

Jay Borchert, Amy Cooter, Jane Rochmes, Claire Herbert, Jon Tshiamala, Katie Harwood, Elizabeth Sinclair, Carmen Gutierrez, Joanna Wu, Clara Rucker, Michelle Hartzog, Tyrell Connor, Madie Lupei, Brandon Cory, Elizabeth Johnston, Ed-Dee Williams, Steve Anderson, Megan Thornhill, Tyler Sawher, and Da Eun Jung.

We are also indebted to our colleagues whose advice helped to shape the design and implementation of the data collection. We thank Sarah Burgard, Elizabeth Bruch, Bill Axinn, Yu Xie, Jennifer Barber, Sandra Smith, Bruce Western, Becky Pettit, Chris Winship, Rob Sampson, Dave Kirk, Chris Wildeman, Kristin Turney, Sara Wakefield, Chris Uggen, Megan Comfort, Andrea Leverentz, Issa Kohler-Hausman, Shawn Bushway, John Laub, Mario Small, Scott Allard, Kurt Metzger, David Martin, Steve Heeringa, Brady West, and Zeina Mneimneh.

Lastly, this project would not have been possible without the generous support of multiple funders. The Russell Sage Foundation was the source of funding at two critical points in the project: at the launch of data collection in earnest, when it provided our first external funding, and as the project neared completion for analysis and writing. We also appreciate support from the William T. Grant Foundation, the Berkeley Population Center at the University of California–Berkeley, the Berkeley Sociology Department, Berkeley's Social Science Matrix and Institute for Research on Labor and Employment, the National Institute of Justice (2008-IJ-CX-0018), the National Science Foundation (SES-1061018, SES-1060708), and the Eunice Kennedy Shriver National Institute of Child Health and Human Development (1R21HD060160 01A1); and the center grants from the Eunice Kennedy Shriver National Institute of Child Health and Human Development to the Population Centers at the University of Michigan (R24 HD041028) and at UC Berkeley (R24 HD073964). The project also benefited from pilot funding from the Office of the Vice President for Research, Rackham Graduate School, Department of Sociology, Joint PhD Program in Sociology and Public Policy, National Poverty Center, and the Center for Local, State, and Urban Policy at the University of Michigan.

Chapter 1 | Introduction

PETER IS A white man, born in the late 1970s. Two themes have, sadly, echoed through his life—substance abuse and incarceration. Peter reported that he began experimenting with drugs at a heartbreakingly early age. He was only six, he said, when he first tried marijuana and various prescription drugs. At eight, he began drinking alcohol and moved on to cocaine within a year. By the time he was incarcerated in state prison at seventeen, Peter was an addict, using these drugs daily. It is perhaps unsurprising that Peter dropped out of high school. However, he earned his GED when he was eighteen—and in prison.[1]

Although Peter was only seventeen when he entered state prison for the first time, he already had a long criminal history by that age. He was arrested for the first time at eleven for "driving away" and again the following year for breaking and entering.[2] Three years later, at the age of fifteen, he was hauled in again on another breaking-and-entering charge. In each of these felony cases, Peter was convicted as a juvenile. In total, as a juvenile, he was sentenced to probation twice and juvenile detention twice. Twice he escaped from juvenile custody. A few months before his eighteenth birthday, Peter pled guilty to two more felonies—armed robbery and breaking and entering. He would spend the next four and a half years incarcerated in state prison. When he was admitted, he reported that he had a mental health problem. He also reported that, in addition to all the other drugs, he had started using heroin daily. Over the course of this sentence, Peter lived in ten different prisons, not including the reception center and release preparation. For the most part, he was a "good" prisoner; in addition to earning his GED, he was cited for misconduct only four times— twice for "out of bounds" (being somewhere you are not supposed to be), once for gambling, and once for interfering with justice—and spent a total of eighteen days in solitary confinement.

Peter was released to a community corrections center in late 2000, but he did not remain on the outside for long. Three months later, he was

1

arrested and pled guilty to three felonies: receiving stolen property, fleeing justice, and unlawful driving away. He reentered prison in mid-2001.
Prior to this second incarceration in state prison, Peter was living with his
aunt in an upper-middle-class suburb of Grand Rapids. The suburb was
almost entirely white, and only a small fraction of its residents lived below
the poverty line. His father lived in the same town, and while we do not
know exactly where Peter spent his childhood, it may well have been in
this environment. Peter served less than two years of his six-year sentence.
In contrast to his previous stay, he experienced far fewer moves between
prisons, being housed in four different prisons. He was charged with three
out of bounds and unauthorized cell occupation misconducts, for which
he spent about a week in solitary confinement.

Peter was released onto maximum parole supervision in early 2003.
Immediately after his release, he lived with his father, but less than two
weeks later he moved back in with his aunt. He spent about a month and
a half with her, then moved to a new residence in Grand Rapids, where
he lived for only a month before being arrested once again, for burglary
and obstructing justice. He pled guilty and was again sentenced to prison.
He spent a few months in jail before being transferred to prison, where he
remained for six years, until late 2009, when he was again released onto
maximum parole supervision.

Once again, however, Peter was rearrested within a few months. He
pled guilty to felony breaking and entering and felony home invasion
in early 2010, at which time he was readmitted to prison. He was almost
thirty-two and now a father; despite earning a GED, he had never worked
in the formal labor market. Peter was not released from prison again until
late 2012, after our study follow-up. Despite absconding (failing to report
to his parole officer) several times, Peter managed to stay out of prison for
almost a year and a half before being returned in early 2014.

Peter's experiences in early adulthood were not uncommon among
young men who are imprisoned during this critical life stage. Yet not all
young men who are imprisoned in their early adult years spend so many
of the subsequent years in prison, as Peter did. Consider Luke, a young
black man also born in the late 1970s. Luke experienced his first arrest at
age seventeen, but he does not appear to have been prosecuted, as he had
no juvenile record. Nevertheless, like many of the young men we studied,
Luke did not finish high school. He first became involved with the adult
criminal justice system at age eighteen, when he was arrested for home
invasion—his only arrest on record. On that charge, he spent nearly four
months in pretrial detention, pled guilty, and was sentenced to five years'
probation in a special probation program for young offenders. Placed

under maximum supervision, he was ordered to undergo alcohol and drug testing and to enroll in a GED program.

Luke successfully complied with these conditions. Each of his drug tests as a probationer came back negative, and he earned a GED in the spring of 1998. In addition, Luke was employed in every quarter but one between his arrest and early 2000. Luke occasionally worked retail jobs but found most of his jobs through temporary services agencies. Of the eleven calendar quarters in which Luke was employed, he worked at least one temp job in eight of them. Despite sometimes working ten different jobs in a year, Luke never earned even $10,000. During the three quarters of 1997 in which he was employed, he earned about $8,300 with eight different employers. The following year he worked in all four quarters, earning about $6,400, again with eight different employers. In 1999, Luke again was employed in only three quarters, earning about $5,200 working for ten different firms.

It is unclear exactly what happened to Luke in mid-1999. Something caused him to lose his job and to be placed on electronic monitoring and compelled to enroll in a special alternative to incarceration (SAI) program; sometimes called prison "boot camp," SAI programs are for low-risk offenders who are deemed good prospects for only a short period of incarceration. Luke spent about four months in SAI and was released in the fall of 1999 and placed on probation. He worked in the last quarter of 1999 and the first quarter of 2000. But he did not work for a full year—a year that ultimately led to his imprisonment. According to his probation records, he absconded from probation several times in the first few weeks after his release from SAI. He was apprehended and sent to state prison as a technical rule violator (TRV) in the spring of 2001.

At the time of his imprisonment, Luke was single and did not have any children. He reported no mental illnesses or substance use. He was living with an uncle in a midsize city near Grand Rapids. The neighborhood was overwhelmingly white and had a low poverty rate. Luke served his prison sentence exclusively in a facility for younger inmates. He remained imprisoned for about half of his three-year sentence. His early release probably resulted from good behavior—he was not charged with any misconduct during that time. While he was incarcerated, each of his twelve drug tests came back negative.

In late 2002, Luke was released from prison into a community corrections center in Grand Rapids where he lived for a month before moving back in with his uncle. Six months later, Luke was formally paroled onto minimum supervision. After another six months, Luke's girlfriend moved in with him at the same residence. They would live together at least as long as we were able to follow Luke's residential history—into 2005.

After his mid-2003 parole, Luke found employment—again through a temporary staffing agency. He earned $4,300 in the third quarter of 2003, and over the next year he worked mainly in manufacturing, bringing in $21,000 from jobs at six different firms. In the following year, he again worked mainly for temporary staffing agencies, earning about $20,000 with eight employers. Although Luke reported no substance use prior to prison and consistently tested negative in prison, he began to test positive while on parole. In late 2004, he tested positive in three successive tests. However, his last test before he was discharged from parole came up negative.

Luke was discharged from parole in mid-2005. Over the next year and a half, he worked in metal manufacturing, earning about $30,000. Then he transitioned away from that type of work and into another employment arena—perhaps having found more of a passion than a means of subsistence. At age twenty-eight, Luke began working for a fitness club. He continued to work almost exclusively in fitness through the end of our follow-up in 2009. Over two years in that line of work, he earned about $29,000 per year. Luke is one example of a success story in the transition to adulthood after prison.

Peter and Luke are just two of the millions of young adults who have come into contact with the criminal justice system in the United States. One-third of young adults can now expect to be arrested by the time they turn twenty-three.[3] Nor are Peter and Luke unique in their experiences with imprisonment and reentry so early in life. Each year, 100,000 young adults ages eighteen to twenty-four are released from prison nationwide.[4]

These young adults, including Peter and Luke, experience imprisonment during a critical developmental period in their lives: the transition to adulthood. During this period, which spans roughly age eighteen to twenty-five, critical life events typically occur: school completion, first full-time employment, departure from the childhood household, marriage, and childbearing.[5] Crucially, the transition-to-adulthood period sets the stage for later adult life by establishing long-term developmental trajectories. It is a period when human capital is often acquired through postsecondary education and initial work experiences, when the foundation for economic independence is established, and when long-term relationships are formed, including those that will lead to marriage, parenthood, or both. Yet the transition to adulthood is also a time of risk. Substance use and criminal activity peak during this life stage,[6] and mortality from preventable causes like accidents, homicide, suicide, and drug overdoses is also more common at this age.[7] Research demonstrates that successfully navigating the challenges of the transition to adulthood—however one defines success—requires both the "scaffolding" of family support and engagement in positive institutions like colleges and job training programs.[8]

Their low educational levels and struggles in the labor market had made both Peter and Luke members of a particularly vulnerable subset of this age group whom policymakers and researchers have come to call "disconnected" young adults.[9] Disconnected young adults are neither in school nor working (nor looking for work). Many are entangled in the criminal justice system. Concern for disconnected youth and their futures and an interest in developing policies to reconnect them to supportive social and economic institutions have grown more or less steadily since the late 1990s, when the employment of young adults with low levels of education—particularly black men—failed to rebound in line with the economy as a whole. Because this period also followed over three decades of increasing incarceration, disconnectedness among young black men has been attributed in part to incarceration and its effects.[10] Derek Neal and Armin Rick, for instance, attribute lack of black socioeconomic progress since 1965 in part to the effects of high rates of incarceration among black men.[11]

Today conservative estimates suggest that around one in sixteen Americans between the ages of sixteen and twenty-four are neither in school nor working.[12] Those most at risk of joining the ranks of the disconnected are young people from low-income families who grew up in high-poverty neighborhoods served by low-quality schools. They have been let down by core social institutions that failed to provide them with the scaffolding during the transition to adulthood that their middle-class peers often do not even realize they rely upon and benefit from.[13] Because young people of color disproportionately experience these disadvantages—and also face additional barriers such as labor market discrimination, criminal justice contact, and lack of access to social networks that can connect them to meaningful entry-level work—they are disproportionately likely to become disconnected young adults.[14] At the same time, many young adults, including young adults of color, exhibit incredible resilience, and somehow manage, as Luke did, to engineer a successful transition to adulthood.

The successes of young men like Luke provide an opportunity to build new knowledge about how to provide better scaffolding for Peter and those like him. How is it that Peter and Luke had such different experiences after their imprisonment? More broadly, what leads some young men but not others to exhibit resilience in the face of the seemingly overwhelming adversity of growing up in poverty and becoming ensnared by the criminal justice system? What can we learn from these differences that could be applied to help formerly incarcerated and disconnected young men more generally?

The goal of this book is to understand how some young men exiting prison are eventually able to achieve some of the key markers of adulthood while others are not. Although prior research has examined the transition to adulthood among young people from low-income families and studied the lives of young adults at high risk of becoming disconnected, little prior work has focused on how this most vulnerable group of young adults moves from adolescence into adulthood. Our central argument is that the immediate post-prison experience is key to successful transition to adulthood among formerly incarcerated young men. The social contexts, institutional involvements, and social supports that welcome (or neglect) these men upon release are just as significant for their capacity to reintegrate into society as their pre-prison backgrounds, disadvantages, and experiences.

In short, new trajectories are possible. Race, however, constrains these possibilities. Race plays a huge role in determining the contexts, institutions, and social supports to which young men have access and influences the quality of their experiences in these contexts and institutions. Among the formerly incarcerated, young black men face steeper hurdles to overcome, and their post-prison trajectories reflect these deeper challenges.

Throughout this book, we document the challenges and achievements of 1,300 young men like Peter and Luke who left Michigan's prisons in 2003 and whom we followed over time in administrative records. We examine the roles of race, social support, neighborhood contexts, and key institutions like the labor market, the criminal justice system, and educational institutions. Our study of the struggles and achievements of young men like Peter and Luke is grounded in two bodies of research, both of which are intimately tied to contemporary and historical racial inequalities: the transition to adulthood in twenty-first-century America, and the U.S. criminal justice system in the era of mass incarceration. Next, we discuss each in turn.

THE TRANSITION TO ADULTHOOD IN TWENTY-FIRST-CENTURY AMERICA

Today's young adults are coming of age in an era significantly different from that of past generations. Historically, conceptualizations of the transition to adulthood focused on a single idealized timing and sequence of life transitions. Completion of education, in this model, led to employment; stability in employment led to the solidification of a romantic partnership and marriage; and marriage led to the establishment of a new household, one that soon included children. This sequence of events in the normative transition to adulthood—which was typical mainly only of the white middle class—was supposed to occur by one's midtwenties.[15]

Today the scholarly understanding of the transition to adulthood has broadened to encompass many possible pathways.[16] The underlying reality has changed as well: this period of life has become elongated, complicated, and uncertain.[17] Some young adults drop out of school to work; others delay entry into the labor market. Some become parents in their teens, and without stable partners; others delay parenting until well into their thirties. Marriage is rarer and delayed, as compared to previous decades, while cohabitation is more prevalent. Particularly for those from more advantaged backgrounds, an elongated pathway to adulthood has emerged, what Jeffrey Arnett calls "emerging adulthood," in which the responsibilities of adulthood are put off and the early midtwenties become an age for extended education and personal exploration, identity construction, and human capital development.[18]

These changes in the transition to adulthood have corresponded with other social and economic changes. A chief explanation for the elongation of the transition to adulthood is the need for more postsecondary education in the modern economy.[19] College enrollments have been steadily increasing. According to the National Center for Education Statistics (NCES), undergraduate enrollment increased by 27 percent at degree-granting postsecondary institutions between 2000 and 2017, when enrollment was 16.8 million students.[20] Even as more young people have enrolled in college, they have taken longer to complete their degrees. Only 58.3 percent of individuals who enrolled in two- or four-year degree programs in 2012 had completed their degree by 2018.[21] Prolonged schooling pushes back the beginning of careers, childbearing, and marriage, particularly for young adults from middle-class families.

When today's young adults do enter the labor market—either after college or in lieu of it—they experience shorter job tenures and change employers more often than past generations at the same age, and more than today's older workers.[22] Thus, it takes them longer to establish themselves in a good job, and their chances of working for the same employer for an entire career are much lower. Today's young adults are also earning less in real terms and are therefore unable to establish their own households.[23] Perhaps as a result of this economic uncertainty, young adults today are much more likely to return to live with their parents. Even in the 1990s, 40 percent of young adults were living with their parents at some point in their twenties.[24] These patterns are evident not just in the United States but across most developed countries, suggesting that fundamental changes in the global economy are at least partially responsible for delayed economic and residential independence.[25] As the transition to adulthood has been elongated worldwide, parental support is increasingly necessary.

As the objective experience of the transition to adulthood has become more uncertain and variable, so too have young people's subjective understandings of what it means to be an adult, even if older generations have not updated their views.[26] The public discussion of "boomerang" children returning to the parental nest when they supposedly should be on the path to becoming economically independent is suffused with worry about a "failure to launch," with long-term negative implications for both parents and their adult children. Young people themselves, however, have adopted more nuanced understandings of what it means to become an adult.[27]

Although today's young adults still understand adulthood in terms of the traditional markers, they construct adult identities much more flexibly, viewing them as building blocks from which they can construct multiple pathways to adulthood. Feeling like an adult has become less closely linked to particular markers of adulthood and a single normative sequence of events.[28] One exception is parenthood, a role that still makes young people suddenly feel like adults. Moreover, role reversals such as returning home after being economically independent are understood by young people as setbacks on the road to adulthood, not as "failures to launch."[29]

These changes in subjective understandings of adulthood also reflect in part the greater diversity of the nation and its young people in particular. For example, multigenerational households are more normative among immigrants and nonwhites, for whom living with one's parents is a way to fulfill family obligations of mutual social, emotional, and financial support that extend throughout the life course.[30] Young adults in less advantaged circumstances may also have little choice but to live in multigenerational households.[31]

Although the lengthening of the transition to adulthood is often experienced as an opportunity for personal exploration and human capital development for young adults from middle-class families, the changing nature of the transition to adulthood is fraught with risks and challenges for young adults from poor and working-class backgrounds.[32] Young adults whose parents have more education and income are most likely to enroll in and complete postsecondary schooling and to find their footing in the labor market, while young adults whose parents have less education are more likely to have children at an early age and to miss out on postsecondary education.[33] Young adults from families in the top quarter of the income distribution receive three times the financial support from their parents as those from the bottom quarter of the income distribution, a difference that amounts to tens of thousands of dollars in early adulthood.[34] In addition, children from middle-class families can rely on their more educated parents to help them navigate contemporary society's complex institutions, anticipating and preventing problems and solving those that arise.[35] As Mary Waters and her colleagues observe, "For the vast majority of youth, [the transition to adulthood] is when the inequalities in our society firm up like hardening cement."[36]

Prior research has also traced these class differences in the transition to adulthood to broader changes in the economy and other core social and economic institutions. Today the social safety net is less generous than in the past, and for those without a college education, changes in the economy—deindustrialization, the decline of unions, globalization—have reduced opportunities for meaningful work or a middle-class income.[37] As a result, the pathway to adulthood for poor and working-class youth has become much more difficult. As Jennifer Silva writes, "The children of the nearly obsolete industrial working-class can be characterized primarily through their struggles to come to terms with the disappearance of the foundational aspects of industrial working class life."[38] In other words, the contemporary economy no longer provides a firm foundation of living-wage employment for the working class. Without a firm economic foundation, young adults feel ill prepared to set up their own households, marry, and become parents.[39]

Multiple studies have pointed out a pattern now exhibited by young adults from poor and working-class backgrounds. Variously called "accelerated adulthood" or "accelerated role transitions," the concept identifies the importance in the lives of young adults of role transitions, particularly early parenthood, occurring before they are emotionally or financially ready.[40] Although having children is not, of course, inherently negative, the current configuration of our social and economic institutions makes it difficult for young people to establish themselves in the labor market or complete education or training while parenting, especially as a single parent. Stefanie DeLuca, Susan Clampet-Lundquist, and Kathryn Edin point to a similar idea, which they term "expedited adulthood": young adults from poor and working-class backgrounds feeling pressured to complete their education or training quickly and to begin work in occupations that promise higher wages for young people but that provide few opportunities for career advancement over the long term.[41] For example, they opt for faster training programs to qualify for positions, such as a phlebotomist or nurse's assistant rather than a nurse, that will move them more quickly toward key markers of adulthood. These findings highlight the importance of scaffolding: the social support from family that provides the resources required to elongate the period of preparation for adulthood. Such scaffolding is much more available to middle-class young people.

These findings also call our attention to the weaknesses of educational institutions that disproportionately serve young adults from poor and working-class backgrounds. Deluca and her colleagues identify a "postsecondary landscape full of snares."[42] For-profit colleges charge high tuition for degrees with low payoff in the labor market; community colleges are less expensive but present challenges to successful navigation to completion owing to inadequate career and college counseling, remedial education that does not grant credits toward a degree, few opportunities to earn and learn at the same time, and limited seats in programs of coursework with the best returns in the labor market.[43] Richard Settersten argues that these problems are representative of a larger failure of institutions that serve young adults, particularly those that serve the poor and working class: they have yet to catch up with the changing nature of the transition to adulthood and the everyday realities and needs of young adults.[44] In contrast, middle-class young adults are ensconced in the generally supportive and developmentally oriented environment of residential four-year colleges during key years of their transition to adulthood.[45]

These labor market and educational challenges facing poor and working-class young adults translate into a higher risk of disconnectedness.[46] Disconnectedness as a young adult is related to poor education and lack of labor market experience in the teenage years,[47] but disconnectedness is not an inescapable state.[48] Two-thirds of young adults who experience a spell of disconnectedness manage to "reconnect" at some point later in early adulthood, and three-quarters of those who reconnect do so through the labor market rather than schooling.[49] These figures suggest that young adults can be resilient and recover from educational and employment setbacks, but they raise the question of *how* young adults are able to do so. They also provide further evidence that conventional notions of the ordering of events in the transition to adulthood—according to which schooling should precede work—do not adequately describe the experiences of today's young adults, particularly those from poor and working-class backgrounds. Indeed, many young adults from such backgrounds work for a time before returning to postsecondary schooling to earn further credentials and advance their careers.[50]

Racial differences are also clearly evident in the transition to adulthood. Class differences in employment, schooling, and early parenthood are paralleled in differences that track race and ethnicity.[51] Young men of color are especially likely to experience periods of disconnection from work and schooling during early adulthood.[52] Black, Hispanic, and Native American young adults are more likely to have grown up in poor and working-class families, but racial differences in the transition to adulthood extend beyond family class background. Young men of color are more likely than their white counterparts to have grown up in poor and violent neighborhoods and to have attended poorly performing and resource-starved public schools as a result of residential racial segregation.[53] Young adults of color are also far more likely to face compounding disadvantages, such as both family poverty and prolonged exposure to poor neighborhoods.[54] Black young adults are more likely than their white peers to return to live with their parents, owing in part to difficulties with other aspects of the transition to adulthood, including work and schooling.[55] As we discuss later in more detail, young people of color are also much more likely to be affected by the growth and increasing punitiveness of the criminal justice system.

In addition, young adults of color are less likely to find entry-level jobs in traditionally working-class occupations that provide a living wage. In their study of the transition to adulthood among young adults in Baltimore, Karl Alexander, Doris Entwisle, and Linda Olson identify what they call "two attainment regimes."[56] By virtue of their social networks based on family and neighborhood connections, young whites from working-class families have better access to entry-level positions in the skilled trades that do not require a college degree. This access reflects the racialized hiring practices in these traditionally white working-class occupations, particularly the use of social networks for hiring or placement in apprenticeships.[57] In contrast, the young black men studied by Alexander and his colleagues primarily had access to low-wage work in the service sector, with few prospects for career mobility. They tended to turn instead to college as a path to higher earnings and stable employment, but this pathway is a longer road to living-wage work. Moreover, completion rates are low for low-resource black students because of the greater challenges they face in navigating institutions of higher education.[58]

In sum, prior research on the transition to adulthood has explored the experiences of the middle class,[59] the working class,[60] and the urban poor,[61] yet none of these studies have focused on the transition to adulthood among those young adults who have been imprisoned. This group, an important subset of the "disconnected," faces an overwhelming array of challenges in constructing lives for themselves during this critical life stage. On the one hand, young adults leave prison at an age when most of their more advantaged counterparts are also still in the middle of the elongated and fractious transition to adulthood. In one sense, it is normative for their age group to continue to pursue education, build a career, and live at home. On the other hand, young adults exiting prison, who are overwhelmingly from poor and working-class families and have low levels of education, are not only behind their cohort on an accelerated path to adulthood but face all the same challenges related to the low-skill labor market and the weakness of the postsecondary educational institutions that serve the poor and working class. Furthermore, they face an additional set of challenges that stem directly from their early and intensive involvement with the criminal justice system, the topic to which we now turn.

RACE, CLASS, AND THE CRIMINAL JUSTICE
SYSTEM IN THE ERA OF MASS INCARCERATION

The tens of thousands of young adults who leave prison every year and confront the challenges of reentry, reintegration, and the transition to adulthood are but one part of a larger story involving the expansion of the criminal justice system and an increasingly punitive social policy regime in the United States. Since the early 1970s, the number of individuals incarcerated in prisons and jails in the United States has risen dramatically. In 1975, the population in jails and prisons on any given day in the United States was roughly 400,000 people, but by 2003—when the young men in this study were paroled from prison—this number had increased more than fivefold, to 2.1 million. Incarceration in prisons and jails peaked at almost 2.3 million in 2009, then declined slightly, to about 2.2 million in 2016.[62] With 698 out of every 100,000 people behind bars, the U.S. incarceration rate is now higher than that of any other country in the world; it is one and a half times Russia's, six times China's, and more than ten times that of the typical nation in Western Europe.[63] In other words, our current regime of mass incarceration, long in the making, is unprecedented relative both to our own history and in comparison with the rest of the world.[64]

Furthermore, the era of mass incarceration has been marked not simply by an expansion of the use of prison sentences to punish individuals convicted of a felony but also by a much broader punitive turn in every corner of the criminal justice system. Pretrial detention in jails and jail sentences have become more common, and convictions have become more common and probation supervision more intensive. Fines and fees deprive defendants of not just their liberty but their economic well-being, and even misdemeanor and civil citations trap the poor in a never-ending cycle of court involvement, opening a gateway into more intensive involvement with the criminal justice system.[65] Police tactics like "stop and frisk" and "order maintenance policing" have subjected many more civilians to harassment and other negative police-civilian interactions in heavily policed minority neighborhoods, where these practices have a negative impact on civic and political life.[66] Not only does such aggressive policing reduce young people's trust in the law and legal institutions,[67] but police violence and deaths are all too common in poor communities of color. Police killings are a leading cause of death for black and Latino young men.[68] Likewise, the policy logic of surveillance and control has gradually crept into many other aspects of our social policy, from "zero-tolerance" school discipline to drug testing of recipients of welfare benefits to the use of police to manage public spaces.[69] As Loïc Wacquant notes, the expansion of a penal logic has coincided with the retrenchment of the welfare state, and incarceration

thus has become an increasingly common policy approach to social problems related to poverty, particularly those related in the public mind to
poverty with racial and ethnic undertones.[70]

The expansion of the criminal justice system is intimately connected
with race, both in its causes and in its consequences. Blacks are almost six
times as likely as whites to be incarcerated in the United States, and Latinos
are two and a half times as likely. On any given day, almost one in ten black
men in their late twenties are incarcerated in jail or prison.[71] The disparate
impact of the criminal justice system is even starker when we look beyond
incarceration. One in thirty-one Americans are under some form of correctional supervision in the United States, including one in eleven blacks and
one in twenty-seven Latinos.[72] The majority of black men with less than a
high school degree experience imprisonment at some point in their lives.[73]

Although increasing crime played a small role in rising incarceration
early in the prison boom, incarceration continued to rise as crime fell
in the 1990s. Longer sentences, a greater likelihood of being sentenced
to prison (particularly for drug crimes), and more returns to prison for
parole violations—the results of "law and order" and "tough on crime"
politics—bear most of the responsibility for the higher rates of incarceration.[74] The primary reason for the increase in incarceration is the passage
by state and federal lawmakers of laws that have made imprisonment
more likely and prison sentences longer.[75] Scholars have identified these
changes as a deliberate response to black Americans' gains from the civil
rights movement and traced them to Republican attempts to split the
white working class away from the Democratic coalition through "tough
on crime" and "law and order" rhetoric that eventually suffused political
views on both sides and framed urban problems as the result of lawless-
ness and criminality rather than poverty and racial oppression.[76] Mass
incarceration can be understood as a continuation of policies of racial
oppression and control with a long lineage in American history, from
slavery to Jim Crow to segregation and now the criminal justice system.[77]

For those seeking to understand the experiences of young adults from
poor urban communities, the criminal justice system is arguably now as
important as the education system or the labor market. Recent research
also shows that the experience of arrest has greatly expanded for young
black men and become "decoupled" from actual criminal behavior.[78]
Furthermore, the high rate at which young black men without a high
school degree are imprisoned suggests that incarceration now constitutes
a "new stage in the life course" that "may collectively reshape adulthood
for whole birth cohorts."[79] Imprisonment now far surpasses other key
events in the transition to adulthood for black men, for whom it is nearly
twice as common as college completion and more than twice as common as

military service. Becky Pettit and Bruce Western argue that deviance has always been higher during adolescence and young adulthood, regardless of race and ethnicity. What is novel about the prison boom is that a form of punishment that was once reserved for the most violent and persistent offenders became normal and widespread under the war on drugs and war on crime, especially for young black men.[80]

The experience of imprisonment has consequences for released prisoners that extend far beyond the period of confinement.[81] Simple involvement with the criminal justice system marks young men with the stigma of a criminal record, and that stigma can exclude them from future opportunities in the labor and housing markets.[82] It also reinforces and perpetuates their disconnection from mainstream institutions. The stigma of a criminal record is a structural stigma.[83] That is, it is propagated and maintained both by institutional policies and practices and by dominant cultural norms rather than simply through individual interactions.[84] Moreover, stigma can harm mental and physical health through the combined effects of stress, social isolation, material deprivation, internalization of the stigma, and health care access.[85]

A robust body of research documents the impacts of imprisonment and a criminal record on education, employment, family formation, health, and civic and political participation. Those who have been imprisoned face discrimination in hiring and are shunted into the secondary labor market, where wages are low, benefits are rare, and there are few opportunities for career advancement; these effects are greater for blacks than whites and are concentrated among those with lower wages.[86] Imprisonment can also interrupt school and the acquisition of work experience, cut off social ties that are important for finding work, and inhibit the "soft skills" that are increasingly important in the modern workplace.[87] Especially for young black men, incarceration, rather than education or work, is often the proximate reason why they leave home for the first time.[88] Men who have been incarcerated are less likely to live with their children or to have regular contact with them, in part owing to the dissolution of their relationships with the mothers of their children that often results from their incarceration.[89] Formerly incarcerated men experience worse mental and physical health, effects that are thought to stem from the loss of social networks and social support, the stressful and isolating environment of the prison, and poor health care in prison.[90] Imprisonment also reduces civic and political participation, not only through formal means such as prohibitions on voting but also through exclusion from political life more generally; this impact has important implications for political representation and power in communities where incarceration rates are high.[91] Low rates of upward intergenerational mobility among blacks may be attributable to the disproportionate incarceration of black men.[92] The disadvantages created by the experience of imprisonment are important to understand as we investigate the experiences of formerly incarcerated young men in Michigan after their release from prison in 2003.

The consequences of imprisonment also extend far beyond the incarcerated individual: the families and communities of the incarcerated experience social exclusion as well.[93] Prior research has documented some of the effects on the social, emotional, and intellectual development of the children of incarcerated fathers,[94] as well as the mental and physical health of both these children and their mothers.[95] Parental incarceration has impacts that accumulate over time: it affects educational outcomes, which in turn have an impact on housing security, political participation, and access to health insurance.[96] The family members of an incarcerated young person also bear the economic costs of their incarceration, such as bail payments[97] and the costs of phone calls and transportation for visits.[98] The incarceration of a family member, in short, reduces a family's wealth and material security.[99]

Incarceration rates are particularly high in poor urban communities, where widespread incarceration erodes the social fabric of the community (by disrupting the social networks that provide informal social control), diminishes political power, and weakens economic foundations.[100] The concentration of children with incarcerated fathers in schools is associated with lower educational attainment for all children in these schools, even for those without incarcerated fathers.[101] Young men coming home from prison thus disproportionately return to families and communities that are the least prepared to assist them in reintegrating into the community and navigating the transition to adulthood. The concentration of incarceration by race and class exposes young black men in particular to this lack of support from family and community.

The prison boom has made the reintegration of former prisoners, about 80 percent of whom are released on parole supervision, newly challenging.[102] Over 620,000 prisoners are released each year.[103] Prior research on prisoner reentry among older populations documents the challenges of reintegration in the era of mass incarceration. Formerly incarcerated individuals face a profound mismatch between the social, economic, and cultural resources with which they leave prison and the institutional and social environments they must navigate upon release.[104] They encounter a low-skill labor market that offers them few opportunities for stable work at a living wage, a punitive parole system focused on surveillance and monitoring rather than reintegration, ubiquitous computerized background checks that make managing the stigma of a criminal record very difficult, and families and communities that are ill equipped to provide social support and economic opportunities. The formerly incarcerated must face these challenges while dealing with the consequences of lifetimes of trauma from exposure to violence, material deprivation, and emotional and physical abuse—including the addictions and mental health problems that developed from these traumas.[105] Prior research on prisoner reentry and reintegration has largely focused on older formerly incarcerated individuals, who make up the vast majority of that population. In this book, we investigate whether those who are released from prison much earlier in their lives fare any better, and we determine who among them is able to transition to adulthood and leave the criminal justice system behind.

The Transition to Adulthood after Prison

We examine the unique experiences of those leaving prison during the transition to adulthood, at ages eighteen to twenty-five.[106] They represent a growing problem: the number of young adults exiting prison and attempting to build new lives for themselves as they transition to adulthood has increased over time. As more juveniles are prosecuted in adult courts and more first-time offenders are sent to prison, increases in incarceration rates for young adults have paralleled overall trends. Between 1990 and 2000, the incarceration rate for those ages twenty to twenty-four almost doubled.[107] According to our data on parolees in Michigan, almost 20 percent of those exiting prison onto parole are age twenty-five or under, and many older prisoners experienced their first release from prison as they were transitioning to adulthood.

Because incarceration separates individuals from social networks and interrupts schooling and employment, it can delay or preclude key life transitions and significantly alter life trajectories. As widespread post-secondary education has lengthened the transition to adulthood,[108] formerly incarcerated young adults may now have even more trouble desisting from crime because adult roles that promote desistance—those related to work and family—are less normative in their age group. In other words, today's young people exiting prison are reentering society during a socially defined life stage in which they have assumed fewer of the roles and identities—full-time worker, parent, spouse—that prior research and theory suggest are critical to desistance from crime. As discussed later, salient life events and role transitions—such as first full-time employment, school completion, and household formation—typically occur during this developmental period. Serving time in prison surely disrupts these events and can set an individual on a trajectory of deeper disadvantage marked by low wages or unemployment, continued involvement in crime, and weak ties to family and institutions.

Further complicating these processes are substance use and mental health problems, which are very common among those who have served time in prison.[109] Fifty-six percent of state prison inmates have a mental health problem.[110] Jason Schnittker estimates that psychiatric symptoms among those who have ever been incarcerated are twice as common as they are among the never-incarcerated population.[111] An estimated 80 percent of incarcerated individuals have some kind of alcohol or drug problem, and 20 percent have a history of injection drug use.[112] In a 1997 survey, 83 percent of state prison inmates reported past drug use, 57 percent reported using drugs in the month prior to their offense, 51 percent reported that they were under the influence of drugs or alcohol when they committed their offense, and 19 percent reported committing their offense in order to obtain money for drugs. Nearly one-quarter of state prison inmates were classified as alcohol-dependent.[113]

Young adults exiting prison are especially vulnerable to experiencing obstacles in their adult transitions compared to those not involved in the criminal justice system.[114] They lag behind their peers in educational attainment and work experience and have experienced childhood disadvantages at alarmingly high rates. One-third of young adults under age twenty-five who were incarcerated in 1997 had parents or guardians who abused alcohol or drugs, 16 percent had lived in foster homes or institutions, and one-third had parents who had themselves served time in prison or jail. Almost 20 percent reported a learning disability, mental or emotional condition, physical disability, or speech disability.[115] Post-prison prospects for transitional-aged young adults are often dim, as the chances of returning to prison within three years range from 40 to 75 percent—a higher recidivism rate than for older prisoners.[116]

For young black men from disadvantaged backgrounds, the situation is even more dire. Young, low-skill African American males are more likely than their white counterparts to experience arrest, incarceration, and community supervision.[117] Their criminal records further marginalize them socially, educationally, and economically by restricting their access to education, housing, and employment.[118] That formerly incarcerated black men experience poor life-course outcomes relative to non-incarcerated subpopulations is well established.[119] Yet our data clearly show substantial racial inequality in life-course outcomes even among formerly incarcerated young adults. Formerly incarcerated young black men lag behind their white counterparts in achieving traditional markers of adulthood: completing education, finding employment, and establishing their own household. This suggests that we have yet to understand the full complexity of the entanglements between contact with the criminal justice system and racial inequality in access to opportunities and successful life-course development.

Given what we know about the dual challenges of the transition to adulthood among poor and working-class youth and the difficulties created by the criminal justice system, it would be easy to assume that almost all young men who leave prison end up struggling as Peter did. Yet Luke's experiences are more common than we might expect. Indeed, many formerly incarcerated young adults leave prison never to return, and as we will see, many do manage to build new lives for themselves anchored by steady employment or sustained enrollment in college. What can we learn from comparing the Peters and Lukes of this world?

OVERVIEW OF THE BOOK

Our goal in this book is to better understand reentry and reintegration for formerly incarcerated young men who are released from prison during the transition to adulthood. To that end, one of our contributions is to describe how they fare after release, both with regard to traditional markers of the transition to adulthood, including education, employment, and residential stability and independence, and with regard to outcomes that are particularly relevant to young men involved in the criminal justice system, including health—as captured by mortality and substance abuse—involvement in violence, and various measures of recidivism. Unfortunately, as we will see, many of the young men in our sample struggled with the transition to adulthood as they also struggled to avoid further involvement in the criminal justice system. Yet we will also see that a significant proportion of them made progress toward economic independence and remained free of the criminal justice system. Thus, a second contribution of this book is to leverage the comparisons we can make between those who struggle and those who make progress to identify some of the factors that can promote a successful transition to adulthood after prison and, by extension, promote successful transitions to adulthood among disconnected young men more generally. Pre-prison experiences are certainly predictive of post-release outcomes in many cases, but here we focus on the post-prison experiences of the young men we study, especially the social supports, social contexts, and institutions that shaped those experiences. Our data generally show that family social supports, neighborhood contexts, and labor market, educational, and criminal justice institutions play an important role in the transition to adulthood after prison. So too does race, both in structuring young men's access to social supports and institutions and, for some outcomes, independently from these factors. To some degree, different pathways to adulthood are available to blacks and whites.

To accomplish these goals, we examine several types of outcomes and their correlates one by one and then investigate how the outcomes cluster over time in the lives of these young men, combining to create different trajectories in the transition to adulthood. In the chapters that focus on specific outcomes—GED, college enrollment, health (as measured by mortality, substance use, and involvement in violence), employment and earnings, and residential stability and independence—we present our findings in a common structure. We first describe how the outcomes vary both over time after release and with regard to race. Then, drawing on prior research and the transition-to-adulthood conceptual framework to develop possible explanations for the patterns we see, we present analyses that identify the primary factors that explain these patterns. In so doing, each chapter consistently examines themes related to race, social supports, contexts, and institutions.

We believe that this book will be of interest to multiple audiences, including researchers, policymakers, and practitioners. For those interested in the transition to adulthood, this book addresses the experiences and challenges of young men whose transition to adulthood was interrupted by imprisonment, a particularly vulnerable group of young adults who have not been separately studied before. The experiences of these young men have wider implications for understanding the transition to adulthood among poor and working-class young adults more generally. For those interested in efforts to reconnect disconnected young adults to work and schooling, this book provides a case study of a population of disconnected young men who faced some of the most difficult challenges to reconnecting. For those interested in the criminal justice system and its collateral consequences, this book documents the roles played by early and ongoing involvement with prison and parole in the lives of the formerly incarcerated. And finally, for those interested in prisoner reentry, reintegration, and recidivism, this book explores the reentry outcomes of a subset of recently released prisoners who reentered society at the peak age for both criminal offending and substance abuse. Policymakers and practitioners may wish to skip ahead to chapters 8 and 9, where we describe the various life trajectories of the young men in our study, summarize key findings, and discuss implications for policy and practice, before returning to the domain-specific chapters (chapters 3 through 7) that are of most interest to them.

This book is part of a larger mixed-method project on prisoner reentry and reintegration in Michigan, the Michigan Study of Life after Prison, which includes a prior book on prisoner reintegration based primarily on qualitative interview data from a sample of predominantly older, formerly incarcerated individuals.[120] This book focuses on formerly incarcerated young adults, foregrounds what we have learned from our administrative data, and engages directly with the transition to adulthood after prison and with disconnected youth, including new data on education and health.

Chapter 2 explains how we studied the transition to adulthood after prison. It elaborates the conceptual framework that guides our study, including our emphasis on contexts, institutions, and social supports. It then describes the data and methods we employ and documents the early experiences of the young men we study, including their experiences before, during, and immediately after release from prison. Chapter 2 also explains how this book builds on and extends our prior research on prisoner reentry and reintegration.

Chapter 3 begins our examination of the educational experiences of formerly incarcerated young men with an investigation of their efforts to earn a GED, a critical educational credential for those who have not graduated from high school. The GED is important both for the labor market and as a prerequisite for college enrollment and many job training or certification programs. A GED was particularly important for the young men in our study, as only 8.5 percent of them had a high school degree at prison entry. Those who avoided criminal justice involvement as adolescents and those from more advantaged neighborhoods and better public schools were most likely to have a high school diploma. This chapter examines who earned a GED, when they did so relative to their imprisonment, and what social supports, contexts, and institutional factors were associated with a greater chance of earning a GED. The hopeful news is that 74 percent earned a GED at some point. Of those, about one-quarter earned a GED in the community before their imprisonment, one-third earned it in prison, and the remainder earned it after release—about half of them in the community and half during a subsequent prison term.

The results of this chapter point toward criminal justice institutions and prior academic preparation as important determinants of GED receipt. Young men who persisted in high school longer before dropping out and were more involved in the criminal justice system as measured by prior adult probation and length of time in prison were more likely to earn a GED at some point. Young men with more pre-prison employment were also more likely to earn a GED. Blacks were less likely to earn a GED, even net of these factors. Evidence that blacks are more likely to repeat the GED exam in order to pass suggests that aspects of academic preparation that we are unable to measure directly may play a role in these racial differences. Nevertheless, the young men in our sample appeared to be taking advantage of GED opportunities in prison when they could, suggesting that expanding opportunities for education in prison could be productive.

Chapter 4 continues our examination of education with an investigation of postsecondary enrollment. Many young men in our study embraced further education: 28 percent enrolled in college at some point after their release, typically many years after release and typically in community colleges or for-profit colleges. Few, however, were able to complete a degree, at least not in the time frame we observe. College enrollment showed distinct racial patterns consistent with prior research on disconnected youth and racialized pathways during the transition to adulthood. Blacks were more likely to enroll in college, especially those who earned a GED in prison, but tended to do so after having experienced some success in the labor market, as higher earnings are predictive of college enrollment among blacks. Social support from romantic partners was also predictive of college enrollment among blacks. On the other hand, continued contact with the criminal justice system was negatively related to college enrollment; returning to prison at any point was associated with lower odds of postsecondary enrollment for both blacks and whites. Coupled with what we know about college enrollment and completion from prior education research, our findings indicate that college enrollment could serve as an important pathway to adulthood for formerly incarcerated young men, but also that stronger supports may be required to help them select appropriate colleges and complete degrees.

Turning to health, chapter 5 emphasizes the two most salient health risks faced by young adults: substance use and violence. Consistent with prior research on the formerly incarcerated, we see very high risks of mortality among formerly incarcerated young men relative to others their age. We find stark racial patterns in health risks post-release, with substance abuse being the primary risk for whites and violence the primary risk for young black men. For example, before prison, young white men were more likely to have abused opioids, cocaine, and alcohol, whereas young black men tended to be marijuana users. In the extreme case—fatality—young white men died almost exclusively from overdose and young black men were almost exclusively victims of gun violence.

Our results indicate that the criminal justice system's response to the risks of substance abuse emphasizes monitoring and punishment rather than effective treatment. Despite young white men's more serious substance abuse histories and greater risk of overdose, young black men were slightly more likely to be tested for substance use by their parole officers. Young white men had greater access to residential drug treatment through parole, but these programs were almost never long enough to be considered effective by contemporary standards of care. Arrest and jail confinement were practically universal, as almost every young man in our sample was arrested at some point after his release.

Health is one domain in which there are strong and consistent patterns over time in health risk. Those young men who engaged in serious substance use before prison were more likely to do so after release, and those young men who were involved in violence before their imprisonment were likely to become involved in violence after their release. These findings suggest that improving the health of formerly incarcerated young men will require stronger interventions than those currently available, and ones based on indicators of prior health risks. However, experiences during the post-prison period are important determinants as well. This chapter shows the role of social context in the health of formerly incarcerated young men. Whites who returned to their pre-prison neighborhood were more likely to test positive for drugs after release. Reconnecting young men to education and employment appears to have protective health effects, as young black men who were employed had lower rates of substance use and arrests for violent crimes, and young white men who enrolled in college were less likely to be arrested for violent crimes.

Chapter 6 examines the labor market experiences of formerly incarcerated young men, including finding employment and maintaining employment, as well as the trajectories of their employment and earnings over time. The findings paint a relatively bleak picture of the labor market struggles of these young men. Although almost all found some form of formal employment at some point during the six years we follow them, job instability was a critical challenge. Rates of employment were actually highest in the period immediately after release, then declined over time. By seven years after release, only 28 percent of formerly incarcerated young men had worked for four consecutive calendar quarters in the formal labor market. Those who maintained employment, however, did experience some earnings growth.

Here too we find important racial disparities. Young black men experienced lower employment rates, greater job instability, and lower earnings when working than young white men. Earnings growth was greater among black men, but primarily because they started with lower earnings. Racial differences in labor market outcomes are only partly explained by lower levels of education and pre-prison work experience among young black men and their concentration in neighborhoods with high unemployment rates. Although substance use is associated with job loss, it does not help to explain racial disparities in job stability, as whites are more likely to engage in alcohol and hard drug use. These findings on job loss and job stability should reorient our thinking about the sources of the employment challenges faced by formerly incarcerated young men. Although stigma is certainly important for understanding why they struggle to find jobs, there is also a larger story about maintaining employment once a job is found. Racial differences in employment are also not simply a function of differential stigma.

This chapter then probes deeper into the nature of work for formerly incarcerated young men. To understand how these young men are able to position themselves in the labor market, this chapter examines the industries in which formerly incarcerated young adults were most likely to find jobs and the likelihood of stable employment in different industries. Formerly incarcerated young men who did find work were concentrated in a small number of industries: temporary labor, food service and restaurants, construction, some forms of manufacturing, and retail. Here too there were racial disparities, which helps us to understand differences in earnings and job stability. Young black men were concentrated in industries where turnover was higher and earnings were generally lower, while white workers were much more likely to be employed in more stable jobs with higher earnings. For example, whites often worked in construction (15.3 percent versus 2.7 percent), while black workers were much more likely to be employed in temporary labor (29.1 percent versus 16.9 percent). These findings suggest that improving the employment of formerly incarcerated young men will require improving their prospects for securing higher-quality jobs rather than simply finding them any employment.

Chapter 7 focuses on residential stability, a key challenge for formerly incarcerated young men and a critical foundation for long-term reintegration. Where and with whom did these young men live in the months and years after their release from prison? Which young men were able to form their own independent households and which remained reliant on institutional housing or family members? This chapter shows that formerly incarcerated young men experience very high rates of residential instability, particularly in the period immediately following release. The typical young man in our study moved three times per year—or at about three times the rate at which housing scholars and advocates classify someone as housing-insecure. Housing is a domain in which the impact of family support was readily evident. About half of the young men we study moved in with a parent upon release; the remaining lived with other adult relatives (16 percent), a romantic partner (12 percent), or friends or siblings (12 percent). Those who lived with parents experienced greater residential stability. Contrary to conventional wisdom, however, only about three in ten formerly incarcerated young men returned to the home where they lived before prison. Whites were more likely to experience residential instability than blacks, owing in part to higher rates of substance abuse among formerly incarcerated white men. Among those of the same race, young men who returned to poor neighborhoods were more likely to experience residential instability. These findings suggest that support from families is critical to the residential stability of formerly incarcerated young men, but that when families lack the resources to provide much more than a place in the family home, the goal of residential independence will be elusive for most formerly incarcerated young men.

Our examination of residential instability also reveals the role of the criminal justice system in generating residential instability by disrupting residential stays. In the two years after release, more than seven in ten of the young men we study lived at some point in institutional or other non-private housing, including criminal justice facilities, treatment programs, and motels. Young men who were held in criminal justice facilities or residential treatment programs did not always return to their former home — a pattern that is associated with future residential instability. Rather than providing a foundation for reintegration or stability, the criminal justice system makes the transition to adulthood after prison more challenging.

While chapters 3 through 7 treat outcomes separately, chapter 8 investigates their interrelatedness and their associations with recidivism. It examines how individual trajectories of education, substance use, employment, residential independence, and involvement in crime and the criminal justice system come together in the post-prison lives of formerly incarcerated young men. In showing that there are multiple pathways through adulthood for these young men, this chapter identifies five distinct trajectory groups and then examines how pre-prison, in-prison, and immediate post-prison experiences are related to who ends up in each group. The hopeful news is that about one-quarter of the young men we study appeared to have successfully transitioned to adulthood and escaped involvement in the criminal justice system. These young men avoided substance use and recidivism and eventually became stably employed, although they were less successful at achieving residential independence. An additional 8 percent also avoided substance use and recidivism but experienced lower employment rates and eventually enrolled for a sustained period of time in college. Whites were more likely to be in the former group and blacks were more likely to be in the latter. The young men in these two groups were best positioned for success by their pre-prison experiences and post-release circumstances. They experienced the least criminal justice involvement earlier in their lives and left prison with higher levels of education and prior work experience. They also returned to less disadvantaged neighborhoods than the young men in the other groups.

At the other end of the spectrum were the young men who persisted in criminal justice involvement and experienced little employment or further education. Accounting for about one-quarter of our sample, these young men were equally likely to be black as to be white, and they all ended up back in prison at some point during the observation period. They experienced criminal justice involvement at an early age, were least likely to be involved in in-prison rehabilitation programs, and were most likely to have had substance abuse problems before their imprisonment and to have been diagnosed with a mental illness before prison entry. They also returned to some of the most disadvantaged neighborhoods and tended to experience high rates of residential instability in the first year after release.

The remaining two groups are especially interesting, because they complicate the simple binary between success and failure. One group, whom we label "the disconnected," avoided substance use and further criminal justice involvement but also experienced low rates of employment and did not enroll in college. Representing one-fifth of our sample, these young men were disproportionately black, had the lowest levels of human capital, and returned to some of the most disadvantaged neighborhoods in the state. Like those in the first two groups, however, they were not typically involved in the criminal justice system early in their lives.

The final group, whom we call "the unsettled," made up one-quarter of the formerly incarcerated young men we study. These young men straddled prosocial and antisocial institutions. They experienced some criminal justice involvement after release, as measured by arrests, but did not return to prison. At the same time, they experienced moderate levels of formal employment throughout the period of study, reflecting an underlying job instability. Members of this group were distinguished from others by early and intensive criminal justice contact during their pre-prison lives and by higher rates of substance use and mental illness.

Collectively, these findings paint a bleak picture of the challenges of the transition to adulthood after incarceration, but they also offer a glimmer of hope. On the one hand, formerly incarcerated young men must navigate the challenges of high-poverty neighborhoods, where crime is common and job opportunities are few; enter an unforgiving labor market already disadvantaged by low levels of education; conform to the rules of a criminal justice system more interested in surveillance and control than rehabilitation and reintegration; and find stable housing with few material resources to draw upon. A substantial number face these challenges while managing the added burden of addiction and mental illness. We should not be surprised, then, that many end up back in prison or enter the ranks of the disconnected, unable to secure steady work, enter school, or find stable housing.

And yet a substantial number overcome these challenges and make significant progress toward traditional markers of adulthood while escaping the criminal justice system. To some degree, these formerly incarcerated young men are more advantaged than others in terms of human capital and the depth of their prior contact with the criminal justice system, but they also are able to capitalize on family resources and avoid the most disadvantaged neighborhoods. Still others find themselves somewhere in between—experiencing some progress but struggling to maintain it as they remain enmeshed in the criminal justice system. They too tell us that, with the right interventions, different outcomes are possible.

With that glimmer of hope in mind, the concluding chapter explores the implications of our findings for both the transition-to-adulthood literature more broadly and for policies to improve the well-being and long-term life outcomes of formerly incarcerated young adults. In chapter 9, we revisit the literature on disconnected young adults to discuss policies that might provide them with stronger scaffolding and support as they rebuild their lives after prison. How might we intervene to improve college completion rates among those who enroll, assist more formerly incarcerated young adults to enroll in college, or facilitate postsecondary enrollment earlier in the post-release period? How might we change the criminal justice system, particularly parole, to be supportive of the developmental needs of those just released from prison rather than simply punitive and surveillant? What might help the young men who successfully avoid reimprisonment but struggle to find stable employment? How can we help remove these and other obstacles encountered by young men who have been released from prison as they transition to adulthood?

Chapter 2 | Studying the Transition to Adulthood after Prison

DESPITE THE MAGNITUDE of the increase in incarceration and the new scope of community criminal justice supervision,[1] social scientists are only beginning to understand the experiences of young men directly affected by these trends, particularly what happens when they reenter society. The life-course framework provides theoretical grounding for our investigation of the transition to adulthood after prison. In this chapter, we describe the key elements of the life-course framework and explain how this model of human development can help us understand the transition to adulthood after prison. We also introduce the data and methods on which our study relies and give an overview of the characteristics of the young men in our study sample.

THEORETICAL FRAMEWORK: LIFE-COURSE THEORY AND THE TRANSITION TO ADULTHOOD

The life-course framework is a developmentally informed theoretical perspective that emphasizes the connections between different stages in the life course. As Robert Sampson and John Laub put it, "The life-course perspective highlights continuities and discontinuities in behavior over time and the social influences of age-graded transitions and life events."[2] A central assumption of this framework is that events (such as marriage, employment, school completion) are linked over time and that the sequences and patterns of events must be examined.[3] Thus, the framework focuses on the role of salient life events in structuring developmental trajectories and life transitions, such that "each [life] stage represents a launching point for the next."[4] The life-course framework therefore suggests that formerly imprisoned young adults are likely to face especially strong challenges in making the transition to adulthood because of the interruptions they have experienced in normatively sequential connections between critical life events (for example, the connection between first employment and departure from the childhood household), as well as the compounding nature of early events in establishing trajectories of advantage or disadvantage over the life course.

"Trajectories" and "transitions" are the two primary concepts that link individual experiences over the life course and structure life outcomes.[5] Trajectories are long-term patterns or sequences of behaviors and social roles. For example, by decreasing the time an individual has to devote to schooling, intensive employment during adolescence or young adulthood may prevent the accumulation of human capital and block the transition to higher-wage work.[6] Transitions are discrete changes in roles and behaviors connected to "salient life events" such as marriage, school completion, or entry into military service.[7] For instance, the accumulation of human capital while parents are providing material support allows individuals to make the transition to work and eventually establish their own household. Life-course research attempts to understand variations in trajectories and transitions, focusing on the intergenerational transmission of disadvantages, historical events,[8] and structural positions like gender, race, and class.[9]

In the developmental period of becoming an adult, important transitions are made and long-term life trajectories are established. Dennis Hogan and Nan Marie Astone emphasize that the transition to adulthood is a process rather than a discrete event.[10] Life events may hasten or interrupt the transition or change its direction. For example, military service may delay schooling, marriage, or parenthood, but it may also pay dividends—in particular by providing skills valuable to the labor market. The life-course framework highlights the importance of early life events in creating and maintaining inequality, since events during the transition to adulthood can establish lifetime trajectories, what Glen Elder calls the "accumulation of disadvantage."[11] Because transitions and their effects are reversible, however, and trajectories can be shifted, some researchers choose to focus on resilience, or "how some individuals succeed in the face of difficult circumstances."[12]

We take a sociologically informed perspective on the transition to adulthood that emphasizes the role of institutionally created "pathways" that structure the transition to adulthood.[13] For example, access to higher education is generally restricted to those with either a high school diploma or a GED. Sociologists also emphasize social contexts and social bonds. Institutions often treat young people from lower-class backgrounds and minority groups with less care and consideration than those from middle-class white backgrounds, who are better able to present themselves as conforming to middle-class social norms.[14] Deepening the impact of norms, social bonds to conventional others facilitate informal social control as individuals seek to maintain relationships by conforming to "conventional" roles.[15] Social bonds can also be important sources of social support. Social contexts influence the networks that individuals form and the resources to which they have access. We develop these ideas later as they apply to formerly incarcerated young adults.

Criminologists have fruitfully employed the life-course perspective to understand desistance from crime, a process that, once complete, constitutes a life-course transition that changes an individual's long-term behavioral trajectory. Sampson and Laub have developed an "age-graded theory of informal social control" to explain changes in delinquency and criminality over the life span.[16] Informal social control, a product of both interpersonal ties and participation in social institutions, emerges from "the role reciprocities and the structure of interpersonal bonds linking members of society to one another and to wider social institutions such as work, family, and school."[17] They argue that opportunities springing from class, race, and family background in childhood and adolescence affect informal family and school social controls, which in turn affect delinquency. Antisocial behavior that arises from this background continues into adulthood in part because of the weak personal and institutional ties also formed through earlier delinquency. In the normative case, on the other hand, adult social bonds—particularly those resulting from marriage, employment, and military service—deter adult criminality through informal social control.[18] Positive transitions, or "turning points," occur when social ties are changed so as to increase social control, establish productive daily routines, and stabilize prosocial roles, all of which increase the likelihood of desistance. Such changes may also separate individuals from criminal peers—prime examples are getting married or joining the military.[19] In contrast to this notion of social control, Shadd Maruna emphasizes changes of self-concept that come from new roles and relationships or from maturity through aging—such as beginning to think of oneself as prosocial rather than antisocial.[20]

This prior research on the life course, the transition to adulthood, and desistance from crime has important implications for the study of prisoner reentry and reintegration among young adults. First, it motivates our own study by suggesting that this already vulnerable population may face additional challenges as a consequence of their past and ongoing involvement in the criminal justice system. Prison interrupts schooling and employment, separates prisoners from social supports,[21] attaches stigma that affects employment and access to institutions of higher education,[22] and may establish trajectories of long-term disadvantage. Moreover, if the experience of early criminal justice system contact and incarceration separates young people from supportive family members by severing or weakening social ties, they will have fewer social resources upon which to draw as they attempt to rebuild their lives after prison.[23]

Yet, with its emphasis on resilience, the protective effect of strong social bonds and supportive social contexts, and the role of life events in precipitating transitions, the life-course framework also suggests that these disadvantages may be reversible for some young adults. Prior research and theory suggest that social contexts structure access to the social supports and informal social control necessary to transition away from crime and substance abuse and toward work and education. Social contexts and institutions provide structured daily activities that impose informal social control, affect investments in conventional institutions and social bonds, and transform identities.

The life-course framework also suggests that experiences and outcomes after prison will be related to one another, both over time and across life-course domains such as work, education, residential stability, and health. Early post-release experiences can either provide a strong foundation on which young men's future successes will be built or undermine their initial attempts at reintegration, setting them on trajectories of long-term disadvantage and struggle. For example, early post-prison success in finding a job or enrolling in college might lead to stronger identification with prosocial roles and set the stage for long-term changes in substance use, involvement in violence, or residential instability. In contrast, struggles with employment in the months after release may dissuade formerly incarcerated young men from following through on sobriety goals or educational plans and lower the costs for them of returning to criminal activity to make ends meet. Accordingly, we pay special attention to the relationship between events in the first year of the post-release period and long-term outcomes, and we carefully examine the impact of successes or failures in one domain on outcomes in others.

CONCEPTUALIZING THE TRANSITION TO ADULTHOOD AFTER PRISON

We draw upon the transition-to-adulthood theoretical framework to conceptualize our empirical analysis of the reentry and reintegration experiences of young adults leaving prison. As outlined in figure 2.1, we conceptualize the life trajectories of young men leaving prison as starting before their incarceration in prison and as influenced by their pre-prison, in-prison, and post-release experiences. That is, transitions and turning points may occur in all of these time periods and may also be influenced

Figure 2.1 Conceptual Model of the Transition to Adulthood after Prison

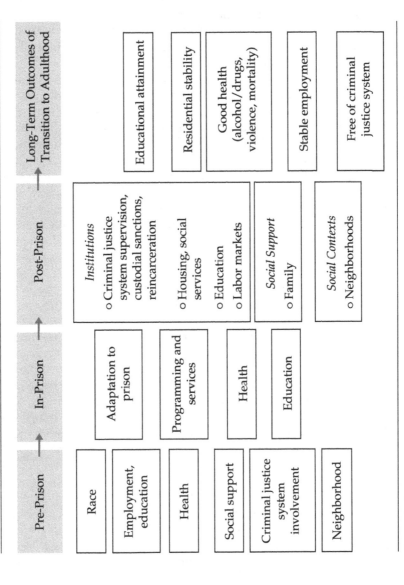

Pre-Prison	In-Prison	Post-Prison	Long-Term Outcomes of Transition to Adulthood
Race	Adaptation to prison	*Institutions*	Educational attainment
Employment, education	Programming and services	o Criminal justice system supervision, custodial sanctions, reincarceration	Residential stability
Health	Health	o Housing, social services	Good health (alcohol/drugs, violence, mortality)
Social support	Education	o Education	
Criminal justice system involvement		o Labor markets	Stable employment
Neighborhood		*Social Support*	Free of criminal justice system
		o Family	
		Social Contexts	
		o Neighborhoods	

Source: Authors.

by the young men's social contexts, social supports, and institutional experiences in these periods. Consistent with the life-course framework, we emphasize that the sequencing of events should be viewed as potentially (although not necessarily) variable, as should the timing of experiences; in other words, some transitions may overlap or even revert backwards and need to be repeated. In short, we envision multiple pathways to adulthood after release from prison and deploy our data to understand the diversity and structure of those pathways.

Our key markers of the transition to adulthood appear to the far right of figure 2.1 and include education completion, stable employment, good health, residential stability and independence, and freedom from further involvement in crime and the criminal justice system. In addition to being the markers of adulthood widely adopted in recent research on the transition to adulthood,[24] these outcomes, even as their order and frequency have changed and become more variable over time, continue to be considered by young adults from all family backgrounds and racial groups the anchors for their understandings of what it means to be an adult, as consistently shown by research on young adults' subjective feelings of adulthood.[25] Rather than assuming a particular sequence of events, our analyses inductively identify from the data various sequences and their relative frequency (see chapter 8).

The core empirical chapters of this book examine each of these longer-term outcomes and their interrelationships. Achievement of these markers in the first year after release was relatively rare (see table 2.1). Only 7 percent of the young men continued their education after release, and only 54 percent found employment in the formal labor market. Average earnings were low, only $1,555 per calendar quarter. The typical member of our sample lived independently for only eighty-seven days of the first post-prison year. Eleven percent tested positive for alcohol or drugs, and on average the young men in our study spent six and a half days in residential substance abuse treatment. Racial inequalities were already evident at one year after release. Employment and earnings were notably higher among whites than blacks. Although positive substance use tests were more common among blacks, whites spent more time in residential treatment.

To the far left of figure 2.1, we include critical pre-prison experiences and characteristics. Our conceptual model suggests that race, prior human capital, health behaviors, social support, criminal justice involvement, and neighborhood context play important roles in later experiences, including in-prison, after prison, and over the long term, by establishing early life trajectories. Although such trajectories are interrupted by imprisonment, they partially determine the social, economic, and cultural resources on which young men can draw later in life. These pre-prison characteristics

Table 2.1 Background Characteristics and Pre- and Post-Prison Experiences, by Race

	Overall		Blacks		Whites	
Variable	Mean	Standard Deviation	Mean	Standard Deviation	Mean	Standard Deviation
Pre-prison criminal justice system interactions						
Age at first arrest	15.4	2.5	15.5	2.5	15.4	2.5
Juvenile commitment (%)	0.44		0.43		0.45	
Number of arrests	3.2	2.0	3.1[a]	1.9	3.3[a]	2.1
Number of convictions	3.5	2.1	3.2[a]	1.9	3.7[a]	2.2
Number of post-conviction fines	1.1	1.2	0.8[a]	1.1	1.4[a]	1.3
Number of post-conviction probations	0.8	1.0	0.8	0.9	0.8	1.0
Number of post-conviction custodies	2.3	1.5	2.1[a]	1.3	2.5[a]	1.6
Age on entering prison	20.8	2.0	20.9	2.0	20.7	2.0
Demographics						
Foster care history	0.09		0.11[a]		0.07[a]	
Has dependent	0.41		0.49[a]		0.33[a]	
Ever married	0.05		0.05		0.06	
Pre-prison human capital development						
High school graduate	0.09		0.09		0.08	
Earned GED	0.61		0.46[a]		0.74[a]	
Employed	0.71		0.65[a]		0.76[a]	
Lived independently	0.63		0.65[a]		0.61[a]	

(Table continues on p. 34)

Table 2.1 Continued

	Overall		Blacks		Whites	
Variable	Mean	Standard Deviation	Mean	Standard Deviation	Mean	Standard Deviation
Pre-prison mental health and substance use						
Mentally ill	0.20		0.09[a]		0.29[a]	
Daily alcohol use	0.11		0.08[a]		0.13[a]	
Daily marijuana use	0.27		0.28		0.27	
Daily stimulant use	0.07		0.06		0.08	
Daily depressant use	0.03		0.02[a]		0.04[a]	
Prison experiences						
Months in prison	22.2	19.1	24.0[a]	20.3	20.9[a]	17.9
Earned GED in prison (%)	0.31		0.27[a]		0.36[a]	
Had misconducts (%)	0.61		0.66[a]		0.56[a]	
Days in solitary	11.4	67.7	11.1	56.6	11.6	76.2
Social context in first post-prison year						
Days in Detroit	54	118	107[a]	150	8[a]	42
Tract disadvantage score	0.53	1.19	1.36[a]	1.11	-0.22[a]	0.63
Tract affluence score	-0.38	0.56	-0.37	0.50	-0.39	0.61
County crime rate per 1,000	6.12	2.78	7.39[a]	2.71	4.97[a]	2.31

Criminal justice system interactions in first post-prison year						
Electronic monitoring (%)	0.36		0.30[a]		0.41[a]	
Number of parole violations	1.14	1.35	1.12	1.43	1.15	1.28
Number of arrests	0.54	0.78	0.60[a]	0.79	0.49	0.77[a]
Days held in custody	47.6	83.3	48.0	81.3	47.2	85.1
Human capital development in first post-prison year						
Continued education	0.07		0.06		0.07	
Employed	0.54		0.41[a]		0.65[a]	
Earnings	$1,535	$2,428	$950[a]	$1,850	$2,093	$2,736[a]
Days lived independently	87.2	121.4	84.1	122.6	89.9	120.3
Positive drug tests (%)	0.11	0.22	0.14[a]	0.25	0.08[a]	0.19
Days in residential treatment	6.5	21.5	4.4[a]	19.3	8.2[a]	23.0
N	1,300		612		688	

Source: Michigan Study of Life after Prison.

Notes: Fourteen individuals who are Asian and Native American are grouped with whites. "Stimulants" are mainly cocaine but also include methamphetamines and prescription stimulants such as Ritalin and Adderall. "Depressants" are mainly heroin and prescription opioids but also include sedatives, tranquilizers, barbiturates, and benzodiazepines. "Continued education" indicates that the young man either earned a GED or enrolled in college in the first year after prison. The tract and county variables are averages over all of the characteristics of the residential addresses where a young man lived during the first post-prison year. We lack a non-institutional neighborhood address in the first post-prison year for twenty-four individuals. The disadvantage and affluence scores were generated via factor analysis and are orthogonal to each other. The disadvantage score loads on percent black, poverty and unemployment rates, female-headed households, and welfare receipt. The affluence score loads on higher education, professional and managerial occupations, and higher median income. Because of multicollinearity between the indicators, these scores are preferred over the individual indicators. Data for 2003 Michigan parole cohort age 18–25 at parole, followed through 2009.

[a] The difference between the black and white means is statistically significant (at $p \leq 0.05$).

and experiences will also structure the resources and constraints to which young men have access in prison and their capacity to take advantage of such opportunities or to remain resilient to the difficulties of life in prison (see the second column of figure 2.1).

Young men exiting prison between the ages of eighteen and twenty-five had pre-prison experiences marked by significant struggle and disadvantage, as shown in table 2.1. They also had considerable involvement with the criminal justice system even before their imprisonment. They were age fifteen on average at the time of their first arrest, and 44 percent were incarcerated as juveniles. They averaged 3.2 arrests and 3.5 felony convictions and entered prison on average at age twenty-one. Whites in our sample typically had more arrests and more felony convictions than blacks prior to their incarceration, which probably reflects a combination of different types of crimes and more lenient treatment by the criminal justice system. With regard to demographic characteristics, 9 percent had been in foster care and 41 percent had dependents (almost exclusively children). Blacks were more likely to have experienced foster care and to have children than whites. Only 5 percent of all young men had been married. The picture that these figures paint is fairly grim: based on what these young men experienced before they entered prison, many left prison with low levels of social support.

The pre-prison experiences of these young men were also marked by significant disadvantages in human capital development and mental health. Only 9 percent had a high school degree at prison entry. An additional 61 percent had a GED, although this was much more common among whites than blacks, and many of these GEDs were earned during prior periods of imprisonment, as we will see in the next chapter. Seventy-one percent had been formally employed; only 63 percent had lived independently before prison. Prior employment was more common among whites, while independent living was slightly more common among blacks. Mental health problems were identified in 20 percent at prison entry, as measured by self-reports of diagnoses, hospitalizations, or prescriptions for mental health problems. Serious substance use problems were also evident. Eleven percent reported daily alcohol use, 27 percent reported daily marijuana use, 7 percent reported daily stimulant use (mostly cocaine, methamphetamines, and prescription drugs), and 3 percent reported daily depressant use, primarily opioids. Mental health problems, alcohol use, and depressant use were more common among whites.

These racial differences in pre-prison experiences tell us that there are racial differences in the processes by which young white men and young black men end up in prison. As discussed earlier, young black men face a much higher risk of imprisonment than young white men owing to greater surveillance and more punitive treatment by the criminal justice system and fewer employment and educational opportunities. In other words, it is much rarer for a young white man to end up in prison relative to other young white men than it is for a young black man to end up in prison relative to other young black men. Indeed, imprisonment has become a new stage in the life course for young black men, especially those without a high school degree.[26] Somewhat paradoxically, this means that young white men who are imprisoned face different rates of certain disadvantages than young black men who are imprisoned. Young black men's imprisonment typically has its roots in lack of economic opportunities, the war on drugs, and greater police presence in poor black neighborhoods,[27] as indicated by higher rates of drug crimes and the firearm violence associated with the drug trade. The sources of young white men's imprisonment typically lie in the criminalization of mental illness and addiction, as evidenced by higher rates of diagnosed mental illness and abuse of hard drugs, such as opioids and cocaine, as well as alcohol. Such racial differences in the pathways into prison are important to keep in mind as we consider the different challenges and barriers that young black and white men face after prison.

As described earlier, the life-course framework's emphasis on transitions and trajectories suggests that early experiences after release from prison may be especially important for determining longer-term trajectories (see the third column of figure 2.1). Qualitative research has documented the optimism of most incarcerated individuals at the moment of release, suggesting that they could maintain the motivation to work, enroll in school, and stay clear of further involvement in crime if they could access supportive social institutions and contexts.[28] Initial successes may lead to future opportunities as well as future exposures to even more supportive institutions and contexts, in a virtuous cycle. For example, early success in the labor market or schooling may mitigate to some degree the stigma of a criminal record in the eyes of employers or landlords. Moreover, stable housing may be the foundation upon which other aspects of successful reentry rely.[29] Without stable housing, a young man recently released from prison can find it challenging to find and maintain employment, family connections, and health care and to avoid substance use.[30] Together, these ideas suggest that we should observe some degree of "path dependency," as early outcomes are predictive of later trajectories.

Our conceptual framework emphasizes three key concepts that appear throughout our analysis of these outcomes: social support, social contexts, and institutions. Our data allow us to measure these concepts primarily through households, institutional living arrangements, neighborhoods, the criminal justice system, involvement in the formal labor market, and educational institutions.

Families, Households, and Alternative Living Arrangements

Households are a potentially important context for young adults who have recently left prison, particularly during the transition to adulthood. Incarceration almost invariably disrupts ties to family members, romantic partners, and children.[31] Thus, individuals exiting prison often find themselves living in shelters, residential treatment programs, or other institutional contexts. Previous research has found high rates of housing instability and homelessness among former prisoners.[32] For vulnerable young adults, the household context proves to be a critical determinant of their short-term material well-being. Given the role of family in supporting young people during schooling, residing with family may make further education possible.[33] In a very real sense, family may be the *only* source of social support for those who have been incarcerated in prison and thereby separated from other networks. Yet we know little, even descriptively, about the household contexts to which formerly incarcerated young adults return after their release or how these contexts affect their employment, education, substance use, or recidivism outcomes. Our data shows only about three-quarters of these young men age twenty-five and under moving to private homes when they were first released from prison.

Households and families have largely been conceived in the transition-to-adulthood literature as a source of material support and stability,[34] as the provider of scaffolding that enables continued schooling, and as a source of socialization during childhood and adolescence that instills cultural skills and attitudes.[35] Little attention has been given to the other types of living arrangements that our data show are common among the formerly incarcerated, such as residence in shelters or treatment centers. Yet the life-course framework suggests multiple additional ways in which households and other living arrangements may affect young adults during the transition to adulthood, both positively and negatively. Young adults living with family in particular may be accountable to household members; for them, the mechanisms of informal social control may constrain criminal activity and substance use and encourage schooling or work. Family roles and the expectations that go with them can also reshape self-concepts and identities. For example, John Schulenberg and his colleagues find that family responsibilities often precede a decline in substance abuse, but that substance use among young adults tends to increase once they leave the family home.[36] For those living in institutional settings, rules and staff supervision may impose formal social control. Families and households may also provide access to social capital. Household members may provide information about employment or schooling opportunities or provide access to a wider social network of "weak ties" that can provide such information.[37] On the other hand, family role expectations can also create stress and lead to negative decisions if an individual is not equipped to meet them. This "role strain" may prompt either a return to illegal activities in order to meet household material needs or renewed substance abuse to cope with the resulting stress.[38] Similarly, families and households may be sources of emotional conflict. Frequent conflict or emotional abuse in the household may also create stress and prompt poor coping responses such as substance abuse or violence.[39]

The possibility of countervailing positive and negative effects of families and households suggests that returning to the pre-prison household can be either positive or negative, depending on the nature of the household and the individual's relationship to it. For those from potentially harmful household environments, returning home may prove disadvantageous. Furthermore, for those with serious mental health and addiction problems, the services in institutional contexts may be protective.

Neighborhoods

Neighborhoods are another context that may be critical for reintegration. Neighborhoods with high unemployment, poverty, and crime rates are likely to provide young adults with fewer resources to support the transition from prison to work, lower levels of social control, and greater opportunities to return to crime.[40] Many former prisoners return to very disadvantaged neighborhoods characterized by poverty, joblessness, and high rates of crime and disorder.[41] Returning to disadvantaged neighborhoods after prison has been shown to increase the risk of recidivism and to reduce employment.[42]

There are stark racial differences in the neighborhoods to which prisoners are released.[43] Whites enter and exit prison from less disadvantaged neighborhoods than do blacks.[44] Blacks do tend to move to poorer neighborhoods than whites after prison, but mainly because of the more general landscape of residential segregation by race rather than the impact of incarceration itself. Moreover, only whites experience worse neighborhood conditions after prison than before, but blacks experience greater residential instability.[45]

Table 2.1 shows that these patterns among the general post-prison population are also reflected among the young men in our study. To measure neighborhood context, we use two scales that combine multiple indicators.[46] The disadvantage scale includes poverty, welfare receipt, single-parent families, unemployment, percent black, and high school dropout rate. The typical young black man lived in a neighborhood with a disadvantage score that was 1.36 standard deviations higher than the state average, while the typical young white man lived in a neighborhood that was 0.22 standard deviations *below* the state average. In addition, whites tended to return to counties with lower crime rates and to spend less time living in Michigan's largest city, Detroit. Both whites and blacks, however, tended to live in neighborhoods with similar levels of affluence. The affluence scale combines college education, professional or managerial occupations, and high median income.[47] Both whites and blacks were more likely to live in neighborhoods that were below the state average on the affluence scale. Table 2.2 shows more detailed neighborhood measures by race for the first year after release.

Neighborhoods have received little attention in the transition-to-adulthood literature, but they can play an important role in establishing life-course trajectories.[48] We expect that young adults returning to disadvantaged neighborhoods will have greater difficulties finding and maintaining employment, pursuing education, complying with parole requirements, and staying away from crime and substance abuse—each of which can establish trajectories of disadvantage. Prior research suggests five processes through which neighborhoods may affect formerly incarcerated young adults. First, disadvantaged neighborhoods tend to exert lower levels of informal social control over their residents and to have higher rates of crime and disorder.[49] Former prisoners who return to neighborhoods with lower social control will face fewer barriers to returning to crime and substance abuse and therefore may also see employment and education as less appealing. Second, returning to disadvantaged neighborhoods located in local labor markets with higher unemployment rates (like central cities) may increase unemployment and recidivism. County unemployment has also been found to influence the employment prospects and recidivism of former prisoners.[50] Third, residents of disadvantaged neighborhoods, particularly African Americans, are socially isolated from networks that might provide information about employment and education.[51] Young adults returning to such neighborhoods therefore cannot rely on neighbors for help with jobs or schooling. Local conditions may also affect the availability of resources for education. Fourth, in what is known as "spatial mismatch," disadvantaged neighborhoods are often located far from jobs.[52] Although social service providers tend to be concentrated in poor neighborhoods, the greater need for services among residents of these neighborhoods can make it harder for them to secure employment, training, or addiction-related services.[53] Lastly, differential opportunity theory suggests that disadvantaged neighborhoods provide more opportunities to engage in crime and substance abuse, both of which may lower prospects for employment or schooling.[54] Disadvantaged neighborhoods also have a higher concentration of former prisoners and higher rates of alcohol and drug use.[55]

Table 2.2 First Year Post-Prison Neighborhood Contexts, by Race

	Overall		Blacks		Whites	
	Mean	Standard Deviation	Mean	Standard Deviation	Mean	Standard Deviation
Poverty rate	0.18	0.12	0.24[a]	0.11	0.13[a]	0.09
Unemployment rate	0.09	0.05	0.11[a]	0.05	0.06[a]	0.03
Did not graduate (%)	0.20	0.09	0.23[a]	0.09	0.17[a]	0.08
Single mothers (%)	0.26	0.14	0.35[a]	0.13	0.17[a]	0.10
Black (%)	0.35	0.37	0.63[a]	0.32	0.10[a]	0.16
Median income	$44,471	$16,359	$36,966[a]	$13,851	$51,217[a]	$15,487
Owner-occupied (%)	0.66	0.18	0.59[a]	0.16	0.73[a]	0.17
Same address (%)	0.75	0.085	0.74[a]	0.08	0.76[a]	0.08
Professional (%)	0.24	0.10	0.22[a]	0.10	0.26[a]	0.09
High income (%)	0.22	0.13	0.17[a]	0.10	0.26[a]	0.13
On assistance (%)	0.09	0.09	0.12[a]	0.10	0.07[a]	0.08
N	1,300		612		688	

Source: Michigan Study of Life after Prison.

Notes: Each indicator is an average over all of the neighborhoods, defined as census tracts, in which each individual lived in the first year after prison. Twenty-four individuals did not have a known non-institutional residential tract during the first post-prison year. See figures 2.A1 and 2.A2 for the distributions of pre-prison and post-prison neighborhood disadvantage. Data for 2003 Michigan parole cohort age 18–25 at parole, followed through 2009.

[a] The difference between the black and white means is statistically significant (at $p \leq 0.05$).

Institutions

Three critical institutional contexts can impact young men's transitions to adulthood after prison: the labor market, educational institutions, and the criminal justice system. Given their lack of work experience and low levels of education, many former prisoners are relegated to the "secondary labor market," which refers to jobs where turnover is high, schedules are variable, wages and benefits are low, and opportunities for promotion and wage growth are few.[56] These characteristics of the low-skill labor market may lead to economic insecurity, residential instability, trouble meeting family and partner role expectations, and lack of commitment to work, but they may also motivate young adults to attempt to build their human capital through further education. In addition, the stigma of a criminal record, both formal and informal, reduces one's chance of being hired.[57] Indeed, a vast industry works to maintain and distribute criminal record information, making the management of a stigmatized identity in the labor market particularly difficult.[58]

Educational institutions can reduce these problems by developing human capital, but we know little about how often or with what success formerly incarcerated young adults pursue GEDs, job training, or college degrees. Educational institutions are variously viewed by scholars of poverty and inequality as either engines of social mobility[59] or reinforcers of class and racial privilege that sort students on the basis of social and cultural capital and the capacity to comport with white middle-class norms.[60] The notion of the "school-to-prison pipeline" takes this idea even further, arguing that the disciplinary procedures of public schools combine with the surveillance and punishment of the criminal justice system to push young people of color away from educational opportunities and toward the carceral state.[61] It is probably safe to say that most of the young men in our study who were imprisoned early in the life course did not find their secondary schooling experiences to be supportive or enabling, given the low rates of high school completion described earlier.

After release from prison, community colleges and for-profit colleges are the primary educational institutions open to formerly incarcerated young men. Such institutions have high enrollment rates but low completion rates, for several reasons: the academic preparation of their students is poor, and they need to take remedial courses that do not provide credit toward a degree; career and college counseling resources are limited; and courses in the fields with the greatest returns in the labor market are oversubscribed.[62] Students who enter college later in life have more trouble finishing their degrees, owing in part to other life responsibilities such as work and parenthood.[63] We examine the extent to which formerly incarcerated young men enroll in postsecondary institutions and how successful they are at completing degrees or certificates during their transition to adulthood.

Exposure to the criminal justice system before prison may have long-term consequences that cascade through early life, prison, and reentry experiences, including the transition to adulthood. Earlier and more frequent arrests result in longer criminal records, which can lead to harsher sentences, more stringent treatment in prison, and more intense supervision after release.[64] More frequent arrests, convictions, and punishments during adolescence and early adulthood can interrupt schooling and prevent a young adult from accumulating work experience.[65] These setbacks delay post-prison adult transitions as the criminal justice–involved try to rebuild their lives on weak human capital foundations. Substance use that begins with experimentation can intensify into abuse as individuals find themselves with few licit opportunities and instead turn to illicit work in the drug economy.[66] Finally, if the experience of early criminal justice system contact and incarceration separates young people from supportive family members by severing or weakening social ties, they are left with fewer social resources upon which to draw as they attempt to rebuild their lives after prison.[67] The structural stigma that can result from contact with the criminal justice system can also have negative effects on physical and mental health.[68]

Experiences *during* prison also can affect future life trajectories, in theory both positively and negatively. On the one hand, access to health care, mental health and addiction treatment, and educational opportunities in prison can shift life trajectories in a positive direction.[69] If prison creates a break from substance abuse and involvement in violence, offers access to medical care, and provides time for human capital development, it can anchor a turning point or transition.

Unfortunately, prisons in the United States typically fail to deliver on such potential: supports and services are often hard to come by, and the quality of services in prison is typically low. Moreover, countervailing effects of the prison environment—such as the risk of violent victimization, social isolation from family and other sources of social and emotional support, and the regimentation of prison life—may hinder or harm the social, emotional, and cognitive development of young adults.[70] Solitary confinement in prison may be especially damaging to the developmental process.[71] Such prison experiences can reinforce previously accumulated disadvantages and fix rather than alter life trajectories that include criminal behavior. To the extent that the experience of imprisonment in the United States might represent an improvement in circumstances, such an improvement is actually a reflection of lack of economic and educational opportunities and other institutional supports outside of prison as well as the high risk of violent victimization in poor communities, especially as experienced by young black men from poor and working-class families.[72] Indeed, in her research Megan Comfort found that young formerly incarcerated men understand prison as the kind of time for reflection and life planning that young adults from middle-class families are provided in other institutional contexts, particularly college.[73] But when young men return to the disadvantaged environments from which they entered prison, gains they may have made during incarceration can be lost.[74]

Table 2.1 describes some of the prison experiences of the formerly incarcerated young men we study. They spent on average twenty-two months in prison during their latest prison term, and blacks spent about three months more in prison than whites. Thirty-one percent earned their GED in prison, but this was more common among whites (36 percent) than blacks (27 percent). On the other hand, 61 percent received some sort of misconduct violation while in prison, which was slightly more common among blacks (66 percent) than whites (61 percent). Misconduct citations in prison are one potential indicator of difficulties adjusting to the prison environment, which are most common among younger prisoners.[75] On average young men spent a total of 11.4 days in solitary confinement, an average that did not differ by race.

The influence of the criminal justice system does not stop when a young adult leaves prison. In Michigan, over 90 percent of those released from prison are released onto parole supervision. Parole is a social institution intended to carry out a multifaceted set of policies that allow the criminal justice system to supervise released prisoners as they reenter society. Parole systems incorporate numerous interventions into the lives of the formerly incarcerated, including supervision (at several levels) and electronic monitoring as well as special conditions of release that are applied to some but not all.

On the one hand, parole interventions are intended to facilitate parolees' access to both social supports and social control (formal and informal) in an effort to assist them in transitioning away from crime and substance abuse and into work and education. This suggests that intense parole supervision—which can require formal work, schooling, drug testing, and electronic monitoring—may be associated with parolees achieving greater residential stability, being more successful at employment and educational enrollment (GED or postsecondary), lowering their substance use, and avoiding rearrest. On the other hand, the very nature of parole supervision—whose emphasis has shifted from rehabilitation to surveillance and control—may negatively affect the transition to adulthood.[76] Parole requirements that restrict access to communication, people, or residences may exacerbate the felon stigma in the labor and housing markets and lead a young man to abscond, thus making formal employment and schooling impossible. More intense supervision may put him at greater risk for parole sanctions, as minor crimes (such as drug use or fighting) and noncriminal behavior (breaking curfew, consuming alcohol) can lead to transition-halting incarceration spells.[77] Even when minor offenses lead to so-called "intermediate" sanctions that fall short of return to prison, those sanctions may disrupt employment, residential stability, and schooling.[78] These arguments suggest that parole supervision intensity and electronic monitoring are associated with greater risk of parole violations, absconding, arrest, and return to prison, all of which are associated with residential instability and lower employment and schooling.

Furthermore, parole violations are central to the "revolving door" of prison: technical rule violations yield over one-third of prison admissions.[79] Technical rule violations are failures to conform to the rules of parole, not new crimes that would ordinarily lead to imprisonment. Examples include curfew violations, alcohol and drug use, absconding, or refusing to comply with treatment or other required programming. Even while admissions for new crimes fell in the late 2000s, parole violation admissions continued to rise.[80] Moreover, racial and class disparities similar to those for incarceration in prison are also evident for the intensity of community correctional supervision.[81] Differential application of the conditions that must be met for parole may exacerbate these disparities.[82]

Young men in our study who left prison had considerable difficulty escaping further criminal justice system involvement, as shown in table 2.1. Thirty-six percent experienced electronic monitoring on top of their routine parole supervision in the first year. Each individual had on average one parole violation, and half were arrested at some point in the first year after release. The typical individual was held in custody for forty-eight days during his first year, or just over a month and a half.

A STUDY OF 1,300 FORMERLY IMPRISONED YOUNG MEN

We set out to understand how and why some formerly incarcerated young men escape involvement in the criminal justice system and establish conventional lives for themselves—marked by avoidance of substance abuse and violence, further education, employment, and residential stability—while others do not. What pre-prison characteristics and experiences, in-prison experiences, and post-release experiences, social contexts, and institutional encounters are associated with a greater chance of successful transitions to adulthood, and which are associated with continued instability, poor health, and continued involvement in the criminal justice system?[83] Understanding which formerly incarcerated young men are most or least likely to recover from early-life imprisonment is a critical first step toward developing policies and interventions to improve their long-term outcomes and those of disconnected young adults more generally.

This study focuses on data from the Michigan Study of Life after Prison, which includes information on 1,300 Michigan parolees that we assembled with the cooperation of the Michigan Department of Corrections (MDOC). The data used in this book include a two-thirds sample of all male parolees age twenty-five and under who were paroled from Michigan prisons to Michigan communities in 2003.[84] This data set is unique in its detailed, longitudinal information on the social contexts of a vulnerable population. The data set is also approximately half black and half white, allowing us the opportunity to examine differences in the transition to adulthood by race.[85] This research design represents a departure from prior research on the transition to adulthood, which has typically relied either on nationally representative longitudinal survey data[86] or qualitative interview data collected in a small number of cities or towns.[87]

This study leverages the comparative advantage of longitudinal administrative data. First, like survey data, the data set allows us to follow the young men we study over time as they transitioned to adulthood, measuring intermediate processes and longer-term outcomes in fine-grained temporal detail. Second, it provides data on many young men who are typically underrepresented in or excluded from traditional social science data sources. When they are present in such data sources, they are rarely included in sufficient numbers to study variation among them in outcomes. Instead, researchers typically compare criminal justice–involved young men as a group to others who are not criminal justice–involved—a strategy better suited to answering research questions about what differentiates those who experience incarceration from those who do not. Third, the data set allows us to study a population that is not only extremely difficult to follow using survey-based methods but also traditionally excluded from survey data.[88] Survey sampling frames are typically based on the non-institutionalized population and also often miss young people who are only tenuously attached to households and are highly residentially mobile.[89] Fourth, administrative data allow us to measure in detail various forms of involvement with and punishment within the criminal justice system, from more common measures like arrests, convictions, and returns to prison to harder-to-measure experiences like custodial parole sanctions, short jail stays, and parole-mandated residential treatment programs.

The Michigan Study of Life after Prison is distinctive both in the breadth of information it covers—few previous studies have detailed longitudinal data on returning prisoners, and even fewer have any information on neighborhood context—and in its geographic scope. Previous studies that collect data on former prisoners have been limited to individual cities and cover a relatively short follow-up period.[90] By contrast, this study covers the entire state of Michigan, including suburbs and rural areas where former prisoners are increasingly found,[91] and follows formerly incarcerated young men for at least six years. Moreover, no previous study of which we are aware has been able to examine the interrelationships between pre-prison background, social contexts, institutional involvements, and key indicators of the transition to adulthood, such as employment, education, substance use, and recidivism, among a large sample of formerly incarcerated individuals in the age range that captures the transition to adulthood.

The primary sources of data are MDOC databases that track prisoners, parolees, and probationers under MDOC supervision. The records we have extracted and cleaned cover a wide but variable length of time for each parolee that includes (a) pre-release background, for example, demographics, education, detailed criminal history, pre-prison address, addiction assessments, in-prison educational assessment tests, prison behavior problems; (b) the prison spell that ended in 2003 and the subsequent parole period, which we term the "focal prison spell"; and (c) prospective data on neighborhoods and living arrangements and on supervision conditions, employment, substance use tests, and measures of crime and recidivism.[92] These data are supplemented by Census Bureau data on neighborhoods, unemployment insurance records, court records, police arrest data, mortality records, records of GED test-taking and completion from the State of Michigan's Parchment database, and records of college enrollment from the National Student Clearinghouse. The case notes that parole agents write and update regularly on each parolee provide another key source of data. Our research team developed essential expertise in reading and coding case notes (which include many abbreviations and terminology particular to MDOC) in collecting the prospective data on parolees' residential addresses, living arrangements, and employment after prison. Detailed information on how we measure particular variables is introduced throughout the book as the variables are analyzed.

We would note that our decision to employ administrative data represents important trade-offs. First, administrative data contain only information that is captured in government databases. As a result, it provides little to no information on community involvement, subjective understandings of adulthood, identity development, or self-concept, all of which would need to be collected directly from research subjects. Second, our measures of behavior and experiences are limited to those detected and recorded by government agencies. Thus, for example, our measures of employment cover only formal employment, and our measures of criminal activity are measures of only criminal activity recorded by the criminal justice system. This limitation may lead us to undercount crime that is undetected or overcount crime that is falsely attributed to the young men in our study. A third trade-off is generalizability to the nation as a whole: the complexities and inconsistencies of administrative data systems require concentrating data collection in a single state.

We note two other features of these data that are important for readers to keep in mind. One is that the population we are studying is highly selected on childhood disadvantage. Individuals who end up in prison at a young age come almost uniformly from poor and working-class families, and many of the adults in these families also face challenges with employment stability, substance abuse and other mental health problems, and involvement in the criminal justice system. Even though we have few measures of family-of-origin socioeconomic status, we are confident that there is less variation on this dimension than in the typical social science survey sample. A second consequence of our decision to sample individuals who have experienced imprisonment at a young age is that associations between variables in our data measured prior to this time may be different from what one would expect to see in a more general sample.[93] In other words, because we have implicitly conditioned on imprisonment in young adulthood by studying only those who experienced imprisonment, associations between variables determined earlier in life that affect imprisonment may be different in our sample. For example, it is typical to see employment during adolescence as negatively associated with high school completion.[94] In our sample, however, once we limit to those who eventually end up in prison, employment during adolescence is actually positively associated with pre-prison educational attainment (see chapter 2).

We primarily use two types of statistical techniques to analyze these data. Chapters 2 through 6 uses discrete time-event history models, implemented as multinomial logistic regression models.[95] Such models allow us to examine the association between both time-constant and time-varying characteristics of individuals and the specific life events that are indicators of the transition to adulthood, such as GED receipt, college enrollment, finding or losing a job, being arrested, or achieving residential stability. Time-constant characteristics include race and other demographic characteristics, pre-prison criminal history, substance use, and prison experiences. Examples of time-varying characteristics, which can change after release, include substance use, social contexts, and criminal justice contact. These models predict particular transitions, such as transitions into and out of employment. A key advantage of such models is that, as logistic regressions, their results can easily be converted into marginal effects, which show the association between a change in an independent variable and a change in the probability of the outcome event or transition. Chapter 7 focuses on describing trajectories over time and their variations across people using group-based multi-trajectory models.[96] Such models allow us to describe outcome trajectories in different domains and examine the associations between them, as well as between pre-prison, in-prison, and initial post-release experiences and different long-term life trajectories. All appendix tables, designated in text with an A in the numbering, are available via the online appendix at https://www.russellsage.org/publications/after-prison.

Because our study covers a single state, it is especially important to understand the ways in which Michigan may be unique compared to other parts of the country. One is Michigan's economy. Michigan is known both for a robust public system of colleges and universities and for manufacturing employment. In 2017, manufacturing accounted for almost 14 percent of employment, the third-highest percentage of any state.[97] The falling number of high-paying working-class jobs has negatively affected the economic well-being of Michigan families. Median family income in real terms has fallen over the last several decades. For instance, the median family income of white families living in the Detroit metropolitan area was $74,400 (in 2016 dollars) in 1970 but only $49,100 in 2016.[98] Even before the Great Recession in 2008, Michigan experienced relatively high unemployment rates. Unemployment in Michigan stood at 7.5 percent in June 2003, the year the young men in our study were paroled from prison. By the end of the Great Recession six years later, unemployment in Michigan had risen to 14.5 percent.[99] Michigan's central cities, to which many of the young men in our study returned after prison, have long been known for crushing unemployment and joblessness rates, especially for black men. The Great Recession hit men, the less educated, and blacks especially hard.[100]

With regard to the criminal justice system, Michigan's rates of incarceration and parole are close to the national averages.[101] With its population size, Michigan also accounts for a nontrivial share (4 to 5 percent) of the nation's parole population.[102] Compared with state corrections practices across the nation in the same time period, Michigan's rates of parole revocations to prison were much lower: in 2007, Michigan's parole revocation rate was 6.6 percent, while the national average was 11.4 percent.[103] However, the average time served is longer for Michigan prisoners than for inmates in any other state. In 2009, the average length of time an individual served in prison in Michigan was 4.3 years, a 79 percent increase from 1990, when the Michigan average was 2.4 years.[104] State officials attribute the increase to harsher sentencing practices by judges and longer minimum sentences encoded into law by the state legislature.[105]

Finally, Michigan is also known for racial inequality. It has long been a state with high segregation, owing to the concentration of black residents in central cities and, more recently, in inner-ring suburbs around Detroit.[106] Racial gaps in economic well-being in Michigan's largest metropolitan area—Detroit and its suburbs—have actually grown since 1970. The median income for black families, $33,600 (in 2016 dollars), is now only 52 percent of the median income of white families. Whereas 40.9 percent of black children lived in poverty in 2016, up from 28.2 percent in 1970, only 14 percent of white children lived in poverty in metro Detroit.

The Great Recession hit black homeowners in Michigan particularly hard. Fifty-three percent of black households owned their home in 1970, and 49 percent did in 2008, but only 40 percent of black families owned their home in 2016, compared to 77 percent for whites. Home values among blacks also fell sharply. The median value of black owner-occupied residences grew slightly between 1970 and 2008, from $105,600 to $109,800 (in 2016 dollars), but then fell to $57,000 in 2016, compared to $154,600 for white homes. Blacks are also much more likely to live in concentrated-poverty neighborhoods—those where more than 40 percent of families are poor—than in 1970, when fewer than 2 percent of blacks living in metro Detroit lived in such neighborhoods, compared to one-third in 2016. For whites, by contrast, this figure grew from less than 1 percent to only 4 percent in the same period.[107]

Reynolds Farley attributes these changes to fundamental changes in Michigan's economy, including the decline in working-class jobs that pay a living wage, the demand for higher levels of education in the workforce, and the failure of educational institutions, particularly public schools, to keep pace with these changes and effectively serve black residents.[108] In 2016, fewer than one in ten black men and only 14 percent of black women ages twenty-five to thirty-nine had a college degree, proportions that have barely increased since 1980. In contrast, almost 40 percent of white women and 35 percent of white men in metro Detroit had a college degree in 2016.

This chapter has explained the theoretical framework that guides the study, described the data and methods it employs, and introduced the reader to the characteristics of the young men in our study. The next chapter begins our in-depth analysis of their experiences, focusing on their educational experiences before and during their imprisonment.

Chapter 3 | Education, Part 1: The GED

Pathways to economic self-sufficiency and independence typically involve early employment experiences, the completion of high school, and long-term employment. Educational investments are particularly critical because they can connect young men to long-term employment—a mark of successful transition to adulthood that provides identity and life satisfaction, creates external incentives (for example, commitments and informal social control) to desist from crime, and reduces one of the main incentives to return to crime: the need for income. Setbacks during the transition to adulthood—not completing high school, discontinuing further education, and being unemployed—put youth at risk for becoming "disconnected": a state of not being enrolled in any schooling, being unemployed, and having no high school diploma or GED.[1] Those who do not complete high school become ever more likely to work at low-wage jobs or to be unemployed.

The experiences of young, incarcerated men are often consistent with a "disconnected" narrative of struggles with schooling and work. Jeremiah, a black man born in the early 1980s, grew up in a poor city in the western part of Michigan; his experience illustrates the challenges of schooling and work for those who become involved in the criminal justice system at an early age. He was placed on juvenile probation at age fourteen and was incarcerated in a juvenile detention center after violating the terms of his juvenile probation. Around the same time, he dropped out of middle school. Jeremiah never started high school and began smoking marijuana at age fifteen; he was a daily marijuana smoker by the age of twenty-two.

At seventeen, Jeremiah landed his first formal part-time job, at a fast-food restaurant. He was employed there for less than half a year, during which time he earned a total of just over $400. He would not be employed in the formal labor market again until after his release from prison in 2003.

51

However, he would become persistently involved in the adult criminal justice system. Jeremiah was arrested at age seventeen for driving a car without insurance. A month later, he was arrested for breaking and entering. As a juvenile, he received a deferred judgment, which would have been cleared from his record if he had completed probation successfully. A little more than a year later, however, he pled guilty to unarmed robbery, receiving a two-week jail sentence, a $500 fine, and probation for an additional year. A few months after he completed probation, Jeremiah was arrested and prosecuted again. He pled guilty to several theft-related property offenses, including breaking and entering and second-degree home invasion. He was sentenced to two years of probation—with a term of confinement to be served if he violated probation. Ten months later, he was arrested again, resulting in his commitment to state prison for the first time.

Jeremiah was released onto maximum parole supervision in 2003, at which time he moved in with his mother. As a special condition of his parole, he was required to pursue a GED. He struggled initially on parole. In the first three months after his release, he spent several nights on three different occasions in a community corrections center, a custodial sanction that is an alternative to reimprisonment for parole violators. Despite that setback, Jeremiah then experienced a period of stability when he found work at a metal manufacturing firm. He was employed at that firm during the second and third quarters of his first post-prison year, earning nearly $4,400, mainly during the first quarter of his employment. While he was employed, Jeremiah did not test positive for substance use, but he did immediately before and immediately after he was working.

After losing his manufacturing job, Jeremiah continued his substance use and involvement with the criminal justice system and experienced only sporadic employment. All told, in the first year after his release, he absconded from parole three times. Each time a warrant for his arrest was issued. About five months after his release, he was arrested for resisting and obstructing a police officer, pled guilty, and spent two weeks in jail. A few months later, he was formally cited for violating parole and served thirty-two days in jail and seventy-one days in a facility for technical rule violators (TRVs). That parole violation coincided with his last quarter of employment before he was returned to prison. Jeremiah was returned to prison less than a year after his release on another resisting and obstructing charge, to which he also pled guilty.

Jeremiah was released from prison a second time in 2005—again on maximum supervision. He again struggled on parole, repeating his patterns during his prior release, including absconding within a few months. Less than three months after his release, he was cited for violating parole and placed on electronic monitoring for one month. Despite these challenges,

Jeremiah again found work fairly quickly. Unfortunately, he was unable to maintain it. He worked through a temporary services firm for about half a year, during which time he earned only about $2,400.

Nine months after his second release from prison, Jeremiah pled guilty to malicious destruction of property. He was imprisoned a third time—this time for just over thirteen months. During that period of incarceration, Jeremiah earned a GED, which he received about one month before he was released. Upon release, Jeremiah returned again to live with his mother and her partner. He again found work through a temp agency, where he earned about $3,500 in two quarters of employment, his last period of employment in the formal labor market. In early 2008, Jeremiah was arrested again, this time for breaking and entering and receiving stolen property. After pleading guilty, he was returned to prison for fourteen months. Soon after his release in early 2010, he was arrested for and pled guilty to a charge of domestic violence. As a result, he was returned to prison a fifth time. After his release, Jeremiah started college. At the age of thirty-one, he enrolled in the local community college as a full-time student.

Prior research shows that, nationwide, incarcerated men like Jeremiah have lower levels of educational attainment. According to one survey by the National Center for Education Statistics, the highest level of educational attainment for 30 percent of prison inmates is less than high school.[2] For many, early offending and involvement with the criminal justice system precludes school completion, compounding their human capital deficits during the transition to adulthood.[3] Early school noncompletion can put young men who were disconnected prior to prison at a higher risk for continued disconnection after prison. When released from prison, human capital deficits become a significant barrier in the labor market, often leading to chronic unemployment and an increased risk of recidivism. In growing recognition of the importance of school continuation and the immense human capital deficits among prison inmates, correctional institutions have increasingly offered several forms of basic educational programming, including adult basic education (ABE), adult secondary education (ASE), and vocational training. Because so many prison inmates have never completed high school, prison-based education tends to focus on developing ABE skills and completing the general educational development (GED) certificate. As of 2003, most prisons offered GED classes, and an estimated 19 percent of inmates had earned their GED or high school equivalency during their incarceration.[4] The postsecondary landscape of correctional institutions, however, has shrunk since Pell Grant restrictions were implemented in 1994, an important matter to which we return in chapter 9.[5]

In this chapter, we assess the respective roles of contexts, institutions, and social support in fostering or inhibiting secondary educational attainment, primarily GED completion. We are interested in understanding the educational trajectories among incarcerated men, including both the completion of a high school diploma before prison and GED attainment before, during, or after prison. We start with an overview of secondary education in the context of prison and the GED specifically, then lay out the factors that may affect high school and GED attainment among incarcerated young men. We discuss various explanations for how those factors might play out before finally examining the data to determine which of those explanations is supported.

Previous research identifies several important factors associated with educational attainment, including an individual's neighborhood context, racial background, prior human capital investments, school contexts, and early criminal justice involvement.[6] Institutional settings include schools and adult and juvenile criminal justice institutions. As a quantitative measure of social contexts, we utilize an index of neighborhood socioeconomic status (SES). Social supports are measured based on pre- and post-prison living arrangements. We also assess racial differences in prior schooling and work experience, which we would expect to influence future educational attainment.[7]

The educational outcomes considered here include GED attainment before, during, and after prison as well as high school completion prior to prison. To track GED test-taking and receipt, we rely on data from the GED testing service provided by the Michigan Department of Corrections. These data allow us to track individuals' attempts to take GED subject tests through September 2015, including the dates on which subject tests were attempted, dates of repeated tests, and dates of completion and award.[8] Our data also allow us to examine whether an individual earns a GED in prison or while in the community. Thus, we differentiate between young men who earned a GED during their focal prison sentence and those who earned a GED during another custody spell or in the community.[9]

Our analysis shows that pre-prison human capital investment—as measured by level of completed schooling and by work experience—is an important factor in whether young men earn a GED while incarcerated. The human capital deficits of many young incarcerated men are larger than in the general population, but variations among them in these deficits are significant. We find that young men who completed more years of schooling during adolescence were more likely to earn a GED, either in prison or in the community before prison.

Race also plays an important role in our analysis. Young men who have experienced longer spells of disconnection during the transition to adulthood may have more difficulty participating in and completing the educational programming that can help them reconnect to mainstream institutions, and this risk factor strikes black men particularly hard. In our sample, black men had slightly lower levels of schooling completed before prison (mean = 10.27 years) compared to their white peers (mean = 10.41 years), although these differences were not statistically significant. Moreover, blacks also had lower levels of employment in the formal labor market prior to entering prison than whites: 12.8 percent of blacks were employed in the formal labor market before prison compared to 15.7 percent of whites. We argue that low GED attainment among black men is likely due to racialized inequalities in access to school resources, neighborhood contexts, and prior human capital investment opportunities.[10]

Neighborhood and school contexts also influenced educational outcomes. Young men from high-poverty neighborhoods were less likely to enter prison with a high school diploma, but they were no less likely to have earned a GED before their imprisonment. Their school contexts, including class sizes and average test scores, helped them earn GEDs but did not facilitate high school completion. We suspect that although these more positive school contexts did not help the young men in our sample avoid prison, they did better prepare them for later educational attainment. Young men who had been employed in the formal labor market before prison were more likely to have earned a high school diploma or their GED in the community prior to entering prison, although the data cannot tell us whether this points to the necessity of a diploma or GED for getting a job or to factors in labor market participation that help students earn these credentials.

Lastly, institutional settings are crucial to understanding educational attainment among formerly incarcerated young adults. The prison setting facilitates GED attainment. We suspect that institutional policies that require prison inmates to earn GEDs for parole eligibility provide a strong incentive for completing the certificate. Outside of prison, the consequences of criminal justice involvement for GED attainment varied with respect to stage in the life course: early criminal justice contact—juvenile justice involvement—decreased the chance of high school completion. However, adult criminal justice involvement increased the chance of earning a GED in the community prior to entering prison independent of age of incarceration.

THE GED AND PRISON-BASED EDUCATION

The GED provides the opportunity for those who did not complete a high school degree to acquire a credential that is the equivalent of a high school diploma. First developed for returning veterans after World War II, the GED has become relatively common in the United States, accounting for nearly 12 percent of all high school credentials annually.[11] The GED exam covers five topics: mathematics, science, social studies, writing, and reading. GED recipients tend to be different from high school graduates: they are more likely to be men, less likely to have parents with a college education, more likely to come from a single-parent household, and more likely to come from a socioeconomically disadvantaged background.[12] Prior research has found several factors to be associated with earning a GED: socioeconomic status, prior test scores, having or expecting a child, and (perhaps unsurprisingly) highest grade level completed.[13]

Since the GED signals a person's human capital (as well as being an outright requirement for many jobs), it may offer several immediate benefits to its recipients, including the expansion of labor market and postsecondary education opportunities.[14] Nevertheless, the value of the GED has been subject to debate. Prior studies have yielded mixed evidence with respect to the GED's benefits as a credential. In a seminal piece, Stephen Cameron and James Heckman find no difference in the average earnings of GED recipients and high school dropouts.[15] John Tyler, Richard Murnane, and John Willett, on the other hand, find positive effects of a GED on earnings among recipients with relatively low levels of job skills and among those who score just high enough to pass the exam.[16] They also find that the GED tends to increase earnings for whites but not for blacks. Contra Cameron and Heckman, some evidence suggests that earning a GED has a positive effect on wages for individuals who earn the credential compared to those who drop out of high school.[17] Looking at further educational attainment rather than wages, other research suggests that earning a GED increases the probability of college attendance and college course completion.[18]

While debates persist over the utility of earning a GED for people generally, even less is known regarding its potential benefits for prison inmates. Nevertheless, many prison systems require inmates who have not earned a high school credential to pursue a GED. Just as some of the young men in our sample were entering prison in 1998, Michigan's Public Act 320 established the requirement that prison inmates serving a minimum sentence of two years or more earn their GED or high school diploma for parole eligibility.

Among prison inmates, a GED might offer several benefits. First, a GED can help to improve an individual's labor market prospects.[19] John Tyler and Jeffrey Kling find evidence that receiving a GED leads to a short-term boost of post-release earnings among blacks but not among whites. Since many jobs require at least a high school diploma or its equivalent, a GED can assist those who would otherwise be closed off from such positions in the formal labor market.[20] Second, some evidence suggests that earning a

GED in prison can improve health outcomes among incarcerated men.[21] Third, previous research suggests that prison inmates who earn a GED are less likely to participate in criminal behavior.[22] Lastly, earning a GED allows individuals, including the formerly incarcerated, to pursue post-secondary education options.[23]

HIGH SCHOOL DIPLOMAS, GED TEST-TAKING, AND GED ATTAINMENT

Relatively few men in our sample (8.5 percent) earned a high school diploma before prison, and there was no significant difference in this rate between black and white men. In our sample, 968 individuals (74.4 percent) earned a GED at some point in time. More than one-quarter of those who earned a GED did so in the community prior to prison, and approximately one-third (32 percent) earned the credential during their focal prison spell. The remainder obtained their certificate after prison in the community or during a later prison spell.

Unlike high school graduation, there was a substantial racial gap in GED attainment (see figure 3.1). About nine in ten whites in our sample earned their GED at some point, compared to seven in ten blacks. This disparity was present prior to prison and persisted through the focal prison spell. Prior to entering prison, we observe a racial gap in GED attainment in the community. Among whites, 38 percent earned their GED in the community before prison relative to 20 percent of blacks. A relatively smaller proportion of our sample earned their GED after their focal prison spell. Some earned their GED in the community after prison (5.7 percent), and others recidivated to prison and earned their credential during their new custody spell (5.9 percent). Racial disparities in GED attainment persisted during prison and after release. During the focal prison spell, we observe a persistent black-white gap in GED attainment, even when holding constant the time spent in prison (see figure 3.2). We suspect that this racial gap reflects prior racial differences in school opportunities, which is also consistent with the evidence on repeated exams, which we consider next.

Repeated Exams

To examine preparedness and ability to complete the GED, we also look at young men's repeated attempts to pass the GED exams. We use the term "repeaters" for individuals who repeated one or more of the subject area tests. Students can retake subject area tests as many times as necessary, conditional on the availability of testing dates. We interpret a greater

Figure 3.1 Timing of High School Diploma and GED Receipt, by Race

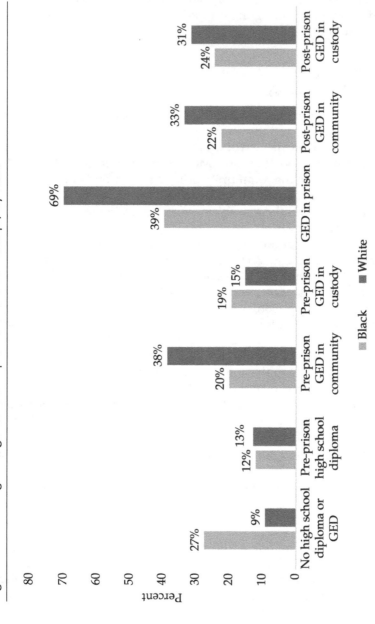

Source: Michigan Study of Life after Prison.
Note: 2003 Michigan parole cohort, followed through 2009. Pre-prison GED percentages are among those with no high school diploma. GED in prison percentages are among those entering prison with no diploma or GED. Post-prison GED percentages are among those leaving prison with no diploma or GED.

Figure 3.2   Probability of Earning a GED during the Focal Prison
Sentence, by Race and Time

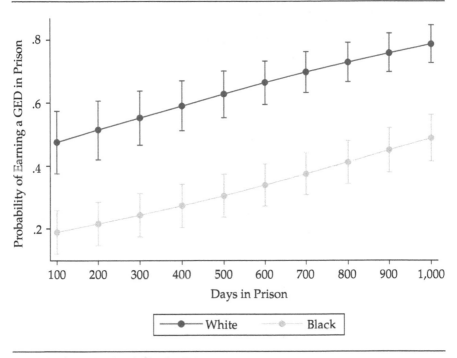

Source: Michigan Study of Life after Prison.
Note: Focal prison sentences end with 2003 parole (various prison entry dates).

number of repeated exam attempts as indicative of larger deficiencies in
prior human capital acquisition. Our analysis finds significant racial disparities in who repeated the GED exam, as well as in who repeated specific
subject tests (see table 3.A1). In our sample, 158 young men (12 percent)
repeated one or more GED subject tests. Blacks were significantly more
likely to repeat a GED subject test (70 percent). Although most of the young
men who repeated the test eventually earned their GED (78 percent), they
naturally took longer to earn the credential. The fact that blacks were more
likely than whites to repeat each subject test, and that black GED earners
had a higher average number of attempts than white GED earners did,
suggests that blacks were less likely than their white counterparts to successfully complete the exam. Repeated exam attempts provide additional
evidence of racial disparities in prior human capital accumulation.

THE IMPACT OF CONTEXTS, INSTITUTIONS, AND SOCIAL SUPPORTS ON EDUCATION ATTAINMENT

In this chapter, we assess variations in high school and GED completion based on contexts, institutions, and social supports (see chapter 4 on post-secondary education). First, we examine the importance of prior human capital attainment in shaping later educational outcomes. In the context of educational attainment, we find that earlier human capital attainment provides a foundation for future learning. We next look at the role of social and school contexts, briefly summarizing the mechanisms thought to link each to educational outcomes. Finally, we focus on the role of institutions—the labor market and the criminal justice system—and social supports in relation to GED and high school completion. After discussing how these factors may be related to educational attainment, we look at the actual results: what paths do incarcerated young men follow—before, during, and after prison—as they set out to achieve (or turn away from) a high school diploma or its equivalent?

Race and Human Capital Investment

Young black men are more likely than other demographic groups to have experienced disconnection.[24] It is worth exploring whether our data can illuminate the extent to which this disconnection is the result of either obstacles these young men face in the present (such as individual or institutional racism) or of past societal failures to provide them with the tools—the human capital—to navigate the transition to adulthood. Human capital development is important because it provides the foundation for the future accumulation of additional skills and knowledge. According to human capital theory, individuals acquire important skills for future productivity through on-the-job training and schooling. Those who acquire more human capital have a relative advantage over their peers in preparing for and completing a GED exam. Schooling provides the formal, institutional basis on which individuals develop the important skills and abilities needed for further educational achievement. These resources are cumulative: they are acquired and refined from one grade level to the next.[25]

Prior research documents the variations in human capital development by race. Racial gaps in reading and math scores begin in childhood and widen during elementary school.[26] Schools appear to play a significant role in the black-white achievement gap. On average, black children are more likely to attend high-poverty schools with lower-quality teachers, lower-quality facilities, and fewer resources.[27] Other research suggests that racial gaps are produced by differences in school resources, teacher expectations, family background, peers, and track placement.[28] Given the prior research that documents black-white achievement gaps and higher rates of disconnection among black men, we view race as a fundamental axis along which structured inequalities manifest to create both educational deficits[29] and disconnection among black men.[30] Taken together, we suspect that cumulative disadvantages experienced by black children will correlate with lower levels of GED completion.

Neighborhood Socioeconomic Status

We also examine how pre-prison neighborhood contexts relate to GED and high school completion. In this chapter, we measure neighborhood contexts using census tract median family income, which is a measure of neighborhood socioeconomic status. We suspect that pre-prison neighborhood SES can affect high school and GED completion primarily through the availability of resources, including economic and social capital. Previous research has documented the extent to which neighborhood contexts can influence educational outcomes.[31] Sean Reardon shows that the black-white differences in school poverty are strongly correlated with black-white achievement gaps within school districts.[32] Thus, we can expect that resource deprivation will negatively influence educational outcomes, and these patterns are likely to be concentrated among young black men, who more often attend high-poverty schools.[33] Ann Owens finds that living in a high-poverty neighborhood with higher unemployment and more single-mother households reduces the probability of high school completion.[34] The quality of the school a child attends depends on more than simply access to tangible resources; students from more affluent neighborhoods may also benefit from attending schools where peers have higher levels of achievement or where there is greater access to positive role models that facilitate positive educational outcomes.

Outside of schools, another way in which neighborhood SES may influence educational outcomes is through differential access to social capital. Those from relatively more affluent neighborhoods may benefit from enhanced information channels, norms and effective social control, or expectations that can facilitate educational outcomes, whereas educational outcomes may be diminished for individuals who lack these forms of social capital.[35] Other neighborhood characteristics, including the physical environment, the presence and degree of violence, and concentrated disadvantage, can adversely influence educational outcomes.[36]

Secondary Schools

Inequality in school contexts may lead to differential rates of GED or high school completion as well as racial disparities in these outcomes. Overall, we suspect that inequality in schooling can affect the quality of the investments in students' human capital, which subsequently influences GED or high school completion.

There are several ways in which racial disparities in school quality can affect disparities in GED completion. First, student-teacher ratios have been shown to vary across race. Meredith Phillips and Tiffani Chin find that the classrooms of children from majority-minority secondary schools have higher average student-teacher ratios compared to majority-white schools.[37] Higher student-teacher ratios can affect student achievement by reducing the amount of time teachers can spend with each pupil. With opportunities for high-quality learning thus diminished, individuals who attend schools with higher student-teacher ratios may be less likely to complete their GED or high school diploma.

Another way in which school quality can affect these outcomes stems from differences in teacher quality. Compared to their counterparts elsewhere, teachers in high-poverty schools and majority-minority schools have attained lower levels of education, accrued less experience (owing to high levels of turnover), and mastered less subject-matter knowledge.[38] The probability of completing a high school diploma or GED may be reduced for those who attend schools with lower teacher quality.

Lastly, fewer resources, as indicated by the number of dollars spent per student, may be another aspect of the impact of school quality on GED or high school completion. Although previous research has found weak associations between school expenditures and achievement,[39] it may nevertheless be the case that school expenditures affect educational outcomes by determining the availability and quality of learning materials. We suspect that several relationships will emerge from the prior research on school contexts. First, we expect to observe a positive relationship between a school's performance—indicated by higher average math and English test scores—and its students' future GED and high school completion. Second, we expect that students in schools with a higher student-teacher ratio will be less likely to earn a GED or high school diploma. Lastly, we suspect that students in schools with more resources—measured by dollar expenditures per student—will be more likely to obtain a GED or high school diploma.

As previously discussed, black children are more likely to attend high-poverty schools with fewer resources, poorer teacher quality, and larger student-teacher ratios.[40] Thus, differences in school quality may reproduce or worsen racial gaps in achievement that can lead to racial disparities in GED or high school completion.

Criminal Justice Institutions

The criminal justice system itself could have both positive and negative influences on educational outcomes. We expect these effects to vary largely with the type of criminal justice contact and supervision (arrest, probation, or incarceration). Most studies have examined how early criminal justice involvement (juvenile arrest) affects educational outcomes, and they have consistently reported a negative association between juvenile arrest and educational attainment.[41] Several theoretical frameworks posit a negative effect of criminal justice sanctioning (punishment) on educational outcomes.[42] Social control theory suggests that criminal justice sanctions can weaken an individual's attachment to mainstream institutions, resulting in diminished educational outcomes. Labeling theory posits that early criminal justice sanctions (juvenile arrest or probation) have a detrimental effect on educational outcomes as individuals internalize negative labels that discourage school performance. Rational choice theory argues that individuals may opt out of additional schooling if they perceive that completing school will offer few benefits.[43] Taken together, these theoretical perspectives suggest that early criminal justice contact has negative consequences for educational attainment.

Yet criminal justice institutions might also have a positive effect on educational attainment. As mentioned earlier, Michigan now requires those under adult probation supervision to earn a high school diploma or GED, and most prison inmates must do so in order to be eligible for parole.[44] Taken together, the institutional policies that incentivize educational attainment are expected to be associated with positive educational outcomes. Therefore, adult criminal justice contact—adult probation supervision and imprisonment—might improve educational outcomes. We also expect that the duration of a prison spell will positively correlate with GED attainment, since longer prison terms allow prisoners more time to prepare for the exam and expose them to more institutional resources that can help them in those preparations.

Pre-Prison Employment

Early employment experiences can play an important role in establishing pathways through the transition to adulthood, and these experiences may influence educational outcomes as well as economic ones. Besides setting a foundation for transitioning into full-time work, first-time employment experiences can provide a source of attachment to mainstream institutions that promote prosocial behaviors[45] and motivate stable employment and the education investments necessary to achieve or maintain it.[46] Early employment experiences may translate into educational attainment for several reasons. First, employers may encourage employees to pursue additional education to enhance their productivity, perhaps through increased compensation based on new educational attainments. Second, employment may prevent young people from dropping out of school by reinforcing the positive effects of educational investments. Finally, employment may reduce young people's free time, thus indirectly influencing educational outcomes by helping them avoid early criminal justice involvement. Conversely, employment may also reduce the time a student devotes to education—there are only so many hours in the day.

Social Bonds, Social Control, and Family Support

Sociologists argue that social bonds, or "informal control mechanisms," play an important role in the transition to adulthood.[47] Social bonds are strengthened when individuals are attached to the labor market, family, and other mainstream institutions, such as schools. According to Sampson and Laub, social bonds "create interdependent systems of obligation and restraint that impose significant costs for translating criminal propensities into actions."[48] Social bonds not only provide a strong disincentive for criminal behavior but also help to foster prosocial behaviors. Other research suggests that family members in particular provide informal social control, fostering prosocial behaviors.[49] We expect that strengthened social bonds will be associated with prosocial behaviors—in this case, the completion of a high school diploma or GED. We focus on several dimensions of social bonds: employment in the formal labor market, living arrangements before and after prison, and family attachments.

Family members—children, spouses, parents, siblings—may also offer important forms of social, emotional, and economic support. The literature on prisoner reentry often stresses the importance of family relationships for successful reintegration.[50] Family support can help young men during the reintegration process by providing housing, food, and other daily necessities, allowing them to focus on education. That said, not all family ties make education easier: we hypothesize that individuals with children will be more likely to obtain a GED, as early childbearing can be disruptive of schooling, specifically, high school completion.[51] Thus, young men in our sample who had children might have been less likely to earn a high school diploma.

WHO COMPLETES HIGH SCHOOL EQUIVALENCY, AND WHEN?

Pre-prison contexts, institutions, and social support are expected to influence educational outcomes among young criminal justice–involved men. We examine bivariate associations between pre-prison experiences and characteristics and (a) earning a high school diploma before entering prison and (b) earning a GED in the community before entering prison. We caution that these results are not meant to indicate causal relationships and thus should be interpreted as descriptive of who does and does not attain these educational credentials.

Earning a High School Diploma before Prison

Figure 3.3 shows key characteristics of individuals who received a high school diploma before prison relative to individuals who did not earn a high school diploma or GED prior to entering prison.[52] We assess neighborhood SES, criminal justice supervision, social bonds, and race. Our results provide descriptive evidence that young men from more affluent neighborhoods who also had more work history were more likely to complete their high school diploma. Moreover, individuals with early criminal justice contact were less likely to complete their high school diploma.

Our analysis shows that high school diploma earners were ten percentage points more likely to have resided in a neighborhood with a median income of $50,000 or more. Our results also show that coming from a neighborhood with a concentration of individuals with low levels of educational attainment was negatively associated with earning a high school diploma before prison. Those who graduated from high school before prison were twenty percentage points less likely to have resided in an area where 20 percent or more of the population over age twenty-five lacked a high school diploma.

Institutions play a relatively strong role in high school completion prior to prison. Our expectation that formal employment would be positively associated with high school completion, since early employment might foster prosocial behaviors and a continued attachment to schooling, is borne out by our results. Although the vast majority of both groups had pre-prison employment in the formal labor market, we see that diploma earners (87 percent) were twenty-four percentage points more likely to be employed before prison compared to individuals who did not earn a diploma or GED before prison (63 percent). Second, early criminal justice involvement tended to disrupt progress toward graduation, consistent with prior literature.[53] The timing here is crucial. Criminal justice involvement

Figure 3.3 Key Differences between Those Who Earned a High School Diploma before Prison and Those Who Did Not Earn a Diploma or GED before Prison

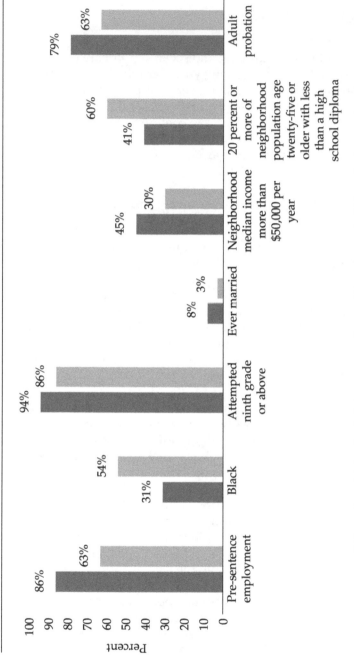

Source: **Michigan Study of Life after Prison.**
Note: Focal prison sentences end with 2003 parole (various prison entry dates).

at younger ages—indicated by a juvenile commitment, juvenile probation, and age at first arrest—is negatively associated with earning a diploma. The bivariate results indicate that those who completed high school prior to entering prison were twenty-five percentage points less likely to have had a prior juvenile commitment, twenty-nine percentage points less likely to have been on juvenile probation, and twenty percentage points more likely to have experienced their first arrest at eighteen or older rather than as a juvenile.

Finally, social bonds are positively associated with earning a high school diploma before prison. We suspect that individuals who earned a high school diploma were more likely to marry, given that prior research shows an association between educational attainment and marriage.[54] Our bivariate results indicate that those with a pre-prison high school diploma were five percentage points more likely to have ever been married.

Earning a GED before Prison

Figure 3.4 shows key factors that are associated with earning a GED in the community before prison relative to not earning this credential or completing high school prior to prison.[55] Prior human capital investment, race, and institutions appear to be important factors for GED attainment in the community.

Young men with higher levels of human capital are more likely to earn a GED. Human capital matters, we argue, because it captures the acquisition of the educational skills that are necessary for GED completion. Our analysis provides supporting evidence for this claim. Young men who attempted to complete at least ninth grade or higher were eight percentage points more likely to earn their GED in the community before prison. There were large racial disparities between young men who earned a GED and those did not. Young black men were twenty-three percentage points less likely to earn a GED compared to their white counterparts.

Institutional settings also shape differential patterns in GED attainment in the community before prison. First, young men who were employed before prison were more likely to earn a GED in the community before prison. Those who did so were twenty-three percentage points more likely to have had formal labor market employment before prison. We caution against interpreting the directionality for this association too quickly. On the one hand, as prior research suggests, earning a GED credential can facilitate labor market entry and employment.[56] However, prior work experience may indicate a commitment to prosocial behaviors, such as the pursuit of education.

Figure 3.4 Key Differences between Those Who Earned a GED in the Community before Prison and Those Who Did Not

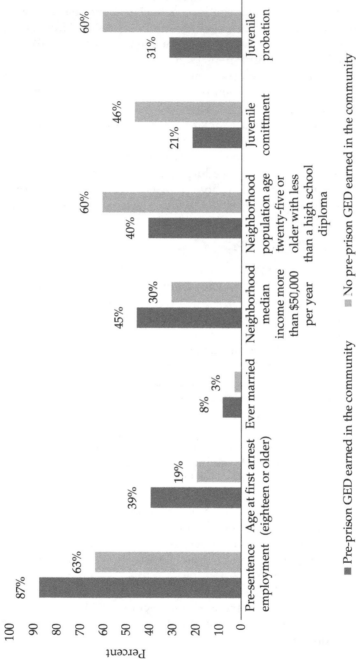

Source: Michigan Study of Life after Prison.
Note: Focal prison sentences end with 2003 parole (various prison entry dates).

Young men who became involved in the criminal justice system as adults were also more likely to have earned a GED before prison. Unlike high school completion, which is impeded by early criminal justice supervision, young men under adult probation supervision were sixteen percentage points more likely to have earned a GED in the community before prison. We suspect that the standard requirement that individuals enroll in adult education facilitates their earning a GED while they are on probation.

Some evidence does suggest that social bonds play an important role in facilitating the earning of a GED in the community before prison. The results indicate that those who had been married were more likely to have completed their GED in the community prior to entering prison. Young men who had been married were four percentage points more likely to have completed a GED in the community before prison.

GED Attainment during Prison

We now compare individuals who earned a GED in prison to those who earned a GED previously in the community. Nearly one-third of our sample earned a GED during their focal prison spell. Figure 3.5 presents key results from regression models that compare those who earned a GED during their focal prison spell to those who earned a GED prior to prison.[57] We compare men who earned in-prison GEDs to those who had previously earned a GED because we believe that the former are more comparable than those who earned neither a GED nor a high school diploma. This comparison helps us understand the difference between those who earned a GED in prison and those who earned a high school diploma or GED prior to entering prison. Surprisingly, there is little evidence suggesting that years of prior schooling, social bonds and family support, or neighborhood SES are related to earning a GED in prison. Rather, an important factor in whether men earn a GED in prison is the time they spend incarcerated. One additional year in prison increases the probability of earning a GED in prison by 9.7 percentage points, suggesting that more time in prison gives young men the time to prepare for and successfully complete the exam. School context also influences whether young men earn a GED in prison or in the community: the K-12 income-adjusted math and reading score and the student-teacher ratio are negatively associated with earning a GED in prison versus in the community. A one-unit increase in the income-adjusted math and reading percentile decreases the probability of earning a GED in prison by one percentage point. In addition, a one-unit increase in the K-12 student-teacher ratio that a young man experienced decreases that probability by 4.5 percentage points.

Figure 3.5   Differences in the Probability of Incarcerated Young Men
Earning a GED in Prison Compared to Earning a GED
in the Community before Prison, by Various Predictors

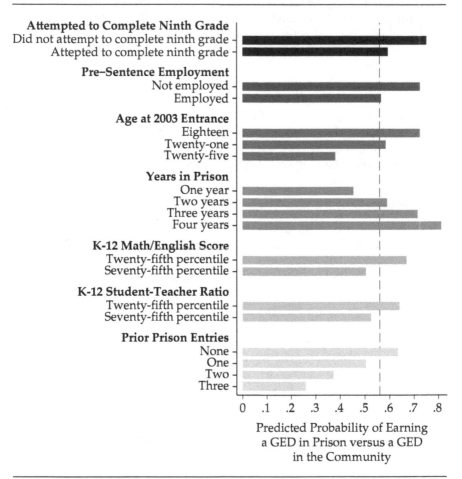

Source: Michigan Study of Life after Prison.
Note: Focal prison sentences end with 2003 parole (various prison entry dates).

We can also compare individuals who earned a GED in prison to those
who entered prison without a GED and did not earn the credential in
prison. Figure 3.6 displays key factors from a regression model predicting whether an individual will earn a GED in prison.[58] The results indicate that race, prior human capital investment, time spent in prison, and
supervision level in prison were associated with earning a GED in prison.

Figure 3.6   Differences in the Probability of Earning a GED
in Prison Relative to Not Earning a GED in Prison,
by Various Predictors

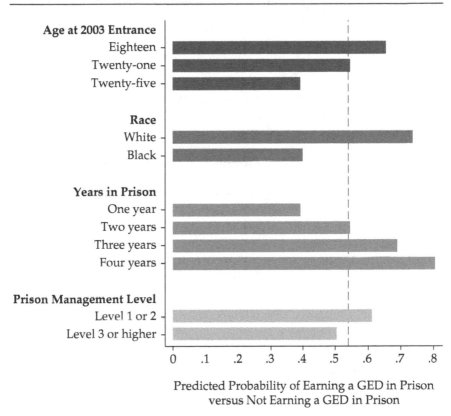

Predicted Probability of Earning a GED in Prison
versus Not Earning a GED in Prison

Source: Michigan Study of Life after Prison.
Note: Focal prison sentences end with 2003 parole (various prison entry dates).

Racial disparities between those who earned a GED in prison and non-GED earners are also apparent. Our results indicate that young black men were 33.7 percentage points less likely to obtain a GED in prison. Among all potential GED earners entering prison, 73.8 percent of whites earned a GED compared to 40.2 percent of blacks. As with the previous comparisons, longer periods spent in prison increased the probability of earning a GED in prison. Our results indicate that an additional year in prison increased the probability of earning a GED by 15.1 percentage points. Moreover, our results suggest that higher levels of security in prison were negatively associated with earning a GED there. Our estimates indicate that being on a higher management level—level 3 or higher—decreased the probability of earning a GED by 10.7 percentage points, probably because prisoners at higher management levels often have fewer opportunities to participate in programs.

CONCLUSION

Young formerly incarcerated men typically face significant human capital deficits even before they are incarcerated. As was the case for Jeremiah, these deficits include early substance use and juvenile justice system involvement, which lead to dropping out of school—sometimes prior to high school—and minimal (if any) involvement in the formal labor market. The state of disconnection that results is a key reason that many young men end up incarcerated. And the stigma associated with their incarceration perpetuates their disconnection from mainstream institutions even after they are released.

Educational attainment can help formerly incarcerated men reconnect to institutions that are likely to reduce recidivism among them and increase their labor market participation. We have examined the role of institutions, contexts, and social support in the efforts of formerly incarcerated young men to earn a GED or high school diploma. Those with more pre-prison human capital are relatively advantaged in the quest to earn a GED, a finding that partially explains why black men are significantly less likely to earn a GED. We suspect that black men's lower levels of GED attainment are due to longer spells of disconnection and racial differences in pre-prison human capital development that are partly attributable to poorer school quality. As a result, incarcerated black men struggle to earn a GED both prior to incarceration and during their incarceration spell, and failure to earn this credential can lead to further disadvantages after they are released. Like Jeremiah, they may struggle not only to earn a GED in prison but also to find gainful employment after release. Eventually— perhaps a decade or more later—many of these now older men return to school (see chapter 4).

Our analysis also examined which institutions, contexts, and social supports influence GED attainment and high school completion. Social bonds—in particular, having ever been married—are positively associated with having earned a GED in the community or a high school diploma prior to entering prison, although this result probably reflects the effect of education on marriage rather than the reverse. However, there is little evidence suggesting that social bonds and family support are related to earning a GED at future times.

In examining the role of neighborhood and school contexts, we find some evidence to suggest that school contexts matter for pre-prison educational attainment and earning a GED in prison versus earning a GED before prison. Our measure of the proportion of individuals in the neighborhood over age twenty-five with less than a high school education suggests that growing up in a disadvantaged neighborhood reduces the chance that a young man will attain a high school diploma or GED in the community before prison. Moreover, young men who come from more affluent neighborhoods are more likely to have completed their high school diploma or GED in the community before prison.

Institutional settings are also critical to understanding GED and high school completion. These include early experiences with the criminal justice system and early labor market attachment. All else being equal, those who have stronger labor market attachment and who avoid early criminal justice contact are more likely to complete their high school diploma or GED before entering prison. Earning a GED in the community or during incarceration is often facilitated by adult criminal justice supervision, but hindered by early criminal justice supervision (juvenile probation or juvenile commitments). Thus, whether criminal justice supervision facilitates or hinders educational attainment depends on when it occurs in the life course. For those who earn a GED in prison, we suspect that it is the institutional policy requiring a GED for parole eligibility that pushes young men to earn the credential, both by motivating them to prepare for taking the GED tests and by improving their access to GED preparation. That longer prison terms are positively associated with earning a GED reflects, we believe, the extra time that these prisoners have to prepare for the exam, as well as their access to institutional resources that aid them in preparing for it.

Chapter 4 | Education, Part 2: Postsecondary Enrollment

COLLEGE ENROLLMENTS HAVE risen quickly over recent decades, from 25.7 percent among eighteen- to twenty-four-year-olds in 1980 to 41.2 percent in 2010.[1] Over this period, the economic importance of a college degree has also increased as wages for high school graduates have stagnated[2] and the need for skilled workers has increased with the growth of industries like health care and technology.[3] Given the potential payoffs of a degree—or the cost of not having one—it is not surprising that participation in postsecondary education has risen. In turn, these shifts in postsecondary education have shaped the transition to adulthood itself, prolonging the period of emergence from adolescence to full adulthood and contributing to shifts in the patterning of other life events, such as entering the labor market, achieving financial independence, and starting a family.[4]

Degree completion, however, has not kept pace with the rise in enrollments. Nearly two-thirds of recent high school completers are enrolling in two- or four-year colleges,[5] but only about half of these students earn a credential.[6] Thus, although enrollment rates increased by 60 percent from 1980 to 2010, degree completion increased by only 40 percent.[7] At the same time, the cost of college has increased drastically, such that the student debt burden, particularly for those who do not finish, has grown to unsustainable levels.[8] Thus, for both good and ill, college is an important gateway (or barrier) to a successful transition to adulthood and to both inter- and intragenerational social mobility. This chapter evaluates the place of college in the transition to adulthood of formerly incarcerated young men.

A college education may be especially influential for formerly incarcerated young men for several reasons. Education can help to develop skills and build résumés that improve formerly incarcerated young men's tenuous viability in the labor market[9] and also, as an important prosocial institution, help them reintegrate into their communities and with their peers. In addition, research suggests that college is extremely important in breaking the link between a father's incarceration and his child's social exclusion.[10] This happens not only when the child attains a college degree but also when the father does. In other words, in addition to contributing to their own successful transition to adulthood, earning a college degree may be consequential in the ability of formerly incarcerated young men to break the chain of social exclusion for their children.

Although we cannot test such effects directly, simply understanding the prevalence and quality of college enrollments is an essential first step in evaluating how college may mitigate the effects of incarceration on the transition to adulthood and beyond. Accordingly, this chapter comprehensively examines the postsecondary enrollment patterns of formerly incarcerated young men. In particular, we describe the quality of those enrollments in terms of their sector, status, and duration and investigate the factors that predict who is more likely to return to school after release and when they are most likely to return.

Recall that Jeremiah, whom we introduced at the beginning of the previous chapter, struggled mightily with substance use and sporadic employment, earned a GED in prison, and eventually enrolled in community college. His decision to enroll in college, many years after his first release from prison, turns out to be more common than one might expect. Dennis, a white man born in the early 1980s who grew up in a white middle-class suburb of Detroit, experienced a somewhat different educational trajectory during adolescence but nonetheless also enrolled in college later in life. Like Jeremiah, Dennis did not finish high school and became a daily substance user at an early age. He dropped out in the eleventh grade, and that same year he made a brief foray into the formal labor market, working in one calendar quarter and making $200. Around the same time—at age sixteen—he began using drugs and alcohol. Dennis's first arrest and sentence were for arson. He was placed on probation, during which time he attended GED courses at a community college and earned a GED. Yet soon thereafter, he served three months in jail for assault and battery. Dennis was imprisoned about two years later for a technical probation rule violation related to his substance abuse. By the time he was admitted to prison, he was using alcohol and marijuana every other day and experimenting with the hallucinogen LSD. There is some evidence that Dennis was using drugs to "self-medicate": when he was admitted to prison in 2003, he reported having a mental illness.

Dennis spent four months in state prison and was released onto parole under medium supervision in mid-2003. As a special condition of parole, he was required to complete a psychiatric evaluation and to participate in mental health treatment programming. A month later, after he tested positive for drugs, his supervision level was raised to maximum and he entered residential treatment. After three months in treatment, Dennis returned to live with his mother and worked a series of different jobs, including temporary jobs, a job in the packaging industry, a job in the recycling industry, a job at a fast-food restaurant, and a job at a big-box retailer. During those six months, Dennis earned about $4,000 in total, mainly from the big-box retailer.

Less than six months after he was released from prison, Dennis pled guilty to assaulting a police officer and was sentenced to another prison term. He served nearly three years in prison and was released onto minimum parole supervision in late 2006. Upon his release, Dennis moved in with his girlfriend, who lived in an apartment only a few minutes from his mother's home. He also found relatively stable employment at a furniture store throughout 2007 and 2008—earning between $1,000 and $5,000 each quarter. In 2008, he also started working at a manufacturing plant. Despite his relative residential and employment stability, Dennis continued to run afoul of the law; he committed violent offenses and offenses related to substance use, including driving under the influence and assault with a deadly weapon. In the fall of 2008, he was sentenced to prison again. In 2012, after his latest release from prison, Dennis enrolled half-time in a program at a local community college.

How common is enrollment in college among formerly incarcerated young men, and how should we understand college in their transition to adulthood? This chapter uses data from the National Student Clearinghouse (NSC) to examine college attendance. The data extend through the end of 2013, a full decade after the young men in our sample were paroled. As it becomes increasingly common for students to return to school at older ages, such a follow-up is essential to producing a comprehensive account of enrollment behavior. Because this follow-up is longer than for our other outcomes, this chapter does not assess the *effect* of returning to school, but rather focuses on factors that might contribute to this return and the kinds of postsecondary educational experiences we see in our sample. We illustrate descriptively the timing of enrollments and the sectors in which they occurred, which we divide into four categories: three in the not-for-profit sector—two-year institutions, public four-year institutions, and private four-year colleges—and one category for for-profit institutions. To begin to unpack the importance of education in the transition to adulthood for young men returning from prison, we then consider who returns to school after prison and how the timing of their enrollment relates to their criminal justice involvement, employment, and other markers of stability.

Two important limitations of the NSC data should be kept in mind as we discuss these findings. First, each institution reports to the National

Student Clearinghouse voluntarily; thus, coverage is not perfect. However, we do not believe this poses a significant problem for our sample, as the rate of reporting in Michigan exceeded 80 percent overall—and 90 percent for public two- and four-year schools—by 2004.[11] Second, the NSC only began collecting data on whether students were degree-seeking in 2009. This supplemental information was not yet widely reported at the time of our data collection and is not available in our data. Thus, we cannot claim that all men in our data were enrolled in college-level courses. Rather, some may have been enrolled in remedial coursework, GED classes, or certificate programs. Although this circumscribes some of the inferences we might be able to draw, we consider all of these forms of continuing education to be important because any enrollment is likely to facilitate (and signal to others) important involvement in a prosocial institution during the transition to adulthood.

We begin by describing the frequency and character of enrollments in our sample. The remainder of the chapter attempts to explain the puzzle that emerges from this picture: enrollments among formerly incarcerated young men, especially black men, increased as time went on, with a peak around 2010. To guide our analysis, we propose two sets of hypotheses. The first, in a variant of relative risk aversion, is that these men were more likely to enroll when the total cost of college was lower and the relative expected return was greater.[12] The second is simply that those who were more firmly embedded in the criminal justice system—specifically those whose lives during the "traditional" postsecondary years (ages eighteen to twenty-two) were more often interrupted by their involvement in the justice system—were less likely to enroll. Neither of these hypotheses, however, appears to explain the findings from our data.

TYPES AND TIMING OF POSTSECONDARY ENROLLMENT

When they entered prison for the incarceration spell ending in 2003, only 40 percent of the men in our sample had earned a secondary degree, and only 3.5 percent had ever enrolled in college courses (see table 4.1).[13] An additional 23 percent of black men and 33 percent of white men earned a GED while in prison; 55 percent of black men and 81 percent of white men thus possessed a secondary degree credential at the time of their release in 2003. As a result, although very few incarcerated young men completed high school, the proportion with a secondary degree upon release was on par with the high school graduation rates in Michigan (82 percent and 59 percent for white and black students in Michigan in 2010, respectively).[14] Although GED credentials are likely to reflect lower levels of academic

Table 4.1   Education at Prison Release

	Black		White		Total	
	N	%	N	%	N	%
Less than high school	42	6.95	23	3.35	65	5.03
Some high school	217	35.93	103	14.99	320	24.79
GED in prison	144	23.84	231	33.62	375	29.05
GED before prison	128	21.19	263	38.28	391	30.29
High school	46	7.62	45	6.55	91	7.05
Some college	23	3.81	22	3.20	45	3.49
Missing	4	0.66	0	0.00	4	0.31
Total	604	100	687	100	1,291	100

Source: Michigan Study of Life after Prison.
Note: Michigan 2003 parole cohort, release years 2000–2003.

preparation than a traditional high school degree,[15] they nevertheless indicate baseline eligibility for postsecondary education among formerly incarcerated men.

Figure 4.1 illustrates the number of men in our sample with an NSC-reported enrollment in each quarter. New enrollments (beginning in each quarter) are represented by the darkest shade of the stacked bars and enrollments that end in each quarter are represented in the lightest.[16] This figure shows a steady increase in the number of men enrolled up to a peak of around 7 percent of our sample (ninety-three men) per quarter in 2010–2011. Although total enrollments in any given quarter tend to be dominated by those continuing from a prior quarter, it is also true that more individuals began enrollments as time went on, up to a peak of around 2.4 to 3.4 percent of our sample who began new enrollments per quarter between the fall of 2009 and the winter of 2012. However, there is also an early peak in enrollments in the winter and fall of 2004, suggesting that at least some of the men may have attempted to follow the "traditional" path of completing school before entering the labor market, by enrolling relatively soon after release. Nevertheless, most enrolled later. Additionally, note that even with the increasing number of new enrollments, the medium shade "persisting" portion of the stacked bar does not grow much beyond 2010, because a large number of men also ended their enrollments each quarter. These later returns to schooling indicate that the men were enrolling in their mid to late twenties, and that many were still enrolled in their thirties.

Overall, 28 percent of the men in our sample (364 of 1,291) eventually returned (or attempted to return) to school after their release from prison

Figure 4.1 Beginning, Persisting, and Ending Enrollments, by Quarter, 2003–2014

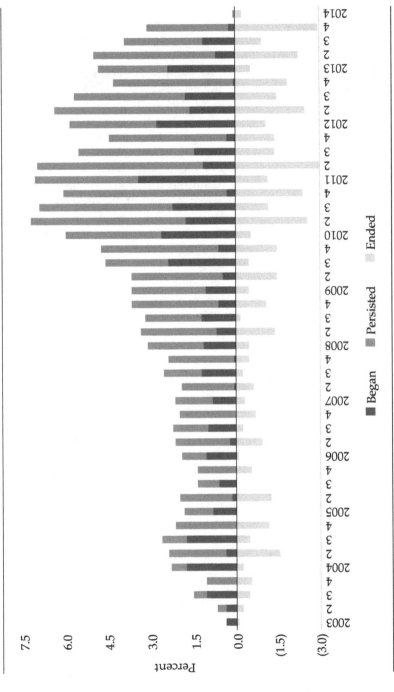

Source: Michigan Study of Life after Prison.

in 2003. However, these enrollments were generally short-lived. Among those who enrolled, the median length of their persistence in school by the end of 2013 was the equivalent of approximately one full-time semester; only about one-quarter of the men who enrolled did so for the equivalent of more than one full-time year. By comparison, 65 percent of first-time college students at or below the poverty line in Michigan had enrolled for more than one full-time equivalent (FTE) year within six years of enrollment, according to data from the Beginning Postsecondary Students Longitudinal Study (BPS-2004) for the entering college cohort of 2004.[17] This suggests that young men transitioning to adulthood after prison experience considerable difficulties in college persistence, even compared to other disadvantaged students. Although this does not necessarily mean that the time, effort, and money spent in pursuit of postsecondary education were misplaced, it raises important questions about the relative risk of the financial and labor market insecurity associated with college enrollments for formerly incarcerated young men. The lack of sufficient post-enrollment employment, health, or housing data for our sample precludes any investigation of the *returns* to schooling, but descriptive evaluations of patterns of enrollment offer suggestive evidence that our sample enrolled primarily in relatively high-risk postsecondary institutions. To examine this further, we turn next to the sector, status, duration, and timing of enrollments.

Sector and Status of Enrollments

Figure 4.2 is a spine plot that illustrates the breakdown of enrollments by institutional sector and student enrollment status; the width reflects the percentage of enrollments in a given sector, and the height reflects status. Each one of the 566 observations in this figure reflects the commencement of a new enrollment period (as shown in the black bars in figure 4.1), which may be composed of several calendar quarters or reporting periods from the NSC.[18] It is important to note the prevalence of enrollments reported by the NSC as "withdrawn." As many as 26 of the 364 men in our sample with NSC records may never have achieved active enrollment status. Overall, this would reduce the enrollment rate in our sample from 28 to 26 percent.

The average enrollment in our sample was undertaken at a public two-year institution on a half-time basis (meaning that one FTE year would take four semesters or six academic quarters). This is what we would expect, based on the average enrollment behaviors of low-income students in Michigan.[19] The next most common institutional context for enrollments in our sample was for-profit colleges—the fastest-growing sector of U.S. postsecondary education.[20] Although they accounted for only 4 percent

Figure 4.2   Relative Frequencies of College Enrollment Sector
              and Status, 2002–2014

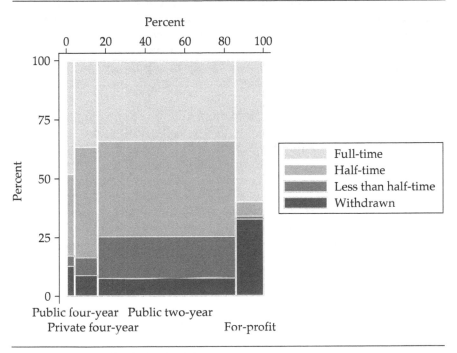

Source: Michigan Study of Life after Prison.
Note: 2002 enrollments occur for individuals released before their 2003 parole date. See
chapter 2, note 92.

of students enrolled in two-year colleges in the 1990s, for-profit colleges
accounted for 9 percent of associate's degrees.[21] However, for-profit institutions have also been accused of taking advantage of poor students. Their
graduation rates may be higher overall, but so are their students' debt and
unemployment rates.[22] The labor market stigma of an online for-profit
education[23] combined with that of a criminal record[24] may make these men
especially unlikely to benefit from these credentials in the labor market,
increasing the relative burden of student debt associated with this postsecondary sector.

It may seem that the prevalence of for-profit enrollments shown in figure 4.2 is somewhat exaggerated owing to the number of these enrollments
that were withdrawn. In fact, however, for-profit enrollments are likely
to be *more* common than the figure suggests, as only about 30 percent of

for-profit institutions (weighted by student enrollment) reported to the National Student Clearinghouse during our observation period, 2003 to 2013.[25] Figure 4.3 illustrates the types of institutions that our young men attended over time, by initial enrollment status and sector.[26] This allows us to get a better sense both of when they were choosing to enroll as well as whether any observed trends may be related to increases in reporting to the NSC. The figure shows that the number of enrollments in the private four-year and for-profit sectors increased markedly in the latter half of our observation period.[27]

It may be that labor market hardships due to the economic recession in 2008 contributed to the uptick in new enrollments beginning in 2009. In fact, a study released by the Pew Research Center in 2009 found that a record number of eighteen- to twenty-four-year-olds were enrolled in college in October 2008 and that this increase was driven by community college enrollments.[28] Additionally, the National Student Clearinghouse reports that the number of students over the age of twenty-four enrolling for the first time in 2008 increased by 20 percent over the previous year.[29] The trends in our data appear to mirror these larger national trends, albeit perhaps a year behind.

Institutions and Degree Attainment

Were any of the men in our sample likely to have actually improved their labor market position by returning to school? As mentioned earlier, persistence in our sample was very low: the average student enrolled for the equivalent of only one semester. However, the NSC does identify 5.5 percent of the students in our sample (twenty young men) as having earned a degree by January 2014: five bachelor's degrees, nine associate's degrees, and three certificates; for two graduates, no degree type was reported. Although low, this proportion is not vastly dissimilar from the graduation rates of first-time college students who were at or below the poverty line in Michigan in the 2003–2004 academic year, especially when considering only associate's or bachelor's degrees.[30] By 2008–2009, only about 8 percent of the BPS-2004 sample had earned an AA or BA.[31] Thus, the degree (that is, noncertificate) graduation rate of those in our sample who enrolled—about 4 percent—was roughly half that of poor first-time college students in Michigan in 2003. Moreover, because of the preponderance of late enrollments (2009 or later) in our sample, half of our students could not be followed for the full six years that the BPS-2004 uses to calculate these graduation rates. The BPS-2004 finds that the average student took forty-two months, or three and a half years, to earn a terminal associate's degree, with at least one break; that means that it is not altogether unlikely

Figure 4.3 Timing of Enrollments by Sector and Status, 2002–2014

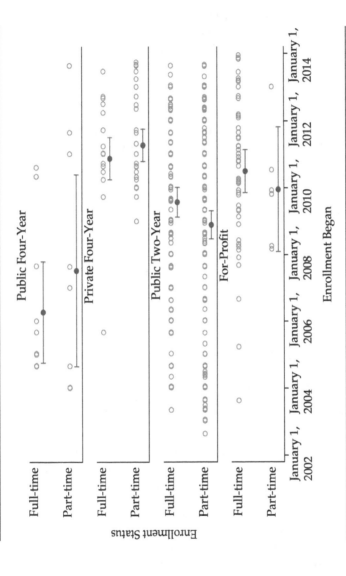

Source: Michigan Study of Life after Prison.
Note: Lighter dots indicate the start dates of individual enrollments, by quarter. Average enrollment date and a 95 percent confidence interval are represented in the darker shade. Part-time status refers to enrollments reported as half-time or less than half-time by the NSC. Enrollments with "withdrawn" status are omitted. 2002 enrollments occur for individuals released before their 2003 parole date. See chapter 2, note 92.

that some formerly incarcerated men earned a degree after our observation period. Had we followed up later, we might have observed an even more similar graduation rate. In either case, education was likely ongoing for at least some young men in our sample at the point of data collection in 2013, even as most were entering their thirties.

Given that only twenty of the men who enrolled earned any kind of credential, more detail is needed to understand the extent of college persistence in our sample. Figure 4.4 shows the duration of enrollments by sector and enrollment status. Like figure 4.3, these observations pertain to unique enrollment spells, as opposed to individual men, who may have had multiple spells. Overall, enrollments in our sample typically lasted for about a year, regardless of the sector or status. Note that with the exception of the for-profit sector, these enrollments were very likely to have been part-time (a status that includes students enrolled less than half-time).[32] It is not surprising, therefore, that so few men appear to have earned credentials. Nevertheless, it may be that some of these men improved their labor market standing through their participation in postsecondary education. Prior research has shown that individuals earn 5 to 10 percent more for each full-time equivalent year spent in community college, even without a degree.[33] On the other hand, it is also possible that, without a credential, these human capital gains do not overcome the mark of a criminal record and that, rather than reaping financial benefits, these students may primarily experience the financial burden of paying for school.

The risk faced by our sample in terms of debt accumulation and devalued credentials may be exacerbated by the type of institutions they attended. Table 4.2 shows the institutions in the private and for-profit sectors most commonly attended by men in our sample. Enrollments in the private not-for-profit sector were dominated by two institutions, Baker College of Flint and Davenport University. Both are career colleges that emphasize technology and health and have several campuses across Michigan as well as significant online programming. In other words, these institutions share many of the characteristics of heavily advertised and largely online for-profit institutions like the University of Phoenix, ITT Technical Institute, and Ashford University. The prevalence of these types of institutions in our sample may reflect preferences for flexible application and start dates and degree programs designed to produce credentials for direct entry into growing technical fields.

Recent research illustrates the prevalence of enrollments in short-term certificate programs at private or for-profit trade schools among low-income emerging adults.[34] This work effectively demonstrates the draw of these programs, which advertise the ease of getting started by offering flexible applications, start dates, and hours and promising an "insta-career."

Figure 4.4   Enrollment Duration by Sector and Status, 2002–2014

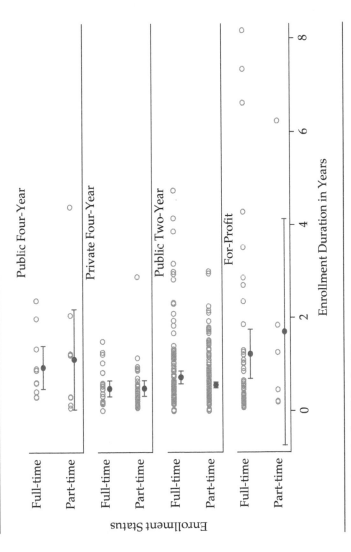

Enrollment Duration in Years

Source: Michigan Study of Life after Prison.
Note: Lighter dots indicate the duration of individual enrollments, in years (days, divided by 365). Average duration and a 95 percent confidence interval are represented in the darker shade. Part-time status refers to enrollments reported as half-time or less than half-time by the NSC. Enrollments with "withdrawn" status are omitted. 2002 enrollments occur for individuals released before their 2003 parole date. See chapter 2, note 92.

Table 4.2 Total Person-Quarters Ever Enrolled at Private and For-Profit Colleges Most Commonly Attended, 2002–2014

Private Four-Year College	Quarters		Individuals	
	N	%	N	%
Baker College of Flint	111	57	35	67
Davenport University	49	25	9	17
Other	35	18	8	15
Total	195	100	52	100

For-Profit Institutions	Quarters		Individuals	
	N	%	N	%
University of Phoenix	82	29	21	27
ITT Technical Institute	59	21	14	18
Ashford University	24	9	7	9
Other	37	13	10	13
Total	202	100	52	100

Source: Michigan Study of Life after Prison.

Note: Individuals may attend multiple institutions. 2002 enrollments occur for individuals released before their 2003 parole date. See chapter 2, note 92. Data for 2003 Michigan parole cohort age 18–25 at parole, followed through 2014.

The research also illustrates the pitfalls of programs that lock students into a course of study with no opportunity for exploration, little potential for transferability should they decide to change direction, and no recourse for these students when they are left with considerable debt and little credit.[35]

Unfortunately, given how few credentials are reported to the NSC, it appears that the young men in our sample were very likely to experience these pitfalls. In fact, they may have hit our sample exceptionally hard. ITT Technical Institute, which was one of the three most-attended for-profit institutions among those in our sample, has since lost its accreditation and was shut down in 2016. Subsequently, it undoubtedly became more diffi-cult for the ITT Tech students in our sample to have their credit recognized either on the labor market or at other universities. Further, as of January 2019, the Flint Campus of Baker College was also set to be closed as part of a consolidation effort.[36] Although this closure was unlikely to directly impact the men in our sample, this decision suggests that the Flint campus was not a particularly strong site of investment for the institution in the preceding years. Put simply, the postsecondary enrollments pursued by low-income young adults often lead to low or even negative financial returns, and the enrollments of formerly incarcerated young men are no exception.

Black-White Differences in the Timing of Enrollments

Much of the literature on incarceration and its effects on later outcomes focuses on disparities between blacks and whites after release, particularly with regard to their employment opportunities.[37] Black and white men in our sample enrolled in postsecondary education after release at slightly different rates. Black men were somewhat more likely to enroll than white men, at 30.6 percent versus 25.7 percent, respectively.[38] Although this dif-ference is not quite statistically significant at conventional levels ($p = .053$), race is a stronger bivariate predictor of enrollment than various markers of criminal justice involvement and pre-prison disadvantage, including age at first arrest, number of arrests, racial composition and poverty of pre-prison neighborhood, and history of mental illness or substance abuse ($p > .1$ for each). Therefore, racial differences in postsecondary enrollments warrant closer consideration.

Figure 4.5 plots the duration, timing, and sector of enrollments for white and black men separately. Overall, these plots look quite similar. There is no noticeable difference in the sector of enrollments, and apart from four for-profit outliers for black students, enrollment durations also seem similarly clustered at less than two years. Moreover, there do not appear to be any strong relationships between status, sector, or duration of

Figure 4.5   Sector, Timing, and Duration of Enrollments, by Race,
2002–2014

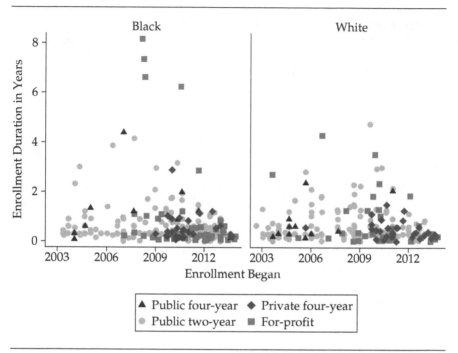

Source: Michigan Study of Life after Prison.
Note: 2002 enrollments occur for individuals released before their 2003 parole date. See chapter 2, note 92.

enrollments that differ between the two groups. However, one difference is that enrollments seem somewhat denser after 2009 for black students than for white students.

Table 4.3 confirms these impressions. There is no significant difference in the status, sector, or persistence of individual enrollments between black and white men in our sample. However, while both black and white men were more likely to enroll in the latter half of our observation period, this jump in enrollments was significantly greater among black men. This racial difference in enrollment rates may reflect the disproportionate impact of the 2008 recession on employment for black men relative to white men. For every percentage point increase in the Michigan unemployment rate during the 2008 recession, the unemployment rate increased by nearly 2 percent for black men.[39] Perhaps one compelling reason why more

Table 4.3   Black-White Differences in Enrollments, within Ten Years
after Release, 2002–2014

	Black	White	T-test P-value	Significant Difference
Status (n)	306	267	573	
Withdrawn	12%	12%	0.922	
Part-time	49	50	0.722	
Full-time	39	38	0.666	
Sector (n)	303	263	566	
Public two-year	69%	71%	0.653	
Public four-year	4	5	0.576	
Private four-year	12	12	0.931	
For-profit	16	13	0.327	
Start of enrollment (n)	306	267	573	
Percent before 2009	30%	41%	0.004	***
Percent 2009 or later	70	59	0.004	***
Persistence (n)	306	267	573	
Less than half a year	66%	61%	0.218	
Half a year to one year	20	21	0.844	
One to two years	10	13	0.215	
Two years or more	5	6	0.571	

Source: Michigan Study of Life after Prison.
Note: 2002 enrollments occur for individuals released before their 2003 parole date. See chapter 2, note 92. Data for 2003 Michigan parole cohort age 18–25 at parole, followed through 2014.
Significance stars for *t*-tests of differences between white and black sample: $^+p < .1$, $^*p < .05$, $^{**}p < .01$, $^{***}p < .001$

formerly incarcerated young black men returned to school beginning in this period was that it had become more difficult to find a job.[40]

RELATIVE RISK AND CONTINUED CRIMINAL INVOLVEMENT

So far, we have demonstrated that education was an ongoing endeavor for a significant proportion of the young men in our sample. Those who returned to the school environment appear mainly to have pursued associate's degrees and technical credentials, primarily at community colleges, for-profit institutions, or trade schools and typically at half-time status.

Reported enrollments peaked in 2010, perhaps owing at least partially to a combination of improved reporting by private four-year institutions and the impact of the Great Recession. Blacks were slightly more likely to enroll than whites, and this gap was more pronounced after 2008 than before, possibly reflecting different labor market experiences. In this section, we develop two sets of hypotheses as to why certain formerly incarcerated young men were more likely to enroll and to persist in postsecondary education, with a special focus on these racial differences.

First, given the nature of our sample, we make informed assumptions about the impact of larger processes of accumulated disadvantage and involvement in the criminal justice system on educational trajectories.[41] We posit that educational interruption or momentum is one dimension along which the likelihood of enrollment may be shaped. Second, regarding the observed racial differences in the likelihood and timing of enrollments, we propose a variation on relative risk aversion that takes into account the labor force advantage of white working-class men relative to their black peers.[42] We return to this explanatory framework shortly.

Criminal Justice Experiences and Interrupted Educational Momentum

During their incarceration, young men in our sample were necessarily precluded from participation in traditional educational institutions. Some may have found themselves unable to finish high school or pursue their GED (outside of prison), while others were directly impeded in their postsecondary plans by incarceration.[43] In either case, incarceration constituted a serious break in their (potential) educational momentum. Research has shown that "momentum" is important to postsecondary degree attainment. Controlling for family background and academic preparation, students are more likely to complete a degree if they begin college directly after high school or if they continue to take courses during the summer term.[44] Turning this hypothesis into a question we can directly ask of our data, we predict that the younger a man is at his first arrest and the older he is at release, the less likely he will be to return to school.[45] Therefore, our first guiding theory is related to the degree of criminal justice involvement as it might affect educational opportunities. Simply, we expect that those who spent a greater share of their emerging adulthood years entangled with the criminal justice system (for example, those who were first arrested at younger ages and who spent more time in prison) and those who continued to be involved in the criminal justice system after their 2003 release were less likely to enroll in postsecondary education.

We acknowledge the possibility that prison itself might actually *create* educational momentum by requiring men who might not have pursued a GED to do so, thereby increasing their eligibility for postsecondary enrollment relative to similar peers who avoided incarceration.[46] However, within our sample of incarcerated men, it is more likely that those with greater criminal justice involvement experienced greater educational interruption and therefore had less momentum. Specifically, after controlling for whether men earned a GED while incarcerated, we expect that those with earlier first arrests and later releases will be less likely to enroll after release.

Of course, involvement in the criminal justice system did not end when these men left prison. In the best-case scenario, they were under ongoing supervision through parole. Many were rearrested or reincarcerated in this period, and some continued in prohibited or criminal behavior that led to further criminal justice involvement. For these men, our decision to consider all enrollments after their 2003 release as "post-prison" is essentially an arbitrary one, and we expect that any ongoing involvement in the criminal justice system will be negatively associated with college enrollment.

Relative Risk Aversion Theory

Richard Breen and John Goldthorpe assume that individuals seek to at least reproduce, if not surpass, their parents' class status.[47] Therefore, different individuals have different definitions of "success" that are not predicated on any cultural influence but rather are associated with their particular class origins. Investments in education present one important pathway to achieving socioeconomic mobility, and students evaluate the risk associated with either continuing school or entering the labor market against their relative definitions of success. Breen and Goldthorpe dub this "relative risk aversion." The risk associated with pursuing the next level of education is a function of the subjective likelihood of attaining that level of education or that credential and the total cost of doing so. Breen and Goldthorpe argue that the subjective likelihood of success is important because students who attempt a given level of education and fail may face more barriers to achieving their status aspirations than students who do not attempt the same level of education (both because of the mark of failure and the forgone labor market experience). Unfortunately, the risk of failing in college was extremely high for every young man in our sample. It may then be that the men who enrolled were those who believed that they would be no worse off if they tried and failed than if they did not try at all. These are likely to be the men who faced the greatest labor market stigma and for whom the total cost of postsecondary education was lowest.

The total cost of postsecondary education can be understood as both the price of attending and the amount of foregone earnings while enrolled. Again, this cost has a relative impact on risk because tuition costs are less prohibitive for families with more wealth. A traditional interpretation of Breen and Goldthorpe's relative risk aversion theory, therefore, would imply that individuals with more resources are more likely to enroll. This theory assumes the "traditional" student, who decides whether or not to enroll in college directly after high school and who, perhaps more importantly, has parents who will pay most or all of the tuition. Calculations of risk may differ for individuals who are deciding whether to enroll after a period away from school, like the young men in our sample. The cost of forgone earnings may weigh more heavily in this population, particularly given that, with little or no accumulated wealth, they may have been more likely to pay for college themselves. In this regard, black would-be students may have faced *lower* costs than whites because, relative to their white counterparts, their labor market disadvantages were disproportionately compounded by the stigma of a criminal record.[48] There is also evidence that stable and lucrative blue-collar work, such as in construction, was more accessible to white men, and that even those black men who did find such work were paid less.[49] Thus, the cost of returning to college in terms of forgone earnings may have been lower for black men, possibly contributing to the higher enrollment rates we described earlier. This hypothesis is also consistent with the increase in enrollments around 2008, when the Great Recession drove unemployment rates up, perhaps reducing the perceived risk of returning to school for many men, irrespective of race. Thus, while a traditional reading of relative risk aversion would predict a positive association between financial resources and enrollments, the labor market precarity and lack of wealth in our sample might instead lead us to hypothesize a negative relationship between earnings and enrollments.

For men whose economic position is as precarious as that of the men in our sample, the cost of tuition, even at community colleges, is a significant burden. Having strong ties to significant others who might share this burden by caring for children, helping to pay bills, or directly paying tuition may be an important predictor of the ability to enroll in college. We might expect that men who lived with their parents (or other older relatives) were likely to have high social and financial support and relatively lower financial independence (or to be less of a financial burden) than those living with a romantic partner or in other private arrangements. Vast racial differences in wealth,[50] however, may mean that these resources were more available to whites than blacks, even if they lived in similarly impoverished neighborhoods. Our best proxy for the potential for social support is living arrangements. Accordingly, we expect that living with a parent or older relative increases the likelihood of enrollment. Furthermore, we would expect a larger benefit to living with parents for whites. This hypothesis reflects a more traditional interpretation of relative risk aversion.

PREDICTORS OF ENROLLMENT

Having discussed the educational experiences of the men in our sample— when they enrolled, the types of schools in which they enrolled, their enrollment status, and their persistence—we next unpack these findings by investigating who experienced these various educational outcomes. In particular, we are interested in understanding who *ever* enrolled and whether any time-varying factors help predict enrollment in a given calendar quarter after release.[51]

Our results confirm that race is among the most important factors in predicting who would enroll after release, but overall we find little support for the hypotheses described here. Unsurprisingly, those with a secondary credential at the time of their release were more likely to enroll in college. However, there is little evidence among our sample of educationally interrupted young men that the *extent* of that interruption predicted enrollments. Further, although we find that earnings in the year immediately after the 2003 release positively predict enrollment *at some point* among black men, we find no relationship between earnings in one quarter and enrollment in the following quarter for either black or white men. Additionally, neither analysis finds any effect of living with a parent or older relative compared to other private residences. For brevity, figures 4.6 and 4.7 present only the coefficients that test our key hypotheses.

Who Enrolls in Postsecondary Education?

We begin by evaluating the question of who is likely to enroll in postsecondary education during the transition to adulthood after prison. As in other chapters, we present results from logistic regressions using marginal effects, which can be interpreted as the change in probability of the outcome associated with a one-unit change in the predictor.

We test whether educational interruption or relative risk aversion theories correctly predict the likelihood of ever enrolling in postsecondary education among the young men in our sample. To measure educational interruption, we include age at first arrest, age at 2003 release, and number of months in prison during the focal incarceration.[52] We also include indicators for whether secondary credentials were earned before, during, or shortly after incarceration. The variables used to test the relative risk aversion hypothesis are highest quarterly earnings (logged) within a year of release, living arrangements immediately after release, and the jobless rate in the neighborhood of release. Importantly, our hypotheses suggest that certain variables may predict enrollments differently for white and black men. Accordingly, results are reported separately by race in figure 4.6.[53]

Not surprisingly, men with more education prior to their incarceration were more likely to enroll in college after release. Secondary education is divided into five categories, by credential and timing: GED earned prior to the 2003 incarceration, GED earned during the 2003 incarceration, GED earned in the first year after the 2003 release, high school degree (all earned prior to the 2003 incarceration), or no secondary degree (the reference group). For men with a secondary degree by their 2003 release, the likelihood of enrollment increased around fifteen percentage points—about a twofold increase in the *odds* of enrollment—over those with no secondary degree, all else constant. If interruption to young men's *traditional* schooling years is important to their likelihood of enrollment, we might expect that those who earned a high school degree before prison would benefit relative to those who earned a GED in prison. On the other hand, prison itself might *create* educational momentum for those who would not otherwise have completed a secondary credential but were required to do so by MDOC. If this is the case, we might expect that earning a GED *during* prison could increase the likelihood of continuing education after prison relative to those who had earned their GED previously. There is no evidence, however, to support either of these ideas: there is no statistically discernible difference in the likelihood of enrollment (1) between men who earned a high school degree compared to those who earned a GED, or (2) between men who earned their GED before their 2003 incarceration, those who earned it during incarceration, or those who earned it just after release.

Our primary indicators of educational interruption—age at first arrest, months in prison, and age at 2003 release—also provide no evidence that men who experienced relatively less disruption to the traditional education trajectory were more likely to enroll in postsecondary education after release. Of course, this does not suggest that educational interruption and momentum are unimportant to lifetime educational attainment. Rather, it suggests that within our sample of young men, who all experienced significant educational interruption during the period traditionally associated with completing school, there is no *further* association. These analyses also control for factors that should be indicative of the intensity of criminal justice involvement, such as number of arrests, convictions for violent offenses, and prison management and conduct, none of which predict enrollments.

There is some evidence, however, that earnings influenced formerly incarcerated young men's likelihood of college enrollment. In our sample, black men were more likely to enroll in college after their 2003 release if

Figure 4.6   Differences in the Probability of Ever Enrolling in College, by Various Predictors

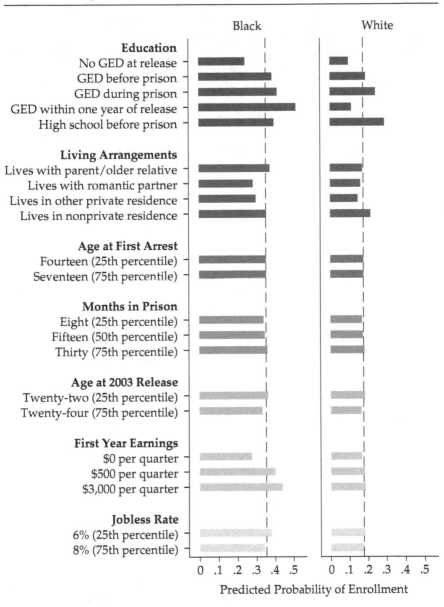

Source: Michigan Study of Life after Prison.
Note: Data for 2003 Michigan parole cohort age 18–25 at parole, followed through 2014.

they had higher earnings in their first year out of prison. This was not the case among white men. Our variable for earnings in the first year after release captures the highest earnings in a single quarter within the first four quarters after release. For each unit increase in the natural log of highest quarterly wages among blacks, the likelihood of enrolling in college increases by about two percentage points. The median black individual in our sample had no earnings in any of the first four quarters after release, and only one-third exceeded $500. Thus, the likelihood of enrollment for a black man at the sixty-seventh percentile of first-year earnings is about twelve percentage points higher than for a black man at the fiftieth percentile.[54] Although this appears to contradict our theory that men who earned less would perceive less risk of forgone earnings in returning to school and therefore would be more likely to enroll, this conclusion may be somewhat premature.

First, it is interesting to note that, among zero earners in the first year after release, blacks and whites were equally likely to enroll (25.5 percent and 23.6 percent, respectively). Yet among wage earners, black men were significantly more likely to enroll than white men (38.7 percent versus 27.0 percent, respectively), despite the fact that they earned significantly less money in their highest earning quarter on average. Conditional on having *some* earnings, then, it may be that lower earnings potential among black men does motivate enrollment. Second, because earnings tended to be extremely low prior to the recession of 2008, it could be that only those men who were doing relatively well after release felt any impact from the recession at all. In fact, men who returned to school in 2009 or later were more likely to experience a downward earnings trajectory or consistent lack of formal employment.[55] Our adaptation of the relative risk aversion hypothesis may therefore be better tested on later earnings rather than on earnings in the first year after release.

We also consider the possibility that living arrangements after prison, as reflections of the amount of social and financial support available to young men, shaped their likelihood of enrollment. We would expect those living with a parent or older relative (the reference group) or those living with a spouse or romantic partner to experience more social and financial support than those in other private living arrangements or in shelters or treatment facilities. Because living with a romantic partner may signal additional financial responsibility as much as it does support, and because these men had taken other traditional steps toward adulthood, we might expect living with parents to be the favorable living arrangement for encouraging enrollments. For the most part, it was indeed the case that men who returned to a living arrangement other than with their parents or an older relative at release were somewhat less likely to enroll in college. However, none of these differences are statistically significant.

When Do Formerly Incarcerated Young Men Enroll in Postsecondary Education?

Because enrollments in our sample were spread out over the entire decade of our follow-up—illustrating the protracted nature of education in the transition to adulthood—we consider in this section whether any post-incarceration experiences predict enrollment timing. Unfortunately, although our data on enrollments from the National Student Clearinghouse extend through the end of 2013, the rest of our data extend at best to 2010, at which point only about half of the observed enrollments had occurred. Thus, the following analysis (figure 4.7) considers the factors that predict enrollment only for those who returned to school relatively early.[56] As we saw in figure 4.5 and table 4.3, black men were especially likely to enroll later in our observation period. Thus, to account for any potential differences in the consideration of time-varying factors between white and black men, we present results by race, as in the previous section.

Even considering the limitation of omitting enrollments after 2010, the available window of observation—which includes men as young as eighteen at the outset and as old as thirty-two at the end—is apt for an investigation of education in the transition to adulthood after prison. Time is considered in quarters since release.[57] In considering several key time-varying variables, we extend our ability to test the hypotheses addressed earlier: earnings in prior quarter, whether an individual had a GED by the current quarter, and living arrangements. We construct the latter set of variables as mutually exclusive indicators of living arrangements at the beginning of the quarter. Further, to account for ongoing criminal justice involvement, we include time-varying indicators of substance abuse tests, arrests since release, and absconding. Finally, under the assumption that the perceived costs of enrollment may be lower if more options are available within a short commuting distance, we include county-level measures of college density, which is time-varying due to residential mobility.

Figure 4.7 presents the results by race.[58] Several of these variables—GED, quarterly earnings, living arrangements, and jobless rate—parallel those that were addressed in the models described earlier, which were restricted to static estimates from the year following the 2003 release. Because of this difference, and because the current models are restricted to enrollments occurring before 2010, the estimates from these coefficients may differ from those presented earlier. Indeed, although GEDs are highly predictive of whether men in our sample enrolled at any point after release, the time-varying indicator of GED credentials is only predictive of enrollment in a given quarter for black men, not for white men (see figure 4.7). We can think of two possible explanations for this finding. The first is in

Figure 4.7   Differences in the Probability of Quarterly Enrollment, by Various Predictors

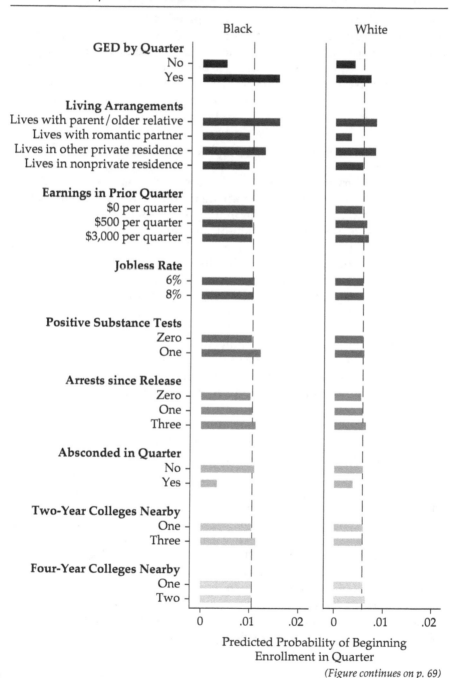

Predicted Probability of Beginning
Enrollment in Quarter

(Figure continues on p. 69)

Figure 4.7   *Continued*

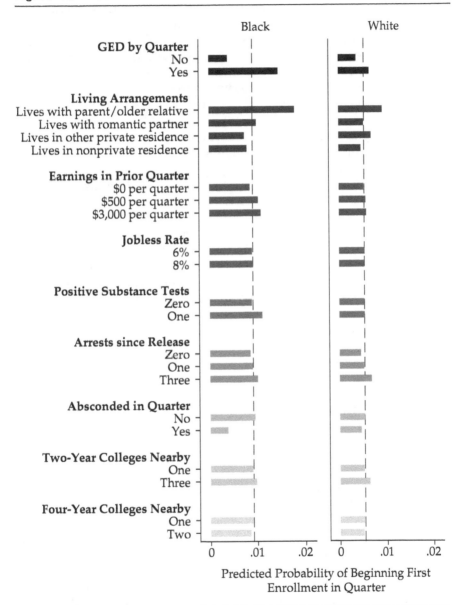

Source: Michigan Study of Life after Prison.
Note: The first panel plots results from a model predicting all enrollments from release to the end of 2010. The second panel plots results from a model predicting only the first enrollment after release, before 2010. Data for 2003 Michigan parole cohort age 18–25 at parole, followed through 2014.

keeping with our relative risk aversion hypothesis: the effect of racial dis-crimination in the labor market may be strongest for black GED holders, a credential that employers may associate with a prison term; if this is the case, returning to school may have felt more worth the risk to blacks with a GED, even if the expected return was no greater. Alternatively, employers' association of a GED with a prison term could reflect the fact that blacks in our sample were twice as likely as whites to earn a GED after their 2003 release; thus, the time-varying GED variable captures more behavior that is truly time-varying—in that it captures *ongoing* education—in the black sample. This possibility is also consistent with the hypothesis that GED coursework is important for building momentum that might help young men continue their education.

By using time-varying measures, event history analysis also permits a finer-grained picture of the importance of earnings relative to the logistic regressions presented earlier. Specifically, we examine how income in one quarter is related to enrollment in the next. One might reasonably suggest that most potential students consider their earnings more than a calen-dar quarter in advance of making an enrollment decision. Although this is probably true when possible, this kind of advanced forecasting was often difficult in our sample of young men, whose earnings were extremely vola-tile. Moreover, because these men largely attended institutions that offered rolling admissions and allowed students to begin classes in either the fall or the spring, or even more frequently, quick decisions to apply and enroll were possible. Nevertheless, we find no relationship between earnings in the prior quarter and the likelihood of enrollment among either black or white men. This is contrary to our relative risk aversion theories, in both their traditional and updated forms, which hypothesize that men take their earnings into account when considering the total cost of postsecondary enrollment. Although this does not preclude the possibility that the reces-sion of 2008 gave more men an impetus to return to school beginning in 2009, it does suggest that short-term fluctuations in wages were not pri-mary drivers of college enrollment.[59]

We find that those in "other" private living arrangements on the first day of the quarter were in fact less likely to enroll than those living with a parent or older relative, but that these differences are not statistically significant.[60] In contrast, those who lived in a nonprivate arrangement (for example, those who lived in a treatment facility, were jailed for a short period, or were homeless) were significantly less likely to enroll—probably because each of these situations almost necessarily hinders an individual's ability to attend school. Individuals living with their parents at the begin-ning of the current quarter had the best odds of returning to school for the first time in a given quarter.

Overall, few other time-varying variables were predictive of enrollment. The exception is for white men, who were extremely unlikely to return to school for the first time, and somewhat less likely to begin any enrollment, in a quarter in which they had tested positive for drugs. Note that simply being tested for drugs is not associated with any difference in the likelihood of enrollment for either black or white men. Number of arrests since release is also not statistically significant in predicting enrollments in a particular quarter, and neither is absconding. Taken together, these findings suggest that the transition to adulthood of our formerly incarcerated young men was already so shaped by involvement in the criminal justice system that additional contacts—in the form of arrests or monitoring, such as drug testing—seldom produced even more disadvantage until they led to serious sanctions, like a period of confinement. Further, the educational and labor market contexts in which our young men lived, as measured by county joblessness and the prevalence of two- and four-year public colleges, do not appear to have shaped their enrollment decisions in the short run. Given the shared context of extreme structural disadvantage in our sample, it may be that more idiosyncratic, personal, and unobservable characteristics are better indicators of enrollment.

CONCLUSION

There are many barriers to returning to school for those who are incarcerated in young adulthood, including relatively low educational achievement prior to incarceration, few financial resources to put toward education, and the emotional and scheduling stresses of being on parole. Despite these challenges, 28 percent of the young men in our sample attempted to enroll in a postsecondary institution at some point between their release in 2003 and the end of 2013. Like Jeremiah, most of them enrolled part-time at a community college and did so for the equivalent of one full-time semester on average. These lower-intensity enrollments reflect larger national trends: lower-income and older students are entering postsecondary education in larger numbers, but the majority fail to complete a degree or a certificate. Enrollments in our sample also reflect national trends in the growth of for-profit education: enrollments (or attempted enrollments) in institutions like the University of Phoenix, ITT Technical Institute, and Ashford University were common among our young men. Attendance at private career colleges with multiple campuses, flexible enrollment, and significant online programming was also common. These types of institutions are known to produce relatively high debt burdens with relatively low labor market returns. Thus, while considering the potential benefits of education, it is also important to recognize that many of the returning students in our sample may not in fact have been better off after their enrollment than their peers who never pursued postsecondary education.

Of the 338 men in our sample who successfully enrolled in postsecondary education, only twenty (or about 6 percent) earned a degree or certificate. Like Dennis, most were in their early thirties by the time they completed a two-year degree. Although the completion rate in our sample was considerably lower than the 20 percent degree or certificate completion rate for students at or below the poverty line in Michigan, at least three points should be kept in mind. First, certificates from private trade schools may have been underreported by the NSC during our observation period. Second, the Michigan statewide estimates are based on a six-year follow-up period, which was not available to us for half of the students in our sample (those who first enrolled after release in 2009 or later). And finally, the statewide estimates include women, who may graduate at different rates from men.

Overall, enrollment patterns in our data, in terms of enrollment destinations and persistence, suggest that efforts at postsecondary education after incarceration may not be producing the labor market returns that no doubt motivate formerly incarcerated young men to enroll. This descriptive account of enrollments benefits from an exceptionally long follow-up period, covering an entire decade after our sample began parole. Given their protracted schooling in the transition to adulthood—as these young men pursued more education and did so at older ages—such a follow-up is critical to an accurate picture of participation in postsecondary education. However, because our enrollment data extend significantly beyond our employment data, and because such a large proportion of our enrollments did indeed occur in this later period, we cannot directly test the outcomes associated with schooling. Instead, we attempt to understand what made some men in our sample more likely than others to enroll.

The best predictors of enrollment are race, prior educational attainment, earnings shortly after release, and living arrangements. Although we found only partial support for our two theories specific to education and incarceration—a theory that enrollments are less likely among those whose "traditional" schooling years have been disrupted by their criminal justice involvement, and a recasting of relative risk aversion theory specific to the labor market realities of formerly incarcerated men, it is noteworthy that the variables that emerged as the most significant are those that have tended to be of most interest in the transition-to-adulthood literature: race, schooling, employment, and residential independence. Overall, education and earnings at release are positively associated with postsecondary enrollments, echoing research that depicts role transitions as clustered in the life course.[61] In the regression models that predict whether or not men in our sample would ever enroll after release, both black and white men were significantly more likely to enroll if they had earned a secondary credential by the time of their 2003 release. Two other effects, however, differed somewhat by race, with associations tending to be more significant for black men: highest quarterly earnings in the year after release were predictive of enrollments only for black men; and the time-varying indicator for GED attainment was also only significant for black men.

GED and first-year earnings are two of very few variables that predict enrollment.[62] It is therefore quite noteworthy that the predictive power of these experiences differs by race. All told, race remains one of the best predictors of enrollment in our sample, with black men being more likely to enroll. This in itself may offer some support for the relative risk aversion hypothesis, in that the labor market prospects of black men with a criminal record are especially low and the perceived risk of taking time away from the labor market for education, even with the extremely high likelihood of failing to earn a credential, may not be as strong a deterrent for black men as for their white peers. Furthermore, it may well be that black men with relatively "high" earnings in the year after release (essentially, those with nonzero earnings) were precisely those who were most likely to feel the impacts of the recession and thus be motivated to return to school later in our study period. There is little evidence, however, of short-term decision-making on the basis of prior quarterly earnings up to 2010.

Importantly, our data show that many formerly incarcerated young men *wanted* to pursue postsecondary education, but that very few of them had the resources to benefit from this motivation. Given the potential of education to break the link between incarceration and social exclusion, both intra- and intergenerationally,[63] greater effort should be made to support these young men in getting into postsecondary institutions and completing degrees or certificates. Low-income, first-generation college students in general face challenges in gathering information from their social networks about potential careers and how to pursue them. This increases the likelihood that they will enroll in "insta-career" technical programs, with little knowledge of what the training actually entails, and subsequently drop out.[64] This calls for more information, not only about growing technical fields and the training they require but also about the types of programs that are best designed to see students through from enrollment to employment. Policy around information dissemination is never simple, but if the promise of postsecondary education is to be met for formerly incarcerated young men, improving it should clearly be a goal of parole reform. We return to such policy considerations in the concluding chapter.

Chapter 5 | Health and Risky
Health Behaviors

EDWIN, A YOUNG black man, was first arrested on drug charges at age seventeen. His arrests and drug tests indicate consistent involvement in the drug trade, as well as drug abuse, during the next decade. Yet his "official" involvement in violence did not begin until much later. When he was in his late twenties and back in prison, Edwin spent thirty days in solitary confinement for fighting. After he was released, he was arrested for domestic violence. Although he later enrolled in community college, he also consistently tested positive for drugs throughout his parole.

Douglas's patterns of substance use and violence were more severe, began earlier, and ran deeper. Douglas, who was white, first tried alcohol when he was in the first grade. His substance abuse progressed such that, by the time he could drink legally, he was drinking two fifths of liquor daily and smoking marijuana weekly. His arrest history included several charges of driving under the influence and domestic violence, suggesting that his substance use and violence were intertwined. His involvement in drug abuse and violence deepened as he got older. In his early twenties, he began to use cocaine, and a few years later he was arrested for domestic violence. A year later, he was arrested for drug possession and assault on a police officer—all signs of his continuing difficulty navigating drug addiction and managing social relationships. Shortly thereafter, he entered substance abuse treatment, where he remained for one month. After leaving treatment, Douglas moved in with a girlfriend and enrolled in community college, eventually earning a certificate in his early thirties.

Despite their struggles, Edwin and Douglas were able to meet more transitional markers than Rodney and Trevor—two young men who ultimately succumbed to health risks associated with their age group. Rodney, a young black man, was not arrested for the first time until he was twenty years old. He had no juvenile record and no record of substance use. However, at that time he was on probation for what may have been a domestic violence offense—he had been ordered to avoid a particular person and to seek mental health treatment. Thus, his mental health and difficulty maintaining healthy interpersonal relationships seem to have contributed to his involvement with the criminal justice system. Rodney was imprisoned after being arrested on a felony drug charge while on probation. Soon after he was released from prison, Rodney struggled to find a job and began testing positive for drugs. Less than a year later, at age twenty-five, he was shot and killed.

Like Douglas, Trevor—who was also white—began using drugs in early childhood, smoking marijuana as early as third grade. He had juvenile justice contact even before he became a teenager and started drinking alcohol in his midteens. At age seventeen, he was arrested for drunken driving and sentenced to probation. While on probation, he was arrested on several theft and fraud charges before being sentenced to prison in his early twenties. After prison, Trevor entered substance abuse treatment, where he stayed for seventy-five days—just shy of the recommended three months, but far longer than most men stay. Still, he could not seem to find a job or shake the reach of the criminal justice system. Old warrants and charges such as obstructing justice kept him cycling in and out of technical rule violator (TRV) facilities. A year and half after he was released from prison, Trevor died in a car crash. He was twenty-six.

These young men's stories highlight the main risks to male youth undergoing the transition to adulthood in the United States, whether they have been incarcerated or not: risky health behaviors. As Edwin's and Douglas's stories illustrate, risky health behaviors have negative consequences for life-course transitions regardless of when in their life course young men become involved with violence and substance use. Employment opportunities were closed to them and their educational achievement was delayed because of their substance use, but also because each of them struggled to negotiate interpersonal relationships without resorting to violence. As Rodney's and Trevor's stories illustrate, engaging in risky health behaviors can also lead to the most serious of negative consequences for health: an early death. In addition, the deaths of these two young men demonstrate the stark racial divide in mortality causes across the United States. Between 2000 and 2015, firearm homicide was consistently the leading cause of death among fifteen- to thirty-four-year-old black males. During the same period, threats to the lives of young white men shifted: in 2013, drug overdose surpassed motor vehicle accidents as the leading cause of death among fifteen- to thirty-four-year-old white males.[1]

In this chapter, we examine patterns of mortality and involvement in two particularly risky health behaviors, substance use and violence.

Looking at these behaviors from a health perspective is not the only way to study them, but this approach allows us to focus on the consequences for the people engaged in them. Broadly, health behaviors are "personal behaviors that influence health, morbidity, and mortality." In the United States, health behaviors explain "about 40 percent of premature mortality as well as substantial morbidity and disability."[2]

Violence and substance use are two socially proscribed and risky health behaviors that often lead to contact with the criminal justice system. These behaviors are highly correlated with their health-related consequences, especially mortality. The perpetration of violence is deeply but not perfectly intertwined with the likelihood of becoming a victim of violence — particularly of homicide — just as substance use and overdose are linked.[3]

Criminal justice–involved men commonly engage in risky health behaviors that contribute to their eventual incarceration and their post-release premature deaths. Prior to their incarceration and after they were released, the young men in our sample engaged in violence at high rates, as measured by quarterly arrests for violent offenses,[4] and in substance use, as measured by quarterly positive tests for any drug.[5] Similarly, many of these men were involved in the drug trade — as indicated by arrests for drug-related crimes.[6]

These measures of involvement in substance use and violence, which are derived from administrative criminal justice data, have limitations that are important to understand. Each indicator of involvement in a risky health behavior is a function of both the behavior of the individual and the behavior of the criminal justice system. We can only observe the perpetration of violence that the police observe. Although most arrests for violent offenses result from citizen calls for service,[7] fewer than half of violent victimizations — 43 percent in 2018 — are reported to police.[8] Compounding that fact, police make arrests in response to only a fraction of the violent crimes reported to them. Fewer than 40 percent of robberies and only about 60 percent of aggravated assaults occurring in jurisdictions policed by more than one hundred officers were cleared by arrest in 2013; these rates have been stable since 1981.[9] The number of their arrests for violent offenses, therefore, almost certainly understates these young men's involvement in violence. Similarly, we observe only substance use that was tested for and detected. If parole agents did not test parolees, we cannot observe their drug use. Given the intense surveillance of parolees, this particular factor is less important than others. In our sample, only seventy-two men (5.54 percent) were never tested after they were released. That said, the tests themselves are imperfect indicators; they err on the side of false negatives and do not detect substance use when it has occurred. For some substances, false negative rates are as high as 25 percent, whereas false positive rates — signaling use when there has been none — do not exceed

3 percent for any substance.[10] Moreover, the life histories we constructed suggest that even regularly tested men who seemed to be using drugs heavily, as evidenced by their record of entering residential treatment or being arrested for driving under the influence, were able to avoid detection at least some of the time. Thus, the prevalence of substance use is also likely to be higher than we are able to report.

Even though young white men are more likely to die from overdoses and young black men are more likely to die from firearm violence, the young black men in our sample were more likely than their white counterparts to both engage in violence and test positive for drugs after prison. Prison experiences themselves did not predict post-prison involvement in risky health behaviors in our sample, despite considerable variation in our sample in the length of prison stays, number of misconduct violations, and time spent in solitary confinement, each of which has been theorized to exacerbate post-prison mental illness, substance use, and violence. Instead, the young men resumed their pre-prison risky health behaviors after they were released. Early criminal justice system contact and risky health behaviors before prison are among the strongest predictors of such behaviors after release from prison.

Disadvantaged post-prison social contexts also contribute to these patterns of behavior in racially distinct ways. The environments to which whites returned seem to promote substance use, whereas blacks returned to places that seemed to promote violence. On a more positive note, meeting transitional markers before, during, and after prison can counteract the deleterious influence of young men's post-prison social environments. After prison, young white men who continued their education and young black men who found employment were less likely to commit violence or use substances.

In the sections that follow, we discuss post-prison patterns of mortality, substance use, and violence among the young men in our sample. We then draw on work on the social determinants of health, stigma, and stress to explain how those patterns may have been generated. Finally, we explain what our empirical work reveals about the post-prison patterns of substance use and violence in these young men.

MORTALITY, SUBSTANCE USE, AND VIOLENCE DURING THE POST-PRISON TRANSITION TO ADULTHOOD

Within nine years of being paroled, 3.4 percent of young black men and 3.8 percent of young white men in our sample had died.[11] These rates exceed those for men of similar age in Michigan.[12] However, they mirror those reported for other samples of young, criminal justice–involved men who were followed for comparable periods.[13] In addition, the deaths of our young parolees followed a racialized pattern that reflects national trends. Of the twenty-one deaths among young black men, nineteen were homicides, and guns were involved in eighteen of the deaths. Only one was an overdose. Of the twenty-six deaths among the young white men, sixteen were overdoses. Only one was a gun homicide. In addition, it is likely that two of three motor vehicle–related deaths also involved substance use.[14] Trevor, for example, died in a car accident on a major holiday that is often celebrated with alcohol. The stark racial divide in cause of death suggests racially divergent pathways into adulthood that are directly connected to two risky health behaviors in which young men commonly engage: substance use and violence.

Pre-Prison Patterns of Violence and Substance Use

Prior to their incarceration, young black men were more likely to have been involved in violence. As shown in figure 5.1, sixty-five percent of young black men in our sample had been arrested for a violent offense, whereas only 60 percent of the white men had been. Likewise, 32.1 percent of young black men had used a gun in a prior offense, whereas only 11.5 percent of young white men had done so.

The racial divide in violent offending seems to have emerged over time. Both young black men and young white men were typically first arrested at about age fifteen. At first arrest, young black men were statistically no more likely than young white men to have committed a violent offense (33.5 versus 29.7 percent), although they were more likely to have used a firearm during that first offense (15.4 percent versus 5.2 percent). As their pathways from first arrest to prison evolved, however, young black men and young white men committed different types of violent offenses. Young white men were at least twice as likely as young black men to commit some types of violence, including injurious motor vehicle offenses (13.1 versus 5.8 percent), rape (8.2 versus 4.1 percent), and other sex offenses (8.7 versus 4.1). Robbery, which is more prevalent, drives racial differences in violent offending. Before prison, blacks were more than twice as likely as whites to be arrested for robbery (23.7 percent versus 10.4 percent). Aggravated assaults do not differ by race.

Patterns of pre-prison substance use also diverge racially. Whites started using drugs and alcohol more than a year earlier than blacks. On average, whites were 13.6 years old when they first tried drugs or alcohol, whereas blacks were 14.8 years old. Moreover, whites were more likely than blacks

Figure 5.1   Prevalence of Pre-Prison Involvement in Violence and Substance Use, by Race

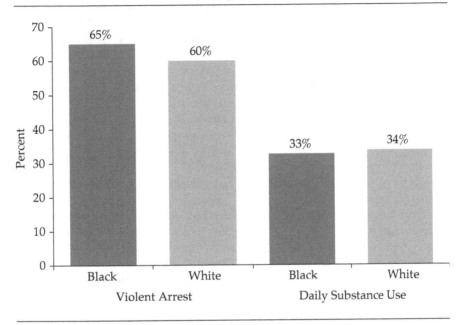

Source: Michigan Study of Life after Prison.
Note: Percentages reflect the probability of ever being arrested for a violent crime or of self-reporting the daily use of drugs or alcohol prior to the focal prison spell, which ended with the 2003 parole (various prison dates).

to initiate their substance use with alcohol rather than marijuana or other drugs (60.5 percent versus 39.5 percent). Whites' preference for alcohol and blacks' preference for marijuana persisted at least until they were incarcerated as young men.

Young men of both races reported to prison officials at intake that they used alcohol or drugs at similar rates before prison, as is also shown in figure 5.1. About one-third of young white men and one-third of young black men used drugs or alcohol daily; about half used them weekly. However, the types of substances that they reported using differed. Before prison, 43.6 percent of blacks used marijuana weekly, whereas only 37.8 percent of white men did. By contrast, young white men were more likely than young black men to use alcohol (33.4 percent versus 21.2 percent), cocaine and other stimulants (16.1 versus 11.9 percent), and heroin and other depressants (4.8 percent versus 2.1 percent) weekly.

Post-Prison Patterns of Violence and Substance Use

Despite their post-prison mortality differences, figure 5.2 indicates that young black men were more likely than young white men to engage in both violence and substance use after prison. As their mortality rates suggest, blacks were more likely than whites to be arrested for a violent crime in any post-prison quarter (6.9 percent versus 4.3 percent). Although gun violence was less frequent than nongun violence, young black men were four times as likely as their white counterparts to be arrested with a gun in any post-prison quarter (1.8 percent versus 0.4 percent).[15] However, these race-dependent differences in violence seem to be attributable mainly to the frequency of arrests for violence. In their first post-prison release year, blacks (47.4 percent) and whites (44.0 percent) were about equally as likely to engage in violence. This slight and not statistically significant difference persisted: over the next six years, 49.1 percent of whites and 53.5 percent of blacks were arrested for a violent offense. However, among those who were arrested for a violent offense after prison, young black men were arrested more frequently than young white men: 1.9 times versus 1.5 times.

Perhaps surprisingly, young black men were also more likely to test positive for any type of drug use than young white men after prison. During the seven years after their release, young black and white men were about as likely to be tested in any given post-prison quarter: 60.3 percent versus 60.6 percent, respectively. However, young white men were far more likely to *never* be tested after prison. Of the seventy-two men who were never tested, fifty-two were white. Still, among the tested, young black men tested positive in 23.6 percent of quarters, whereas young white men tested positive in only 17.8 percent of quarters. In addition, nearly two-thirds of blacks tested positive after prison, whereas about half of whites did. Higher rates of testing positive among blacks relative to whites may be related to their preferred substances. Marijuana, with more black users, can linger in the body for weeks, whereas alcohol, which is preferred by whites, clears within hours.[16]

Entering residential substance abuse treatment after prison did not seem to depend on positive drug tests. In any post-prison quarter, whites had a 10.8 percent chance of receiving residential substance use treatment, whereas blacks had a 7.6 percent chance. These rates are high relative to the general population.[17] This supports Benjamin Cook and Margarita Alegría's finding that the criminal justice system increases access to treatment.[18] When they did get treatment, however, these young men did not stay long enough for it to be effective. On average they spent only 27.3 days of the recommended three months in treatment.[19]

In sum, after prison we see high rates of mortality, substance use, and violence for all young men in our sample. However, young black men were

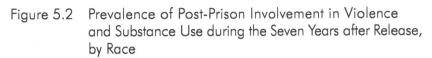

Figure 5.2   Prevalence of Post-Prison Involvement in Violence
              and Substance Use during the Seven Years after Release,
              by Race

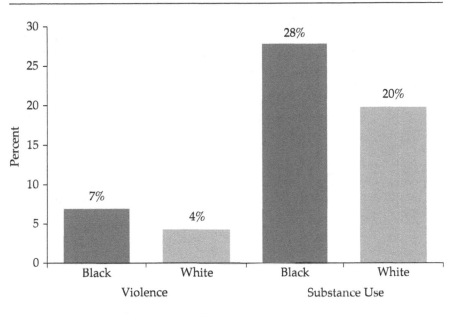

Source: Michigan Study of Life after Prison.
Note: Percentages reflect the quarterly post-prison probability of being arrested for a
violent crime or testing positive for substance use, conditional on being tested. Data for
2003 Michigan parole cohort, followed for seven years after release.

more likely to test positive for drugs and to be arrested for violent offenses
after prison than young white men. These differences did not exist before
prison, suggesting that differential prison experiences or differential post-
prison environments may have contributed to this divergence. In the following section, we discuss these potential explanations for risky health
behaviors during the post-prison transition to adulthood.

EXPLAINING RISKY HEALTH BEHAVIORS DURING THE POST-PRISON TRANSITION TO ADULTHOOD

Much of the transition-to-adulthood literature focuses on questions of
whether, when, and how young people meet structural markers that signify
adulthood, such as completing their education, finding employment,

establishing residential independence, entering into romantic partnerships, and building families.[20] How the *health* of young people is impacted as they transition from adolescence into adulthood has also been explored, with a particular focus on the effect of role transitions on mental health and substance use.[21] Less studied is the impact of role transitions on violence, although explaining violence, which occurs mainly in adolescence and young adulthood, has long been a focus of criminological inquiry.[22]

Extremely disadvantaged young men who are imprisoned during the transition to adulthood are exceptionally likely to engage in risky health behaviors. Yet risky health behaviors are not all that exceptional for young people as a whole: they engage in violence and substance use at higher rates than people in all other age groups.[23] Nevertheless, if risky health behaviors become regular or routine, they can threaten young people's physical and emotional well-being and delay or even abort their adult transitions. In this section, we explain how young men might become involved in substance use and violence and why those behaviors might persist or even be exacerbated during and after prison.

Neighborhood Disadvantage and Post-Prison Risky Health Behaviors

The primary correlate of health and health behaviors is poverty. Poorer people have consistently been found to be less healthy than wealthier people.[24] According to Bruce Link and Jo Phelan, the robustness of this relationship indicates that poverty is a fundamental cause of ill health.[25] Fundamental causes are those that constrict both access to resources to promote health and the ability to leverage those resources.[26] Even as common health risks evolve with medical progress, fundamental causes like poverty remain key predictors of ill health because they determine access to health-promoting resources and impact risks for multiple diseases and health disorders. Another example of a potential fundamental cause is stigma, which constrains resources, thwarts social relationships, and exacerbates stress among people who are systematically devalued and discriminated against.[27] Fundamental causes are associated with multiple health outcomes, through multiple risk factors, mechanisms, and pathways that reveal new connections between fundamental causes and outcomes as more is learned about them. In particular, the relationship between poverty and poor health persists as more becomes known about it, and it can be expected to persist until the fundamental cause—poverty itself—is addressed.

Fundamental cause theory is typically applied to explain health disparities between people. Yet social contexts can also be impoverished. In neighborhoods, disadvantage is the analog to poverty. Poor health and risky health behaviors are robustly and disparately concentrated in disadvantaged neighborhoods.[28] Therefore, it is reasonable to propose that neighborhood disadvantage, which constrains collective resources,[29] may be a fundamental cause of differential engagement in risky health behaviors between individuals and neighborhoods.

Prior research on violence supports this argument. The relationship between neighborhood disadvantage and poor health holds for violence as well. Violence as measured through victimization surveys, crime statistics, calls for service, and homicide rates is concentrated in disadvantaged neighborhoods and has been for decades.[30]

To explain why violence is disparately concentrated among poor people who live in disadvantaged neighborhoods, Bruce Western argues that poverty promotes violence through three mechanisms related to resource deprivation: chaos (instability), diminished social control, and a culture of violence.[31] Home environments can be chaotic as unemployment crowds extended and unrelated families into small apartments.[32] Proximity then foments stress and interpersonal conflict,[33] and this household instability aggregates at the neighborhood level, where evictions prompt routine population turnover, turning neighbors into strangers and undermining the trust and social cohesion necessary for collective efficacy.[34] In such environments, young men who have neither observed nor experienced peaceful conflict resolution turn to violence to resolve conflicts. Thus, the culturally accepted means of settling conflict becomes to fight it out—or at least to look like you will.[35]

These fundamental associations between risky health behaviors and neighborhood disadvantage have implications for racial disparity in risky health behaviors such as those in our sample. In the United States, both individual poverty and neighborhood disadvantage are highly correlated with race. More than a century of segregationist public policies at the local, state, and national levels have corralled black people into disadvantaged neighborhoods, subjected them to state-sanctioned violence, deprived them of the potential to build wealth through homeownership and entrepreneurship, and devalued their property by locating environmental hazards nearby.[36] The inevitable result of these policies is that black people are poorer than white people and black neighborhoods are more disadvantaged than white neighborhoods.[37] Moreover, the differences in terms of disadvantage by nearly all socioeconomic measures between white and black neighborhoods have been and continue to be so stark that few white neighborhoods can be found that are as disadvantaged as the poorest black neighborhoods.[38] Similar levels of racial disparity in neighborhood poverty and other forms of disadvantage, such as crime rates, are evident in our sample (see chapter 2).[39]

To explain observed racial differences in violence across neighborhoods, Robert Sampson and William Julius Wilson point to the incomparable state of disadvantage in which blacks live relative to whites.[40] They posit a multitude of mechanisms that link neighborhood disadvantage to racial disparity in violence through multiple pathways stemming from resource deprivation. Western echoes many of their arguments: family disruption promotes neighborhood instability and violence, and population turnover reduces informal social control, removing an important counterweight to violent behavior.[41]

Sampson and Wilson also observe that disadvantaged neighborhoods lack political power because they are socially isolated.[42] As a result, they cannot garner enough resources to deter violence, invest in infrastructure, or promote development.[43] Perniciously, this structural disadvantage shapes "cognitive landscapes," or shared expectations about how the community can operate. In the absence of optimism about neighborhood norms, structure, and governance, cynicism sets in, perpetuating collective feelings of inefficacy.[44]

As presented by Western and by Sampson and Wilson, neighborhood disadvantage is a fundamental cause of violence.[45] Moreover, profound disparity in disadvantage between black and white neighborhoods is a fundamental cause of racial disparity in violence. Through many mechanisms, disadvantage deprives neighborhoods of the resources they need to prevent violence and to address it when it occurs—and black neighborhoods are more disadvantaged and therefore more resource-deprived than white neighborhoods.

To our knowledge, the argument that neighborhood disadvantage may be a fundamental cause of substance abuse has not been made. For adults, fundamental cause theory can plausibly explain substance abuse, a health outcome with negative consequences concentrated in disadvantaged areas.[46] Neighborhood disadvantage is associated with multiple negative substance abuse outcomes, including addiction and mortality.[47] Multiple risk factors, mechanisms, and pathways explain these associations, including disparate exposure to drug markets, drug supply chains, and alcohol outlets[48]; differential exposure to structural stress and stigma[49]; and inadequate medical and mental health care that promotes self-medication.[50] These pathways implicate access to different structural resources—from health care to policing—in substance abuse. Finally, these pathways have shifted over time in response to the political and social environment, as drug use shifted from heroin in the 1970s to crack cocaine in the 1980s, to methamphetamine in the 1990s, to prescription opioids in the early 2000s, and back to heroin and illegal synthetic opioids today.[51] We find evidence that neighborhood disadvantage may be a fundamental cause of substance abuse in adulthood.

Incarceration, Stigma, and Post-Prison Risky Health Behaviors

In life courses shaped early on by neighborhood disadvantage, incarceration is one potential consequence of substance use and violence that may impact health and health behavior. Prison incarceration may improve the physical health of inmates who enter prison from disadvantaged neighborhoods where health care is scarce and violence threatens lives.[52] However, most inmates experience deteriorating mental health during incarceration. Depression intensifies and persists post-release.[53] In addition, physical health improvements made during incarceration tend to dissipate after release, when medical care again becomes scarce and risky health behaviors that threaten mortality, such as substance use and violence, become more likely.[54] After prison, the weight of the evidence indicates that incarceration carries collateral consequences that negatively impact the physical and mental health of former prisoners.[55] To explain this, incarceration has been characterized as both a *chronic strain* and a *primary stressor*.[56] Chronic strains persist over long periods of time—such as years of incarceration. Primary stressors spawn a proliferation of secondary stressors that cascade across life-course domains. The dissolution of a relationship, for example, can cause psychological distress and substance use, acrimony and violence, and financial strain.

Incarceration sparks secondary stressors at two times in particular: when people are incarcerated and after they are released. Secondary stressors that proliferate during incarceration include the intended consequences of punishment, such as isolation from family and friends and the incidental stressors associated with "doing time."[57] An example of the latter, and a primary burden of prison, is boredom.[58] The overabundance of idly spent but heavily policed time can rob inmates of self-conceptualizations, self-efficacy, and self-control.[59] Each of these consequences may be particularly salient during the transition to adulthood, which has been characterized as a time when young people construct identities, build self-control, and exercise more self-efficacy on the path to independence.[60]

Time in prison is also spent in close quarters with other men, with whom living conditions such as noise, cleanliness, and safety levels must be negotiated. The potential for interpersonal conflict and violence is ever present.[61] Witnessing violence or feeling the threat of violence can decrease happiness, foment psychological distress, and promote further violence.[62] Prisoners in the United States are more than three times as likely as non-incarcerated people to report recent psychological distress, and younger inmates report distress at higher rates than older inmates—14.9 percent versus 9.5 percent.[63] Inmates who have trouble adjusting to prison are more likely to engage in violence during incarceration.[64] Serious misconduct violations can then lead to solitary confinement, which can adversely affect mental health, cognitive ability, and social functioning.[65]

Although in-prison secondary stressors can lead to risky health behaviors after prison, "incarceration's most powerful effects might emerge only after a sentence has been served."[66] Post-release secondary stressors can proliferate across life-course domains, reducing post-prison education, employment, and housing opportunities; inhibiting the continuation, reestablishment, and development of social relationships; and spawning individual responses to stigma that further delay adult transitions and promote risky health behaviors.[67]

Post-release secondary stressors are mainly attributable to the stigma associated with having been imprisoned. Jason Schnittker and Michael Massoglia define stigma as "a mark that sets an individual apart from others."[68] Stigmatization happens in stages. First, stigmatized people are devalued—they are seen as "less than" others. Then they are discriminated against—they are treated differently than others. Finally, their reactions to being stigmatized can backfire and perpetuate their stigmatization. Stigmatized people often internalize and conform to the stereotypes associated with their status. Alternatively, they may try to cope with, address, and overcome stigma by concealing their status from others, educating others about their status, or withdrawing from others.[69]

Among the formerly incarcerated, these coping strategies typically backfire.[70] Trying to conceal a prison record can reinforce negative stereotypes about former inmates' untrustworthiness. Trying to educate people about the discrimination faced by people with criminal records can generate backlash. And more fundamentally, the very notion of "reentry" precludes withdrawal. To reintegrate, formerly incarcerated people must engage with institutions that stigmatize them and with people who discriminate against them.[71] Barred from voting and from many types of jobs and often ineligible for education loans, welfare, and housing assistance, the formerly incarcerated can find themselves structurally stigmatized by laws and institutions that alienate them from the societies they are supposed to reenter.[72] The formerly incarcerated may also be interpersonally stigmatized and discriminated against by friends and family who avoid them, employers who refuse to hire them, and landlords who refuse to rent to them.[73]

Other Forms of Post-Prison Stigma

Formerly incarcerated men are likely to experience multiple forms of stigma in addition to prison stigma, including age, race, and addiction stigma.[74] These types of stigma can accumulate and compound across life-course domains.[75] In a unique survey conducted by Thomas LeBel, the majority of formerly incarcerated men reported experiencing two to three different types of discrimination as they reentered society.[76] Two-thirds of formerly incarcerated men experienced discrimination related to their incarceration, nearly half experienced race or substance use discrimination, and more than one-third experienced discrimination because they were poor. It should be noted, however, that the people LeBel surveyed were age thirty-six on average. Younger men, especially younger men who have not been imprisoned previously, may not anticipate or fully appreciate these challenges. In a sample of eighteen- to twenty-five-year-olds sentenced to a Texas boot camp instead of prison in 1993, 93.6 percent of respondents agreed with the statement, "Once I get out of here, if I straighten up my life I should not have a problem readjusting back to society."[77] Thus, young people's expectation that it will be easy to reenter society and progress toward adulthood may turn out to conflict with their experience. Misalignment between expectations and experiences during the transition to adulthood can lead to depression, which can promote risky health behaviors.[78]

Stigma and Risky Health Behaviors during the Post-Prison Transition to Adulthood

Stigmatization has been found to negatively impact health and promote risky health behaviors, primarily because of the stressors that proliferate from stigma—depression, anxiety, anger, and erosion of self-efficacy and self-control.[79] Each of these stressors has been found to be associated with substance abuse, violence, or both.[80]

Stigma experienced during the transition to adulthood after incarceration can erode self-efficacy, promote criminal behavior, and encourage withdrawal from conventional lifestyles.[81] When young people build human capital through school and work during the transition to adulthood, their sense of personal control or agency accumulates.[82] Confidence gained in achieving one role builds confidence for achieving other roles.[83] Conversely, continuously confronting obstacles to meeting adulthood markers can lead to depression and disengagement across life-course domains as the possibility of achieving new roles seems to become more remote.[84] Similarly, desisting from criminal behavior engenders a sense of entering adulthood, whereas persisting in criminal behavior does the opposite.[85]

Social Relationships, Adult Transitions, and Post-Prison Risky Health Behaviors

Although stigma can motivate risky health behaviors after release from prison, other aspects of the post-prison environment can help young men avoid them. In particular, receiving social support after prison can help young people desist from crime, avoid substance use and violence, and transition to adulthood. Social support offsets the stress associated with stigmatization.[86] Social support provides the most crucial assistance in a successful reentry because it is material in nature (housing and transportation), as opposed to simply informational (guidance) or emotional (love and empathy).[87] Although being connected to family and friends can reduce social isolation and promote social reintegration over time, young people are most immediately challenged upon release in simply meeting their basic needs (food, clothing, and shelter).[88]

Younger and first-time inmates may enjoy more post-prison social support than their older and recidivist counterparts because they have not yet become "long standing sources of trouble and conflict at home [who] have likely disappointed or alienated . . . family and friends."[89] However, reconnecting with family, friends, and romantic partners can also promote risky health behaviors because interpersonal relationships can be stressful as well as supportive.[90] For example, the increasing economic pressure on the family when a young man returns home can promote family conflict and violence.[91] Family conflict that occurs after prisoners return home is associated with depression, substance use, family violence, and reincarceration.[92]

Transitioning to Adulthood, Health, and Post-Prison Risky Health Behaviors

Early educational and labor market success can set the stage for successful transitions to adulthood and reduced involvement in risky health behaviors.[93] On the other hand, young men who cannot find employment or achieve residential independence because they have few opportunities or are stigmatized are more likely to resort to illegitimate means of supporting themselves, such as the drug trade, which promotes substance use and violence.[94]

Education should, in theory, reduce substance use and violence. Research on the relationship between education and health consistently indicates that more highly educated people are healthier, although whites seem to benefit more than blacks from higher levels of education.[95] If education is associated with better health because it enables individuals to change their social context to promote a healthier lifestyle, perhaps this benefit is less available to blacks because they are less socially mobile than whites.[96] For example, in a nationally representative sample of young adults transitioning to adulthood, 24 percent of black males, as compared to 7 percent of white males, experienced the highest levels of personal and neighborhood disadvantage as adolescents and saw "almost no" social mobility within fifteen years.[97]

As young criminal justice–involved men age into their midtwenties, they tend to desist from antisocial behavior and to seek employment.[98] But employment is a two-edged sword: it can promote or deter substance use and violence.[99] Employment can be a stabilizing activity through which formerly incarcerated young men construct identities and build a sense of personal control. Yet employment also provides the means to buy drugs and alcohol and can promote violence through stress and interpersonal conflict.[100] Moreover, substance use is common among coworkers in many jobs accessible to people with felony records, such as those in the restaurant industry.[101]

Parole Supervision, Adult Transitions, and Post-Prison Risky Health Behaviors

Parole supervision seeks to promote the successful reentry of formerly incarcerated people into the community, in part by monitoring and attempting to deter risky health behaviors. Most parolees are subject to supervision conditions intended to deter violence, such as restrictions on their possession of weapons. Likewise, most parolees are subject to supervision conditions that prohibit substance use, even including the use of legal substances such as alcohol. However, substance use can be actively monitored and potentially deterred in ways that violence cannot.

Random drug testing and sanctions for testing positive, such as revocation of parole or elevated supervision levels, are meant to deter substance use. Higher supervision levels may create a greater deterrent effect through more frequent testing. However, prior research indicates that there seems to be a threshold after which higher supervision levels become both onerous and counterproductive: violations and revocation become more likely, and deterrent effects level off.[102]

In addition to variation in supervision levels, parole supervision *regimes* also vary. As defined by Ryken Grattet, Jeffrey Lin, and Joan Petersilia, a supervision regime is "a legal and organizational structure that shapes the detection and reporting of parolee deviance."[103] How often a person tests positive for substance use depends on how often he is tested, which is determined by his supervision level, which is determined within the supervision regime to which he is assigned.

In Michigan, there is reason to suspect that blacks and whites are subject to different supervision regimes. Parole supervision regimes operate at the county level, and white and black populations are unevenly distributed across the state. Blacks are clustered in urban areas, whereas whites live throughout Michigan.[104] In addition to the implications of geography, we see evidence that whites and blacks are subject to different parole supervision regimes. For example, we previously mentioned that blacks are more likely to be tested in any given quarter and less likely to never be tested while on parole. In addition, blacks' and whites' supervision levels vary. Blacks are more likely than whites to be released under more intensive parole supervision (27.9 versus 20.5 percent). Whites, who are less likely to serve their minimum sentences, are more likely to be released into corrections centers where they are supervised more intensely (25.3 percent versus 15.9 percent).[105] Prior research suggests that the more moderate policies to which blacks are subject may more effectively reduce their substance use.[106]

Race and Post-Prison Risky Health Behaviors during the Transition to Adulthood

As we proceed from explaining how young men might become involved in risky health behaviors to determining how they do so, a final note on race is warranted. There are many reasons to suspect that, relative to young white men, young black men differentially engage in risky health behaviors after prison. The neighborhoods that young black men grow up in and to which they return from prison are far more disadvantaged than those of their white counterparts. As racial minorities, blacks are more likely than whites to experience compound post-prison stigma that can negatively impact their capacity to find employment, live independently, and maintain overall health.[107] Moreover, the weight of the evidence suggests that, relative to young white men, young black men lack employment opportunities and their lives are not as enriched by educational experiences. This does not mean, however, that young white men are not also at risk of involvement in substance use and violence after prison. Relative to young white men who have not been incarcerated, the young white men in our sample were extremely disadvantaged. Similar forces of stigmatization and deprivation are likely to promote their involvement in post-prison risky health behaviors. Nonetheless, these racial differences suggest that the post-prison trajectories of risky health behaviors should be modeled separately for young black men and young white men. We take that approach in our analyses.

DETERMINANTS OF POST-PRISON INVOLVEMENT IN RISKY HEALTH BEHAVIORS

We now turn to an empirical investigation of post-prison involvement in substance use and violence among transition-aged young men.[108] Our analyses include indicators that capture the predictors of post-prison risky health behaviors discussed earlier: pre-prison physical and mental health; involvement in risky health behaviors before, during, and after prison; criminal justice contact before and after prison; transition to adulthood markers achieved before, during, and after prison; and various measures of the post-prison social context. Although we cannot directly measure stigma, we include indicators of secondary stressors of incarceration: first-time inmate status, solitary confinement, time incarcerated, and misconduct violations.[109] In the sections that follow, we discuss how the predictors presented in figures 5.3 and 5.4 impact post-prison involvement in violence and substance use for young white men and young black men.

Violence during the Transition to Adulthood after Prison

Early and more intense involvement in the criminal justice system is associated with greater post-prison violence. Relative to those who were not incarcerated as juveniles, spending time in juvenile detention was associated with a 1.8-percentage-point (26 percent) increase in the quarterly chance of being arrested for a violent offense for young black men and a corresponding 1.3-percentage-point (30 percent) increase for young white men. If neighborhood disadvantage is a fundamental cause of violence, experiencing incarceration as a child or adolescent may be a consequence of it. Juvenile incarceration may also be a primary stressor that propagates violence.

Deeper criminal justice system involvement, as measured by prior arrests, also seems to propagate violence, a finding that supports prior research. Even a single arrest has been shown to have lasting consequences for homicide victimization and mortality.[110] On average, the men in our sample experienced three prior arrests, which seem to have compounded their post-prison involvement in violence. For blacks, each additional pre-prison arrest was associated with a 0.6-percentage-point increase in the quarterly post-prison probability of being arrested for a violent offense; the corresponding increase for whites was 0.2 percentage points.

As figure 5.3 illustrates, involvement in violence before, during, and after prison is robustly related to continued violence after prison. Again, violence seemed to propagate violence, particularly for young black men, who lived in the most disadvantaged neighborhoods. A prior arrest for a violent offense was associated with a 2.0-percentage-point increase in the probability of being arrested for a violent offense after prison, but only among blacks. Similarly, being cited for violent misconduct was associated with a corresponding 1.6-percentage-point increase in post-prison violence only for blacks. Thus, a young black man who had been arrested for a violent offense before prison and who also committed a violent misconduct in prison had more than a 10 percent chance of being arrested for a violent offense after prison.

Young white men were not immune from the perpetuation of violence. After prison, some young men of both races established and perpetuated trajectories of violence. For young black men, being arrested for a violent offense in the prior quarter was associated with a 4.3-percentage-point (62 percent) increase in the quarterly probability of an arrest for violence. For young white men, the corresponding increase was 3.6 percentage points (83 percent). Notably, the association between current and recent violence was more than twice as strong as the association between current and temporally distant violence for young men of both races—suggesting an escalation of behavior that could be identified and interrupted.

Surprisingly, the prison experiences captured by our data—with the exception of engaging in violence—were not associated with post-prison violence. First-time and returning prison inmates did not differ in their likelihood of engaging in violence after prison. Likewise, months spent in prison, citations for conduct violations, and time spent in solitary confinement did not predict post-prison violence. If secondary stressors of incarceration impact inmates' risky health behaviors, their effects may pale in comparison to the generalized prison experience and the post-prison stigma faced by parolees.[111]

A unidirectional relationship between substance use and violence was present in all time periods—a finding that accords with Jonathan Caulkins and Peter Reuter's conclusion that "clearly a considerable proportion of crime and violence is caused by, not merely correlated with, substance abuse."[112] For young black men, daily drug or alcohol use before prison was associated with a 2.0-percentage-point increase in the quarterly post-prison probability of violent arrest. For young white men, the corresponding increase was 1.3 percentage points. Moreover, the magnitudes of these relationships between pre-prison substance use and post-prison violence paralleled those between pre-prison violence and post-prison violence. Thus, regardless of race, prior substance use seems to be at least as large a contributor to post-prison violence as prior violence.

After prison, however, substance use was related to continued violence only for young white men. After prison, prior-quarter positive substance use tests were associated with an increase of 1.5 percentage points (35 percent) in the quarterly probability of violence for whites. Young whites' preference for alcohol may explain the deeper correlation between post-prison substance use and violence for them. According to Harold Pollack, "alcohol is *immediately* involved in far more homicides than any illicit substance" (emphasis added).[113] Moreover, alcohol use and violence are correlated with the experience of incarceration. About 40 percent of people incarcerated for violent crimes were drinking when they committed them.[114] Troublingly, for young white men, substance use may also promote violence in the home, which can endanger romantic partners, children, and roommates. Living independently at the start of the quarter was associated with a 1.3-percentage-point increase in the probability of arrest for violence later in the quarter only for whites.

Meeting transition-to-adulthood markers may help young men of both races exit trajectories of violence. Meeting educational markers seemed to protect young white men from post-prison violence. Being enrolled in college in the prior quarter was associated with a 2.4-percentage-point (56 percent) reduction in young white men's quarterly post-prison probability of being arrested for violence. Pre-prison educational attainment also seemed to help young black men avoid violence. For blacks, finishing high school was associated with a 2.5-percentage-point (36 percent) reduction in the likelihood of being arrested for violence in any post-prison quarter. In addition, young black men seemed to benefit from post-prison employment, whereas young white men did not. For blacks, being employed in the prior post-prison quarter was associated with a 1.8-percentage-point (26 percent) reduction in the quarterly probability of arrest for violence.

Substance Use

As was the case with violence, predictors of post-prison substance use emerged early in the life course among the young men in our sample. Many of them, like Douglas and Trevor, began using drugs and alcohol in early adolescence—or even childhood. These early experiences with substance use seemed to be perpetuated across time, through the prison context, and into the post-prison context.

As shown in figure 5.4, substance use before prison was robustly related to substance use after prison—but only for young white men who started

Figure 5.3 Differences in the Probability of an Arrest for a Violent Offense in a Calendar Quarter during the Seven Years after Release, by Various Predictors and Race

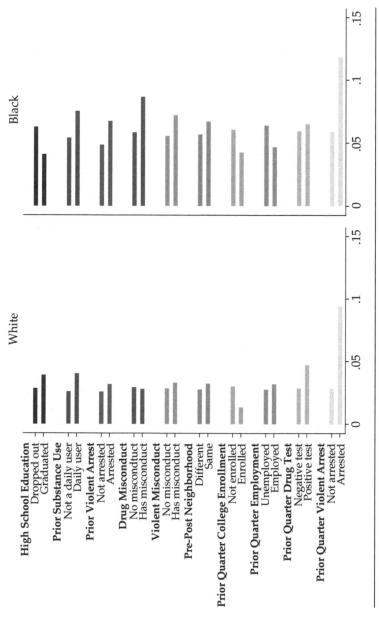

Source: Michigan Study of Life after Prison.
Note: Based on models in tables 5.A1 and 5.A2. Data for 2003 Michigan parole cohort, followed for seven years after release.

using drugs, particularly alcohol, earlier in life. Daily drug or alcohol use prior to prison was associated with a 5.7-percentage-point increase in the quarterly post-prison probability of substance use only among whites. Young white men who did not use drugs daily before prison had less than a 20 percent chance of testing positive in any post-prison quarter, whereas those who did use drugs daily had more than a 25 percent chance.

By contrast, substance use during and after prison promoted continued post-prison substance use for all young men. Drug misconduct during prison was associated with a 9.3-percentage-point increase in the quarterly post-prison probability of testing positive for blacks and a 9.9-percentage-point increase for whites. These young men had high average quarterly probabilities of testing positive. Therefore, for young black men, these relationships meant that the average probability of testing positive rose from 27.8 to 37.1 percent, while young white men's average probability of testing positive rose from 19.8 to 39.7 percent.

After prison, young black men who tested positive in the previous post-prison quarter were 26.0 percentage points more likely to test positive in the current quarter—their probability of testing positive nearly doubled. For young white men, the corresponding increase was 17.9 percentage points—again, nearly double the baseline probability. The magnitudes of these relationships, particularly in relation to the smaller magnitudes of the more temporally distal relationships, indicate strong continuity in substance use that may be indicative of addiction.[115] Moreover, familiar environments may have assisted in the perpetuation of substance use.[116] For whites only, returning to the same neighborhood was associated with a 5.0-percentage-point increase in the quarterly post-prison probability of testing positive.

As with violence, what does *not* predict post-prison substance use is also notable. Again, the available recorded prison experiences—aside from continued involvement in substance use—were not associated with post-prison substance use. In addition, whereas prior substance use predicted prior violence, violence before, during, and after prison did not predict post-prison substance use. If violence predicted substance use, it was either violence that occurred very early in life or as a result of witnessing or being victimized by violence.[117]

As with violence, helping young men build the scaffolding of their adult transitions—before, during, and after prison—may reduce their involvement in substance use after they are released. Notably, graduating from high school was associated with a 16.7-percentage-point decrease in young white men's probability of testing positive for substance use in any post-prison quarter. To contextualize that number, white high school graduates in our sample had a 3.1 percent chance of testing positive in any post-prison quarter, as compared to nearly 20 percent for white dropouts. For young white men, earning a GED during prison was also associated with reduced post-prison substance use. Earning a GED in prison was associated with a 7.9-percentage-point decrease in the quarterly post-prison chance of testing positive. The finding that earning a GED does not confer the same benefits as graduating from high school adds another dimension to prior research that compared the labor market outcomes of high school graduates to those of GED earners and concluded that GED earners come up short.[118]

Perhaps more concerning is that young black men who earned GEDs in prison did not even see those benefits—a finding that supports prior research indicating that whites reap more health benefits from education than blacks.[119] However, there is room for some optimism. For young black men who were able to find post-prison employment, having a job was associated with reduced substance use. Being employed in the prior post-prison quarter was associated with a 5.1-percentage-point reduction in blacks' quarterly probability of testing positive for drugs. Young white men, on the other hand, did not see a similar benefit from employment. Taken together with the violence outcomes, continuing education after prison seems to protect young white men, but not young black men, from risky health behaviors. In contrast, post-prison employment seems to protect young black men, but not young white men, from risky health behaviors.

Finally, young black men were less likely to engage in substance use under some types of post-prison criminal justice supervision. Electronic monitoring in the prior quarter was associated with an 11.0-percentage-point decrease in the post-prison probability of testing positive in the current quarter for blacks—a 40 percent reduction. In addition, being on medium relative to minimum parole supervision at the start of the quarter was associated with a 9.0-percentage-point reduction in young black men's probability of testing positive later in the quarter. Young white men did not see similar reductions; that difference is probably attributable to differences in the parole supervision regimes to which whites and blacks are exposed. Notably, intensive supervision was not associated with reduced substance use, suggesting that there may be a threshold of supervision after which it becomes counterproductive.[120] Thus, less intensive approaches to parole supervision, such as electronic monitoring rather than residential placement, may better protect formerly incarcerated young men's health as they rebuild their lives after prison.

How Social Context Shapes Post-Prison Involvement in Substance Use and Violence

To examine how disadvantaged neighborhoods shape racial differences in violence and substance use outcomes, we add a neighborhood disadvantage

Figure 5.4 Differences in the Probability of a Positive Drug Test in a Calendar Quarter during the Seven Years after Release, by Various Predictors and Race

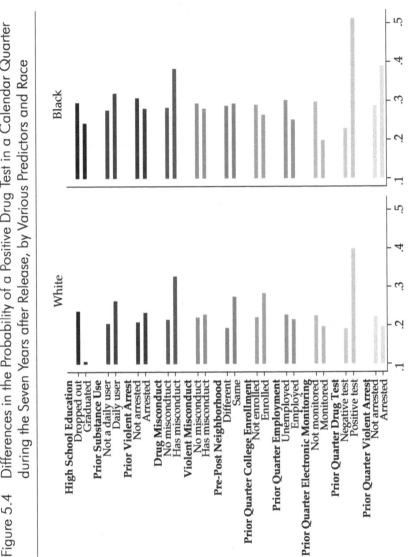

Source: Michigan Study of Life after Prison.
Note: Based on models in tables 5.A1 and 5.A2. Data for 2003 Michigan parole cohort, followed for seven years after release.

Table 5.1   White-Black Difference in Quarterly Probability of Arrest
for Violence or Positive Substance Abuse Test during
the Seven Years after Release, with and without Controlling
for Neighborhood Disadvantage

	Violence		Substance Use	
	Baseline	Controlling for Neighborhood Disadvantage	Baseline	Controlling for Neighborhood Disadvantage
White versus black	−0.028*	−0.028*	−0.037*	−0.027

Source: Michigan Study of Life after Prison.
Note: Full models available in table 5.A3. Data for 2003 Michigan parole cohort age 18–25 at parole, followed through 2009.
* Statistically significant at $p \leq 0.05$.

index (see chapter 2) to models that regress violence and substance use on race, while controlling for pre-, in-, and post-prison characteristics and experiences.[121] We present the results in table 5.1.[122]

Neighborhood disadvantage does not explain racial differences in post-prison violence. After accounting for all of the other variables in the model, accounting for neighborhood disadvantage does little to explain racial differences in violence. Nor does neighborhood disadvantage itself explain involvement in violence among either whites or blacks. In contrast, neighborhood disadvantage does account for much of the racial differences in substance use. Accounting for neighborhood disadvantage was associated with a one-percentage-point reduction in the association between being black and post-prison substance use—a reduction that renders the association of race and post-prison substance use statistically insignificant. If young black men lived in more advantaged neighborhoods, they might be less likely to engage in post-prison substance use. Alternatively, if young white men lived in less advantaged neighborhoods, they might be more likely to engage in substance use after prison.[123]

CONCLUSION

The lives of many of the young men in our sample revealed patterns of behavior that included substance use, violence, or both. These patterns varied in the point in the life course at which they began. Some started in adolescence, some early in the transition to adulthood, and some, disturbingly, in early childhood. Once initiated, many of these young men, whose eventual incarceration distinguished them from other young men, continued to engage in these risky health behaviors as they transitioned into adulthood. Drug use and interpersonal violence became ever-present in their lives, with early post-prison experiences shaping how their later lives unfolded.

Both of the life stories presented at the beginning of this chapter indicate that over time substance use can lead to violence—but generally not the other way around. As Douglas's experience illustrates, enrolling in college may help some young white men overcome their struggles with substance abuse and interpersonal violence. Enrolling in community college after he exited substance abuse treatment seems to have given Douglas a stepping-stone into adulthood. As Edwin's experience illustrates, however, similar strides made toward educational achievement may not be as beneficial for blacks as they are for whites. Edwin persisted in substance use, even when he was paroled. Douglas eventually completed his degree, but Edwin did not. Still, both Douglas and Edwin survived into adulthood—unlike Rodney and Trevor, neither of whom established a foothold in education, employment, or even consistent social support from family. For these and the rest of the young men in our sample, disadvantaged social contexts shaped their involvement in substance use and violence.

After controlling for pre-, in-, and post-prison health, criminal justice involvement, and achievement of transition-to-adulthood markers, post-prison neighborhood disadvantage did not seem to promote violence in either young white or young black men. Nor did neighborhood disadvantage explain racial differences in post-prison violence. On the other hand, post-prison neighborhood disadvantage did increase the probability that young white men would engage in substance use after prison. Moreover, young white men from the most disadvantaged neighborhoods—the neighborhoods most similar to those of young black men—were most likely to test positive for substance use after prison. Neighborhood disadvantage did account for racial differences in substance use. Therefore, we find some evidence that neighborhood disadvantage may be a fundamental cause of substance use and racial differences in substance use. Contrary to our expectations, however, we do not find evidence that neighborhood disadvantage fundamentally causes violence or racial differences in violence.

Interestingly, in-prison secondary stressors of incarceration were not associated with post-prison substance use or violence for young men of either race, a finding that may support Schnittker and John's assertion that the stigma associated with incarceration—and not necessarily the incarceration experience itself—has the greatest impact on post-prison health.[124] Therefore, we cannot rule out the possibility that prison stigma and other types of stigma influence young men's post-prison involvement in substance use and violence. For example, the relationship between juvenile incarceration and post-prison violence may represent both a consequence of neighborhood disadvantage and a primary stressor that proliferates violent tendencies across the life course.

Likewise, the struggles that these young men faced as they transitioned to adulthood can be interpreted as evidence that they confronted considerable stigma—both prison and race stigma—on parole.[125] Employment and earnings were very low in our sample—and they were even lower for young black men (chapter 6). Few young men achieved residential independence, and residential independence rates were lowest for blacks (chapter 7). The young white men who did achieve some independence were more likely to engage in violence or, if they returned to familiar neighborhoods, to engage in substance use, suggesting that stress, rather than social support, might have been at work.[126]

Relative to employment and education, residential independence has received less attention in transition-to-adulthood studies. But achieving independence is more important to young adults than achieving the other markers of adulthood.[127] Young people who have achieved residential independence are more likely to report that they feel like adults than those who are employed full-time or have completed their education.[128] However, the racial disparity in employment, earnings, and residential independence that the young men in our sample confronted suggests that young black and young white men may experience residential "independence" in substantively different ways. When young white men live independently, they may do so on their own with a full-time job, which can promote violence and substance abuse through many mechanisms.[129] By contrast, young black men may be dependent on their romantic partners, who may nudge them toward more prosocial behavior.[130] As research on the transition to adulthood progresses, more attention should be paid to racial differences in the experience of independence and its consequences for substance use, violence, and subsequent adult role transitions.

Meeting education and employment markers has a complicated relationship to risky health behaviors that varies by race before, during, and after incarceration. Pre-prison high school graduation rates among formerly incarcerated young men in our sample were abysmally low: fewer than 10 percent of the men in our sample finished high school (chapter 3). However, those who did graduate seemed better able to avoid risky health behaviors than those who dropped out. Young men of both races who finished high school were less likely to engage in violence and substance use after prison—even when they lived in the most disadvantaged areas.

During and after prison, however, young white men were more likely than young black men to benefit from the investments they made in education, a finding in accord with prior work on the returns to education in the United States: white people see greater returns than black people.[131] Young white men were about 25 percent more likely to earn a GED in prison, which is associated with reduced post-prison involvement in substance use. Likewise, if they enrolled in college after prison, young white men were also less likely to engage in violent behavior—even when they lived in a disadvantaged neighborhood that promoted violence.

Young black men did not experience similar post-prison health benefits of college enrollment, which may be because they delayed furthering their education. The follow-up period for substance use and violence ended seven years after release from prison in 2003 for our study sample. Most of the black men enrolled in college after 2010—at least six years after release (chapter 4). Additionally, although young black men and young white men were equally likely to enroll in college during the first seven years, they might have been enrolling for different reasons. Black men may have enrolled to earn their GED, whereas white men who already had a GED may have enrolled in postsecondary education.

Perhaps because their in-prison educational attainment was poor relative to young white men, post-prison employment benefited young black men. Young black men were less likely than young white men to be employed in any post-prison quarter (chapter 6). Yet post-prison employment was associated with reduced post-prison involvement in substance use and reduced violence for young black men. Therefore, the young men least likely to find employment after prison were the most likely to benefit from doing so, which suggests that even as late as early adulthood, formerly incarcerated young black men can begin to overcome their educational deficits through labor market participation—if they can also overcome prison and race stigma.

Finally, this chapter demonstrates that more attention needs to be paid to the pivotal role of health and health behaviors during the transition to adulthood. Risky health behaviors such as violence and substance use can derail, delay, or even abort adult transitions. These threats to successful life-course development need to be examined and understood in a more robust transition-to-adulthood framework that recognizes that some young people struggle to meet the markers of adulthood for structural and cultural reasons that can be addressed through more effective public policies. Similarly, healthy behaviors, such as establishing and maintaining supportive relationships, can enrich the lives of young people and support them as they age into and through adulthood, whether they experience incarceration or not. These potentially beneficial health behaviors need to be examined, understood, and fostered in relation to the achievement of transitional markers that indicate successful life-course development.

Chapter 6 | Employment

ACADEMICS AND POLICYMAKERS share the belief that stable employment will improve the life chances of young adults who have just been released from prison.[1] Stable employment allows young adults to lessen their financial dependence on others and develop job-specific skills, and it is generally associated with greater rates of employment and higher wages in later adulthood.[2] For young adults with criminal records, stable employment in the formal labor market can inhibit criminal activity by creating a stake in conformity,[3] reducing the time spent around others involved in criminal activity,[4] and providing a source of income outside of criminal activity.[5] Indeed, some previous research has found that employment and earnings growth are important predictors of desistance from recidivism,[6] though the evidence is somewhat mixed.[7] In addition, stable employment provides those who have been to prison with a sense of self-efficacy, fulfillment, and control over their future.[8]

However, seeking to improve the life chances of recently released young adults through stable employment may be misguided if such employment is not widely attainable by them. As a group, those who have been to prison are likely to have struggled with finding and maintaining employment even in the absence of imprisonment, owing in part to having lower levels of educational attainment,[9] cognitive skills,[10] and prior work experience.[11] These issues are especially salient for young adults who have spent time in prison, since their education and work opportunities are likely to have been interrupted by contact with the criminal justice system. Time spent in prison may also erode the skills and social connections that are useful in securing stable employment.[12] Finally, young adults with criminal records face discrimination in the labor market on the basis of those criminal records.[13] These factors are compounded by recent work trends in the United States that have made low-wage employment increasingly precarious.[14] In particular, young adults without a college degree (like those in

132

our sample) have become less likely to find employment that enables them to achieve economic self-sufficiency.[15]

Consider the experiences of Johnny, a black man born in the early 1980s who grew up in a poor neighborhood in a medium-sized industrial city in central Michigan. Johnny began using marijuana and alcohol at age eleven. As his preteen and teen years unfolded, he accumulated an extensive juvenile history, probably because of his involvement in a gang. He was committed to a juvenile detention facility six times and sentenced to two juvenile probation terms. By the time Johnny turned eighteen, he had neither worked in the formal labor market nor graduated from high school, having dropped out in the eleventh grade. A few months prior to his eighteenth birthday, Johnny was arrested and pled no contest to multiple violent crimes, including assault with great bodily harm and carrying a concealed firearm. He was subsequently committed to the Michigan Department of Corrections, where he would spend the first five years of his transition to adulthood.

Having committed many misconduct infractions in prison, Johnny served almost twice his minimum sentence. During that time, however, he also earned his GED. Paroled onto maximum supervision, he moved in with his grandparents in another central Michigan city. Johnny's special conditions of parole reflect prior gang involvement and his potential for substance abuse. He was not to associate with gang members and had to abide by a curfew. He could not own or use a pager or cell phone. And he was ordered to complete and pay for substance abuse treatment. Though he never received residential treatment, he also never tested positive for any substance while on parole. Otherwise, Johnny seems to have struggled with complying with parole supervision, cycling between his grandparents' apartment and a detention center for parole violators. In the year following his release, he was also arrested multiple times: three times for obstruction, one time for drunk and disorderly conduct, and two times for domestic assault. Eventually he moved back to his hometown to live with his mother again.

Despite struggling on parole, Johnny found a job soon after he was released and remained employed for five quarters, throughout 2004. However, perhaps because he continued to be arrested and incarcerated periodically, he struggled to maintain stable employment at the same job and did not appear to be employed full-time. He held three jobs in those five quarters: one at a supermarket, one at a gas station, and one through a temporary services firm. He earned between $700 and $2,000 in each quarter except the last one, during which he seems to have worked for only a few days. Johnny would not hold another job in the formal labor market for the next five years, mainly because of his continued involvement in the criminal justice system. He did, however, enroll part-time in community college for one semester in early 2005.

In late 2005, Johnny was arrested a seventh time, this time on more serious charges that included home invasion, assault with a deadly weapon, and resisting arrest. As a result, Johnny was imprisoned and remained so until the spring of 2008, when he was paroled again. He returned to live with his mother but was recommitted to prison within six months after being arrested for carrying a concealed weapon and pleading guilty to possessing a firearm. He remained in state prison through the end of our follow-up in 2009.

Johnny's sporadic, part-time, and inconsistent employment history is consistent with recent research, both quantitative and qualitative, that provides corroborating evidence that post-prison employment stability is rare. Naomi Sugie collected daily measures of job searching and work from men recently released from prison in Newark and found that the employment search for the wide majority of men could be characterized by what Sugie calls "foraging" for short-term, precarious income-generating opportunities.[16] Focusing on young adults in particular, Robert Apel and Gary Sweeten examined post-incarceration employment trajectories using the National Longitudinal Study of Youth 1997 and found that only 19 percent of young adults obtained what they term "stable employment" after incarceration.[17] And in *Homeward*, a study of recently released adults in Boston, Bruce Western finds that young adults generally experience intermittent work or continuous unemployment in the first year after exiting prison.[18]

We understand less, however, about the factors that may explain variation in the extent to which young adults find stable employment after release from prison. In this chapter, we help to fill this gap in empirical knowledge using our sample of young men released from Michigan prisons in 2003. We base our analyses on quarterly data collected from Michigan's unemployment insurance office between the years 2000 and 2010, alongside criminal justice and demographic data described elsewhere in this volume. The Michigan unemployment insurance data capture almost all employment undertaken in the formal labor market in the state of Michigan. From these data, we know how many employers an individual had and the earnings from each of those employers during each quarter, as well as the detailed industry classification of each employer. In sum, we are able to examine the post-release employment outcomes of all men in our sample for six years after the sampled release.

We first describe several post-release employment outcomes for the young men in our sample: how likely they were to find employment, how likely they were to be lifted out of poverty by employment, and how likely they were to maintain employment once employed. Though most young men in our sample had a record of employment at some point in the six years after the focal prison spell, employment rates at any point after release were low: no more than one-third of these young men were employed in any given quarter. Further, the jobs that most young men found right after being released from prison left them stuck in poverty, and a considerable portion of those who were employed in one quarter were no longer employed in the next.

We also look at how likely the young men were to reach a measure of *stable employment*, which we define as having a record of employment in four consecutive quarters (though not necessarily with the same employer) after the focal prison spell. Though the choice of this length of time is somewhat arbitrary, using four quarters as a measure captures an intuitive understanding of what stable employment signifies by excluding those who experienced breaks in employment due to seasonal changes in demand, which is common in industries like construction and retail, where many of these young men worked.[19] We find that most men in our sample did not reach this measure of stable employment over the six years after release from prison. Those who did worked most commonly in the blue-collar industries of manufacturing and construction, but a sizable portion of the young men who found stable employment did so at restaurants or through temporary help agencies.

In our descriptive examination of post-release employment outcomes, we focus on variations in the attainment of employment outcomes by race. Audit studies have convincingly demonstrated that low-wage employers discriminate against black job applicants, offering them fewer jobs[20] and lower wages[21] than similar white applicants. Further, this discrimination is exacerbated when comparing black and white job applicants with criminal records[22] and may be driven by a perception of the criminality of black men[23] that is driven in part by racial inequalities in criminal justice contact.[24] Research has also found that black job seekers are disadvantaged in their access to mainstream ties and institutions that can connect them to job opportunities,[25] as well as in their ability to leverage their social ties to obtain a job.[26] Finally, as shown in table 2.1, young black men in our sample generally experienced greater disadvantage than young white men in our sample along a host of other dimensions—prior criminal justice contact, education, prior work history, and post-prison neighborhood disadvantage—that were likely to affect their employment outcomes. Consistent with these theoretical predictions, we find that young black men were less likely to find employment, less likely to have earnings above the poverty line when employed, more likely to lose employment, and less likely to reach our measure of stable employment.

In our final analysis, we specify and estimate a regression model that predicts whether or not a young man in our sample will attain stable employment within the first three years after release from prison, based on demographic information, human capital attainment, neighborhood opportunities, and prior criminal justice contact, measured at the time of release. Though this regression does not allow us to make causal inferences, it does allow us to understand which variables are robustly associated with finding stable employment when taking other plausible factors into account. We find that, even after controlling for the confounding variables just described, young white men in our sample were significantly more likely to attain stable employment than young black men. Measures of human capital are also positively associated with attaining stable employment; we additionally find associations between some (but not all) measures of criminal justice contact and attainment of stable employment.

POST-RELEASE EMPLOYMENT OUTCOMES

Figure 6.1 plots the probability of employment in each quarter after release from prison, with trend lines for all young men and for black and white men separately.[27] The proportion of men who were employed spikes immediately after release and plateaus at just over 30 percent in quarters 2 through 4 after release. Subsequently, the probability of employment declines, dipping under 25 percent three years after release and under 20 percent six years after release. The incidence of employment after release from prison and these trends in employment over time are generally consistent with other studies.[28] Employment rates may spike soon after release due to close parole supervision immediately after release, as searching for or maintaining employment in the formal labor market is a requirement of parole in Michigan.[29]

Racial differences in the proportion of individuals in our sample employed in each quarter after prison are striking. Black men were employed at much lower rates in all quarters after release. The probability of employment peaked for black men at 23 percent in the third quarter after release and steadily declined to under 10 percent seven years after release. In comparison, white men reached 40 percent employment in the second quarter after release, and over 30 percent were employed through five years after release.

Such low rates of employment after release from prison (for young men of all races) portend ill for the idea that employment can be the main pathway to improving the life chances of young men who have spent time in prison. Further, the extent to which post-prison employment can positively affect the life chances of these men depends not only on the incidence of

Figure 6.1   Proportion of Men Employed during the Twenty-Four Calendar Quarters after Release

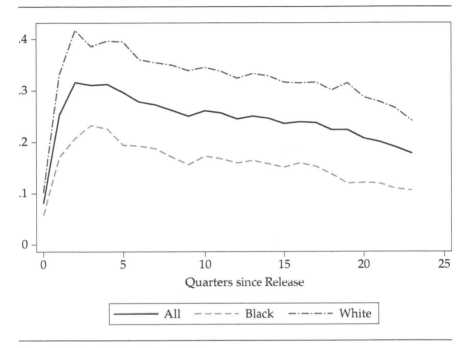

Quarters since Release

——— All   – – – – Black   –·–·–·– White

Source: Michigan Study of Life after Prison.

employment but also on the financial benefits received from employment. Well-paying employment should increase the likelihood of engaging in healthy behavior and maintaining residential stability (see chapters 5 and 7 for some evidence on this topic), and there is some evidence that employment quality more generally reduces future criminal justice contact.[30] We measure the financial benefits of employment using a simple dichotomous measure that indicates whether an employed individual earns enough—among all jobs recorded in the unemployment insurance data set—to move above the poverty line for a single person under the age of sixty-five. In the state of Michigan during the time period of our study, this line was set at earnings of $2,835 per quarter.

Figure 6.2 shows trends over time in the proportion of employed young men in our data who earned more than this poverty threshold in any quarter after release from prison. We find that, in the first year after release from prison, only a little over one-third of young men who found employment

Figure 6.2   Proportion of Employed Men with Earnings above
the Poverty Line during the Twenty-Four Calendar
Quarters after Release

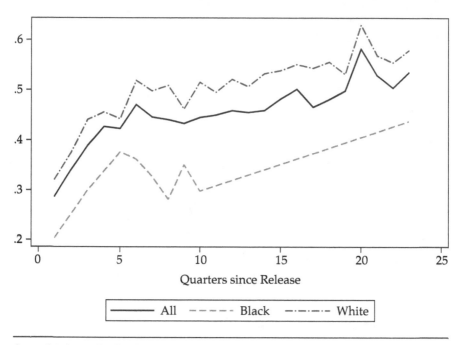

Quarters since Release

— All   – – – – – Black   – · – · · – White

Source: Michigan Study of Life after Prison.

earned enough to get out of poverty. The proportion of employed young
men who earned above the poverty line did grow over time; at the end
of our observation period in 2009 (six years after their release in 2003),
about half of employed men earned above the poverty line. Still, given
that employment did not lift a large percentage of young men out of poverty, it is unclear whether the purported benefits of employment after
release from prison extended to all. Figure 6.2 also shows a wide racial gap
between black and white young men in our sample in the degree to which
employment reduced poverty. In all quarters after release, employed white
men were substantially more likely to have earnings above the poverty line
than were employed black men.

We next look at whether employment after release from prison was
characterized by concentration among a few young men who were able to
obtain relatively steady employment or intermittent employment among a

Figure 6.3   Proportion of Men Ever Employed during the Twenty-Four Calendar Quarters after Release

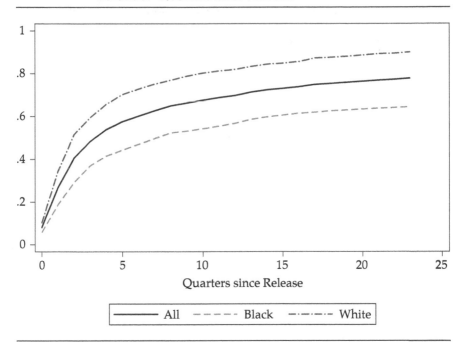

Source: Michigan Study of Life after Prison.

larger group of young men. Figure 6.3 shows trends over time in the percentage of men who had ever been employed since release from prison. Despite low overall rates of employment in any given quarter, we find that most of those in our sample found at least short stints of formal employment at some point after prison. Just over half of the young men in our sample found some form of employment in the first four quarters after release, and roughly three-quarters of them found work at least once within six years after release.

We again find a large racial disparity in the percentage of men who had been employed at some point since their 2003 release. Four quarters after release, 42 percent of black men had recorded employment since prison, compared to 66 percent of white men. This gap persisted in later quarters. Six years after release, only 64 percent of black men had recorded employment, less than the percentage of white men who had recorded employment in the first four quarters after release. In contrast, 90 percent of white men had some recorded employment during this time period. White

Figure 6.4   Proportion of Men Employed in Previous Quarter
              Who Remain Employed in Subsequent Quarter
              during the Twenty-Four Calendar Quarters after Release

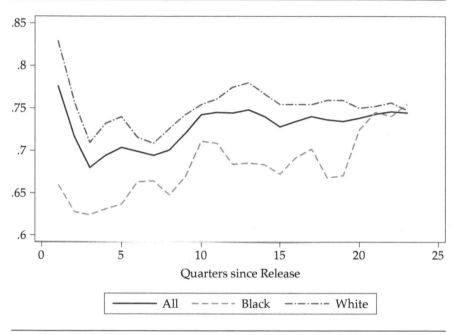

Source: Michigan Study of Life after Prison.
Note: Trend lines have been smoothed.

men, in short, were significantly more likely than black men to participate
in the formal labor market after prison.

The difference in the percentage of men who were employed in any
given quarter after release from prison and the percentage of men who had
ever been employed after release suggests that stable employment is relatively rare for young men after release from prison. One way to measure
this is by the percentage of men employed in one quarter who remained
employed in the next quarter. Over the seven years for which we have data,
72 percent of young men who were employed in one quarter were also
employed in the next. Figure 6.4 graphs this measure of stable employment
for each quarter after release. Eighty-three percent of those who found
jobs in the quarter of their release from prison in 2003 maintained employment in the next quarter. In future quarters, however, employment was

Figure 6.5   Proportion of Men Who Reach Stable Employment during the Twenty-Four Calendar Quarters after Release

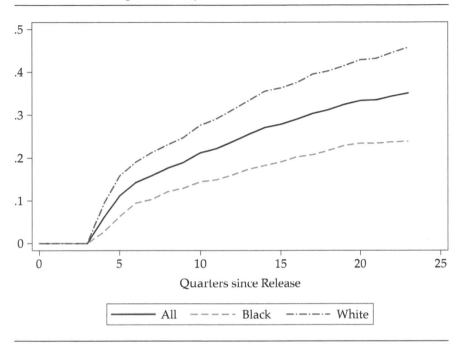

Quarters since Release

All   ----- Black   --·---·-- White

Source: Michigan Study of Life after Prison.

maintained at significantly lower rates, though there was a slight upward trend over time after the initial decrease. Given that fewer individuals were employed in any given quarter over time, this may reflect individuals who were less likely to maintain employment dropping out of the labor market altogether over time. Figure 6.4 also shows that, as with other employment outcomes, young black men fared worse in maintaining employment in consecutive time periods than did young white men.

We also assess the extent to which young men in our sample achieved our measure of stable employment—maintaining employment for four consecutive quarters—after release from prison. Figure 6.5 graphs the percentage of young men who reached this milestone by the quarter after release from prison in which they did so. Within three years after release, slightly fewer than one-quarter of young men had achieved this metric of stable employment, and only 35 percent of young men did so within six years. Notably, young black men were roughly half as likely as young

Table 6.1   Most Common Industries in Which Formerly Incarcerated
             Young Men Find Stable Employment

All (%)		Blacks (%)		Whites (%)	
Manufacturing	27	Manufacturing	22	Manufacturing	28
Construction	10	Limited service eating	14	Construction	14
Limited service eating	10	Employment services	12	Employment services	9
Employment services	10	Health care and social assistance	11	Full-service restaurant	9
Full-service restaurant	9	Full-service restaurant	9	Limited service eating	9

Source: Michigan Study of Life after Prison.
Note: Data for 2003 Michigan parole cohort age 18–25 at parole, followed through 2009.

white men to have worked for four consecutive quarters within six years after release from prison.

Table 6.1 lists the five most common industries in which young men attained this measure of stable employment after release from prison, both among the entire sample of men and among black and white men separately. Manufacturing was far and away the most likely to be the industry in which young men in our sample (both black and white) found stable employment: over one-quarter of those who found stable employment did so in manufacturing. Other common industries in which men in our sample found stable employment included construction, limited-service eating places, employment services, and full-service restaurants.

Again, we find important differences by race: young black men who attained stable employment were more likely to do so in limited-service eating places or employment services, while young white men were more likely to do so in construction. These differences are consequential because the evidence suggests that the quality of employment varies substantially between these industries. Young men in our sample experienced higher wages and longer job tenures in the construction industry than in limited-service eating places (where most of the jobs they worked were at fast-food restaurants) or employment services (where most of their jobs were obtained through temporary help agencies). Further, jobs in construction in the state of Michigan in the mid-2000s were relatively more likely to be unionized, whereas virtually no jobs in limited-service eating places, employment services, or full-service restaurants are covered by unions.[31]

Thus, among the young men in our sample, black men appear to have been doubly disadvantaged in finding stable employment compared to white men: not only were they less likely to find stable employment, but when they did so, they were more likely to find a job in an industry that offered lower job quality.

DETERMINANTS OF ATTAINING STABLE EMPLOYMENT

Overall, the picture we have just painted of post-prison employment trajectories for the young men in our sample is rather bleak. At peak levels of employment after release, fewer than one-third of the young men were employed in the formal labor market, and fewer than half of them were earning enough from this employment to rise out of poverty. Further, a substantial number of young men who were employed in one quarter were no longer employed in the next. As a result, few young men were able to achieve stable employment after release from prison. Finally, we find that young black men in our sample were less likely than young white men to attain all of the positive employment outcomes.

We next examine which characteristics of the young men in our sample are positively associated with attaining our measure of stable employment (working in the formal labor market for four consecutive quarters within three years after release from prison). We focus on demographic characteristics, human capital attainment, health, pre-prison environment, criminal justice contact through the time of release, and post-prison residential environment. We use these data to investigate which factors appear to be most predictive of attaining stable employment, holding other factors constant. In the following, we briefly discuss how the other factors may influence the likelihood of attaining stable employment.

Race

As discussed in the introduction, young black men with criminal records were likely to be disadvantaged in the formal labor market in multiple ways: they were more likely to face discrimination at the point of hire; they were likely to be less able to use their networks to tap into promising employment opportunities; and we know that, within our sample, young black men faced greater disadvantage along many other dimensions that may affect the ability to attain stable employment. Because our data do not directly capture the discrimination that young black men may face in the labor market or their differential ability to leverage networks for employment opportunities, we still expect to see a negative association between being black and attaining stable employment, even after controlling for other observable factors.

Age

Life-course theories point to the importance of age in understanding the trajectories of those who have experienced criminal justice contact. In particular, if age is a proxy for impulsiveness or self-control, individuals may be less likely to experience criminal justice contact as they age, as well as more likely to attain stable employment.[32] Thus, we might find that the men in our sample who were (relatively) older at the time of release were more likely to attain stable employment. However, since all men in our sample were ages eighteen to twenty-five at the time of release, we may not find this relationship if work after release from prison was effective only in providing stability to those who were in their late twenties or older.[33] We measure age at the time of release from prison.

Human Capital

Prior work experience may be positively associated with stable employment after release from prison, for several reasons. For one, prior work experience may act as a credential that makes employers more willing to hire a young man with a criminal record, since he has previously shown that he can participate in the formal labor market. Additionally, prior work experience may develop skills that make it easier to find and maintain employment. Finally, prior work experience may serve as a measure of unobserved traits that make a person a more productive worker. We operationalize prior work experience by the log of the maximum quarterly wages in the year before entering prison for the focal prison spell.

Education may also be positively associated with attaining stable employment. Fewer than 10 percent of the young men in our sample had a high school degree at the time of release; however, about 60 percent had obtained a GED by that time. We expect that having a high school degree or a GED will be positively associated with stable employment, since the attainment of these degrees might signal worker motivation and quality.[34] However, we consider these two credentials separately. Workers with a high school degree necessarily have more years of education than those who have a GED, and research has found that these additional years of education explain differences in employment outcomes between these two groups.[35] Additionally, employers may not value GEDs as much as high school degrees, which they may view as a better indicator of perseverance.[36] (See chapter 3 for further discussion of the advantages and disadvantages of the GED relative to a high school diploma and relative to having no secondary education credential.)

Health

We examine whether two indicators of health—mental illness and a history of substance abuse—are associated with stable employment. As detailed in chapter 5, substance abuse is a risky health behavior that may contribute to future criminal justice contact. Substance abuse has been linked to higher rates of absenteeism among workers, and employers are likely to believe that drug users are worse and less safe workers.[37] Thus, we expect having a substance abuse history to be negatively associated with attaining stable employment. Similarly, we expect that having a mental illness will interfere with the ability to find and keep employment and thus may be negatively associated with attaining stable employment.

Pre-Prison Neighborhood Disadvantage

Growing up in a disadvantaged neighborhood may lead to worse economic outcomes as an adult through several mechanisms.[38] First, children in disadvantaged neighborhoods may be more likely to grow up around peers engaged in criminal or otherwise deviant behavior, and thus they may be more likely to engage in such behavior themselves. Second, children in disadvantaged neighborhoods may be exposed to fewer successful adults who can model and enforce normative behavior. Finally, disadvantaged neighborhoods are likely to have fewer resources available for neighborhood institutions like schools and police forces that can help ensure children's safety and success. While remaining agnostic about the exact mechanisms at play, we examine whether pre-prison neighborhood disadvantage is negatively associated with attaining stable employment after prison. Because we do not have access to the complete residential history of the young men in our sample, we proxy for pre-prison neighborhood disadvantage via a standardized disadvantage score of the census tract in which each young man lived before beginning the focal prison spell.

Prior Criminal Justice Contact

Their criminal records made all of the young men in our sample more likely to face difficulties in the formal labor market.[39] However, we expect that this stigma will differ between young men in our sample depending on the extent of their contact with the criminal justice system. The extent and types of prior criminal justice contact are probably also indicators of behavioral problems that may make it more difficult to attain stable employment. We examine the association between stable employment and several variables reflecting prior criminal justice contact: conviction for a violent crime, conviction for a property crime, conviction for a drug crime, pre-prison arrests, length of the focal prison spell, number of misconducts per year during the sampled prison spell, and being subject to electronic monitoring upon release from prison.

Post-Prison Context

The social context to which the young men in our sample return after release from prison may affect their likelihood of attaining stable employment. One important facet of young men's post-prison social contexts is their living situation. We focus on two types of living situations that theory suggests may facilitate the attainment of stable employment. First is living with parents or older family members. Housing assistance from relatives is a direct measure of material support that may also signal the willingness of relatives to provide emotional support or additional material support on top of housing assistance. Previous research has found that the formerly incarcerated often rely on emotional and material support from adult family members in their search for employment after release from prison.[40] Especially likely to do so are young adults, who are more likely in general to rely on familial assistance in pursuing employment opportunities.[41] The second type of living situation is living with a spouse or a romantic partner. Cohabitation may leave less time to spend with friends who are in frequent contact with the criminal justice system, thus reducing future criminal justice contact and making stable employment more likely.[42] Further, men who live with a romantic partner often say that they are motivated to find work in order to fulfill the role of the breadwinner in their household.[43] We include two indicator variables to measure these living situations: one indicating whether or not a young man lives with a parent or older family member upon release from prison, and a second indicating whether or not a young man lives with a spouse or romantic partner upon release from prison.

Another facet of the post-prison environment that may be consequential for stable employment is return to the same neighborhood of residence before the focal prison spell. Returning to the same neighborhood could be positively associated with attaining stable employment if a young man has social ties in his neighborhood that he can use to find employment opportunities. On the other hand, returning to the same environment as before prison may lead formerly incarcerated young men to experience the same situations and to reconnect with the same individuals that led to their criminal justice contact in the first place.[44] If this leads to an increased risk of future criminal justice contact, then returning to the same neighborhood could limit stable employment. We measure this construct via a variable that indicates whether a young man lives in the same census tract as he did before prison.

Finally, the unemployment rate in the neighborhood in which a young man lives after release from prison may also be associated with rates of future stable employment. When the unemployment rate is low, it is more difficult for employers to find workers, and they may be more willing to hire those with criminal records (and less willing to fire those with poor job performance) than they would be if the unemployment rate were higher. Lower unemployment rates could thus increase the likelihood of attaining stable employment. Richard Freeman and William Rodgers provide evidence in this vein, showing that employment discrimination against former prisoners is strongly correlated with local unemployment rates.[45] We measure neighborhood unemployment rates at the level of the census tract, in the quarter in which each young man was released from prison after the focal prison spell.[46]

PREDICTING STABLE EMPLOYMENT

About 24 percent of the young men in the sample attained our marker of stable employment within three years after the focal release from prison. Using a regression model to control for other variables, we examine the associations between each of the factors described here and working for four consecutive quarters in the formal labor market. This model cannot provide causal evidence about the effects of any of these factors on attaining stable employment. Still, describing the association between each of the potential determinants of stable employment and the actual attainment of stable employment, net of other observable variables, allows us to examine the plausibility of various explanatory factors.[47]

For ease of interpretation, we focus on figure 6.6, which highlights variables that are significantly associated with stable employment in the model and shows the predicted probability of attaining stable employment across different values of these variables, holding the values of all other variables at the sample mean.[48] The vertical dashed red line indicates the average probability of attaining stable employment.

Even after accounting for many observable factors, race is still a salient predictor of attaining stable employment among the young men in our sample. The estimation results suggest that, compared to being white, being black is associated with a nine-percentage-point reduction in the probability of attaining stable employment. As seen in figure 6.6, this effect

Figure 6.6   Differences in the Probability of Achieving Stable
Employment in a Calendar Quarter during the
Twenty-Four Calendar Quarters after Release,
by Various Predictors

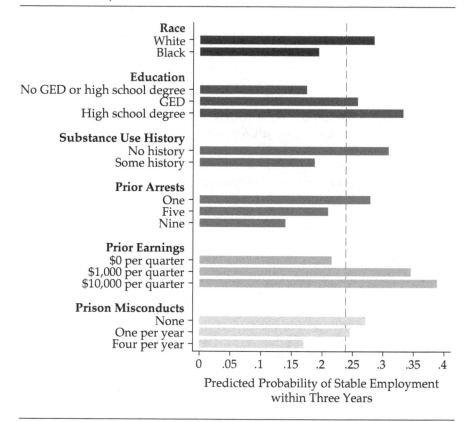

Predicted Probability of Stable Employment
within Three Years

Source: Michigan Study of Life after Prison.

is substantial. When comparing the predicted probabilities of attaining
stable employment across racial categories, holding all else equal, young
white men coming out of prison were roughly one and a half times more
likely to attain stable employment than young black men. Though we
cannot know what mediates the relationship between race and attaining
stable employment after prison, it is possible that racial discrimination
helps to explain this observed relationship.

Measures of human capital—educational attainment and prior work
experience—are also strong predictors of attaining stable employment after

release from prison, consistent with theoretical predictions. Compared to having neither a GED nor a high school degree, having a GED is associated with an eight-percentage-point increase in attaining stable employment after prison, and having a high school degree is associated with a sixteen-percentage-point increase. Again, in relative terms, this is a meaningful difference: the predicted probability of attaining stable employment after prison is about one and a half times larger for young men with a GED—and two times larger for young men with a high school degree—than for young men without a high school degree or its equivalent.

Pre-prison employment is also significantly associated with attaining stable employment after release from prison. Because the extent of pre-prison employment is measured as the log of the maximum pre-prison quarterly wages in the year before prison, the coefficient of 0.018 suggests that a 1 percent increase in maximum pre-prison quarterly wages is associated with an increase in the predicted probability of attaining stable employment after prison of about two percentage points. Figure 6.6 shows that the predicted probability of attaining stable employment is much higher for young men who earned even $1,000 in their most remunerative quarter before prison than for those who were not recorded participating in the formal labor market.

We also find that substance use history is a significant negative predictor of attaining employment stability. All else equal, having a history of substance use appears to reduce the probability of attaining stable employment after prison by twelve percentage points. The predicted probabilities in figure 6.6 suggest that those who did not have a substance use history were over 60 percent more likely to attain stable employment than those who did. This relationship may be driven by employer-driven stigma against drug users; it is also plausible that, because those who used substances before prison were likely to return to using substances after release (as shown in chapter 5), post-prison substance use interfered with their ability to maintain employment.

Finally, we find that two variables related to prior criminal justice contact—the number of arrests before the sampled prison spell, and the number of misconducts per year during the sampled prison spell—are negatively associated with post-prison stable employment after accounting for other factors. Each additional prior arrest is associated with roughly a two-percentage-point decrease in the likelihood of attaining stable employment after prison, whereas each additional misconduct per year in prison decreases the likelihood of attaining stable employment after prison by two and a half percentage points. The number of prior arrests probably reflects the extent of prior criminal behavior or the length of time in which a young man had been entangled in the criminal justice system, both of which may have detrimental effects on post-prison employment outcomes. Meanwhile, it seems plausible that misconducts in prison are a marker of behavioral problems that may make it difficult to hold employment.

What variables were not associated with attaining stable employment? We found that age was not significantly associated with stable employment, perhaps because all men in this sample were of similar age. Mental illness was also not associated with post-prison stable employment, nor was pre-prison neighborhood disadvantage. While some variables measuring criminal justice contact were related to attaining stable employment after prison, many variables—including the types of offenses for which the young man had been convicted, the number of years in prison, whether he was a convicted sex offender, and whether or not he was subject to electronic monitoring upon release from the focal prison spell—were not significantly associated after controlling for other variables. Finally, variables reflecting the post-prison social and economic environment were not significantly related to post-prison stable employment.

CONCLUSION

Stable employment in the formal labor market is an important marker of the transition to adulthood and may be a key pathway along which young men who have experienced incarceration experience upward mobility after they are released. However, consistent with previous research on former prisoners in general, we find that any form of employment in the formal labor market after prison was relatively rare in our sample. No more than one-third of the young men were employed in any quarter after release, and the proportion of them who were employed declined steadily after the first year after release. Further, this employment was not especially well-paying: for over half of the young men in the sample who did find jobs, their wages alone were not enough to move them above the poverty line, let alone help them provide for others. Stable employment was even more uncommon: we find that only about one-quarter of the young men in our sample worked in four consecutive quarters at any point in the three years after release from prison. Distressingly, we find that young black men were substantially less likely to achieve each of the positive employment outcomes that we measure despite lower levels of serious substance use and fewer prior arrests.

We then estimated which factors are significantly associated with finding employment stability. Even after controlling for other factors, we still find a wide racial gap in attaining employment stability after release from prison. Educational attainment and pre-prison work experience are positively associated with attaining employment stability after release from prison, while prior substance abuse, prior arrests, and misconducts in prison are negatively associated with post-prison employment stability.

Our analysis is not without limitations. First, unemployment insurance data include gross quarterly earnings from each employer but do not report hours worked or hourly wages. As such, we cannot know whether an individual is working full- or part-time, or whether changes in gross earnings between quarters are a result of changes in hourly wages or changes in hours worked. More detailed data could help us disentangle whether the rates of poverty seen here even among those who were employed were a function of low wages, low work hours, or both.

Second, the data available to us do not capture the informal, or "gray," economy—that is, the employment that research finds is a common substitute for or supplement to formal employment among the formerly incarcerated.[49] However, we do expect that, because searching for formal employment is a requirement of parole in Michigan, the young men in our sample may have been especially likely to seek stable employment in the formal labor market. Indeed, Josh Seim and David Harding have analyzed a wider sample of released prisoners in Michigan and find that parole supervision increases the likelihood of formal employment.[50] Further, formal employment should be more likely than informal employment to provide stable employment, as well as many of the benefits of employment that are likely to reduce future criminal justice contact.[51]

Third, unemployment insurance data may be subject to underreporting of wages from employers.[52] Also, an estimated 4 percent of waged and salaried jobs across the United States are in categories of formal employment not covered by these data.[53] In Michigan, jobs that unemployment insurance does not cover include certain types of seasonal agricultural workers, low-wage and part-time domestic workers, those doing certain work-relief or rehabilitation work through nonprofits or government agencies, those who earn commissions, the self-employed, and independent contractors, among others.[54] We expect that few individuals in our sample worked in these types of jobs.

Finally, these data do not capture formal employment outside the state of Michigan; as such, sample members who move outside the state during the time frame of our study may be mistakenly coded as unemployed. Fewer than 4 percent of the men in our sample moved out of state at some point while on parole, with an average length of stay out of state while on parole of about seven quarters. Since we have no residential data for those who completed their parole, however, the actual percentage of men who moved out of state during the time frame may be higher.

Despite these limitations, our analyses show that employment may not enable young men to improve their life chances after release from prison.

Even young men like Johnny, who was among those in our sample who briefly attained stable employment, found it difficult to maintain stable employment, lift themselves out of poverty, and desist from involvement in the criminal justice system. Like Johnny, most formerly incarcerated young men face several disadvantages on the labor market: they have low levels of human capital and work experience; they may struggle with substance use or return to the illegal behavior that led to their initial criminal justice contact; and they may face discrimination in the labor market as a result of their criminal record or their race. Further, these young men are trying to find a foothold in life through a labor market in which the work they are qualified to do is increasingly precarious along many dimensions: wages are low; benefits are rare; hours are irregular; and job security is nearly nonexistent.[55] Overall, few young men are able to reap the benefits of a stable job in the formal labor market that lifts them out of poverty. Policymakers should continue to consider how to improve the employment prospects of formerly incarcerated young men and more generally to enhance the life chances of those who face the most challenges in attaining stable employment—perhaps through diversion programs that give young men second chances to avoid criminal records.[56] We return to such policy considerations in the concluding chapter.

Chapter 7 | Residential Stability

FOR FORMERLY INCARCERATED young men, residential security is crucial not only for reestablishing connections to community life but also for successfully transitioning into adulthood. Those who spent their early adulthood in prison have experienced a major disruption in their transition from adolescence into adulthood. They may need to complete formal education, find jobs, and, more generally, plan for independent lives. Establishing a secure and stable residence is a crucial part of the foundation upon which these transitions depend. Without a stable home, it can be difficult to land a job, reestablish relationships, and avoid reoffending or falling victim to substance abuse.[1]

The young men in our sample often experienced considerable residential instability. Consider Shane, a white man born in the early 1980s who grew up in a small city in Michigan's Upper Peninsula. Shane became involved in the juvenile justice system at an early age; at his first arrest, he was only thirteen years old. Shane was incarcerated in juvenile detention three times and sentenced to juvenile probation four times. He experienced his first felony arrest—for breaking and entering—at age fourteen. Shortly after his adjudication as a juvenile, he dropped out of school in the eighth grade. About two months before his eighteenth birthday, Shane was arrested for armed robbery. He was sentenced to a minimum of six years in prison. Unlike many young men who became involved with the criminal justice system early in life, Shane did not report any substance use prior to his imprisonment, and he never tested positive for substance use during imprisonment or while on parole. Nor did he report mental instability. While he was imprisoned, Shane earned his GED.

Shane was released onto maximum parole supervision in mid-2003. He experienced substantial residential instability after prison. Excluding jail, Shane lived in five residences in five different towns in two states in the first year after he was released from prison. Immediately after his release, Shane moved in with a friend in his hometown. He stayed at that address

153

for less than two weeks before moving to a rural area. Less than a month later, he moved out of state and lived by himself for about four months. He then returned to a small Michigan town where he lived for about three months before he was arrested for driving without a license. After the arrest, he moved in with his mother in another small Michigan town. While he was living with her, Shane worked the only job he had ever held in the formal labor market in Michigan, at a fast-food restaurant, where he earned just $135 in the second quarter of 2004. Shane lived with his mother for about three months before he was arrested again for disorderly conduct and served over a month in jail.

Around this time, Shane also became a cocaine addict. He reported that he started using cocaine in his midtwenties and developed a daily habit. After he was released from jail, he moved in briefly with his girlfriend before enrolling in residential treatment. He lived in residential treatment for two months, after which he returned to live with his girlfriend. This was the first time he had left and then returned to the same address and social relationship. He would live with her in the same apartment for the next six months as he was arrested on warrants for failing to appear in court—for which he served less than a week in jail.

While he was living with his girlfriend, Shane enrolled full-time in a state university but dropped out after one semester. He also became a father. About twenty-two months after he had been released from state prison, Shane was arrested for illegally entering someone's property, sentenced to one month in jail, and then returned to prison as a technical rule violator. He was incarcerated for about sixteen months and was released from prison onto maximum parole supervision for the second time in mid-2006. After prison, Shane moved in with his mother, who by now lived in a new town; he stayed with her for a month and a half before absconding from parole. He remained at large for nearly six months. In early 2007, he was arrested in Wisconsin and again returned to prison as a technical parole violator.

Shane was hardly the only young man released from prison who experienced residential instability. Yet despite the apparent importance of establishing a stable residence for successful reintegration after prison release, residential mobility and stability among formerly incarcerated young men have not been systemically studied. This chapter examines the problem, focusing on three specific research questions: How much stability or instability do young men experience in the years after release from prison? Which young men manage to establish stable residences? And what characteristics and experiences are associated with residential mobility and stability?

Our analysis reveals that formerly incarcerated young men experience very high rates of residential mobility, especially during the first year following their release from prison. It also indicates that the criminal justice system itself and residence in a poor neighborhood are key factors that generate residential instability. Meanwhile, support from parents or older relatives plays a key protective role against residential instability.

RESIDENTIAL INSTABILITY AMONG FORMERLY INCARCERATED YOUNG MEN

Although the residential conditions of the broader population of formerly incarcerated people have been reported in previous studies, we know little about the residential stability of formerly incarcerated young men in particular. Previous studies have shown that many formerly incarcerated individuals experience high rates of residential mobility relative to the general population, in part because they frequently move in and out of criminal justice institutions or treatment facilities.[2] They are highly likely to live in high-poverty neighborhoods,[3] and many eventually find themselves homeless.[4] Yet by virtue of their age and less extensive involvement in the criminal justice system compared to older prisoners, formerly incarcerated young men may have more access to supportive people and institutions that can help them with housing. Do formerly incarcerated young men experience residential instability similar to that of older individuals coming out of prison? This section describes the living conditions of our formerly incarcerated young men, focusing on three questions: Where and with whom did they begin their post-prison life? How frequently did they move while on parole? And what types of neighborhoods did they live in during parole?

Residential Mobility and Types of Residences

As shown in figure 7.1, the formerly incarcerated young men in our study moved as often as older formerly incarcerated adults.[5] Almost 90 percent moved at least once, and 47 percent changed their residence four or more times during the parole period. The average individual in our sample moved 4.5 times. Considering that the average parole period is 1.51 years (table 7.A5), this translates into about three moves per year, which is nearly three times the rate of residential mobility generally considered to indicate residential instability.[6]

In addition to frequent residential changes, about three-quarters of our young men experienced at least one institutional (nonprivate) residence,

Figure 7.1   Number of Residential Moves during the First Two Years
after Release, by Race

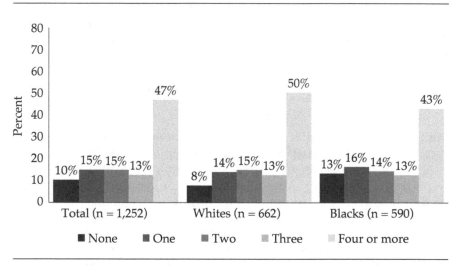

Source: Michigan Study of Life after Prison.
Note: Average number of residential moves: pooled, 4.5 moves; whites, 5.1 moves; blacks, 3.9 moves.

such as a criminal justice facility, a treatment institution, or a motel (see figure 7.2). And about 60 percent were detained in criminal justice facilities at least once. The typical formerly incarcerated young man in our sample experienced such temporary custody 1.2 times while on parole. This means that many engaged in technical parole violations that prompted custody but were not serious enough to warrant a return to prison. These temporary detentions in criminal justice facilities have important implications for residential stability, in that they can frequently interrupt what is an otherwise stable living situation.

The young men in our sample changed residences most often during the first year after prison release. As we see in figure 7.3, the number of residential changes after prison peaked at the third month after prison release and decreased over the two-year period following release. The concentration of residential moves during the first year implies that residential instability is tightly associated with other parole processes, such as discharge from parole, absconding, or custody.

The level of residential instability during parole periods was not very different between white and black subjects. A substantial portion of men in both groups lived in nonprivate residences, and similar percentages of

Figure 7.2   Nonprivate Residences and Custody Spells in Criminal
              Justice Facilities during the First Two Years after Release

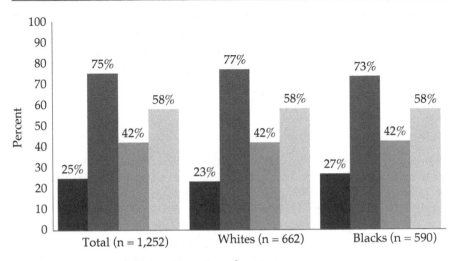

■ Only lived in private housing
■ Experienced nonprivate housing at least once
■ Never detained in criminal justice facility
▨ Detained in criminal justice facility at least once

Source: Michigan Study of Life after Prison.
Note: Average number of times in custody: pooled, 1.2 times; whites, 1.3 times; blacks, 1.1 times.

Figure 7.3   Percentage of Moves in the Community by Month
              after Release

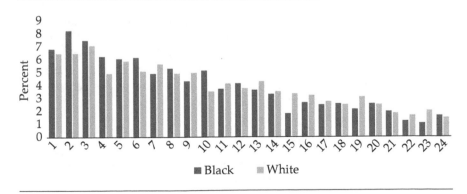

■ Black   ▨ White

Source: Michigan Study of Life after Prison.
Note: First twenty-four months following release from prison. Total moves for two years: black, 1,198; white, 1,661.

black and white young men were temporarily detained in criminal justice facilities. However, as figure 7.1 shows, whites experienced more residential instability than blacks (an average of 5.1 residential moves for whites and 3.9 for blacks). This difference is largely driven by more white men changing residences at least four times (50 percent versus 43 percent among blacks) and more black men not moving at all (13 percent versus 8 percent among whites). These statistics are also affected by the fact that the parole periods for blacks was, on average, shorter than the parole period for whites (see table 7.A5).

Living Arrangements

A substantial number of formerly incarcerated young adults in our sample lived with relatives immediately after prison release.[7] As seen in figure 7.4, 53 percent moved in with one or both parents after release, and about 40 percent moved in with other adult family members, such as spouses or romantic partners (16 percent), siblings or cousins (8 percent), and older relatives other than parents (16 percent). The living arrangements of these young men also varied over the period of parole supervision. Only 19 percent lived with their parents for their entire time on parole (see figure 7.5), whereas 24 percent never lived with a parent during their parole supervision. More than 55 percent moved in and out of a parental home during their parole period (figure 7.4). As discussed later in the chapter, living with family members may signal an important form of social support that aids reintegration by providing a stable foundation of material security. Conversely, never living with a parent or other family member may indicate a lack of social support following release.

Living arrangements after release did vary by race. More whites lived with their parents (59 percent) at their first residence after release than did blacks (47 percent). In contrast, the proportion of those living with other older adults or romantic partners in their first residence was higher for blacks than whites. Among blacks, 20 percent lived with an older family member and 16 percent lived with a romantic partner, while 13 percent of whites lived with an older family member and 8 percent lived with a spouse or romantic partner. If we consider the entire parole period, we see that more blacks had never lived with their parents (21 percent among whites versus 28 percent among blacks).

Neighborhoods

Contrary to conventional wisdom, few formerly incarcerated young adults return to the same addresses or neighborhoods where they lived before

Figure 7.4   Living Arrangements at the First Residence after Release

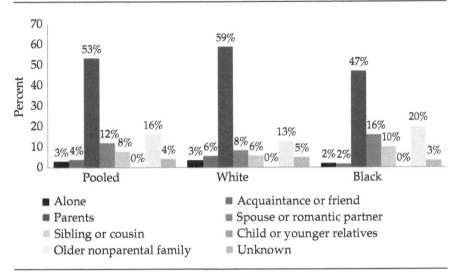

Source: Michigan Study of Life after Prison.

Figure 7.5   Percentage Living with Parents over the Entire Period of Parole

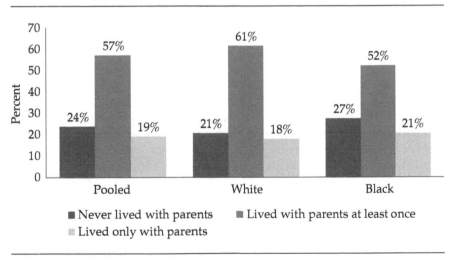

Source: Michigan Study of Life after Prison.
Note: 2003–2009 (various parole end dates).

Figure 7.6   Percentage Who Return to Pre-Prison Addresses
and Neighborhoods at Release

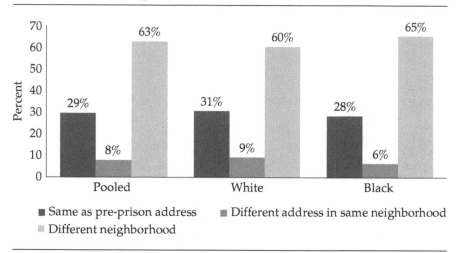

Source: Michigan Study of Life after Prison.

prison. Figure 7.6 shows that only 29 percent of our sample returned to the same address where they lived before prison. Among those who returned to a different home, only 11 percent returned to the same neighborhood where they lived before prison. In addition, the typical formerly incarcerated young man was exposed to disadvantaged neighborhood conditions during the entire period of parole supervision. The young men in our study lived in neighborhoods with relatively high rates of unemployment, poverty, and residential instability.

However, neighborhood conditions varied dramatically by race, reflecting larger patterns of racial and economic segregation.[8] Formerly incarcerated black young men tended to live in predominantly black neighborhoods (mean percent black = 58 percent), whereas whites tended to live in neighborhoods with few black residents (mean percent black = 14 percent). The unemployment rates and poverty levels of the neighborhoods in which blacks lived were also higher than those of the whites' neighborhoods (11 percent unemployment rate and 23 percent poverty rate for black neighborhoods; 7 percent unemployment rate and 14 percent poverty rate for white neighborhoods). The racial difference was less stark for neighborhood residential stability. The percentage of households that had been living in the same residence for at least one year was 70 percent for the typical young black man's neighborhood and only slightly higher at 73 percent for the typical young white man's neighborhood (see figure 7.7).

Figure 7.7   Average Characteristics of Neighborhoods
over the Observation Period

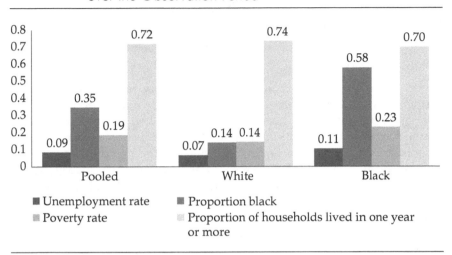

Source: Michigan Study of Life after Prison.
Note: 2003–2009 (various parole end dates).

In sum, this overview of residential stability shows very unstable residential conditions on multiple dimensions. The formerly incarcerated young men in our sample experienced frequent residential changes and often lived in institutional nonprivate residences, particularly criminal justice facilities; in addition, many lived in poor neighborhoods where they had not lived before their imprisonment. Such residential instability was particularly common in their first year after release. Residential instability differed by race. Blacks were less likely than whites to live with their parents but more likely to live with other older relatives. Two-thirds of blacks began their post-prison lives in a different neighborhood from where they lived before prison. Moreover, the neighborhoods that black young men moved to after release were highly disadvantaged.

POSSIBLE EXPLANATIONS FOR RESIDENTIAL INSTABILITY

Consistent with our findings on formerly incarcerated young men, residential instability among the formerly incarcerated has been reported in previous studies as well.[9] A permanent home is effectively a precondition for finding and maintaining employment and avoiding substance abuse and recidivism.[10] To understand how and why such residential instability occurs, we need to know its correlates or predictors. In this section, we discuss three factors that may contribute to residential instability: lack of social support, the intervention of the criminal justice system, and neighborhood conditions.

Social Support

Social support from family members is a primary resource upon which former prisoners rely when finding a place to live after prison.[11] Since they are very unlikely to have the resources to live alone upon release, young men's first residence after prison largely depends upon those who can offer them housing or the financial support they need to live on their own. In prior research, Marta Nelson, Perry Deess, and Charlotte Allen interviewed subjects who were released from New York state prisons and found that their families' provision of housing support in the early period after release was strongly associated with a successful transition to post-prison life.[12] Other studies have also found that formerly incarcerated individuals without long-term family support were more likely to reoffend and have drug abuse problems.[13]

Since the vast majority of the young men in our study had never been married at the time of their 2003 release (96 percent), parents were likely to be their primary providers of resources. As suggested in the life-course literature, young adults receive resources mostly from their parents, who may provide a place to live, financial assistance in the form of rent if their child is living elsewhere, and other social and emotional support.[14]

In addition to parental support, formerly incarcerated young men may also come to rely on others. However, the influence of nonparental relationships may depend on the nature of these relationships. For example, past research has found that a strong bond with a romantic partner or spouse inhibits heavy drinking and drug use and reduces the potential influence of deviant peers,[15] but also that strong bonds with those who abuse substances increase the risk of substance abuse.[16] In addition, sexual activity outside of committed relationships has been found to be associated with greater involvement in criminal behaviors.[17] A few studies have examined the influence of children on their parent's criminal behaviors. Some have shown that living with children may encourage formerly incarcerated young adults to adopt social roles as parents and motivate them to maintain responsibility for their children.[18] Others find evidence, however, that shouldering such responsibility with access to only minimal resources may increase the risk of reoffending due to stress and material need.[19]

As with nonparental kin relationships, friendships are also important sources of social support, but their relationship to housing stability specifically and reintegration more generally is unclear. Friends may provide formerly incarcerated young adults with stable places to live and help deter their future involvement in crime by exerting social control and providing emotional support. Yet renewed associations with friends may also return formerly incarcerated young adults to peer groups that contributed to their initial incarceration and may foster deviant behavior (such as drug use) that can lead to eviction and housing instability.

Custodial Sanctions

Those who are under parole supervision are bound by a set of rules. Violations of those rules can be punished with return to prison or temporary detention in another criminal justice facility, such as a county jail, a treatment program, or a specialized facility for parole violators. These punishments are often called "custodial sanctions" to differentiate them from other possible sanctions, such as an increase in supervision intensity or a verbal or written warning. Violation behavior can include, for example, minor illegal behaviors such as drug use or petty theft, breaking curfew, alcohol consumption, or failing to report to one's parole officer. Custodial sanctions are commonly used in Michigan as an alternative to reimprisonment and are understood by parole authorities as a tool to prevent parolees from escalating to more serious crime.[20] Research on custodial sanctions for parole violations is limited but shows that these sanctions result in a substantial number of individuals being removed from their current residences and sent to jails or treatment facilities.[21] To put this in a broader perspective, about 41 percent of the parole population nationwide were returned to prison in 2002 because they committed a technical violation of their parole or committed a new crime.[22]

Although intended to facilitate former inmates' reintroduction to the community, parole supervision can also be viewed as a means of extending punishment and managing a parolee's behavior.[23] Relative to the rate of reimprisonment for new crimes, the revocation rate due to technical violations of parole has dramatically increased since the 1980s. Jeremy Travis suspects that parole supervision does more to control crime than to reintegrate the formerly incarcerated into their communities, since it removes them from the community as punishment not only for committing new crimes but also for technical violations of the terms of their parole.[24] Additional punitive aspects of parole supervision's reliance on custodial sanctions include disruption to a parolee's livelihood or education and separation from family and friendship networks. And obviously, temporary detention in a criminal facility disrupts residential stability. Thus, spending time in criminal justice facilities, jails, or treatment programs may be strongly associated with the risk of residential instability for formerly incarcerated young adults.[25]

Neighborhood Context

In addition to social support and criminal justice system intervention through custodial sanctions, neighborhood contexts also play a role in prisoner reintegration. Those returning from prison are typically concentrated in a small number of highly disadvantaged neighborhoods.[26] For example, James Lynch and William Sabol found that half of parolees in New York City lived in a few blocks in Brooklyn that were home to only 11 percent of Brooklyn's population.[27] High concentrations of formerly incarcerated individuals in a neighborhood are associated with the breakdown of social cohesion, trust, and informal social control,[28] along with intense supervision by the criminal justice system that may also ensnare other residents.[29]

Neighborhood researchers typically see neighborhoods as disadvantaged when their rates of poverty, residential instability, and concentrated minority populations are high.[30] These characteristics in turn are thought to lead to the breakdown of social cohesion and trust, meaning that such neighborhoods suffer from a lack of informal social support and control.[31] For example, Robert Sampson, Stephen Raudenbush, and Felton Earls argue that neighborhood collective efficacy—the extent to which residents are willing to intervene in the neighborhood for the safety and collective good of the community—reflects levels of mutual trust and shared expectations among neighbors.[32] With regard to crime, a consistent finding is that the rate of crime and delinquency is disproportionately high in neighborhoods with low social cohesion and weakened informal social control.[33]

A counterpart to informal social control is the formal social control exercised by criminal justice actors. Community corrections officers and police are likely to be a more common presence in poor neighborhoods.[34] Prior research suggests that police practices vary considerably across neighborhoods, in such a way that "disadvantaged areas are both overpoliced and underpoliced."[35] On the one hand, poor and nonwhite jurisdictions tend to have less police protection per recorded crime.[36] On the other hand, in more disadvantaged, higher-crime neighborhoods, police are more likely to arrest residents they encounter and to use coercive force and are less likely to provide citizens with assistance and information or to file incident reports.[37] Although we are not aware of any research that examines whether this also applies to community corrections officers, we might hypothesize that similar dynamics are at work with regard to community supervision like parole and probation. If so, that would suggest that former prisoners in impoverished neighborhoods may be subject to greater surveillance and arrest for minor offenses. For parolees, this may directly impact their residential mobility through custodial sanctions for parole violations. Moreover, intense supervision by community corrections officers or police in poor neighborhoods may indirectly encourage individuals on parole to abscond, which can also generate residential instability.

Given that many former prisoners return to disadvantaged and socially disorganized neighborhoods where informal social support and controls are weakened and criminal justice supervision is intense, we expect that formerly incarcerated young men in disadvantaged neighborhoods will more frequently change their residence compared with others who live in relatively less disadvantaged neighborhoods.

Racial Differences in Social Supports, Custodial Sanctions, and Neighborhood Conditions

The challenges faced by formerly incarcerated young men are not likely to be equally distributed across racial groups. Incarceration has become more common in the lives of African American men, particularly those without a high school education.[38] Black men are six times more likely than white men to be arrested and to spend some time in prison during their lives.[39] This concentration of prison time among young black men is also reflected in our sample. Although black young men ages seventeen to twenty-five constituted 47 percent of our sample, only 15 percent of the overall population of that age living in Michigan in 2003 were black.[40]

The disproportionate imprisonment of blacks has been linked with a high rate of family disruption in the black population. According to the U.S. Department of Justice, black children are about nine times more likely than white children to lose a parent to prison.[41] Nonresidential parents or a lack of support from parents may increase young people's likelihood of involvement in crime, and their post-prison life and transition to adulthood may be negatively affected by the lack of continuous parental support. If fewer formerly incarcerated black young men had parents who could provide social support, living with their parents after being released from prison may have had a less positive impact on residential stability among blacks than it did for whites in our sample. Intermediate sanctions by the criminal justice system may also vary between blacks and whites. The criminal justice system tends to treat minority populations more harshly, so its effects on black residential stability may be stronger. Furthermore, black prisoners disproportionately come from disadvantaged neighborhoods to begin with and are more likely to return to such neighborhoods after release.[42] Thus, the consequences of parental support, intervention by the criminal justice system, and neighborhood contexts for residential stability may be different between blacks and whites.

Residential Stability, the Life Course, and the Transition to Adulthood

Formerly incarcerated young adults face a dual transition. The first is their transition from prison to the community, and the second is their transition from adolescence to adulthood. In addition to reestablishing their lives in the community, formerly incarcerated young adults who spent part of their early adulthood in prison often struggle to catch up on key milestones in the transition to adulthood, including completing their education or entering the labor market. Since these life events are also linked to residential mobility, we need to carefully consider them as predictors of residential instability.

Among formerly incarcerated young adults, changing residences may be understood in two different ways. On the one hand, a residential change for an individual who gets a job or enrolls in college can be interpreted as a positive event, just as it would be interpreted for the general population at the same stage of life. In the life-course literature, the residential mobility rate of young adults is shown to peak during the early twenties. For example, 30 percent of twenty- to twenty-four-year-olds in the U.S. population in 2003 had moved into their current residence in the prior year.[43] Similarly, life transition events after release from prison may be a signal that one's livelihood has become more secure and residential stability may therefore be less likely to be disrupted by undesirable situations, such as reinvolvement in crime, drug abuse, or technical violations of parole. For example, receiving high monthly wages from a stable job implies that an individual has enough resources to maintain a residence. Meanwhile, employment may indirectly serve as evidence that a formerly incarcerated young adult is reintegrating into community life. Parole agents may be less likely to impose custodial sanctions on an individual who seems to be succeeding in the labor market. It may be that formal life transition events such as resuming schooling or entering the labor market sometimes require a change of residence. Yet such life transition events should contribute to reduced residential change and greater residential stability in the long run.[44]

PREDICTORS OF RESIDENTIAL MOVES AND LONG-TERM RESIDENTIAL STABILITY

We examine the residential stability of formerly incarcerated young men in two ways. First, we test who is at greatest risk of moving to another private or nonprivate residence and why.[45] In the second part of the analysis, we shift the focus from residential moves to achieving residential stability by examining who *stays* in a private residence for at least one year (our measure of residential stability).[46] In both analyses, we focus on the influence of parental social support, custodial sanctions, neighborhood contexts, and transition-to-adulthood events.

Does Social Support Reduce the Risk of Moving?

The residential conditions of formerly incarcerated young adults depend heavily on their social relationships and on who can offer them a place to live or other support to find and maintain a home.[47] Figures 7.8 and 7.9 show the weekly probability of moving to a new private or a nonprivate (institutional) residence. Living with a parent or older relative reduced the risk of moving among both blacks and whites.[48] Compared to living with a parent or older relative, living with one's own children, other young people, or alone is associated with a 32 percent increase in the probability of moving to a different private residence among whites and a 62 percent increase among blacks.[49] Whites who lived with a romantic partner had a greater probability of moving to a different private residence than those who lived with their parents or with older relatives. Whites who lived with a romantic partner were about one-sixth more likely to move. In general, these significant differences suggest that the support of parents and older relatives protected these young men from the risk of frequent moving during the turbulent period after prison release.[50]

With regard to yearlong residential stability, formerly incarcerated young men who lived with a parent had the highest probability of remaining in the same residence for a year (figure 7.10). This is yet another result suggesting that parents and older relatives serve as a core anchor in maintaining a stable residence. The importance of living with a parent or older relative does not differ by race.

Custodial Intermediate Sanctions and Residential Mobility

Individuals on parole can be temporarily sent to criminal justice institutions, such as jails or treatment facilities, when they violate the conditions of their parole or are involved in minor crimes that would not ordinarily result in incarceration for someone not on parole or probation. Temporary custody may not only disrupt the parolee's current living arrangement but also affect his future residential instability. Our estimates show that individuals who previously resided in a criminal justice facility or treatment institution (after their focal prison stay) were more likely to move (or be moved) into such a facility again rather than stay in their current private residence.

Figure 7.8 Differences in the Weekly Probability of Moving to a New Private Residence, by Individual and Neighborhood Characteristics

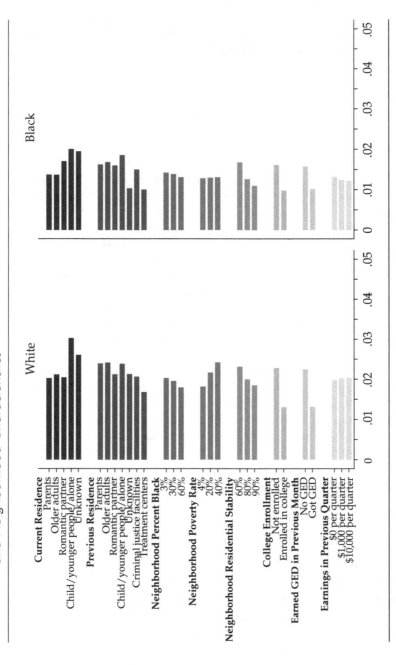

Source: Michigan Study of Life after Prison.
Note: 2003–2009 (various parole end dates).

Figure 7.9 Differences in the Weekly Probability of Moving to a Nonprivate Residence, by Individual and Neighborhood Characteristics

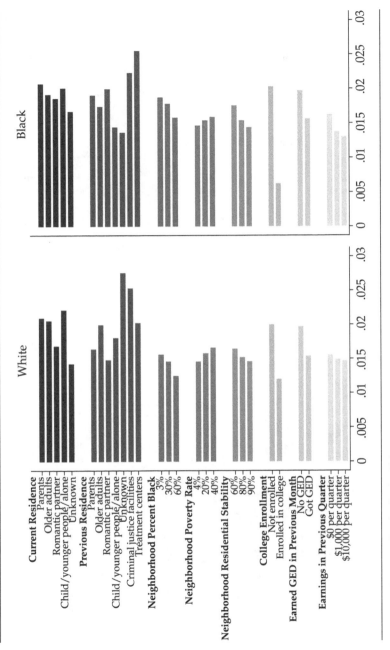

Source: Michigan Study of Life after Prison.
Note: 2003–2009 (various parole end dates).

Figure 7.10 Differences in the Weekly Probability of Attaining Residential Stability, by Individual and Neighborhood Characteristics

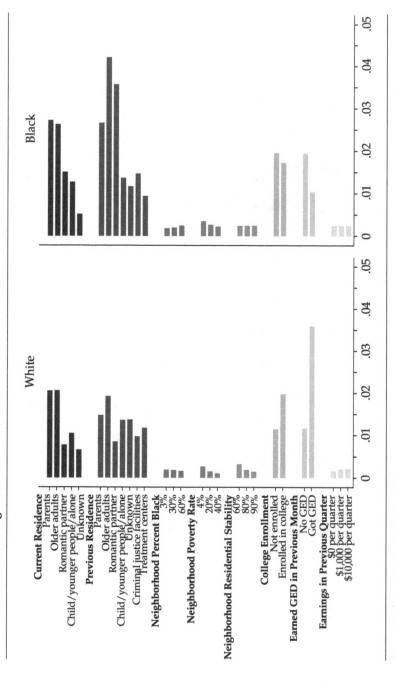

Source: Michigan Study of Life after Prison.
Note: 2003–2009 (various parole end dates).

Among those who were previously detained in a criminal justice facility, the yearly probability of a move into a nonprivate residence was higher by 0.49 among blacks and by 0.21 among whites (table 7.A6). The probability of a move to a nonprivate residence among those who were previously in a treatment facility was 0.22 among blacks and 0.40 among whites.

Experiencing intermediate sanctions in the past is also associated with a lower probability of achieving long-term stability, though only among whites. When they were temporarily detained in criminal justice facilities before living in their current residence, whites experienced a reduction in the yearly probability of achieving residential stability of 0.14. Similarly, white men who had previously lived in a treatment facility experienced a reduction of 0.19. These results imply that the temporary disruption caused by an intermediate sanction may negatively impact future residential stability. However, the results may also reflect the problems that prompted the sanction in the first place.

Neighborhoods and Residential Instability

Neighborhood context is also related to the risk of residential moves. Living in a neighborhood where one's neighbors are more residentially stable (as measured by the proportion who have lived in the neighborhood for at least a year) is associated with a lower probability of moving into another private residence or nonprivate housing. For example, whites who lived in a neighborhood where 60 percent of the residents had lived in their homes for more than one year had a 2.3 percent weekly risk of moving to another private home, whereas those who lived in a neighborhood with 90 percent residential stability had only a 1.8 percent weekly risk of moving. The residential stability of their neighbors also reduced the risk of moving among blacks. In addition, our results show that residentially stable neighborhoods were associated with a greater likelihood of discharge from parole supervision and a lower likelihood of absconding (see tables 7.A8 and 7.A9). This result indicates that a residentially stable neighborhood may play a protective role among formerly incarcerated young men by offering more informal social controls and social supports.

We also find that those who lived in black neighborhoods were more likely to abscond, and that blacks who lived in black neighborhoods were less likely to be discharged (see tables 7.A8 and 7.A9). These results could reflect an overburdened criminal justice system in Michigan's central city neighborhoods, particularly in Detroit, where most black neighborhoods and black parolees are concentrated. In the yearlong residential stability analysis, only neighborhood poverty significantly predicts achieving residential stability, and only among blacks. A ten-percentage-point increase in individuals living below the poverty line is associated with a reduction of 0.025 in the yearly probability of achieving residential stability, a fairly small association.

Life Events and Residential Stability

Finally, we also examined the association between other transition-to-adulthood domains and residential instability. Blacks who had earnings in the previous quarter were more likely to move to another private residence. Given the typically poor neighborhood conditions experienced by blacks in our study, this could reflect movement to a better neighborhood when resources allowed. As for whites, earnings were important to achieving one-year residential stability, although the magnitude of this association was fairly small. Earning a GED was associated with lower residential mobility among blacks, and being enrolled in college was associated with lower residential mobility among both blacks and whites. These educational accomplishments may be not so much a cause of residential stability as a reflection of the opportunities afforded by a stable residential arrangement.

CONCLUSION

Establishing a stable residence upon release from prison is one of the fundamental preconditions for successful reentry and reintegration and an important marker of and foundation for the transition to adulthood. Although many studies have found that residential insecurity is an important predictor of other outcomes, such as recidivism, the factors that affect the residential insecurity of parolees have attracted less attention. In this chapter, we described several aspects of the residential conditions of formerly incarcerated young men and examined the role of social support, criminal justice sanctions, and neighborhood conditions in their residential moves and longer-term residential stability. We came to five key conclusions regarding the residential instability of formerly incarcerated young adults.

First, like Shane, the young man we introduced at the beginning of this chapter, formerly incarcerated young men suffer from high rates of residential instability. While on parole, they experienced more than four residential moves on average. Considering that the average duration of parole supervision in our data was about one and a half years (eighty weeks), this indicates an average of three residential changes per year—a rate higher than in other high-risk populations.[51] Also, this residential insecurity was highly concentrated in the first year following release. At the same time, however, 90 percent of all stable residences—staying in the same private residence for at least a year—were established during the first year following release from prison. Although the first year after release may be turbulent, it is also a critically important period when it comes to settling down in a stable home.

Second, social support from parents and older relatives provides a significant buffer that can protect against residential instability. Among both blacks and whites, living with parents and older relatives reduced mobility and increased the chances of achieving longer-term stability compared to living alone, with one's own children, with younger relatives, or with others. Clearly, parents are a critical form of social support for formerly incarcerated young men. As Shane's experience illustrates, however, social support from parents and romantic partners does not guarantee ongoing residential stability, particularly in the face of ongoing involvement with the criminal justice system.

Third, custodial sanctions imposed by the criminal justice system play a role in residential instability. Almost 38 percent of all spells in private residences ended when a parolee was detained in jail or ordered to a treatment facility. In addition, previously experiencing a custodial intermediate sanction increased the risk of future moves to nonprivate residences. Those whose prior residential events included being detained in a detention facility or treatment institution were more likely to move out of their current residence and into another nonprivate residence. This result implies that intermediate sanctions not only temporarily disrupt residential stability but are also associated with future residential instability.

Fourth, poor and residentially unstable neighborhoods may predict greater residential turnover and a lower probability of achieving a year-long stable residence. One interpretation of this finding is that negative outcomes in some domains (including residential insecurity) are attributable to the lack of informal social control and low social cohesion in poor neighborhoods. The association between disadvantaged neighborhood conditions and the residential instability of formerly incarcerated young men may also be a consequence of the concentration of formal surveillance by the criminal justice system in impoverished neighborhoods, or the poor housing conditions and generally high residential turnover commonly found there.

Lastly, life events such as earning money from work, getting a GED, and enrolling in college are also associated with residential stability, although again, we caution that our associational analysis is unable to convincingly demonstrate causal effects. Enrollment in college in the previous month was significantly associated with a young man's greater probability of remaining in his current residence instead of moving to another private or nonprivate residence. Among blacks, earning a GED lowered residential instability. Higher earnings in the prior calendar quarter were associated with a greater chance of achieving long-term residential stability, although only among whites.

These results suggest that residential stability and other aspects of the transition to adulthood are closely intertwined. In the next chapter, we explore in greater detail the interconnections between outcomes in various life domains and how they combine to generate trajectories during the transition to adulthood after prison.

Chapter 8 | Transition-to-Adulthood Trajectories

THE LIFE-COURSE FRAMEWORK that has guided our study emphasizes the role of critical life transitions in setting the stage for future long-term trajectories. Recall from the introduction that trajectories are long-term patterns, or sequences of behaviors or outcomes. One person's labor market trajectory may involve attending college after high school, entering the labor market after college, and holding a series of jobs with increasing responsibility, autonomy, and compensation, culminating in retirement; another individual's trajectory may involve school dropout followed by intermittent and unstable employment interspersed with criminal ventures and custody in the criminal justice system. We can conceptualize life trajectories as domain-specific (employment, housing, health, and so on), and a particular life trajectory as built up from sets of interrelated domain-specific trajectories.

Transitions are key life events—such as school completion, prison release, marriage, or parenthood—that form the building blocks of life trajectories. Transitions can also shift trajectories over the long term. The previous five chapters of this book examined specific events or transitions in detail and in relation to other events, including earning a GED, enrolling in college, substance use and violence, finding and losing employment, and achieving residential stability. From those chapters we learned how often these events or transitions occurred for formerly incarcerated young men and what early life, in-prison, and post-release experiences were most predictive of these events or transitions. We are now positioned to understand how various life events and transitions are linked together in longer-term life trajectories.

In this chapter, we examine outcome trajectories over time. This will show us how specific events or transitions are patterned over time (the domain-specific trajectories), and how various trajectories in different domains are

175

related to one another, allowing us to answer a number of the important research questions that motivated this study. First, what are the various domain-specific trajectories that formerly incarcerated young men experience after their release from prison? To answer this question, we examine criminal justice system involvement, substance use, postsecondary enrollment, employment, and residential stability. (GED attainment is too rare after release to include in these analyses.) Second, how are these domain-specific trajectories linked together to form larger life trajectories? To answer this question, we identify patterns of domain-specific trajectories that commonly co-occur, allowing us to describe distinct compound trajectory groups in the data as well as the domain-specific trajectories on which they are built. Third, which young men experience each of these compound trajectories, and what prior experiences are most salient in sorting individuals into these trajectory groups? To answer this question we examine the association between various demographic characteristics as well as pre-prison, in-prison, and post-prison experiences and the cross-domain trajectories. We do so by employing group-based multi-trajectory models, a statistical method that extracts from the data groups with similar trajectories in domain-specific outcomes.[1]

GROUP-BASED MULTI-TRAJECTORY MODELS

Both the life-course and transition-to-adulthood frameworks emphasize the importance of examining trajectories rather than point-in-time measures to more completely understand outcomes. Single point-in-time outcomes may poorly summarize post-release experiences, particularly if those experiences evolve in fits and starts as individuals wrestle with the joint processes of reintegration and desistance.[2] Moreover, point-in-time measures, even if measured at many time points, may not fully capture the divergence in trends across individuals because the measures are "noisy," meaning that they neither entirely capture the construct of interest nor capture only the construct of interest. Many noisy measurements captured over time and compared between individuals can create a more accurate representation of the underlying construct than a single point-in-time measure.[3] From a policy perspective, overemphasizing point-in-time measures or specific achievements can lead to development of incentives (goals and metrics) that, divorced from context, no longer correlate with holistic, successful life-course development.

Furthermore, a persistent methodological shortcoming of the transition-to-adulthood literature has been its inability to consider more than one transitional outcome at a time or to consider the relationships between more than two outcomes at a time.[4] Without the ability to consider adult transitions in their entirety, it is impossible to capture the interrelationships between experiences in multiple domains. Meanwhile, the criminological literature has been hampered by its lack of attention to the totality of interactions with the criminal justice system when predicting life-course outcomes. Group-based multi-trajectory models overcome these limitations, providing a tool to examine both trajectories of specific outcomes over time and to consider multiple outcome trajectories simultaneously.[5]

Consistent with the life-course and transition-to-adulthood frameworks, we group and describe post-prison trajectories with a recent extension to group-based trajectory modeling (GBTM) called group-based multi-trajectory modeling (GBMTM). GBTM was developed to study the life-course development of criminal justice–involved individuals like those in our sample.[6] In identifying "latent" groups of individuals who follow similar outcome trajectories, the models produce three pieces of information: the number of groups that best describe the data; a description of the average trajectory for each group; and an estimate of the probability that each person belongs to each group.[7]

We use GBMTM to model the transition-to-adulthood process, for which we have indicators of transitional marker achievement in five domains: education, employment, justice system involvement, residential stability, and substance use. We examine how the achievement of each transitional marker relates to the achievement of the other markers. The software models each of the outcome trajectories separately and in conjunction with each other to produce multi-trajectory groups that characterize the post-prison life-course outcomes of the young men in our sample, beginning at prison release and following them at six-month intervals through the last observation year for each marker.

After identifying and describing the post-prison transition-to-adulthood trajectories, we examine the characteristics of the members of each multi-trajectory group to determine which individuals cluster differentially into trajectory groups. The post-prison trajectory groups then become our dependent variables in a series of multinomial logit models. These models allow us to examine which individual characteristics and pre-prison and in-prison experiences are associated with membership in each trajectory group.[8]

Domain-Specific Outcome Measures

We focus on five post-release transitional marker outcomes: residential independence, formal labor market participation, college enrollment, substance use, and criminal justice system contact. Similar to the definition used in chapter 7, residential independence, recorded by parole agents, is defined as living outside of an institution and apart from parents or older relatives. Employment in the formal labor market is measured using quarterly unemployment insurance records from 1997 to 2010, as in chapter 6. Educational attainment is measured as it is in chapter 4—as enrollment in a postsecondary educational institution, whether or not for a degree program. We have created six-month (half-year) indicators for each outcome. We follow postsecondary enrollments for ten years after prison, whereas we follow residential independence and employment for only five post-prison years.

For criminal justice–involved young people, desisting from crime is viewed as critical to transitioning to adulthood.[9] To examine desistance, we also created indicators of a lack of continued criminal justice contact by measuring the post-prison half years during which the young men were neither arrested nor incarcerated. We follow arrests and incarcerations for seven years after release. Finally, we also track substance use as measured by drug and alcohol screening tests administered by parole agents while our subjects were on parole supervision (a variable amount of time that differed across subjects but did not extend beyond 2011; see chapter 5). For consistency with other measures, we code our substance abuse variable so that it reflects the absence of positive substance use tests.

Key Predictors of Group Membership

Consistent with prior chapters, we focus on measurable explanations for group membership related to prior criminal justice involvement, history of substance abuse, demographic characteristics (particularly race), social contexts, social supports, and institutional attachments and entanglements. This chapter's indicators of juvenile justice system contact include age at first arrest and commitment as a juvenile. We use complete arrest, conviction, and punishment records, which allow us to account for and examine which criminal justice system contacts determined eventual incarceration.[10] Human capital indicators include measures of the progress each young man had made in his adult transition before prison: whether he had finished high school, earned a GED, ever held a job, or lived independently. We also have pre-prison indicators of parenthood and marriage. Health measures include self-reported mental illness and self-reported daily substance use before imprisonment.

With regard to social context, we observe the neighborhood (census tract) characteristics of each young man's first post-prison neighborhood. Because many neighborhood metrics are highly correlated, we created standardized, orthogonal neighborhood disadvantage and advantage scores.

As described in chapter 2, the disadvantage score captures percent black, median family income, poverty and unemployment rates, the proportion of residents with less than a high school degree, and the percentage of households that received public assistance and were female-headed. The affluence score captures the percentage of people who had jobs in managerial professions and college degrees, the proportion of families whose income exceeded $75,000, and the median income. We also control for county crime rates.

Finally, we examine prison experiences during the focal prison spell. We include months in prison, number of misconduct violations, and number of days spent in solitary confinement, which may exacerbate mental illness and substance use.[11] We also determine for each young man whether he earned a GED while imprisoned.

TRAJECTORY GROUPS AMONG FORMERLY INCARCERATED YOUNG MEN

The GBMTM model produced five latent trajectory groups.[12] We named the trajectories to highlight the key differences between them, not to comprehensively summarize the experiences of the young men who followed each trajectory across all five domains. These groups are displayed in figure 8.1. The columns are the groups, with the column heading showing the name we have given to the group and the percentage of individuals who fall into the group. There is one row for each of the five transitional marker variables that inform the trajectory analysis. The graphs in each cell of the grid show the average trajectory over time among the members of the group for the variable in question. For example, the graph in the top left corner shows the average probability of being enrolled in post-secondary education over time since release for those individuals who were in the "persisting" group.

The time scale on the x-axis of each graph is half years, or six-month intervals (in other words, the number 20 on the x-axis corresponds to twenty half years, or ten years). Note also that all the variables in the rows are coded so that higher values are better from the perspective of the transition to adulthood (being enrolled in college, living independently, being employed, avoiding arrest or custody, and having no positive drug test). It is also worth noting that there could be many possible multi-trajectory groups, since we are trying to summarize the coevolution of outcomes in five different domains. However, the fact that there are only five groups means that the statistical model has done a fairly efficient job of summarizing very complex data.

Figure 8.1   Group-Based Multi-Trajectory Model Results: Five Groups on Different Post-Prison Pathways

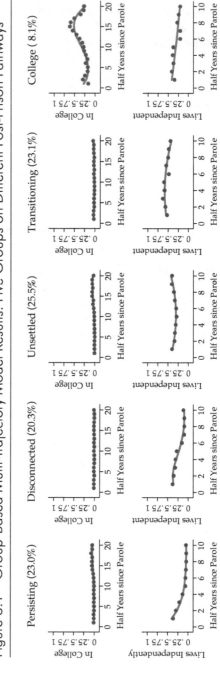

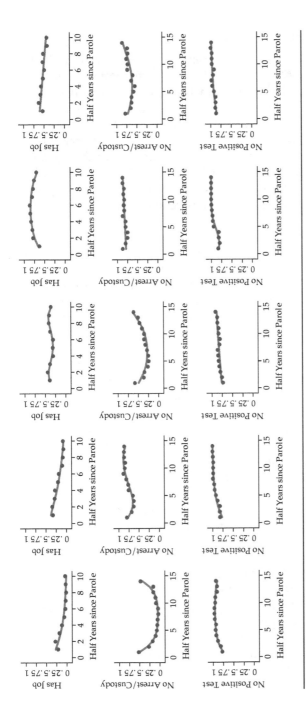

Source: Michigan Study of Life after Prison.

The Transitioning Group

We begin with the group we call "transitioning," which includes almost one-quarter of the sample (23 percent). Relative to the young men who followed other trajectories, individuals in this group most consistently met a majority of the adulthood markers. "Transitioners" were unlikely to attend college. However, they maintained a high probability of employment (approximately 75 percent or greater) and a moderate probability of living independently (approximately 50 percent or greater), although their ability to maintain their independence declined over time. Additionally, these young men were increasingly likely to avoid arrest and incarceration during follow-up and increasingly likely to avoid positive substance use tests.

We interpret the existence of this sizable group as grounds for both optimism and pessimism. On the one hand, that almost one-quarter of our sample experienced some measure of persistent success in the labor market while avoiding the traps of substance use and further criminal justice involvement suggests that many formerly incarcerated young men can successfully reenter and reintegrate with society. On the other hand, at less than one-quarter of the sample, this group is far smaller than we would like; in fact, the vast majority of the young men in our sample were experiencing considerable challenges in transitioning to adulthood. Moreover, the absence of a strong link between labor market success, as measured by steady employment, and residential independence is also cause for concern. The employment that these young men were able to obtain did not provide an economic foundation strong enough to enable them to build stable lives on their own. This is consistent with the findings from chapter 6 on the challenges encountered by formerly incarcerated young men in maintaining long-term, stable employment at a living wage.

We can develop a better understanding of the experiences of the young men in the transitioning group by examining a few of their lives in greater detail. Luke, whom we met in the first chapter of this book, was one of the transitioners.[13] Recall that Luke dropped out of high school and was placed on probation on a home invasion charge. At first he did well: he earned a GED and worked in a series of short-term jobs in retail and temporary labor. Then a probation violation led to his imprisonment. Following his release, Luke moved in with an uncle and started a long-term relationship with a girlfriend. The couple stayed together through the end of our follow-up, and through multiple residential moves. Although Luke never returned to school and did continue to use drugs, he worked a series of increasingly better-paying and more stable jobs, from temporary labor positions and short-term manufacturing positions to a more stable job in metal manufacturing; he eventually found a long-term stable career in the fitness industry. He was discharged from parole three years after it began and experienced no further contact with the criminal justice system.

Another young man on the transitioning trajectory was Jared, a young white man who was born in the early 1980s. He first interacted with the juvenile justice system at age fourteen and was placed on probation twice as a juvenile. Growing up, Jared attended two high schools in his hometown, a small city in the middle of Michigan, but he graduated from neither. He earned a GED at nineteen after taking preparation courses at a nearby community college.

Prior to and after he earned his GED, Jared struggled to gain a footing in the labor market. At age seventeen, he landed his first job in the formal labor market, in a retail store, and earned about $1,500 in his first calendar quarter of work. During the same quarter, he earned another $300 at a second job, which he continued working in the following quarter, earning about $600.[14] Jared was unemployed for about a year beginning in early 1998. Toward the end of the year, he worked very briefly at a restaurant, earning just $175 in the calendar quarter. During that quarter, Jared was arrested for the first time as an adult, at age eighteen. He was arrested on two charges—breaking and entering and receiving stolen property—and was sentenced to probation. He was also ordered to get substance abuse treatment—our only indicator that Jared may have been using drugs or alcohol.

In the spring of 1999, Jared again found work at a local business. He worked there during two calendar quarters, earning about $650 in the first and $120 in the second, after which he found a higher-paying job in construction. He worked for one quarter in that job, earning about $1,500. Jared was then unemployed, and early in 2000 he was arrested again—this time for breaking into a car. Jared remained on probation after the car break-in, but special conditions were applied; he was placed on electronic monitoring in lieu of jail after the adjudication of the case in late 2000. Jared was not arrested again until the summer of 2001, when he was charged once again with felony breaking and entering, but this time with an additional felony charge of safe breaking. Jared was then sentenced to a minimum of two years in state prison.

At the time of his imprisonment, Jared had no children, was not married, and reported no mental illness or substance use. He was living with his mother in a condominium complex in a suburban community near his hometown, which was almost exclusively white. The poverty and unemployment rates were relatively low. Jared served the bulk of his sentence in a minimum-security facility about a day's drive from home. He served over three-quarters of his twenty-four-month sentence. About one year into that sentence, he was charged with his only misconduct—for possessing dangerous contraband—and he spent three days in solitary confinement.

Jared was released onto minimum parole supervision in the summer of 2003. He was not drug-tested while on parole but passed all his tests while incarcerated. After prison, Jared again lived with his mother. About five months after he was released, he moved in with a girlfriend in a nearby city. About fourteen months later, Jared and his girlfriend moved back to the city where his mother lived. They stayed there for another six months— until Jared was discharged from parole in early 2005. Through 2010, Jared had no further interactions with the criminal justice system.

During the follow-up period, Jared never returned to school. Although he was consistently employed, with one exception he did not stay with the same employer for more than a year. Jared earned higher wages than other men in our sample. About six months after he was released, he landed his first post-prison job at an auto detailing shop. He worked there until mid-2004, earning about $5,500 during each of three quarters. Then he worked at a car wash for not quite a year, during which time he earned just under $13,000. After he stopped working at the car wash, Jared worked a temp job, earning $6,100 in just one quarter. That was followed by work at an auto parts manufacturer for six months, during which he earned about $7,500. Then he returned to working for the temporary services agencies, earning about $8,100 over three quarters. When he was twenty-seven, Jared landed a metalworking job, which he held for about eighteen months—his longest stretch at any single employer— and in which he earned about $35,000. Although Jared struggled to maintain the same job over time, he generally seemed able to find jobs that afforded him middle-class earnings.

The Continuing Education Group

About 8 percent of the young men in our sample fell into the "continuing education" trajectory group. They were distinct from the other groups in their increasing likelihood of enrollment in postsecondary education. Like the transitioners, these young men increasingly avoided contact with the criminal justice system and avoided substance use. However, they struggled to meet the other markers of adulthood. Their initially moderate probability of employment and potential for independence diminished over time. Finding it increasingly hard to find employment five years after release may have motivated their continuing education, which peaked a few years later. That these young men had the means to enroll in postsecondary education despite meager earnings suggests that they relied heavily on social support from parents or older relatives, who were probably less disadvantaged than the parents and older relatives of the young men on other trajectories.

The experiences of this group also suggest the possibility of multiple pathways to adulthood after prison. Some of those who struggled to maintain employment in the labor market after prison could instead further their education to improve their skills. This is consistent with prior research showing that young adults from working-class and poor backgrounds who are not able to secure living-wage jobs in the skilled trades often return to school later in life.[15] This pathway is more commonly taken by blacks than whites, owing to the challenges that blacks face in securing jobs in the skilled trades. Enrollment in postsecondary education may also provide an alternative, albeit short-term, source of income in the form of financial aid stipends for living expenses.[16]

Edwin's story illustrates the struggles endured by many in the continuing education group before enrolling in college, including drug addiction, minor but persistent criminal justice contact, and residential and relationship instability. Edwin, a young black man born in the early 1980s, was arrested only once as a juvenile, at age sixteen, and received neither juvenile probation nor juvenile detention. He dropped out of high school in the eleventh grade. Around that time, at age seventeen, he became involved with the adult criminal justice system. Edwin was arrested twice within the span of a few months, first for misdemeanor destruction of property, and the second time for felony assault with a dangerous weapon. As part of a plea deal, the assault charge was dismissed, and he received a two-year probation sentence for the destruction of property charge. Shortly after his second arrest, Edwin started his first job in the formal labor market, working as a janitor in the Grand Rapids area, but lasted only one or two days. He would not work in the formal labor market again until after his release from prison in 2003.

Unfortunately, Edwin did not meet the conditions of his probation. He was arrested several times in 2000—every time for felony drug charges. Those charges resulted in short jail sentences ranging from two weeks to four months and the suspension of his driver's license for six months (because some of the charges were related to transporting narcotics). Edwin was not arrested during the following year, a year marked instead by a success: he returned to school and earned a GED. Yet he was arrested again on a felony drug charge in mid-2002. This time he was sentenced to a minimum of one year in state prison. At the time of his imprisonment, Edwin reported no mental illness or substance use, but he had at least one dependent child. He would father more children over the next few years.

Prior to his state prison sentence, Edwin was living with his mother in Grand Rapids, the county seat of Kent County in western Michigan, and the second most populous city in Michigan, behind Detroit. Grand Rapids is a majority-white city, but the neighborhood where Edwin grew up was majority-minority. Crime, unemployment, and poverty rates were higher on average in that neighborhood than in the rest of Grand Rapids, but the neighborhood where Edwin grew up was not considered poor and the unemployment rate was relatively low. Upon entering the prison system, Edwin reported no mental health problems or substance use of any kind. However, his arrest and parole histories indicate that he used drugs consistently prior to and after being incarcerated. Edwin served most of his sentence in a single facility about one day's drive from his mother's home in Grand Rapids. He was incarcerated for seven and a half months. During that time, he was cited for just one misconduct violation, for which he spent two days in solitary confinement.

Edwin was initially paroled under medium supervision in early 2003, at which time he moved in with his girlfriend in Grand Rapids. Less than two weeks after he was released, he was arrested on a drug charge and returned to prison. He was released for the second time in the fall of 2003. His special conditions of parole included receiving substance abuse treatment, for which he was required to pay, and not working in a place where alcohol was served.

Although Edwin had family support and was able to find a job, he continued to struggle on parole. He moved back in with his mother but shuffled between her home and a community corrections center as punishment for technical rule violations. Throughout the fall of 2003, he would spend a few weeks with his mother, then a week at the corrections center. During that time, he was employed at an automobile repair shop, where he earned $1,100 during the quarter.

In the late fall of 2003, Edwin absconded from parole. For several months, his whereabouts were unknown. He ultimately was arrested on the absconding warrant and spent a few months in jail before being transferred to a TRV facility, where he remained for two months. After he was released in the summer of 2004, he returned to live with his mother. Within two months, Edwin had picked up another arrest, tested positive for drugs, and absconded again. He was jailed on the second warrant in the fall of 2004 and released back on parole and to his mother's home a month later.

For a time, Edwin seemed to stabilize in terms of housing, education, and employment. He enrolled in community college and remained enrolled part-time in each semester through the spring of 2006. Likewise, he continued to live with his mother through the beginning of 2006. In addition, he held several jobs throughout 2005. In the first half of 2005, he worked at a fast-food restaurant, earning about $600 in each quarter. In the third quarter of 2005, he worked a construction job, earning about $400. In the fourth quarter of 2005, he worked two jobs, first at a full-service restaurant and then at a store. In that quarter, he earned about $3,000.

However, Edwin also continued to consistently test positive for drugs during this time. Four of six drug tests he took in 2005 came back positive. In addition, he had a few minor run-ins with law enforcement during this period. He was arrested twice in mid-2005: first for drugs, then for a traffic violation. He served two weeks of a two-month jail sentence after the second arrest. In the winter of 2006, Edwin absconded again. A few months later, he turned himself in and was jailed for a month, then transferred to another TRV facility. Three months later, he was returned to state prison as a technical rule violator. He served almost three years in prison.

During this second prison term, Edwin was cited often for misconduct. He was cited for being "out of bounds," once in 2006 and again in early 2007. Then, in mid-2007, he was charged with possession of dangerous contraband; the resulting additional criminal conviction explains why he spent so much time in prison. Later in 2007, he was charged with four more misconducts, including theft. In 2008, he was cited for being out of bounds eight times. For each of those charges, he spent about a week in solitary confinement. In 2009, he spent about a month in solitary confinement for fighting.

Edwin was released from prison onto parole again in the spring of 2009. He moved in with his girlfriend, who lived in a town near Grand Rapids, for about two months before moving in with his grandparents in Grand Rapids. Throughout 2009, all of Edwin's drug tests came back clean. In the fall of 2009, however, Edwin was arrested again—this time on a misdemeanor domestic violence charge, his first violent offense. He pled guilty. Additionally, by 2010 Edwin began consistently testing positive for substance use again. He tested positive in almost every month up until his discharge from parole in the fall of 2010. Edwin did not work in the formal labor market after his second parole. Instead, in the fall of 2009, he enrolled again in community college—as a full-time student this time. He would remain enrolled full-time until mid-2011, when he dropped down to half-time. He then moved to another part of the state and enrolled in a new community college, again half-time.

Edwin's experiences illustrate the importance of social support—in his case, from a girlfriend and his grandparents—for sustained enrollment in college. His experiences also illustrate how college enrollment can sometimes substitute for employment as formerly incarcerated young men transition to adulthood. Douglas, a young white man who was born in the late 1970s and another member of the continuing education group, had similar experiences. After he enjoyed some initial success in the labor market but then got caught up in substance abuse and the criminal justice system, continuing education became his best option for transitioning to adulthood.

Douglas became involved with the juvenile justice system at age sixteen when he was sentenced to juvenile probation. He had his first drink of alcohol at a very young age—just six years old. By the time he was incarcerated in state prison, he was drinking two fifths of liquor daily. At age twelve, Douglas started using marijuana. He continued to use marijuana weekly throughout his adolescence and transition to adulthood. Despite his consistent alcohol and drug use and involvement in the juvenile justice system, Douglas was one of the few young men we studied to finish high school. He spent his adolescence and early adulthood transition years in a small coastal city on Lake Michigan. Almost entirely white, the city had a low per-capita income, and the poverty rate was over 10 percent.

Douglas began working in the formal labor market at age seventeen, before he finished high school. In his part-time job at a hardware store in town, however, he made only meager earnings: during the three quarters he worked there, he never made more than $300 in any quarter. After high school, Douglas enrolled full-time at the local community college. He withdrew after one and a half years and began a roofing job, which he kept for about six months, earning just over $8,000. Six months later, Douglas's parents relocated to Lansing, the state capital, and Douglas moved with them. He worked two jobs over the next six months, one in construction and one in hospitality. He earned about $4,500. After leaving these jobs, Douglas again enrolled in community college, this time only half-time. He remained enrolled for one year.

Douglas's withdrawal from college seems related to his first arrest as an adult. He was sentenced to three months in jail after a traffic offense during which he tried to evade police—a felony in Michigan. His traffic offense, in turn, may have been related to an escalation in his drug use. Around this time, at age twenty-one, Douglas started using cocaine. Whether that initial arrest precipitated a downward spiral or was simply a symptom of it is unclear. However, six months after his initial arrest, Douglas was arrested on a misdemeanor driving under the influence charge and subsequently sentenced to another thirty days in jail. Then, in mid-2001, he was arrested for misdemeanor domestic violence. Although that charge was dismissed, later that year he was arrested for felony breaking and entering. He pled guilty and was sentenced to state prison. At the time of his imprisonment, Douglas was living with his parents in a mostly white working-class neighborhood in Lansing. He reported no mental illness. Douglas served a little over a year of his eighteen-month sentence, during which time he was cited for misconduct twice at the reception center, once for being "out of bounds" and once for unauthorized occupation of a cell. He spent about a week in solitary confinement for each of these violations.

Douglas was released from prison onto minimum parole supervision in mid-2003. His special conditions were limited to completing substance use treatment and paying for it. After he was released from prison, Douglas moved back in with his parents and lived with them for two years. Despite his extensive substance use history, he was not drug-tested while on parole. In the first year after he was paroled, Douglas neither worked in the formal labor market nor went to school. In 2004, he found a construction job in which he earned about $500 in one quarter before becoming unemployed. Toward the end of 2004, he found another construction job. He earned about $3,000 in the quarter but did not maintain that job either. In early 2005, Douglas worked two jobs—one in landscaping and the other in fast food. He earned about $800 before leaving both jobs. During the summer of 2005, Douglas was discharged from parole.

Douglas started using alcohol again after he was paroled in 2003. He also continued to use cocaine, which may have contributed to his continued involvement with the criminal justice system. At the age of twenty-seven, he was arrested for misdemeanor domestic violence. This time he pled guilty and was sentenced to a year of maximum probation supervision, after spending just over two months in jail. Then, in 2007, he was arrested again on multiple charges that included felony drug possession, misdemeanor disorderly conduct, and felony assault of a police officer. He was sentenced to two years' probation. The judge on the case applied many special conditions to Douglas's probation, including a host of fees to be deducted from his wages and drug and alcohol testing and treatment.

Douglas moved back in with his parents, where he struggled to stay sober. When he was tested during 2007, the result was positive. He was not tested after 2007, when he transitioned to minimum probation supervision and moved into a treatment facility. He remained in treatment for one month and shuffled between family members before ultimately moving in with his girlfriend in his hometown. There he remained until the end of our follow-up period.

After relocating to his hometown, Douglas enrolled full-time in community college. He then withdrew and enrolled again several months later, but less than half-time. The following fall, he returned to college full-time. With the exception of one semester, Douglas remained enrolled in community college at least half-time for the next three years, when he completed an associate's degree. Douglas was also employed during this time. For five quarters, he worked in the hospitality industry, earning $4,000 to $4,500 per quarter in the three middle quarters. He was not employed in the formal labor market for over a year between the third quarter of 2009 and into the third quarter of 2010, when he found a job at a full-service restaurant.

Douglas, like Edwin, enrolled and continued in college many years after his initial release from prison, and only after struggling in other domains of life. For both, college enrollment eventually coincided with a period of relative calm and seems to have represented a new start in life. We return to the potentially transformative role of college enrollment for formerly incarcerated young men, and for "disconnected" young men in general, in the next chapter when we discuss policy options for better supporting them through the transition to adulthood.

The Persisting Group

Another large trajectory group is one we call "persisting" in crime. Twenty-three percent of the sample fell into this category. Relative to the other young men, those in the persisting group most consistently did *not* meet the adulthood markers. Instead, they remained deeply involved in the criminal justice system, maintaining high probabilities of arrest and incarceration. By the fourth post-prison year, it was a near-certainty that persisters would have been incarcerated or arrested at least once every six months. Further examination of persisters' post-prison experiences reveals that they spent much more time incarcerated on average than any other group. On average, persisters spent 1,435 days in custody during the follow-up period, the equivalent of almost four years. Ninety-seven percent were returned to prison at least once during the follow-up period, and 84 percent were convicted of at least one felony during follow-up. Accordingly, by the third post-prison year and continuing until the end of follow-up, persisters had a zero or near-zero probability of employment, independent living, and college enrollment. Moreover, their low rates of measured substance use may reflect long-term incarceration rather than true sobriety.

The existence and relative size of this group can be interpreted in multiple ways. On the one hand, almost one-quarter of our sample persisted in criminal justice involvement and struggled to transition to adulthood by our measures of employment, residential independence, and postsecondary schooling. On the other hand, given the high rates of recidivism consistently reported for the formerly incarcerated, the fact that only about one-quarter consistently remained involved in the criminal justice system over the long term may be grounds for optimism. Because many of the young men in this category returned to prison and stayed there for a considerable period of time, changes in policies around parole violations and criminal sentencing may shrink the number of young men who fall into this group. We return to policy considerations in the next chapter. We also note that persisters were not the only young men in our sample who experienced arrest or custody at some point after release. They were simply the ones whose risk was consistently high.

Peter, whom we also met in the introduction, was a member of the persisting group. Recall that Peter engaged in serious substance use from a very young age and was first imprisoned just before his eighteenth birthday. He would leave and enter prison again two more times before the end of our observation period, experiencing only very short periods of time back in the community before being arrested for new crimes. Although he earned a GED during his first prison spell and became a father, Peter never worked in the formal labor market or pursued further education beyond his GED.

Another young man categorized as persisting was Wesley, a young black man who was born in the early 1980s. Like many young men we studied, Wesley started using alcohol and marijuana at an early age, in his case at age twelve. Two years later, at fourteen, Wesley first became involved with the juvenile justice system: he was sentenced to probation once and committed to juvenile hall once. Perhaps as a result, he dropped out of high school in the ninth grade. He earned a GED at nineteen, while he was incarcerated.

Wesley's first arrest as a juvenile came when he was seventeen. He was arrested for driving without a license, served a short jail sentence, and was put on probation for one year. He did not seem to comply with his supervision conditions. We have no record of Wesley attending school, working, or entering the alternative to incarceration program to which he was assigned. Less than five months later—just before his eighteenth birthday—he was arrested for breaking and entering and fleeing from the police. He was charged, found guilty, and sentenced to one to ten years in state prison.

Prior to his imprisonment, Wesley was single, had no formal work history, and had no dependent children. He had not yet earned a GED. He also reported suffering from mental illness. It appears he used drugs and alcohol to cope with his mental illness. By the time he was incarcerated in state prison, he was drinking daily and smoking marijuana weekly. At the time of his incarceration, Wesley was living with his grandparents in Detroit. They lived in a poor East Side neighborhood that, at the time, was almost entirely black; about one-third of families there lived below the poverty line, and over one-fifth of its working-age residents were unemployed.

Wesley entered prison in mid-2002. He was incarcerated about a year and a half—over one and a half times his minimum sentence—and spent most of that time in a prison for younger inmates. Wesley initially experienced some conduct problems. In the first month, he was charged with misconduct on three separate occasions—for disobeying orders, being insolent, and creating a disturbance. He spent nineteen days in solitary confinement. He fared better at the youth facility, where he was cited four additional times for being out of bounds. There he spent another twenty-one days in solitary confinement. However, a few months prior to his release, Wesley earned a GED.

In the fall of 2003, Wesley was paroled under maximum supervision and required to attend and pay for substance use treatment. Upon his release, Wesley lived with his grandparents, who were now living in a different neighborhood on the East Side of Detroit. About two months after his release, Wesley was arrested for felony breaking and entering. He spent three months in jail before pleading guilty and being sentenced again to one to ten years. Wesley was returned to prison in mid-2004. He would be incarcerated for three and a half years, in six different prisons; his mobility probably resulted from his conduct problems. Over that time he was charged with eleven misconducts—many of them serious—and spent 192 days in solitary confinement. In mid-2004, he was found responsible for theft and alcohol abuse. About a month after that, he was charged with possessing dangerous contraband. After being transferred to a new facility in 2005, he assaulted a staff member and was then transferred to another prison, where he assaulted another staff member. He was transferred again. In 2006, he was found responsible for gambling. In 2007, shortly before his release, he disobeyed an order.

Wesley was released from prison onto minimum parole supervision in mid-summer 2007. The parole board ordered him released into a substance abuse treatment facility. About a week later, he left treatment and absconded from parole. A warrant was issued. Less than two weeks after he was released, he was arrested for violating parole and reimprisoned as a technical rule violator. He remained in prison until early 2008, when he was again released on parole. During this period, he learned that he had fathered a child during his last release from prison.

After his release, Wesley shuffled between several residences. Initially he was staying with an aunt, who after a week moved from downtown Detroit to another neighborhood in Detroit, about five miles away. He stayed with her for two more weeks, after which he moved in with an uncle in a neighborhood in northwestern Detroit. Several weeks later, Wesley was arrested again for breaking and entering with intent and returned to prison. He was twenty-four. This third prison sentence was relatively short. He spent less than a year in prison, during which time he was cited for misconduct only once—for theft.

In late 2009, Wesley was again released on maximum parole supervision and assigned to a parole caseload for people with serious substance abuse problems. He lived for about three months with his mother in another state before he was arrested for trespassing. Extradited back to Michigan, he was diverted to a TRV facility. Wesley spent about two months in that facility and was again paroled under maximum supervision in late 2009. A few months later, a warrant was issued for his arrest. Later that same month, he was arrested again, this time for a home invasion, but the charge was dismissed. The next month he was arrested for assault with intent to murder—a charge that was also dismissed. Three months later, he was arrested again for breaking and entering, to which he pled guilty and again was sentenced to one to ten years. He was recommitted to prison in mid-2010. Over the next four and a half years, Wesley was cited for forty misconducts ranging from being out of bounds to alcohol abuse, theft, fighting, weapons and dangerous contraband possession, and assault resulting in serious injury. At the end of 2014, he was still imprisoned.

The Unsettled Group

Our fourth trajectory group is the "unsettled" group—the largest group at 26 percent of the sample. The young men in this group made some progress on their adult transitions even as they remained involved in the criminal justice system. The unsettled maintained a low but nontrivial probability of employment and independent living (approximately 25 percent) while also sustaining a moderate (25 to 50 percent) probability of arrest or incarceration throughout the follow-up period. They spent more time incarcerated during the follow-up period than any other group except the persisters—an average of 718 days (almost two years). Seventy-two percent were convicted of a new felony during follow-up. As happened with the transitioning and persisting groups, unsettled young men had a near-zero probability of continuing their education in the period after release during which we observed them.

This group is particularly interesting because, following release from prison, many of the unsettled seemed to straddle two worlds—a conventional world characterized by employment and residential independence and another characterized by criminal justice involvement. They moved back and forth between these two worlds as they struggled to build new lives for themselves. Such young men might be most amenable to policy intervention, particularly if we can better understand the unique challenges they face, an issue to which we return in the next chapter. The large size of this group in our data is consistent with prior research characterizing those undergoing the transition to adulthood as "unsettled" as they approach role transitions.[17] The experience of this group is also consistent with a line of research in criminology that examines the "intermittency" of involvement in crime, the challenges of permanent desistance, and the role of employment.[18]

The life histories of Reginald and Adam reflect this unsettledness. Like most of the young men in our sample, Reginald, a young black man born in the late 1970s, did not finish high school. In fact, he dropped out of a Detroit high school in the ninth grade. Around the same time, at age fourteen, Reginald started using marijuana and became a daily user. He started using alcohol soon after, at age fifteen, and became a regular, although not daily, user. Despite dropping out and using drugs and alcohol, Reginald did not have a juvenile record. He first encountered the adult criminal justice system at age seventeen, when he had not yet held a job in the formal labor market. Reginald was arrested for armed robbery, found guilty, and sentenced to two and a half to ten years in state prison. Reginald would ultimately spend the first five years of his early adulthood in prison. During that time, he was shuffled between five prisons in the Upper Peninsula of Michigan.

Reginald earned his GED about midway through his incarceration. Although he was not cited for misconduct often—only about twice per year on average—his violations were more serious. Most of the young men in our sample were cited for offenses related to either being somewhere they were not supposed to be or not being somewhere they were supposed to be (for example, "out of bounds," "unauthorized occupation," and "AWOL" citations). However, Reginald was cited once for threatening behavior, once for an assault resulting in serious injury, and once for substance use, after a positive drug test. In total, he spent three months in solitary confinement for the nine misconducts.

Reginald was released from prison onto maximum parole supervision when he was twenty-two years old. He did not work in the formal labor market after release. His drug tests came back negative through the spring of 2002, when he absconded from parole. A few months later, he was arrested on a felony drug charge, pled guilty, and was sentenced to state prison for a minimum of one year. By the time of his second imprisonment, Reginald had become a father and was living with his mother in Detroit. The central city neighborhood where they lived was overwhelmingly black and middle-class, with a poverty rate under 10 percent and an unemployment rate over 7 percent.

Although Reginald served nearly his entire minimum sentence, he spent far less time in prison during his second imprisonment and was not charged with any misconduct—which probably contributed to his timely release. In the fall of 2003, Reginald was released onto maximum parole supervision and subject to numerous onerous special conditions. He could not own a cell phone or pager, nor could he drive without the consent of his parole officer. In addition, he was required to attend and pay for substance abuse treatment. Reginald was released to his mother's house—she still lived in the same neighborhood—but he alternated between her house and a custodial sanction center for technical rule violators in Detroit. For about six months, he would stay a month or two with his mother, then be detained for a week. During this period, Reginald remained unemployed—at least in the formal labor market.

In the spring of 2004, Reginald absconded from parole. A warrant for his arrest was issued two months later, and he was arrested on that warrant in the winter of 2005. He spent a week and a half in jail and was returned to parole supervision. Reginald moved in briefly with his girlfriend in a West Side neighborhood close to downtown Detroit before entering substance use treatment at a private facility under contract with MDOC, where he stayed for one month. After finishing treatment, Reginald moved back in with his girlfriend. He lived with her for more than six months—a period of relative stability. During this time, Reginald found his first job in the formal labor market, a manufacturing job, which he held only briefly, earning about $1,000 in a single calendar quarter. He would not work again for about two years.

Reginald absconded again in the fall—probably because he had relapsed. When he was picked up two months later, he tested positive for drug use. Reginald moved back in with his girlfriend in a residence where she had moved with her aunt, in the same neighborhood where his mother lived. A month later, he tested positive for substance use and was returned to prison for seven months as a technical rule violator.

Reginald was paroled again in the summer of 2006, with a special condition that gives some insight into his activities over the previous ten years—he was not to associate with any gang members. After his parole, Reginald moved back in with his mother. She had moved to a different house about two miles from her old residence. He stayed with her only three weeks before moving in with his girlfriend in a far West Side neighborhood. He lived there for three months. During this period, Reginald was not working, but he also did not seem to be using: each of his monthly drug tests came back negative until the summer of 2007. However, he had been arrested for possession of marijuana, along with driving on a suspended license, in the fall of 2006. That arrest resulted in a forty-day jail sentence, after which he moved back with his girlfriend. However, their relationship seemed to fall apart at this point. During the winter of 2007, Reginald moved back in with his mother, who appeared to be having some housing stability issues of her own. She had relocated for the third time in less than three years, this time to a neighborhood in northwest Detroit. After about a month, Reginald was again jailed for a month—although it is unclear why.

After that jail spell, and amid several positive drug tests, Reginald found some stability. He lived with his mother for five months and found employment through a temp agency. In the middle of 2007, he earned about $2,000 per calendar quarter for two quarters. He was twenty-eight years old. He would not be formally employed again after 2007, nor would he ever enroll in college. Around the time he left his last job, Reginald also moved out of his mother's house and in with a girlfriend. Aside from periods of incarceration in jail, he would live with her for the next two years. During this period, they would have another child.

Despite attaining some residential stability, Reginald continued to struggle with justice system involvement. By mid-2008, he had absconded from parole again. A few months later, he was arrested and pled guilty to a misdemeanor drug charge. That resulted in a four-month incarceration, after which he returned to live with his girlfriend. Although all of his drug tests in 2008 and most of 2009 came back negative, by the end of 2009 Reginald had started using again. He tested positive for the first six months of 2010, after which he tested negative. During this time he was arrested twice, but not prosecuted, for obstructing justice. In the spring of 2011, Reginald was discharged from parole.

Like Reginald, Adam, a young white man, followed an unsettled trajectory—also owing primarily to persistent substance use. Adam was born in the late 1970s. He started drinking when he was eight years old, and at age ten he began using marijuana. Although he indicated that he used alcohol and marijuana only occasionally, substance use may have played a role in his deep involvement with the juvenile justice system from an early age. Adam was first arrested at age eleven. Between ages eleven and seventeen, he was sentenced to juvenile probation four times and committed to juvenile hall four times. He escaped from custody as a juvenile twice. Given his juvenile history, it is unsurprising that Adam did not finish high school, dropping out in the twelfth grade.

Adam's dropout coincided with his first arrest and conviction as an adult—at age seventeen. The charge was unlawful driving away. He pled guilty to a misdemeanor in the spring of 1997 but was not sentenced to state prison until four months later. Between his conviction and his incarceration, Adam found his first formal job at a fast-food restaurant. He earned about $1,300 before being sent to state prison.

Adam was committed to prison from a white working-class city in southeastern Michigan, where he apparently grew up and to which he would continue to return. His eight-month incarceration seems to have been uneventful. He was not cited for misconduct, nor did he earn a GED. Adam was paroled in the spring of 1998 and ordered to live in a community corrections center, participate in GED courses, and complete substance use treatment. He seems to have complied. Adam earned a GED in the summer of 1998 but would not try to further his education beyond that. Despite his early initiation into alcohol and drug use, later drunk driving incidents and stints in substance use treatment, and despite being drug-tested 222 times between 1998 and 2010, Adam tested positive only twice.

He also began working again. Adam was employed in every quarter between the spring of 1998 and the winter of 2000, working in a wide array of industries; he seemed to take whatever job he could get in the secondary and temporary labor force. He worked in fast-food restaurants, through temporary staffing firms, and in manufacturing. He worked three quarters in 1998, during which he earned about $11,000 from seven employers. He worked all of 1999, during which he earned about $12,000 from six employers. In 2000, he worked only one quarter, earning about $2,800 from two employers.

Adam was discharged from parole in 1998. He was not arrested again until a few months after he had stopped working. In mid-2000, he was arrested for assault and battery. He pled guilty and was sentenced to thirty days in jail and two years' probation. A few months later, however, he was arrested again, this time for misdemeanor drunk driving, fleeing from an officer, and driving away—the same charge as his first adult conviction. He pled guilty and was sentenced to ninety days in jail. Upon his release, more conditions were heaped on him, including maintaining employment and paying court fines, fees, and restitution. We have no record of Adam working in the formal labor market around this time. About six months later, in mid-2001, he was required to enter substance abuse treatment. In 2002, Adam absconded from probation and a warrant for his arrest was issued. At twenty-two, Adam was arrested and recommitted to state prison, where he served out his sentence at a prison for younger inmates. Again, his stay was uneventful. He was not cited for any misconduct and served only ten months of a thirty-month sentence.

Adam was released into a community residential substance abuse treatment program in Detroit and lived there for three months. After release from that facility, Adam moved in with his mother in his hometown, where he was placed on electronic monitoring. He remained on electronic monitoring for three months and was arrested again for misdemeanor drunk driving and felony driving away. He was returned to prison for two years, and once again, he did his time uneventfully.

Adam exited prison onto parole for the third time in 2005. He lived with his grandmother in his hometown for one month before being arrested for disorderly conduct, served a short jail sentence, and was diverted to a TRV facility, where he lived for a little over two months. Afterward, Adam lived with his grandmother for a week and then moved in with his girlfriend in a neighboring town. He lived with her for about five months before moving in with his brother for a little over two months. Then he tried, unsuccessfully, to reconcile with his girlfriend. He moved in with her, but after two days he returned to his brother's place, where he lived for another three months before being arrested on a domestic assault charge. Although the charge was ultimately dismissed, he spent two months in jail. Afterward, Adam moved back in with his brother and was again jailed for a short period of time as a sanction for a parole violation.

By then, Adam was twenty-eight years old. He was still living with his brother in his hometown, where he would stay for three months as he tried to return to work. Again, he found jobs in a variety of industries, from temporary services to manufacturing. He worked for three quarters in 2007, earning about $5,500. Then, perhaps hit by the downturn in the economy in late 2007 and early 2008, Adam was out of work for six months. He found a manufacturing job in 2008 and earned about $5,800 over two quarters.

However, during this time Adam remained continuously involved in the criminal justice system. Over eleven months in 2007 and 2008, Adam was arrested for a parole violation once every other month on average. Each time he would spend between three and seven days in jail. During this period, he mainly lived with his grandparents, although he did live with a new girlfriend for about a month. In the summer of 2008, Adam was again arrested for a more serious offense—misdemeanor aggravated domestic violence. Again, the domestic violence charge was dismissed.

Even as our follow-up period expired, Adam remained involved in the criminal justice system. In the summer of 2010, Adam was discharged from parole. Less than two weeks later, however, he was arrested for trespassing and pled guilty. He received twelve months' probation. In late 2012, Adam was recommitted to state prison, where he remained until mid-2014, when he was discharged on completion of the maximum sentence.

The Disconnected Group

Our final group, comprising 20 percent of the sample, includes those on a trajectory we term "disconnected." Unlike persisters and more like transitioners, those who followed disconnected trajectories experienced some initially moderate levels of arrest and custody but avoided extended contact with the criminal justice system over the long term. About 41 percent experienced incarceration during the follow-up period, and on average they spent only 137 days in custody.[19] Like others, they mostly avoided positive substance use tests. However, these young men also did not participate in the labor market or in educational institutions. Like persisters, the disconnected had a zero or near-zero probability of meeting *any* of the adulthood markers by four years after prison.

This group successfully avoided further involvement in the criminal justice system but had not been rewarded for that with success in other domains. The disconnected group presents us with somewhat of a puzzle: how were they getting by in the medium to long term? Based on the results presented in chapter 7 on residential stability and on prior research on the role of family in providing support for the formerly incarcerated,[20] we suspect that the young men who followed disconnected trajectories were relying heavily on social support from their families and romantic partners to meet their basic material needs. Disconnection and the attendant social isolation carry significant risks for healthy life-course transitions and healthy lives.[21] Of the forty-seven young men in our sample who died within nine years of release, twenty-two had fallen into disconnected trajectories. Rodney's and Trevor's stories illustrate how that can happen.

Rodney, a young black man who was born in the late 1970s, was a member of the disconnected trajectory group. Growing up, he was not involved in the juvenile justice system; in fact, his first arrest did not occur until he was twenty years old. Although he avoided criminal justice contact, Rodney did not graduate from his Detroit high school, dropping out in the tenth grade. He would not go on to earn a GED either prior to, during, or after prison. Rodney started working when he turned eighteen. Initially, he worked odd jobs, earning about $600 in a calendar quarter. Then he got a job at a car wash, where he worked for three quarters, earning about $3,700 in each quarter. He did not work for a year between the fall of 1998 and the fall of 1999. When he went back to work in 1999, he earned less than $1,000 over two quarters of employment. He would not work again until after his release from prison.

Sometime in the first half of 2001, Rodney ran into some sort of trouble with the law in Flint. Although there is no arrest on record, we have a record of Rodney being sentenced to a three-year probation term. Special conditions of his probation hint at interpersonal violence and potential mental health and substance abuse problems. They include a no-contact order with a specific person and a mandate to seek mental health treatment. Similarly, although we have no other record of Rodney working in the formal labor market between the first quarter of 2001 and the third quarter of 2003, his probation records show that he was employed and under medium supervision for six months in 2001. Thus, initially Rodney seems to have done well on probation. In addition to being employed, all of his drug tests in 2000 and 2001 came back clean.

In the fall of 2001, however, Rodney absconded from probation. He was arrested a few months later on a felony drug charge and sentenced to a minimum of seventeen months in state prison. He was released after serving his minimum. Although he spent some time at four prisons after leaving the reception center, Rodney mainly served his time in a facility for younger inmates. His behavior does not seem to have been responsible for his mobility in prison. During his first year of incarceration, he was cited for two misconducts—unauthorized occupation of a cell and fighting—for which he spent a total of just over three weeks in solitary confinement. After his first year, he was not charged with misconduct.

Prior to his parole, Rodney was released from prison into a community correctional center in Detroit in the summer of 2003. He lived in either the center in Detroit or a Saginaw center for the first three and a half months. Rodney was paroled onto medium supervision in the fall. He was supposed to participate in a GED class and complete substance abuse treatment. He does not appear to have done either. After he was paroled, Rodney lived with his grandparents in an apartment in downtown Detroit. Now twenty-four, he worked briefly through a temporary services agency in the early fall of 2003, but he earned less than $100. In the late fall, he tested positive for drug use.

Over the next nine months, Rodney continued to be involved in the criminal justice system, but at a minor level. Although his official state police record shows no new arrests—he had only the drug charge on his record—Rodney continued to serve short jail terms. Five times in the span of those nine months he served three to six days in a correctional center for technical rule violations. Rodney had returned to living with his grandparents when he was shot and killed in the late summer of 2004. He was twenty-five.

Another young man who followed a disconnected trajectory was Trevor, a young white man born in the late 1970s. He was first arrested at age twelve. As a juvenile, Trevor was sentenced to probation twice, committed to juvenile hall once, and escaped from custody twice. By the time he was first arrested, he had been using marijuana for four years. He started at age eight, but reported only occasional use as an adult. Trevor did not start drinking alcohol until comparatively much later, at age fifteen. He also reported using alcohol only occasionally as an adult. Like most of the young men who began using drugs prior to adolescence, Trevor did not finish high school. He dropped out of a high school in Detroit's western suburbs after the tenth grade.

Trevor was first arrested as an adult—for theft—when he was seventeen. However, that arrest was not prosecuted. He would not be arrested again until he was nineteen, when he was arrested on a host of charges, including felony theft, felony fleeing an officer, and misdemeanor drunken driving. He was found guilty of all of these charges and sentenced to two years of probation. After he turned eighteen, Trevor earned a GED and started working. He would work for only one calendar quarter, earning less than $1,200, and would not work again until after his second arrest in 1999. He worked sporadically, earning about $900 in three jobs—one at a car wash, one at a restaurant, and one through a temp agency. After that, he would not work again.

We know very little about what happened to Trevor over the next eighteen months, except that he was discharged from probation at age twenty and did not father any children. At age twenty-one, he was arrested for misdemeanor domestic violence—a charge that was deferred under the Domestic Violence Act. Just a few months later, however, he was arrested and pled guilty to a felony charge of writing fraudulent checks. He was sentenced to a two-year probation term. Trevor violated his probation when he picked up a new arrest about a year later. In early 2002, he pled guilty to felony breaking and entering and was sentenced to one year in state prison.

At the time of his imprisonment, Trevor reported no mental health issues and only occasional marijuana and alcohol use. He was a single twenty-three-year-old man with no dependents who lived with his sister in a working-class suburb west of Detroit. The town was overwhelmingly white and had a low poverty rate. Trevor served not quite eleven months of his twelve-month minimum sentence. During that time, he was cited for two misconducts—out of bounds and unauthorized occupation of a cell. In total he spent four days in solitary confinement.

Trevor was released from prison onto medium parole supervision in early 2003. He moved in with one of his parents (his parents had divorced when he was a child) in a rural part of Michigan. He lived in that parent's household for about two months before he was arrested in a Detroit suburb for driving on a suspended license. He spent a month in jail before returning to his parent's home. In the summer of 2003, Trevor entered substance abuse treatment. He stayed in treatment for ten weeks but then absconded from treatment and from parole for two months. He was ultimately arrested in the fall of 2003 for obstructing justice in the same town where the treatment center was located. He was diverted to a TRV facility, where he lived for another ten weeks before moving back in with his parent in rural Michigan. He lived there for two weeks before he was arrested on an old warrant. After he was released from jail the next day, he absconded. In the spring of 2004, he turned up in a Southern state, where he was arrested on the absconding warrant, returned to Michigan, and again diverted to a TRV facility for ten weeks. When he was released from the TRV, he moved in with his other parent in his childhood home. He lived there for about two weeks before moving in with a friend in Detroit. After August 2004,

Trevor's whereabouts were unknown. On Christmas Eve, he died in an automobile crash in West Virginia. He was twenty-six.[22]

Now that we have some understanding of the five groups that emerged from the trajectory analysis, it is worth pausing to consider some implications of what we have learned at this point about the links between the transition-to-adulthood domains. The analysis thus far suggests that the domains are not as tightly linked together as we might expect based on prior research. First, although substance use is a critical issue after release (chapter 5), the trajectories of positive substance abuse tests look similar for all groups in the longer term. Second, the disconnected and continuing education groups show that there are multiple pathways to desistance from crime other than employment. Indeed, in this population, education and employment may be alternative pathways in the short to medium term, as those who do not find sufficiently rewarding work return to school. Moreover, the disconnected group suggests that alternative forms of social support alone may foster desistance. Third, the unsettled group shows us that a substantial portion of young men who are released from prison combine prosocial pursuits like employment with continued involvement in the criminal justice system. In addition, their membership in this group seems related to persistent substance use.

WHO IS IN EACH TRAJECTORY GROUP?

To better understand the trajectory groups, we need to understand their composition. Table 8.1 shows mean characteristics of the members of each of the five trajectory groups, including their pre-prison criminal justice system involvement, demographic and educational characteristics, substance use and mental illness histories, prison experiences, and social context and intensity of criminal justice monitoring after release. In discussing these results, we emphasize characteristics that are statistically significant predictors of group membership in the multinomial logit regression model predicting group membership (see table 8.A2). In other words, we focus on characteristics that have independent effects even when other characteristics are controlled.

We begin with the transitioning group, as its members include the young men who came closest to success in the transition to adulthood, providing an obvious comparison group for the others. With regard to criminal justice involvement, the transitioners were the oldest at first arrest and the least likely to have been incarcerated as juveniles, although their average age at prison entry was not appreciably different from that of the other groups. This suggests that their adolescent experiences were least likely to

Table 8.1   Mean Characteristics, by Trajectory Group

	Persisting	Disconnected	Unsettled	Transitioning	Continuing Education
Age at first arrest	14.67	16.00	14.85	16.21	15.55
Juvenile commitment	0.57	0.36	0.51	0.31	0.41
Number of arrests	3.60	2.77	3.39	3.12	3.08
Number of convictions	3.54	3.10	3.80	3.39	3.18
Number of fines and sentences	1.03	0.93	1.21	1.31	1.00
Number of probation sentences	0.80	0.79	0.81	0.88	0.66
Number of custody sentences	2.37	2.03	2.57	2.26	2.06
Age on first entering prison	20.51	21.02	20.98	20.91	20.43
Has dependent	0.41	0.41	0.44	0.39	0.33
Has ever been married	0.04	0.07	0.03	0.06	0.06
High school graduate	0.04	0.07	0.09	0.09	0.20
Has earned GED	0.60	0.52	0.59	0.68	0.65
Employed	0.64	0.62	0.73	0.83	0.69
Has lived independently	0.57	0.60	0.73	0.59	0.64
Mentally ill	0.23	0.16	0.19	0.20	0.19
Daily alcohol use	0.13	0.06	0.17	0.06	0.08

(Table continues on p. 204)

Table 8.1 *Continued*

	Persisting	Disconnected	Unsettled	Transitioning	Continuing Education
Daily marijuana use	0.36	0.21	0.34	0.16	0.25
Daily stimulant use	0.12	0.05	0.11	0.02	0.04
Daily depressant use	0.03	0.01	0.05	0.01	0.02
Months in prison	23.62	21.43	20.51	22.94	25.56
Earned GED in prison	0.33	0.29	0.29	0.33	0.37
Had misconduct	0.66	0.58	0.64	0.57	0.52
Days in solitary	21.57	8.31	10.10	6.05	8.93
Return to Detroit	0.24	0.26	0.17	0.17	0.14
Return-tract disadvantage	0.80	0.96	0.64	0.33	0.59
Return-tract affluence	−0.35	−0.36	−0.42	−0.38	−0.27
Return-county crime rate	0.01	0.01	0.01	0.01	0.01
Electronic monitoring at release	0.31	0.34	0.43	0.34	0.33
Supervision level at release	1.64	1.71	1.66	1.75	1.69

Source: Michigan Study of Life after Prison.
Note: Data for 2003 Michigan parole cohort age 18–25 at parole. Characteristics measured at prison entry or at release.

have been disrupted by serious involvement in the criminal justice system. Perhaps as a result, they reported the highest levels of pre-prison education and the greatest likelihood of having worked before their imprisonment. Transitioners also had some of the lowest rates of self-reported substance use before their imprisonment. Together, these patterns suggest that, relative to other young men imprisoned in early adulthood, the transitioners were best positioned to face the challenges of reentry and reintegration after release. They also were the least likely to face particularly challenging neighborhood environments after release, as the neighborhoods to which they returned had the lowest average neighborhood disadvantage score (although the mean was still one-third of a standard deviation more disadvantaged than the average Michigan neighborhood). In addition, they were the least likely to live in Detroit after their release.

The continuing education group members also appeared, owing to their high rates of enrollment in postsecondary education, to be on some sort of pathway to achieving successful transitions to adulthood. However, it is important to remember that this appearance was more promise than realization during the time period when we observed them; by the end of that period, rates of employment and residential independence among them were low and few had earned a degree (see chapter 4). Members of this group had the highest rates of education before their most recent imprisonment. Twenty percent had earned a high school degree, more than double that of any other group, and 65 percent had earned a GED, higher than all groups other than the transitioners. They also were most likely to earn a GED at some point while in prison (37 percent).

Information on their prison experiences and prior criminal justice involvement provides some clues as to how they were able to accomplish this. They spent more time in prison on average than all other groups, and they had the lowest rate of prison misconduct citations, suggesting that they were best positioned to take advantage of prison educational opportunities. They also returned to some of the most affluent neighborhoods, relative to the post-prison neighborhoods of the other groups. More affluent neighborhoods, with more residents who have college degrees, earn higher incomes, and are employed in professional or managerial occupations, may provide the most opportunities to enroll in schooling after release as well as more older, male role models whose own life courses reflect continued education. In sum, the young men who were on a pathway to adulthood involving further education were those best positioned to pursue this strategy after release. They had the most prior education and probably the greatest access to higher education after release. It is important to keep in mind, however, that they enrolled in postsecondary education many years after release, and only after their initial successes with employment and residential independence had proven fleeting (see figure 8.1 and chapter 4).

We now turn to the persisters, those who maintained the highest levels of involvement in the criminal justice system while also experiencing low levels of employment and residential independence. The young men in this group experienced some of the most serious disadvantages, both before and after release. First, they became entangled with the criminal justice system more often and more seriously than did those of any other group: their average age at first arrest was the youngest, at 14.7 years; they were the most likely to be incarcerated as juveniles; they had the largest number of pre-prison arrests; and they entered prison at the youngest ages. Second, prior to their imprisonment, they faced the most challenges with mental illness and substance use: 23 percent were diagnosed with or treated for mental illness, and they had the highest rates of marijuana and stimulant use. Third, their prison experiences suggest that they had fewer rehabilitative experiences in prison. Persisters were the most likely to have a misconduct and spent the most time in solitary confinement. Finally, persisters—along with the disconnected—lived in some of the most disadvantaged neighborhoods and were most likely to be released to Detroit.

Recall that the unsettled group experienced some success with employment and residential independence, but also continued to be involved with the criminal justice system, albeit at a lower level than the persisting group. The unsettled group looks similar to the persisting group with regard to prior criminal justice involvement and substance use. They experienced their first arrest before the age of fifteen on average, were more likely than not to be incarcerated as juveniles, and had more arrests and more custody sentences than other groups. They had higher rates of daily alcohol, marijuana, stimulant, and depressant use than other groups. They also had higher-than-average rates of misconduct in prison, but did not spend as much time in solitary confinement as the persisters. The unsettled were the most likely to be placed on electronic monitoring on release from prison.

After prison, what differentiates the unsettled from the persisters is their labor market experience in the period immediately after release. The unsettled were more likely to be employed in the six months immediately after release (figure 8.1). Further examination of our data shows that they also had higher earnings from employment.[23] However, it was most likely their pre-prison disadvantages that made it difficult for the unsettled to translate some initial successes in the labor market into longer-term stability; relative to the transitioning group, the unsettled had higher rates of pre-prison substance use, a more extensive history of criminal justice involvement, and lower levels of education and pre-prison work experience.

Finally, we turn to the disconnected young men, who had low employment and residential stability but also avoided further criminal justice system involvement. Their previous criminal justice system experiences and pre-prison substance use were very similar to the early lives of the transitioners, but they differed on two potentially important dimensions. First, they had lower levels of education and employment before their imprisonment, suggesting lower levels of human capital development. Second, they returned to some of the most disadvantaged neighborhoods in Michigan and were the most likely to return to Detroit. These two factors combined may explain their low rates of employment. Faced with lesser pre-prison human capital development and greater post-prison distance from jobs, they faced a stark labor market and struggled to find and maintain employment and garner the resources they needed to establish their own households independent of parents and older relatives.

Racial Differences in Group Membership

Earlier chapters have documented racial differences in the transition to adulthood after prison. How do such differences by domain come together in post-prison trajectories? Table 8.2 shows that trajectory group membership does vary by race, although not for all trajectory groups. Blacks and whites were equally likely to be in the persisting group: about 27 percent of both blacks and whites belonged to that group. In addition, although blacks were slightly more likely to be in the continuing education group than whites (8.8 percent of blacks versus 7.0 percent of whites), that difference was relatively small. Blacks were also more likely to be in the unsettled group (21.7 percent versus 18.6 percent). The largest racial differences were between the disconnected and transitioning groups. While blacks were much more likely to be in the disconnected group (27.0 percent versus 14.1 percent among whites), whites were much more likely to be in the transitioning group (33.3 percent versus 15.0 percent among blacks). These racial disparities, which do not reflect involvement in crime because both groups had low criminal justice system involvement, starkly illustrate the racial differences in the transition to adulthood after prison—and the potential reasons behind them.

To understand these racial differences in post-prison trajectories, we estimated a series of multinomial logit models predicting group membership with a race dummy variable as a predictor (coded whites = 1 and blacks = 0). Being in the transitioning group is the reference category for the outcome. This series of models progressively adds more explanatory variables so that we can see whether conditioning on various pre-prison, in-prison, and post-prison experiences can account for the association

Table 8.2 Percentage of Blacks and Whites in Each Trajectory Group

	Persisting	Disconnected	Unsettled	Transitioning	Continuing Education	Total
Blacks	27.5	27.0	21.7	15.0	8.8	100.0
Whites	27.0	14.1	18.6	33.3	7.0	100.0
Overall	27.2	20.2	20.1	24.7	7.8	100.0

Source: Michigan Study of Life after Prison.
Note: Data for 2003 Michigan parole cohort age 18–25 at parole, followed through 2009.

between race and trajectory group membership. If those experiences account for the racial difference, we should see the average marginal effect (AME) on the race dummy variable move toward zero. Table 8.3 summarizes these results, with one set of rows for each comparison between the transitioning group and one of the other groups. Each column adds successively more explanatory variables. Within each row, we provide the AME on the race variable and its standard error and t-statistic. (A t-statistic larger than 1.96 or smaller than −1.96 means that the AME of the race dummy variable is statistically different from zero.) AMEs can be interpreted as the racial difference in the probability of group membership, relative to the probability of membership in the transitioning group.

We start by comparing the persisting group to the transitioning group, since that is where the racial differences are the largest. The first column shows the racial difference with no other variables controlled. The AME of −0.154 tells us that whites were about fifteen percentage points less likely than blacks to be persisters than transitioners. Surprisingly, conditioning on explanatory variables makes the racial difference larger, not smaller, as we might expect. How should we interpret this result? It means that if whites and blacks had the same levels of pre-prison criminal justice involvement and pre-prison substance use and mental health, the racial disparity would be even larger. (The changes in the AME in the other columns are negligible, so we ignore those.) In this sample, whites actually had higher levels of many characteristics that predict being in the persisting rather than transitioning group. They had more prior arrests, convictions, and custody sentences and were more likely to have experienced mental illness and substance use. (Whites, however, did have higher educational attainment and more job experience than blacks.) If whites had the same pre-prison experiences as blacks, they would be even less likely to be in the persisting group, so controlling for those characteristics makes the AME on race larger, not smaller. Note that a similar pattern becomes evident when we try to understand the racial disparity between the continuing education and transitioning groups. Although the initial racial disparity is smaller, making the changes too small to interpret for each variable individually, once all variables are controlled, the racial disparity in continuing education becomes statistically significant.

These somewhat counterintuitive results regarding the persisting versus transitioning comparison stem from an important feature of the population of young men imprisoned at a young age. Recall from chapter 2 that because the rate of imprisonment is much higher for young blacks than young whites, becoming an incarcerated young adult is a much more selective process for whites than it is for blacks. In other words, a white man who ends up in prison as a young adult looks very different from

Table 8.3 Racial Differences (White versus Black) in the Probability of Trajectory Group Membership after Controlling for Explanatory Variables

	Race Only	Pre-Prison Criminal Justice Contact	Pre-Prison Human Capital and Demographics	Pre-Prison Substance Use and Mental Health	Prison Experience	Post-Prison Social Context	Post-Prison Criminal Justice Supervision
Unsettled versus Transitioning							
White	0.014	-0.003	0.009	0.003	0.011	0.010	0.013
Standard error	0.024	0.026	0.027	0.028	0.029	0.036	0.035
t	0.574	-0.129	0.319	0.113	0.369	0.289	0.360
Persisting versus Transitioning							
White	-0.152	-0.177	-0.188	-0.213	-0.220	-0.222	-0.221
Standard error	0.023	0.024	0.025	0.027	0.028	0.033	0.034
t	-6.511	-7.388	-7.380	-7.832	-7.726	-6.645	-6.477
Disconnected versus Transitioning							
White	-0.038	-0.013	0.006	0.024	0.032	0.067	0.063
Standard error	0.023	0.023	0.024	0.024	0.026	0.032	0.032
t	-1.690	-0.553	0.252	0.971	1.232	2.104	1.961
Continuing Education versus Transitioning							
White	-0.016	-0.016	-0.022	-0.018	-0.028	-0.044	-0.043
Standard error	0.015	0.016	0.016	0.017	0.017	0.019	0.019
t	-1.027	-0.988	-1.338	-1.061	-1.639	-2.314	-2.305
N	1,300	1,300	1,300	1,300	1,300	1,281	1,278

Source: Michigan Study of Life after Prison.
Note: Average marginal effects of being white relative to being black as explanatory variable groups are added to a multinomial logit model predicting trajectory group membership. Data for 2003 Michigan parole cohort age 18–25 at parole, followed through 2009.

the typical young white man in the larger population. Young whites who end up in prison often have much more severe disadvantages than their white counterparts more generally. They live in poorer neighborhoods and have a higher incidence of mental health and substance abuse problems than their non-incarcerated counterparts. In contrast, the racialized nature of law enforcement, courts, and corrections ensures that a larger proportion of blacks end up imprisoned at a young age. Young blacks who are imprisoned are more like their non-incarcerated counterparts in the broader black population. Relative to incarcerated white men, incarcerated black men are less likely to have mental health and substance abuse problems, even though they typically grow up in far more disadvantaged neighborhoods. Young black men are also sentenced to prison after fewer offenses than their white counterparts, which may be evidence of more punitive treatment by the criminal justice system. Put differently, the processes of what we might call "selection into prison" are quite different by race, as evidenced by large racial differences in rates of imprisonment. Our sample was selected based on imprisonment at an early age, and whites who experience imprisonment at an early age may be very different from blacks who do so.

The results are slightly different when we compare the disconnected and transitioning groups. In this case, pre-prison criminal justice variables and pre-prison human capital and demographics do completely account for the racial disparity, shrinking it to basically zero (0.006) in the third column from the left. This means that blacks were more likely than whites to be in the disconnected group relative to the transitioning group because of greater criminal justice system contact and lower human capital (pre-prison education and employment). Controlling for other variables as we move to the right increases the disparity further; thus, had whites had the same characteristics as blacks, they would have been even more likely than blacks to be in the disconnected group as compared to the transitioning group. Most of this result is driven by post-prison social context. Had whites been released to the same neighborhoods as blacks, they would have been even more likely than blacks to be in the disconnected group.

If the variables in our study cannot account for racial differences between persisters and transitioners, then what else might? Perhaps there are important unobserved differences by race in our subjects' early life experiences. The "selection into prison" processes are quite different by race, as discussed earlier. Such differences might account for blacks' greater likelihood of continuing their education and their greater likelihood of following disconnected rather than transitioning trajectories.

In addition, we see two possible explanations for blacks' greater likelihood of following a disconnected rather than a transitioning trajectory:

stigma combined with discrimination, and differences in social network support. The impact of the stigma of a criminal record, particularly for employment outcomes, has been extensively studied.[24] In her in-person audit study, Devah Pager finds that the stigma of a criminal record differentially impacts black men relative to white men in terms of their employment prospects.[25] Five percent of black men with a criminal record receive callbacks, whereas 17 percent of white men with a criminal record do, a difference of twelve percentage points. In a subsequent in-person audit study focused on isolating the impact of racial discrimination independent of the stigma of a criminal record, Pager, Bonikowski, and Western find that black men receive a callback or a job offer 15.2 percent of the time, whereas white men are hired or called back 31.0 percent of the time, a difference of 15.8 percentage points.[26] Moreover, they also find that black men are often channeled into lower-prestige and lower-visibility jobs (for example, a position as a busboy rather than a server). Thus, even when blacks are hired, racial discrimination is implicated in relegating them to more precarious work with lower wages.

Racial discrimination and the stigma of a criminal record seem to be linked. In subsequent work on specific industries, Pager finds that restaurants, which tend not to do background checks, are most likely to hire whites with criminal records but least likely to hire blacks with criminal records.[27] In a correspondence audit study, Amanda Agan and Sonja Starr find that the white-black differential in callbacks grew by thirty-six percentage points (from 7 percent to 43 percent) after the passage of "ban-the-box" legislation.[28] Together, these research findings suggest that there is discrimination in the labor market against blacks in general, perhaps in part because employers associate race with a criminal record when they lack information to the contrary. Similar patterns of racial discrimination and criminal record stigma have been observed in housing markets.[29] The combination of discrimination and stigma may therefore account for racial inequality in the post-prison outcomes for the young men in our sample.

Differences in social network support, particularly in the labor market, may also explain residual racial inequality. Deirdre Royster finds that whites are able to monopolize better-paying working-class jobs in industries like construction through the use of social networks for hiring and securing apprenticeships.[30] Sandra Smith finds that blacks are less likely to provide job referrals and references to friends, neighbors, and family members.[31] These arguments are consistent with the racialized trajectories into the labor market among young adults identified by Alexander, Entwisle, and Olson.[32] Future research should investigate the role of social network support in integration into the labor market following prison release among young blacks and whites.

CONCLUSION

This chapter has examined our subjects' trajectories over time with regard to employment, postsecondary enrollment, residential independence, substance use, and criminal justice involvement (arrest or custody). Our aims were to understand how trajectories in these different domains relate to one another and come together to form overall post-prison trajectories and to understand which young men were most likely to experience each post-prison trajectory.

One important finding is that there is considerable variation in post-prison trajectories, and that these trajectories do not correspond to a simple relationship between continued criminal justice contact and outcomes in other domains. Rather than simply focusing on persisters and desisters in our sample, our analysis reveals five trajectories that the young men followed after prison that varied in substantively meaningful ways along multiple dimensions. Two of the post-prison transition-to-adulthood trajectories we identify follow pathways that coincide with expectations about the relationship between criminal justice contact and life-course development. Just under one-quarter of our sample belonged to the "transitioning" group: they avoided criminal justice contact and maintained high employment and moderate residential independence. Just under one-quarter of our sample belonged to the "persisting" group: they experienced high rates of continued criminal justice contact and little employment or residential independence; this trajectory primarily reflected a high probability of reimprisonment and long stays in prison during follow-up.

Over half of the sample belonged to one of three other groups that enrich our understanding of the transition to adulthood after prison. The largest group, at 26 percent of the sample, included "unsettled" young men. They maintained low, but nonzero, levels of criminal justice contact, while also experiencing some formal employment and residential independence. This trajectory seems to capture young men who alternate between conventional pathways to adulthood, such as employment and residential independence, and pathways that prolong their contact with the criminal justice system. The fourth group, at 20 percent of the sample, included those we call "disconnected." They had not achieved conventional markers of adulthood, exhibiting little to no employment or residential independence, but they also had managed to avoid further contact with the criminal justice system. The final group, at about 8 percent of the sample, experienced declining employment and residential independence, but instead of reverting to behaviors that had led to criminal justice involvement, these young men eventually enrolled in postsecondary schooling. This "continuing education" group presents an alternative pathway to adulthood that does not rely exclusively on employment, though it does take longer to make the transition.

A second and related finding from these descriptive results is that many formerly incarcerated young men struggle to transition to adulthood, at least by conventional measures. When outcome domains are considered together, our story line does not improve. On the one hand, more than half of the young men in our sample followed trajectories that exhibited lower initial probabilities of criminal justice contact (25 to 40 percent) that decreased over time. On the other hand, their likelihood of achieving one or more of the traditional markers of adulthood remained low. The average probability of achieving residential independence by the fifth post-prison year was less than 50 percent across all groups. Only among transitioners was the average probability of employment above 50 percent by the fifth year after release. Although individuals on a continuing education trajectory had a 25 to 50 percent chance of enrolling in college during the ten years after their release from prison, that group was the smallest. Many pathways to adulthood seem closed to these young men.

A third key finding concerns the primary predictors of who ends up on which trajectory. The extent of a young man's pre-prison criminal justice involvement is one important dimension. Those who had been more involved in the criminal justice system were less likely to be in the transitioning or disconnected groups and more likely to be in the persisting and unsettled groups. Pre-prison education and employment were also critical. Those with more pre-prison and in-prison education were more likely to continue their education after release, and those with more employment experience were also more likely to be transitioners. In contrast, the disconnected and the unsettled tended to have lower levels of education and employment before their imprisonment. Another important predictor is substance use and mental health. Those who exhibited these problems before prison were more likely to be persisters or unsettled and less likely to belong to the transitioning and continuing education groups. The prison experiences of solitary confinement and misconduct citations were particularly common among persisters, and misconducts were particularly common among the unsettled, suggesting that continuity in antisocial behavior during incarceration predicts post-prison adult transitions. Finally, post-prison social contexts were also different across the groups, with persisters and the disconnected being particularly likely to be released to more disadvantaged neighborhoods. Those in the transitioning group were released into the least disadvantaged neighborhoods, while those in the continuing education group returned to the most affluent neighborhoods.

A final key finding is that there are sizable racial inequalities in transition-to-adulthood outcomes. Young black men experienced poorer transition-to-adulthood outcomes than young white men. Blacks were much more likely to be in the persisting group and much less likely to be in the transitioning group. Blacks were also slightly more likely to be in the unsettled and disconnected groups. We examine several possible explanations for racial inequality in transition-to-adulthood outcomes: pre-prison criminal justice contact, pre-prison achievement of transition-to-adulthood markers, pre-prison substance use and mental health, post-release social context, and post-release criminal justice monitoring. Although pre-prison criminal justice contact, pre-prison employment and education, and post-prison neighborhoods explain why blacks were more likely to be in the disconnected group than the transitioning group, the measures in our data are unable to account for the higher rates of black membership in the persisting group.

The next chapter concludes this book with a discussion of the implications of these findings, both for policy and practice and for our understanding of the transition to adulthood among young people from disadvantaged social backgrounds.

Chapter 9 | Conclusion

OUR GOAL IN this book has been to understand how and why some formerly incarcerated young men are able to escape continued involvement with the criminal justice system and transition to adulthood while others are not. We have considered multiple markers of the transition to adulthood, including employment, further education, residential stability, and health, particularly the two main threats to health during the transition to adulthood: substance abuse and violence. We have examined each marker separately (chapters 3 through 7) and how they relate to one another (chapter 8). Besides individual backgrounds, pre-prison experiences, and experiences in prison, a distinct focus of this study has been the role of post-prison experiences and their impact on longer-term outcomes.

To examine these questions, we collected longitudinal data on a two-thirds random sample of 1,300 men paroled from Michigan prisons in 2003 when they were ages eighteen to twenty-five. These data come from multiple administrative records, including criminal justice records from the Michigan Department of Corrections and the Michigan State Police, death certificate data from the National Death Index, and educational records from the state GED database and the National Student Clearinghouse.

One novel aspect of our data collection was the coding of parole agent case notes to capture information about residences and neighborhoods, including where these young men lived and with whom they lived. The painstaking process of coding the case notes, based on detailed knowledge of the way data are recorded within MDOC, took over two years to complete. We then geocoded these records and linked them to census tracts to provide contextual information from the census and other sources on neighborhood and county characteristics. The resulting data set represents one of the largest and most comprehensive efforts to study young adults' experience of prisoner reentry and reintegration during the era of mass incarceration. Its longitudinal nature allowed us to examine changes over time after release from prison, how processes of reintegration evolved, and how these young men fared into their early thirties.

Our analyses of these data are grounded in a theoretical framework on the transition to adulthood that comes from a life-course perspective on human development.[1] This framework emphasizes the ways in which life events are linked over time, and it orients us toward an examination of trajectories and transitions.[2] Trajectories are long-term patterns or sequences of behaviors and social roles, while transitions are discrete changes in roles and behaviors connected to key life events, like school completion, establishing one's own household, or being released from prison. Transitions have the potential to alter long-term life trajectories. From the perspective of the transition-to-adulthood framework, a critical developmental period in which life trajectories can be determined is late adolescence and early adulthood.[3] Particularly for young people of color and those from poor families, imprisonment represents an all-too-typical life event that marks a discrete change in roles and behaviors.[4] Imprisonment as a life event can change or disrupt life trajectories.

Imprisonment during the transition to adulthood can have multiple repercussions. One possibility is that imprisonment interrupts or even precludes the key life events that typically occur during the transition to adulthood, like completing education, launching a career, establishing a household, or starting a family. In other words, imprisonment may delay or interfere with the transition to adulthood and particularly constrain typical life transitions by setting individuals on life trajectories that are difficult to reverse. Indeed, prior research indicates that imprisonment during this life stage will set an individual on a particularly disadvantaged life trajectory, given the social, economic, psychological, and health-related harms that may result from imprisonment.[5] In the face of these findings, we must keep in mind the potentially negative impacts of imprisonment as we seek to explain variation in the transition to adulthood among formerly incarcerated young men.

On the other hand, for those who were already on a trajectory of disadvantage, prison could represent a positive turning point: a break from the past that creates the possibility of a new life trajectory. The extent to which imprisonment is a transition to a more disadvantaged or more advantaged trajectory depends critically on post-prison experiences and the extent to which those experiences support social and economic reintegration.[6] The transition-to-adulthood framework identifies a set of social, contextual, and institutional post-release factors that could be important at this critical juncture in the life course for those who have been imprisoned: social support, social contexts like neighborhoods and families, and institutions like the labor market, the criminal justice system, and the postsecondary education sector. As our findings also show, race is a critical factor as well. The degree to which a formerly incarcerated young man can take advantage of the resources offered by social supports, contexts, and institutions or, conversely, is put at risk by them depends on his past experiences and characteristics, including his different experiences of imprisonment. For this reason, we also examined a wide array of pre-prison characteristics, from education and work experience to prior substance abuse, and in-prison experiences such as solitary confinement, educational opportunities in prison, and time served.

KEY FINDINGS

Multiple Compounding Disadvantages Early in Life

Young men who are imprisoned during the transition to adulthood are extremely disadvantaged on multiple dimensions of prior life experience. These disadvantages need to be taken into account in understanding their post-release outcomes. In our sample, fewer than 9 percent had a high school degree. These low levels of education partly reflect their high rates of involvement in the criminal justice system, including prior spells in prison and custody in the juvenile justice system, both of which interrupt schooling.[7] On average, the young men were first arrested at age fifteen; 44 percent experienced custody in the juvenile justice system; and they had been arrested 3.2 times, were convicted of 3.5 felonies, and had been in jail or prison 2.3 times. The mean age of entry into prison for the focal prison spell was only 20.8 years. Thus, these young men's educations reflected the educational opportunities available within the criminal justice system: 61 percent had earned a GED by the time they entered prison for the focal prison spell.

Despite the challenges associated with low levels of education and the intensity of their involvement with the criminal justice system, many of these young men had been employed in the formal labor market (71 percent) before prison, and some had lived independently (61 percent). Finally, rates of prior substance use and mental illness were also high, even in our self-report data. Eleven percent were daily alcohol users, 27 percent were daily marijuana users, 7 percent were daily stimulant users, and 3 percent were daily depressant users (primarily opioids). Twenty percent reported one or more signs of a mental health problem in the past, as measured by self-reports of diagnoses, hospitalizations, or prescriptions for treating mental health disorders.

Documenting the Post-Prison Experiences of Young Adults

One contribution of this book has been to document the challenges and hardships that face young adults as they leave prison and attempt to build new lives. The post-prison experiences of the formerly incarcerated young men in our study reflected, at least in part, their early life disadvantages. Continued contact with the criminal justice system was almost universal. Just about every young man in our sample was arrested and spent some time in custody (typically jail) after his release from prison. However, these experiences tended to be concentrated in the years immediately following release for those who were not returned to prison.

These young men also struggled to gain a solid foothold in the formal labor market. Slightly over half found formal employment in the first year after release, and rates of formal employment actually fell over time, consistent with other studies of post-prison employment that use administrative data.[8] Yet despite rates of employment at any point in time that varied from 20 to 30 percent, 78 percent of the young men in our sample worked in the formal labor market at some point in the seven years after their release. This suggests that even those who surmounted the difficulties of finding a job had trouble maintaining employment over time. As chapter 6 documents, their employment stability was lower than that of similarly aged men in a national sample, which may reflect their concentration in a small number of industries where turnover is normally high (such as the temporary labor market) as well as their higher-than-average rates of substance abuse, an important precursor to job loss. Formerly incarcerated young men also face challenges with residential stability and independence. Only about 30 percent of our sample returned to the homes where they lived prior to their imprisonment. The typical individual in our sample changed residences every four months, and three-quarters lived in inherently temporary institutional housing at least once. As chapter 7 shows, such residential instability is closely linked to continued involvement in the criminal justice system.

Trajectories of Successful Transitions to Adulthood after Prison

Despite the many challenges they face, we did see some indicators of successful transitions to adulthood among the young men in our sample. By the end of the observation period, 74 percent had a GED and 28 percent had enrolled in college at some point. Our trajectory analysis in chapter 8 shows that as time passed, around one-third of these young men managed to achieve important measures of success in creating stable lives for themselves, exhibiting incredible resilience in the face of multiple adversities. In the longer term, these individuals escaped from frequent contact with the criminal justice system and avoided substance use while achieving either stable employment (one-quarter) or enrollment in college (8 percent). However, almost none of them achieved residential independence, which we define as living alone or with a romantic partner for one year or more. Another one-fifth of the sample also managed to avoid criminal justice involvement and substance abuse but did not achieve any success in the labor market, enroll in college, or become residentially independent. Of the remainder, about one-quarter remained involved in the criminal justice system, largely as a result of reimprisonment, and another one-quarter achieved some employment success but also remained involved in the criminal justice system through continued arrest and short-term jail custody, often on charges that reflected in part their continued substance use.

In the remainder of this section, we discuss the roles of the three theoretical factors from the transition-to-adulthood framework—social supports, social contexts, and institutions—in structuring these outcomes. We conclude with a discussion of the role of race in the transition to adulthood after prison.

The Roles of Social Support, Social Contexts, and Institutions

Our analysis teases out the roles of three key concepts from the transition-to-adulthood framework for those leaving prison as young adults: social support, social contexts, and institutions. Because the formerly incarcerated leave prison with almost nothing, social supports from family and romantic partners can be essential to reintegration, especially in the early period after release, when meeting their own basic needs for food and shelter can be challenging. Such supports are also critical in the long term, especially when it comes to looking for work, accessing health care and substance use treatment, and enrolling in school.[9] In addition to providing access to resources, social relationships also define social roles, are the source of important sources of identity (parent, partner, son), and exert informal social control through monitoring and structuring of time and routine activities.[10] The social separation created by imprisonment makes the rebuilding of social relationships and social bonds an important part of reintegration after release.

We find the strongest evidence for the importance of social support with regard to residential stability, at least as we can measure social support based on with whom a young man lives. Living with family was critical for residential stability among these young men, as it is for many young adults.[11] As chapter 7 documents, slightly over half of the young men in our sample moved in with at least one parent after their release, and living with a parent was associated with greater residential stability. We also see some evidence of social support for other outcomes. Among blacks but not whites, living with a romantic partner was associated with a greater likelihood of enrolling in college. Among whites but not blacks, living independently was associated with a greater likelihood of arrest for a violent crime. We find no association, however, between social support and employment outcomes or substance use.

Social contexts such as neighborhoods and institutional housing can also influence access to critical resources that support the transition to adulthood and present formerly incarcerated young men with both opportunities and risks. The geographic location of neighborhoods may determine their access to jobs, educational institutions, health care, and other programs. Contexts also influence the people with whom an individual regularly comes into contact.[12] Neighbors, for example, can provide information about job leads or educational opportunities, but they may also facilitate opportunities to return to criminal activity or substance use. Finally, neighborhoods may also influence an individual's chances of future police contact and the intensity of parole supervision. Neighborhood characteristics—such as unemployment rates, poverty rates, and racial composition—and county characteristics—such as proximity to educational institutions, crime rates, and the state of the local labor market—provide our central contextual characteristics. We also examine the consequences for the young men in our sample of returning to their pre-prison neighborhood.

Consistent with theories emphasizing the spatial location of jobs and the importance of job networks in employment searches, those who moved to a high-unemployment neighborhood on release from prison were less likely to find employment. However, once a young man was employed, job loss was not associated with neighborhood context. Residential stability, on the other hand, was. Those who lived in more disadvantaged neighborhoods experienced greater residential instability, as residential mobility is more common in such neighborhoods than in the general population. We also find that, for whites, returning to their pre-prison neighborhood and returning to a more disadvantaged neighborhood were associated with a greater risk of substance use. This finding is consistent with the important role of opportunities to access drugs and other drug users in substance use relapse. Although pre-prison neighborhoods were associated with pre-prison educational outcomes, we found no evidence that post-prison neighborhood contexts impacted post-prison educational outcomes, whether with regard to GED completion or college enrollment. Nor did we find an association between proximity to colleges and college enrollment.

Institutions like colleges, treatment programs, the labor market, and the criminal justice system can also shape the transition to adulthood after prison. Institutions allocate resources, open or constrain opportunities, and provide formal means of monitoring and control.[13] For example, the strength of the local labor market and the nature of low-skill work have important implications for economic and residential stability. On the one hand, the criminal justice system—particularly the rules and practices of parole supervision—can channel resources such as employment opportunities or access to treatment programs or other health care. On the other hand, parole supervision can surveil and punish minor infractions and provide a conduit back into prison. Our measures of institutional involvement focus on parole supervision and other criminal justice contact, enrollment in school, and living in residential treatment programs.

In addition to the role of earlier involvement in the criminal justice system, which reduced high school diploma receipt but increased GED earning, we found two roles for criminal justice contact in the post-release period. Continued contact with the criminal justice system was associated with lower college enrollment and greater residential instability. Both of these associations are consistent with a disruptive effect of criminal justice contact on the transition to adulthood. With regard to educational institutions, we found that higher levels of education were associated with greater chances of finding a job and of keeping a job. With regard to the labor market, the industries in which formerly incarcerated young men were able to find jobs have important implications for employment stability, which differs by industry. We also see some evidence of returns to work experience in other domains. Those who worked in the formal labor market before their imprisonment were more likely to earn a GED, and greater earnings in the formal labor market after release were associated with college enrollment, but only among blacks. Post-prison employment reduced substance use and engagement in violence among blacks, whereas enrolling in college after prison reduced substance use among whites.

Race and the Transition to Adulthood after Prison

Race proved critical in structuring the transition to adulthood, although not always to the disadvantage of blacks or to the advantage of whites. Understanding the role of race requires understanding how race structures imprisonment in the first place, and therefore the different pathways into prison—and into our sample—taken by the young black and white men we studied. As discussed in chapter 1, imprisonment rates are much higher for blacks than whites, so whites who are imprisoned are a much more narrowly selected subset of young white men. Although there are no differences between blacks and whites in our sample in their histories of violent crime, our data suggest that blacks were much more likely to have been involved in the drug trade, as evidenced by higher rates of weapons and drug offenses. In contrast, whites in this age group seem to have ended up in prison more often through serious drug use. Although there are no racial differences in prior substance use, whites were more likely to be users of heroin, cocaine, and alcohol than blacks, whose prior drug use was more likely to be limited to marijuana.

Blacks and whites also had somewhat different experiences in prison. Blacks served more time in prison on average than whites (twenty-two months versus twenty months), largely because they served more time beyond their minimum sentence. While blacks were more likely to be cited for misconduct violations while in prison (66 percent, versus 56 percent for whites), whites spent on average slightly more time in solitary confinement (seventy-six days for whites and fifty-seven days for blacks). Although we did not find that these in-prison experiences were consistently predictive of post-release outcomes, they are suggestive evidence of differential treatment by the criminal justice system that could extend to other parts of the system.

Turning to post-release experiences, we see important differences in the social contexts experienced by blacks and whites that mirror more general societal patterns of racial segregation. After release, blacks lived in more disadvantaged neighborhoods compared to the neighborhoods to which whites returned: neighborhood poverty and unemployment rates were higher and there were more black residents. Given the role of geography and social networks in structuring access to job opportunities, as discussed earlier, this disparity has important implications for employment outcomes. In contrast, we found no racial differences in the use of institutional housing or residential sanctions for parole violations.

We also see in our data somewhat different pathways to self-sufficiency in the post-release period. Among the one-third of formerly incarcerated young men who either attained stable employment or enrolled in college, whites were more likely to be employed and blacks were more likely to enroll in college (chapter 8). This is consistent with prior research by Alexander, Entwisle, and Olson, who find that among young adults from poor and working-class families in Baltimore, whites were more likely to find stable work at a living wage in the skilled trades through their social networks and access to apprenticeship programs, without the need for a college education.[14] In contrast, because blacks were largely shut out of such careers, college was the primary avenue to economic security. More generally, the black men in our sample were less likely than whites to experience most of the positive employment outcomes we measure (see chapter 6). We attribute this to reduced rates of entry into jobs in industries that offer better-quality jobs with greater job security, lower turnover, and higher earnings. For example, whites were more likely than blacks to work in construction but less likely to work in temporary labor jobs. This type of sorting into industry by race exacerbates racial inequalities in earnings.

Other post-release outcomes also differed by race. Perhaps the starkest difference is in mortality: blacks who died during our study period died from homicide while whites died almost exclusively from drug overdoses. Whites were more likely than blacks to receive residential substance abuse treatment in the post-release period, although very rarely did anyone receive the recommended three months of such treatment. Although racial differences in the rate of post-prison arrest for violent crimes were statistically significant but small (because violence in general is rare), whites and blacks differed more dramatically in the specific violent crimes for which they were arrested. Blacks were more likely to be arrested for firearm possession, homicide, and robbery, while whites were more likely to be arrested for sex offenses. Blacks were less likely to complete GED degrees in the post-release period, but as noted earlier, they were more likely to enroll in college.

Few of these racial differences are completely accounted for by the key explanatory variables in this study (social supports, contexts, and institutions). As chapter 8 shows, by the time they were released from prison, blacks were more likely to be on a long-term trajectory of disconnection from the labor market and educational institutions, and they were more likely to be in the unsettled trajectory group characterized by continued but low-level involvement with the criminal justice system (short-term jail custody rather than reimprisonment). The overrepresentation of young black men in this group is completely accounted for by the depth of their prior criminal justice involvement, lower levels of education and work experience, and post-release neighborhoods, but all other racial disparities remain when this study's explanatory variables are controlled. This means that there are important aspects of the racialized transition to adulthood after prison that are not captured by our administrative data. Future research should examine the roles of racial discrimination, enhanced stigma, and the importance of social networks for employment and other opportunities, all of which could disadvantage young black men relative to young white men as they exit prison and attempt to rebuild their lives.

IMPLICATIONS FOR THE TRANSITION
TO ADULTHOOD AND DISCONNECTED
YOUNG ADULTS

In this section, we discuss some of the implications of our findings for our understanding of the transition to adulthood, especially among young men from poor families, and suggest directions for future empirical research. Many of our findings are consistent with the core ideas of the transition-to-adulthood framework. Richard Settersten, Frank Furstenberg, and Rubén Rumbaut have shown that social support is critical to creating a solid foundation of residential stability.[15] In addition, we see evidence of the importance of early life trajectories even in a sample that, like ours, was very homogenous with regard to family background. Pre-prison experiences with work, schooling, and the criminal justice system played a role in life outcomes many years later during the post-release period. Consistent with the framework's emphasis on trajectories, we see links between pre-prison experiences and outcomes in the same domain after release. For example, the strongest predictors of post-release engagement in violence or substance abuse are pre-prison violence and substance abuse, and the quality of schooling experienced in the pre-prison period is predictive of whether a young man would eventually earn a GED.

Consistent with the framework's emphasis on transitions, we also find that trajectories can be changed by key events during the post-release period.[16] This helps us to understand where youth from disadvantaged backgrounds find sources of resilience.[17] We find considerable evidence that early post-prison experiences in life course domains beyond criminal justice contact explain some of the longer-term variation we observe in the post-prison transition to adulthood. Our work therefore also supports prior research that implicates early reintegration experiences in life-course and criminal justice outcomes among the formerly incarcerated.[18] Finally, our data illustrate the importance of examining how pathways to adulthood evolve *over time*. Post-release point-in-time measures of the transition-to-adulthood markers we have studied would have suggested worse criminal justice involvement, education, and health outcomes and better employment and residential stability outcomes than are apparent in our longitudinal data.

The transition-to-adulthood framework emphasizes the role of institutions in defining and creating pathways to adulthood, but the criminal justice system, with some notable exceptions,[19] has received little attention from scholars of the transition to adulthood. Our findings show the power of involvement in the criminal justice system to shape the transition to adulthood, from the role of early incarceration in juvenile facilities in structuring opportunities for education and work to the contribution of parole sanctions to residential instability after release. The power of the criminal justice system to influence the transition to adulthood among disadvantaged young adults goes far beyond the prison. This is evident even in a study that, like this one, focuses on only formerly imprisoned young men. Even after they have been released, and even among those that never return to prison, criminal justice contact continues to play a role in their lives, through contact with police, parole supervision, short jail stays, and custodial sanctions. Future research should delve more deeply into these lesser-researched aspects of the criminal justice system and how they interact with the developmental trajectories of young adults.

Yet our results suggest that the criminal justice system is not uniformly negative in its consequences. One area in which the criminal justice system appears to facilitate new pathways to adulthood is through the educational opportunities it can offer. For the young men in our study, prison was a common time for earning a GED, which can open the door to future college enrollment if the right opportunities are provided. It is worth pausing to reflect carefully, however, on the implications of this finding.

First, the apparent success of the prison in providing an opportunity for young adults without a high school credential to earn a GED is also a reflection of the prior failure of primary and secondary schools in the communities where these young men grew up. Second, how does prison provide young men with the opportunity to earn a GED? We speculate that it does so in part because it provides the time to do so. We also suspect that the requirement that prisoners participate in educational programs as a condition of parole provides an immediate incentive for GED preparation. In addition, rudimentary food and shelter are provided as well as a measure of separation from the day-to-day challenges of life in the community, such as the risks of violence and drugs and alcohol, opening time and space for education that was not previously available to young men from disadvantaged backgrounds. In short, other settings could provide the same time and space to allow young men to invest in their futures without the negative consequences of imprisonment, as we discuss further in the section here on policy implications.

Our results have implications for how future research should approach the role of criminal activity in the transition to adulthood. This study accords with prior research in criminology in finding that there is no simple dichotomy between work and crime.[20] Some young men are engaged in both, and some manage to avoid criminal justice contact despite having little success in the formal labor market. In other words, our study also shows that there are multiple pathways to desistance from crime and escape from the criminal justice system, and that desistance from crime does not always mean success in the labor market or other domains of life. Although one-quarter of our sample eventually experienced steady employment and another 8 percent attained steady college enrollment while staying away from involvement in crime, these individuals did not achieve residential independence. Another group, about one-fifth of the sample, also stayed away from involvement in crime but experienced little employment or school enrollment. Further research is needed to understand how this latter group of young men made ends meet day-to-day and whether their prospects for economic self-sufficiency improved over time.

Formerly incarcerated young men are a subset of the young adults who are the focus of scholarship on "disconnected" young people—those who are neither working nor in school—and our results may have implications for future research on the disconnected as well. Our findings suggest that the challenges faced by disconnected young adults go far beyond the lack of work experience, low levels of education, and experiences of incarceration that are the typical foci of such research.[21] First, many young adults do not have the foundation of residential stability that is a prerequisite for effective engagement with work, schooling, and job training. Some but not all of this residential instability is created by the criminal justice system. Future research should explore the role of residential instability among disconnected young adults more generally. Second, although the transition-to-adulthood literature emphasizes the important role of family and other sources of social support,[22] our results suggest that such support can be important even when families have little capacity for financial support. Future research is needed to understand the precise forms of support that poor families provide and how such support facilitates the transition to adulthood among disconnected youth. Third, neighborhoods may play an important role. For example, young white men who return to disadvantaged neighborhoods after prison are at higher risk of substance use. Neighborhoods are especially important for young people of color who are concentrated in high-poverty and high-crime neighborhoods where opportunities for employment are scarce, neighbors do not have connections to job leads, and opportunities for involvement in crime and substance use are readily available. Although there is a large literature on neighborhood effects on children and adolescents,[23] more research is needed to understand their role in disconnectedness among young adults. Fourth, although young adults are typically thought to be too young to be hampered by the physical health problems common among the poor, our results indicate that greater attention to the mental health of disconnected young adults is necessary. Exposure to violence and other forms of trauma is all too common, and it leads to substance use, aggressive behavior, and other mental health problems in early adulthood that can derail schooling and work and the transition to adulthood more generally.[24]

The young men in our study did not follow the traditional pathways from school to work that were once common during the transition to adulthood, particularly among the middle class. For them, prison was not just a pause in that sequence—it helped to define it. Although few enrolled in further schooling soon after their release, over one-quarter of our sample enrolled in postsecondary education—typically in community colleges and for-profit colleges—several years after their release. Those who did eventually enroll in school tended to work for some period of time first, then enroll in further postsecondary schooling.[25] Thus, their pathways inverted the typical school-then-work sequence.

Based on prior research, we suspect this pattern arose in part because of the work requirements of parole, in part because of the immediate need to work to survive day-to-day, and in part because of what they learned from their experience in the workforce about the importance of education for upward mobility away from the secondary labor market.[26] Further research is needed to understand in more detail the transition from work to postsecondary schooling in early adulthood as well as the actual payoff for young adults from further education after their imprisonment. What are the long-term effects of college enrollment, and who is able to complete a degree or certificate? What characteristics of postsecondary institutions are associated with the greatest chance of completion and of future labor market success? How might we facilitate college enrollment earlier in the transition to adulthood for disconnected young adults? We return to these issues later in our discussion of policy implications.

As already discussed, our results also show that the transition to adulthood is deeply racialized. Race is a robust predictor of many of the individual transition-to-adulthood markers we study in chapters 3 through 7, as well as of most of the trajectories described in chapter 8. This is somewhat surprising given the strong adverse selection among whites into prison relative to blacks, for whom imprisonment is much more common (see chapter 1). For example, formerly incarcerated whites are more likely to have serious substance abuse and mental health problems than blacks, and they experience greater residential instability. The robust role of race is also somewhat surprising given that we have conditioned on many of the factors that are typically thought to explain black-white differences, including pre-prison educational opportunities and work experience, intensity of prior criminal justice involvement and time in prison, and exposure to high-poverty and otherwise disadvantaged neighborhoods. Further research is necessary to continue to unpack the sources of racial differences in the transition to adulthood. Based on prior research, we hypothesize that labor market and housing discrimination as well as social ties to working-class living-wage jobs will at least partly account for the racial differences we are unable to explain with our data.[27] Likewise, cultural adaptations to these strains may promote early transitions that differ by race.[28]

In that vein, we are simply unable to examine a number of aspects of the transition to adulthood after prison with the administrative data we used for this study, particularly psychological and cognitive factors. For instance, psychologists emphasize individual agency and psychological capabilities as drivers of successful life-course trajectories.[29] He Len Chung, Michelle Little, and Laurence Steinberg argue that a healthy transition to adulthood develops autonomy, self-direction, and social competence, which enable a young person to take on new roles and responsibilities.[30] Supportive social bonds and social contexts facilitate these developmental goals by providing safe relationships in which to learn these skills and habits. A social-psychological perspective highlights self-concepts and social and personal identities.[31] Young adults who think of themselves as workers or students will seek out role-appropriate activities and avoid role-inconsistent behaviors. Social bonds and social contexts promote the development or maintenance of self-concepts and identities as social interactions provide cues that reinforce or challenge self-conceptions and allow for identity exploration.[32] In addition to having their own independent effects, these more subjective and interpretive measures are likely to mediate and moderate many of the associations we see in our data. We also wonder specifically about the role of different conceptions of masculinity among formerly incarcerated young men, particularly as masculinity relates to receiving social support, the types of work opportunities available to those with criminal records, and violence and substance use.[33]

IMPLICATIONS FOR POLICY AND PRACTICE

Grounding our analysis of the policy implications of our findings in the transition-to-adulthood framework as well, we are led to two important ideas. First, the framework's emphasis on the potential for transitions onto new trajectories during this critical developmental period suggests that the moment of release from prison is a particularly opportune time to intervene in the lives of formerly incarcerated young men and in the lives of disconnected young adults more generally. The fact that one-third of the young men in our sample were able to escape the criminal justice system when released from prison between the ages of eighteen and twenty-five and go on to accomplish some of the markers of the transition to adulthood is evidence that early life trajectories are changeable, even among extremely disadvantaged and disconnected young men. It is worth remembering that these young men made these changes with few of the institutional and social supports that young adults from middle-class backgrounds can take for granted.

Second, the transition-to-adulthood framework's emphasis on institutionalized pathways to adulthood compels us to determine how to create better institutions to support young adults as they transition to adulthood. In an era when the most advantaged young adults are experiencing an elongated period of early adulthood characterized by continued parental and institutional supports,[34] we cannot expect those who have faced the most disadvantages to navigate the transition to adulthood on their own. Our policies should be aimed at creating effective institutionalized pathways to adulthood for all young adults, not just those who are fortunate enough to be able to attend residential colleges.[35] Indeed, much of what we suggest in this chapter would benefit many young adults from poor backgrounds, not just those who have been to prison or have criminal records. In short, we agree with Michael Wald, who writes: "Youth need time for growth. Society should assume responsibility for youth for much longer periods of time."[36]

One important policy implication of our findings concerns the potential for targeting interventions. Recall from chapter 8 that one-fifth of our formerly incarcerated young men fell into the "disconnected" trajectory group. These young men were neither enrolled in school nor employed but also had little further involvement with the criminal justice system. Their ability to avoid recidivism despite the challenges of being otherwise disconnected from key mainstream institutions suggests that there is considerable potential for successful policy intervention, particularly with regard to labor market–oriented programs. The "unsettled" group also has great potential for policy intervention; these were the young men in our study who experienced some success in the labor market but also occasional and continuing low-level involvement in the criminal justice system. Accounting for over one-quarter of the sample, these young men were achieving important successes in the labor market, at least relative to many of their peers, but fell back into trouble with the law occasionally. Policy interventions that support such young men soon after their release might prove effective in cementing their post-prison gains and preventing future problems.

Improving Educational Institutions

Perhaps our most surprising finding was that a large number of formerly incarcerated young men eventually enroll in college. This suggests that, from a policy perspective, educational institutions such as community colleges can serve as an intervention point enabling many formerly imprisoned individuals to participate in a supportive institution that is primarily focused on human development and learning. Yet we also know that rates of college completion are low, particularly in the types of colleges—community colleges and for-profits—where formerly imprisoned young men typically enroll (see chapter 4). This means that taking full advantage of this potential will require significantly greater support.

Harry Holzer argues that low completion rates at community colleges stem from both student and institutional sources, and that new policy initiatives must grapple with both.[37] Students who are the first in their families to attend college and who come from poor backgrounds tend to enter college without essential academic skills and in need of remedial education. They face competing demands on their time, such as family care responsibilities and work, and they need support if they are to chart their way through complex and bureaucratic institutions like colleges successfully. From an institutional perspective, community colleges tend to suffer from high costs, low instructor quality, lack of available seats in key courses, minimal counseling and advising services, little to no accountability for student retention or completion, and too much emphasis on liberal arts degrees that prepare students to transfer to a BA-granting institution rather than prepare them for the workforce upon receipt of an associate's degree.

What can be done to improve retention and completion in community colleges for students from poor backgrounds? One option is to provide more comprehensive and robust support systems, including child care resources and academic counseling to help students select appropriate courses that will move them efficiently toward degrees with labor market payoffs.[38] Another option is to develop programs that allow students to develop remedial skills while still earning credits toward a degree, either by embedding such skill development in degree courses or by creating hybrid high school and community college programs that facilitate the transition from remedial to credit-bearing courses so that students can envision a pathway to degree completion.[39] A third option is to provide "earn-and-learn" opportunities that simultaneously provide opportunities for work and economic stability while linking training directly to fields in high demand in the labor market.[40] Apprenticeship programs have been particularly successful in this regard.[41] Fourth, when earn-and-learn opportunities are not available, another option is to create "stackable" curricula: pathways to advancement comprising multiple sequential certificates, each of which can be earned relatively quickly.[42] Finally, there is also strong evidence that "back-to-school" programs that involve multiyear residential programs and combine skill-building and remedial education, such as Job Corps, increase the probability of GED completion, vocational certificate receipt, and college attendance.[43] Although successfully implementing such programs would require a significant infusion of resources to community colleges and other program providers, when weighed against the potential public savings from lower imprisonment rates, the fiscal case for such investments in young adults at risk of long-term disconnection is strong.

Furthermore, our finding regarding the relatively long average time between release and college enrollment suggests that efforts to accelerate college enrollment after release could also be productive because young adults could be thus qualified for more lucrative careers more quickly. In addition, prior research finds that providing educational opportunities in prison pays off in terms of lower recidivism rates.[44] How might we facilitate faster enrollment in postsecondary education for formerly incarcerated young men? This is again where the concepts of institutionalized pathways and maintaining momentum (chapter 4) are essential. We could imagine a "prison-to-college" pipeline that starts during imprisonment — first, by providing better preparation for college courses (such as remedial education beyond GED courses) and second, by providing more college courses in prisons.[45]

Currently a significant barrier to such measures is lack of eligibility among prisoners and jail inmates for federal and state financial aid; added during the tough-on-crime era of policymaking, these prohibitions have made it very difficult for colleges to provide education in prisons. A recent federal pilot program to allow prisoners in a select set of correctional institutions to receive Pell grants has been successfully implemented and awaits a formal evaluation,[46] but the time is ripe for dropping this prohibition entirely as well as for extending state need-based financial aid to those who are incarcerated. Similarly, restrictions on federal financial aid for individuals with drug crimes should be lifted. While such changes would make it far easier for individual prisoners to enroll in college programs and use their time in prison productively, they would also change the institutional landscape of higher education in prison. With widespread eligibility for financial aid, colleges — particularly those in the rural areas where many prisons are located — could launch new programs for prisoners knowing that tuition revenue would be available at scale. Moreover, with the same colleges providing courses and programs both inside the prison and in the community, course credits would easily transfer and programs begun in prison could be continued more seamlessly after release. For such programs to succeed at scale, colleges would need to be prepared with more comprehensive student services (see earlier discussion), including the services needed by those recently released from prison, such as addiction and other mental health services and help complying with parole requirements while on campus (for example, encouragement to attend substance abuse treatment, avoid contact with others with a criminal record, and maintain employment).

It will also be important to help young adults who choose to work in the period after release from prison transition to further education at a later time. Recall from chapter 4 that many of the young men in our sample who enrolled in college did so after spending some time in the labor market. This is consistent with prior research on disconnected young adults, which found that three-quarters of those who were disconnected "reconnected" first through work rather than educational enrollment.[47] These findings suggest that more readily available institutionalized pathways are needed to help young adults make the transition from the low-skill labor market to further education. Our current institutional arrangements typically assume a very traditional trajectory from school to work, yet given the challenges of residential stability we have documented, that pathway is unlikely to be viable for many formerly incarcerated young adults. This is a further argument for making available earn-and-learn programs like apprenticeships or industry or sectoral partnerships between employers and community colleges, which could facilitate the transition from work to schooling.[48] The road to a postsecondary credential—whether a vocational certificate, associate's degree, or bachelor's degree—can be a long one for those without a strong academic foundation,[49] so it will often be necessary to allow them to pursue work and schooling simultaneously.

Finally, recall that for many of the young men in our sample the prison itself played an important role by providing an opportunity to earn a GED. As discussed in chapter 2, a GED is an insufficient credential for a living-wage job, but it does open the door to opportunities to further one's education or training.[50] On the one hand, those who manage to earn a GED provide further evidence that time spent in prison could be better leveraged with other educational opportunities, either vocational or postsecondary. On the other hand, their success also implies the failure of other institutions to support and develop incarcerated young people, given that many do earn a GED in prison despite the many challenges of prison life. These challenges include regimentation, lack of control over one's daily life, social isolation, and threats of violence. What prison seems to provide is the time to devote to study, free from immediate worries about one's basic material needs, an environment that offers few other opportunities for using one's time, and a ready cohort of fellow learners. These are some of the same institutional features that young adults from middle-class families experience in residential college settings.[51] New institutional arrangements without the negative consequences of imprisonment are needed to support disconnected young adults, who often fall through the cracks that open up between secondary school and postsecondary education.[52]

Improving the Labor Market

Improvements in education among formerly incarcerated young adults are not enough on their own to improve their employment prospects. Prior research clearly shows that the stigma of a criminal record affects both the probability of finding a job and the types of jobs that a job applicant can find.[53] Yet there is little evidence that individuals with a criminal record actually make worse employees than those without a record.[54] How might public policy reduce the stigma of a criminal record in the labor market? "Ban-the-box" laws may be the most common policy solution: they prevent employers covered by the law from asking about criminal records on job applications, although they do not prevent employers from performing background checks and considering an applicant's criminal record later in the hiring process. Guidelines from the Equal Employment Opportunity Commission also discourage the consideration of a criminal record until a provisional hiring decision has been made.[55] Unfortunately, the limited research thus far on the impact of ban-the-box laws suggests that they may harm employment among African Americans without a criminal record, presumably because employers use race as a proxy for criminal record when they are not allowed to ask about it.[56] It is also unclear how frequently criminal background checks are simply used later in the hiring process.

Another option for dealing with criminal record stigma in the labor market is to increase the availability of record expungement, record sealing, and other practices to remove information about an individual's criminal record from public circulation after some period of time has passed, such as the completion of a prison sentence. Currently, expungement and record sealing are available only to a narrow set of individuals with criminal records and require overcoming significant bureaucratic and legal hurdles.[57] Yet once an individual with a criminal record has avoided a new crime for four to nine years (depending on the type of crime and the age at which it was committed), he or she is no more likely to commit a crime than someone of the same age without a record.[58] Recent research shows that record expungement reduces recidivism and the use of public safety net programs such as welfare,[59] and that losing a job opportunity because of a criminal record increases an individual's chance of recidivism.[60] The effectiveness of expungement or sealing will depend on the regulation of the private companies that collect, store, and sell criminal record information to ensure that they do not report sealed or expunged convictions when providing criminal background checks.[61] Greater enforcement of laws to prevent racial discrimination in the labor market or to limit the exclusion of blacks from employment opportunities by using current workers' social networks for hiring[62] could also help reduce racial disparities in post-prison employment.

However, low rates of employment are not simply a function of difficulties finding a job in the formal labor market, as a stigma-focused explanation would suggest. Three-quarters of the young men in our sample worked at some point in the seven years after release from prison, but many had difficulty keeping jobs. As essential as it is to address stigma and discrimination in the labor market, interventions to reduce job loss are also important. This point is reinforced by the unsettled group that emerged from the trajectory analysis in chapter 7. These young men experienced moderate levels of employment that seemed to stem from lack of job stability coupled with continued drug or alcohol use and justice system involvement. As chapter 5 discusses, this job turnover was related in part to the type of work that formerly incarcerated young men, especially black men, were able to find. Such work is generally low-wage and inherently temporary in nature, and it offers little opportunity for substantial improvements in pay over time. Improvements in the nature of employment relations in the low-skill labor market are an important complement to reducing stigma and discrimination.

How might public policy improve both the experience of work and the pay of formerly imprisoned young adults and others who have experienced disconnectedness? One set of policies would improve job quality by limiting practices like unstable work hours, irregular work schedules, and hiring multiple part-time workers instead of full-time workers.[63] Another set of policies would provide greater opportunities for stable employment to those who have the most trouble finding quality work. Although the currently available evidence suggests that transitional jobs for the formerly incarcerated boost employment only in the short term,[64] longer-term opportunities for subsidized work such as public employment or national service programs could improve employment opportunity and stability.[65] Strategies to improve earnings could also enhance job stability by making work pay. Such policies could include expanded and automatically refunded earned income tax credits, increases in the minimum wage, and expanded collective bargaining rights and protections.[66] Other policies and programs can directly address job retention by addressing the precursors of job loss, specifically those related to stressors at work and stressors outside work. Such stressors might be addressed by caseworker initiatives that include a mental health counseling component to which parolees can turn for intensive social support as they confront these challenges.[67]

Substance Abuse Detection and Treatment

Our results suggest that greater access to high-quality substance abuse treatment would also improve the outcomes of formerly incarcerated young men. A history of substance abuse was particularly common among those in our sample who struggled the most to desist from crime. To better address substance abuse and the involvement with the criminal justice system that can accompany it, we need to identify people who may have problems with alcohol or drug abuse sooner, do the research to better understand the relationships between substance use, violence, and involvement in the criminal justice system, and target interventions to those who need them.

The now-defunct Arrestee Drug Abuse Monitoring (ADAM) program contributed to each of these goals. In various instantiations, the ADAM program surveyed and collected substance use testing data from arrested individuals in select jurisdictions across the United States. In 2013, as many as 83 percent of arrestees tested positive for at least one of ten substances, with substantial regional variation both in the prevalence of substance use among arrestees and in the types of substances used.[68] Moreover, the ADAM program tracked the rise of the current opioid epidemic, noting, "An increasing trend from 2000 to 2013 in the proportion of ADAM II arrestees testing positive for opiates in their systems at the time of arrest was significant in all sites."[69] By the time national attention focused on the issue of opioid abuse, however, the ADAM program had been defunded and little information about where resources might best have been targeted was available. Establishing ADAM-like programs that systematically monitor substance use among arrestees should be a consideration for local, state, and national governments. Such data could be used to identify local, state, and national trends, as well as to direct arrested substance users toward treatment before they are incarcerated in state prison. Furthermore, because alcohol is involved in more violent crimes than any other drug, monitoring alcohol use and abuse among arrestees should be among the priorities of these programs.[70]

As chapter 5 shows, existing interventions provided through the criminal justice system appear to be somewhat poorly targeted: blacks are disproportionately targeted for substance abuse testing—a strategy that does not seem to be particularly effective at detecting use given that whites have more extensive histories of serious substance abuse and a greater risk of overdose death. The young men in our sample came of age even before the current opioid crisis, but still provide evidence of the potential value of greater efforts to provide substance abuse treatment. Almost none of the young men in our sample received residential substance abuse treatment that lasted as long as current guidelines recommend (see chapter 5). The

Affordable Care Act of 2010 (ACA, "Obamacare") requires coverage of mental health services, including addiction services, on par with coverage of other types of health care, and Medicaid expansion should radically improve access to coverage for low-income single men like the formerly incarcerated adults in our sample, at least in states that have adopted Medicaid expansion.[71] It is unclear, however, whether greater availability has resulted in greater use of addiction recovery services in the community by formerly incarcerated young adults.

There is also evidence that intensive treatment programs in prison are effective at preventing relapse after release, particularly those that use a therapeutic community model in which those recovering from addiction live together in their own prison housing unit. Such residential substance use treatment (RSAT) programs have been shown to be more effective than other prison programs in reducing recidivism.[72] Such programs could be significantly expanded to serve more of those in need. Cognitive behavioral therapy has also been found to be effective at building better skills in problem-solving and anger management and at reducing recidivism.[73] In addition, public health experts are increasingly urging correctional institutions to include drug therapies such as buprenorphine for the treatment of opioid addictions in their addiction recovery programs.[74] All such interventions are likely to be even more effective with continuity of care after release in the community.[75] Again, however, we note that although prisons may be available settings in which to administer such programs, we could also imagine community-based institutions that provide the same effective programs without the potentially harmful collateral consequences of imprisonment. Finally, more research is needed to better understand which programs are effective for prisoners with different characteristics and substance use patterns and histories, as most of the evaluation research on such programs is now around two decades old.

Reducing Gun Violence

For more than two decades, gun violence has been the leading cause of death among young black men. Moreover, the public health crisis associated with gun violence among young black men is and has been far deeper than the public health crisis associated with substance abuse among young white men. In 2015, mortality rates due to gun violence among young black men were more than twice as high as mortality rates due to drug overdose among young white men.[76]

Strategies to address gun violence can take multiple forms. The most commonly discussed interventions target the transfer of guns to those who would use them to commit crime.[77] Research has shown that most guns used in crimes were acquired through theft, legal personal sales and transfers, and illegal underground gun market purchases.[78] The volume of such transfers, while low relative to the total number of guns in the United States, is still high. For example, in their analysis of the 2015 National Firearms Survey, Deborah Azrael and her colleagues find that more than 500,000 guns were stolen between 2011 and 2015.[79]

Most of the guns used in crimes were acquired only two months prior to the crime in which they were used—suggesting that interventions to address the situations that promote gun acquisition could be effective.[80] Promising strategies for interrupting the flow of guns into the hands of people who might use them to commit violence include increasing licensing requirements and background checks for person-to-person sales and transfers. Although such interventions target the legal market, Cassandra Crifasi and her colleagues find that, in Baltimore, such restrictions also reduced the availability of guns on the illegal market.[81]

Eliminating the circumstances in which carrying a gun becomes necessary can also reduce gun violence.[82] Patrick Sharkey documents a pronounced reduction in violence in American cities over the past twenty years,[83] but the opposite trend was evident in black neighborhoods.[84] Moreover, during that time gun violence mortality rates among young black men have remained relatively stable, at around 75 per 100,000—and black men more likely than men of all other races to be victims of violence.[85] This suggests that young black men still have reason to feel threatened in their neighborhoods and thus are motivated to carry guns for protection.[86]

How can we make young black men feel safer in their neighborhoods? The answer proposed by Bruce Western seems obvious: make those neighborhoods less violent by alleviating poverty in the ways that we have previously described, which include promoting employment and housing stability.[87] Other interventions might target sources of violence more directly. One of those ways might be to disallow concealed carrying. Research regarding laws that allow concealed gun carrying where once it had been prohibited shows that violent crime rates increased—perhaps because being in possession of a gun increased the chance of it being used.[88] Repealing laws that permit concealed carrying could reduce violence generally.

More specific forms of violence also could be reduced. For example, even as violence has abated in many U.S. communities, police aggression and violence have proliferated, particularly in black communities, where one in 1,000 young black men can expect to die at the hands of police.[89] Police violence has corroded trust between police and disadvantaged minority communities such that people in those communities are less likely to call police or to cooperate with them when crimes occur, potentially to the detriment of public safety.[90] Reducing police violence might therefore go a long way toward repairing police-community relations, enhancing trust in police, and thereby enhancing cooperation with police in the investigation of violent crimes.[91]

Improving Housing Stability

Housing stability is a critical foundation for successful reintegration after prison.[92] Chapter 6 describes the challenges that formerly incarcerated young adults face with housing stability, and it links housing instability to lack of family support, reliance on institutional housing, and residential moves generated by criminal justice system sanctions. Based on these findings, we see two general ways in which housing stability might be improved for formerly incarcerated young adults. One is to help them rebuild and solidify connections to family who might provide social support in the period after release, when it is particularly hard to establish an economic foundation all on one's own. At the most basic level, prisons could do more to facilitate visits and communication by removing barriers to visitation like distance, cost, and unpleasant visitation procedures.[93] Yet more radical proposals also deserve serious consideration. Donald Braman proposes higher wages for prison work that could be used to help support family on the outside.[94] The ability to contribute to family economic well-being even while incarcerated can boost feelings of membership in the family and make sure that families are equipped to help house their loved one upon release. Another option is to help offset the costs of housing a family's formerly incarcerated loved one by loosening restrictions on access to public housing or even including them as dependents for some period of time after release, when benefit amounts from social welfare programs are calculated.

Yet some formerly incarcerated young adults will never be able to rely on family, simply because family members are unavailable or incapable of such support. Thus, a second way to improve housing stability would rely on more robust institutional supports. One critical problem with current institutional housing for formerly incarcerated young adults is that it is almost always designed to be temporary. Temporary institutional housing options do not recognize the long time frame required by this population to achieve residential independence. Our data show that institutional housing options typically include homeless shelters, substance abuse treatment programs, and correctional institutions, all of which are not intended to be long-term residences. Long-term supportive housing is sorely needed. Another model would couple either work or schooling with stable, long-term housing. This strategy would provide young adults without family resources with the residential stability they need to focus on human capital development. We would also note that reducing the frequency of residential moves created by parole sanctions would help as well. Such policy changes would be part of larger efforts at parole reform, to which we now turn.

Fostering Greater Social Support during Incarceration

We found little association between post-prison outcomes and young men's experiences in prison, such as solitary confinement, time served, and misconduct violations. One exception was the opportunity to earn a GED. Nevertheless, despite modest educational advances, there remained a robust continuity between the pre-prison, in-prison, and post-prison violence and substance use behaviors of these young men. Recent research indicates, however, that prisons can interrupt these cycles of violence and substance use by fostering greater social support between imprisoned individuals and their families, through direct contact and regular communication.[95] Policies and practices that facilitate contact with family members—particularly with spouses and children—may reduce recidivism.[96] Removing barriers to visitation (for example, housing prisoners closer to family members or providing subsidies for family members to travel to distant prisons) would be one such intervention, as would facilitating access to telecommunications (such as creating the infrastructure for video calls and reducing the cost of phone and video calls).[97] In addition, prison interventions that foster connections between prisoners and community volunteers, mentors, and clergy in some instances have been found to be even more effective at improving in-prison behavior and reducing recidivism, perhaps because these community volunteers offer "higher-quality" social support without the conflict that often accompanies familial relationships.[98] That these nonfamilial relationships also can foster desistance through social support is encouraging because, by the time they have been incarcerated, many prisoners "have ruined important personal relationships," closing off that vehicle of social support.[99]

Easing the Transition from Prison to Community

Coming home from prison, starting parole supervision, and trying to rebuild one's life can be traumatic—particularly for young people who have not previously made such a transition.[100] Stressors associated with reentry, such as housing instability, unemployment, discrimination, reduced health care, and family tension, can lead to substance use and violence.[101]

Facilitating smoother transitions to the community can help improve the well-being of released prisoners.[102] Although such "discharge programming" is more common in many prison systems than it used to be, only about 10 percent of prisoners in the United States receive it.[103] Especially in states that have expanded Medicaid coverage in the wake of the ACA, discharge programming can promote continuity of medical and mental health treatment for the 44.3 percent of prison inmates with chronic diseases, the 21.0 percent who have had infectious diseases, the 31.6 percent who are disabled, the 36.9 percent who have diagnosed mental health problems, and the 58.5 percent who are dependent on or abuse drugs.[104] But formerly incarcerated young men need more than medical and mental health care to successfully transition into adulthood. We have documented the significant educational, employment, and housing deficits these young men face as they embark on their post-prison lives. Programs targeted to one domain, such as employment, are unlikely to facilitate a complete transition to adulthood in which desistance plays an important role.[105] Programs that systematically assess multi-domain needs and focus services on them to promote the reentry trajectories of the formerly incarcerated have been shown to achieve their objectives.[106] However, many such programs are neither implemented with fidelity nor evaluated with appropriate rigor, so building a knowledge base remains challenging.[107] This is an area in which greater program development and evaluation research are greatly needed.

Making Parole a Supportive Rather than Punitive Institution

Alongside educational institutions and prisons, parole is a central institution in the lives of the young men we studied. Although parole was not always such,[108] contemporary parole has become an institution that too often creates pathways that maintain entanglement in the criminal justice system rather than pathways to opportunity and reintegration. For example, returns to prison for parole violations are a central driver of prison's revolving door,[109] and even lesser sanctions disrupt residential stability and employment.[110] Put slightly differently, rather than prioritizing the rehabilitation and developmental needs of those under its charge, parole currently focuses on monitoring, control, and punishment.[111] For instance, parole officers are held accountable for the crimes committed by the parolees they supervise, but not recognized for positive outcomes like education, employment, or civic participation.[112]

Improving the chances of a successful transition to adulthood for formerly imprisoned young adults requires reforming parole, but how might we do so? At the broadest level, the orientation of parole toward monitoring and control must be reverted to a rehabilitative orientation. One way to do this would be to incentivize individuals on parole to engage in schooling, work, and mental health and substance use treatment. For example, a proposal recently introduced in California would have provided "good time" credits to parolees for completing education, training, and treatment milestones that would reduce their time on parole.[113] Such a policy change is important not only for the message it would send to individuals on parole but for the way it would fundamentally change the work of parole officers, who would be tasked with monitoring and encouraging such activities. Holding parole officers accountable not just for crimes committed by parolees but also for their well-being and human development would incentivize the parole system itself to return to the function it performed before the era of mass incarceration—acting as a broker of social services. Indeed, the intense involvement that formerly incarcerated young men have with parole supervision is a lost opportunity to help them develop sustained connections to supportive institutions and individuals.

Changing the orientation of parole also requires changing how it responds to technical violations of parole that are not crimes (or not crimes that would ordinarily lead to imprisonment). Bruce Western argues that the antisocial behavior of those who have been to prison, such as substance use and violence, is often the result of untreated traumas from early in life, such as being a victim of violence, either in the streets or in the home, being separated from family and loved ones, and witnessing violence.[114] Such traumas need to be healed, as further punishment either does nothing to address the underlying problems or exacerbates them. Viewed in this light, violations of parole conditions can be understood not as signs of resistance to social norms that need to be punished, but as indicators that further support or services are necessary. Although short periods of custody may be necessary in some cases when a parolee is a clear danger to himself or others, the default response should not be reincarceration.

Such changes in the nature of parole would not be cheap to implement, but given the large number of prisoners who are reimprisoned on parole violations, they would presumably pay for themselves over time via lower imprisonment costs.[115] Indeed, large-scale reforms to the broader criminal justice system of the type we propose for parole require shrinking the prison system so that resources can be directed toward social services, supports, and treatment of underlying problems in the community—an idea that has come to be known as "justice reinvestment."[116] Would imprisoning fewer people reduce public safety? There is little evidence that it would, especially as we shrink prisons from their current scale.[117] Recent research shows that even among those convicted of violent crimes, prison does little to reduce reoffending and may even increase future criminal behavior. Even while individuals convicted of violent crimes are incarcerated, their imprisonment prevents less violent crime than we typically assume, in part because only 5 percent of those convicted of a violent crime are rearrested for a violent crime.[118] Preventing a single individual convicted of a violent crime from committing a new violent crime within five years of their sentence requires imprisoning sixteen such individuals.[119]

The high cost and low effectiveness of imprisonment in preventing violent crime is further evidence in favor of a developmentally informed policy approach that focuses on addressing underlying problems. Such an approach would depart from the dominant "persisting" versus "desisting" narrative to develop a robust set of institutionalized pathways to adulthood for formerly incarcerated young men. Moreover, these institutionalized pathways should be robust enough to support the broader population of disadvantaged young adults, many of whom become disconnected from society or unsettled in their lives as they struggle to successfully transition to adulthood in the contemporary United States.

Notes

CHAPTER 1: INTRODUCTION

1. Peter and Luke are pseudonyms, as are the names we use for the profiles presented in later chapters. These profiles are intentionally obfuscated to protect the identities of these young men. We have removed specific dates and geographical information and have also modified non-essential details of their lives and criminal justice system involvement. The profiles are based not only on the narrative parole agent case notes, which were painstakingly coded by our research team, but also on the multiple sources of administrative data on which this study draws (see chapter 2).
2. Driving away is a category of offense in Michigan that includes joyriding (stealing a car without the intent to keep it) as well as taking a vehicle you have access to (a relative's, for example) without the owner's permission.
3. Brame et al. 2012.
4. Uggen and Wakefield 2006.
5. Shanahan 2000.
6. Andrews and Westling 2014; Craig and Piquero 2014.
7. Edwards, Lee, and Esposito 2019; Edwards, Esposito, and Lee 2018.
8. Settersten, Furstenberg, and Rumbaut 2005; Danziger and Rouse 2007; Waters et al. 2011; Swartz et al. 2011.
9. Besharov 1999; Edelman, Holzer, and Offner 2005; Mincy 2006.
10. Holzer, Offner, and Sorensen 2005.
11. Neal and Rick 2014.
12. Fernandes-Alcantara 2015.
13. Besharov 1999; Edelman, Holzer, and Offner 2005; Mincy 2006.
14. Fernandes-Alcantara 2015.
15. Shanahan 2000.
16. Shanahan 2000; Settersten, Furstenberg, and Rumbaut 2005; Arnett 2004, 2006; Schulenberg and Schoon 2013.
17. Schoon 2015; Waters et al. 2011.
18. Arnett 2004.

19. Furstenberg 2008.
20. National Center for Education Statistics 2019.
21. Shapiro et al. 2018.
22. Farber 2007.
23. Bell et al. 2007.
24. Goldscheider and Goldscheider 1999.
25. Bell et al. 2007; Newman and Aptekar 2007; Buchmann and Kriesi 2011.
26. Settersten, Ottusch, and Schneider 2015.
27. Waters et al. 2011.
28. Andrew et al. 2006; Waters et al. 2011; Eliason, Mortimer, and Vuolo 2015.
29. Benson and Furstenberg 2006.
30. Waters et al. 2011.
31. DeLuca, Clampet-Lundquist, and Edin 2016a; Alexander, Entwisle, and Olson 2014.
32. Settersten and Ray 2010; DeLuca, Clampet-Lundquist, and Edin 2016a.
33. Sandefur, Eggerling-Boeck, and Park 2005.
34. Schoeni and Ross 2005.
35. Lareau and Cox 2011.
36. Waters et al. 2011, 202.
37. Silva 2013; Bushway, Stoll, and Weiman 2007.
38. Silva 2013, 146.
39. Waters et al. 2011.
40. For "accelerated adulthood," see Waters et al. (2011); for "accelerated role transitions," see Alexander, Entwisle, and Olson (2014).
41. Deluca, Clampet-Lundquist, and Edin 2016a.
42. Deluca, Clampet-Lundquist, and Edin 2016a, 182.
43. Holzer 2018; Hoxby and Avery 2013; Hoxby and Turner 2013.
44. Settersten 2005.
45. Wald 2006.
46. Edelman, Holzer, and Offner 2005; Mincy 2006.
47. Edelman, Holzer, and Offner 2005.
48. MaCurdy et al. 2014.
49. Hair et al. 2009.
50. Alexander, Entwisle, and Olson 2014.
51. Sandefur, Eggerling-Boeck, and Park 2005.
52. Besharov 1999; Edelman, Holzer, and Offner 2005; Mincy 2006.
53. Sharkey 2013; Perkins and Sampson 2017; Harris and Lee 2012.
54. Perkins and Sampson 2017.
55. Lei and South 2016.
56. Alexander, Entwisle, and Olson 2014.
57. Royster 2003.
58. Holzer 2018.

59. Arnett 2004.
60. Waters et al. 2011; Alexander, Entwisle, and Olson 2014.
61. DeLuca, Clampet-Lundquist, and Edin 2016a.
62. Kaeble and Cowhig 2018.
63. Wagner and Sawyer 2018.
64. Western 2006; Garland 2001.
65. Friedman and Pattillo 2019; Harris 2016; Phelps 2016; Pfaff 2017; Kohler-Hausmann 2018; Dobbie, Goldin, and Yang 2018.
66. Soss and Weaver 2017.
67. Geller and Fagan 2019.
68. Edwards, Lee, and Esposito 2019; Edwards, Esposito, and Lee 2018.
69. Beckett and Herbert 2010; Garland 2001; Simon 2007; Gottschalk 2016.
70. Wacquant 2009.
71. Wagner 2012.
72. Pew Center on the States 2009.
73. Pettit and Western 2004.
74. Travis 2005; National Research Council 2014; Western 2006; Clear 2007.
75. Raphael and Stoll 2013
76. Tonry 1996; Weaver 2007; Western 2006; Hinton 2016.
77. Alexander 2010; Wacquant 2001; Rothstein 2017.
78. Weaver, Papachristos, and Zanger-Tishler 2019.
79. Pettit and Western 2004, 151, 155.
80. Pettit and Western 2004; see also Hinton 2016.
81. Turney and Wakefield 2019.
82. Pager, Western, and Bonikowski 2009; Pager 2003; Leasure and Martin 2017; Evans, Blount-Hill, and Cubellis 2019.
83. Link and Phelan 2001; Hatzenbuehler 2016.
84. Hatzenbuehler and Link 2014.
85. Hatzenbuehler, Nolen-Hoeksema, and Dovidio 2009; Hatzenbuehler, Phelan, and Link 2013.
86. Pager 2007; Western 2002; Bushway, Stoll, and Weiman 2007; Apel and Powell 2019.
87. Kirk and Sampson 2013; Caputo-Levine 2013; Harding, Morenoff, and Wyse 2019.
88. Yi 2019.
89. Western and McLanahan 2001; Swisher and Waller 2008; Geller 2013; Turney 2015; Turney and Wildeman 2018.
90. Sugie and Turney 2017.
91. Manza and Uggen 2006; Gottschalk 2016; Lerman and Weaver 2014a; Weaver and Lerman 2010; Wildeman et al. 2014.
92. Smeeding 2017.
93. Foster and Hagan 2015.

94. Wakefield and Wildeman 2013; Wildeman and Muller 2012; Haskins 2014, 2015, 2016; Turney and Haskins 2014.

95. Foster and Hagan 2017; Lee et al. 2014; R. D. Lee, Fang, and Luo 2013; Turney, Schnittker, and Wildeman 2012; Turney and Wildeman 2013; Wildeman, Schnittker, and Turney 2012.

96. Foster and Hagan 2007.

97. Page, Piehowski, and Soss 2019.

98. Grinstead et al. 2001.

99. Sykes and Maroto 2016; Hagan and Foster 2017.

100. Clear 2007.

101. Hagan and Foster 2012.

102. National Research Council 2007; Pew Charitable Trusts 2014.

103. Bronson and Carson 2019.

104. Harding, Morenoff, and Wyse 2019.

105. Western et al. 2015; Western 2015, 2018.

106. Little prior work has specifically examined the transition to adulthood after prison. One exception is Steven Raphael (2007), who finds that incarceration in early adulthood reduces annual work hours and probability of marriage among young men, but who finds no effect on hourly earnings or living with one's parents. Robert Apel and Gary Sweeten (2010) find that incarceration reduces employment following release, primarily through lack of searching for employment. For conceptual and literature reviews, see Osgood, Foster, Flanagan, and Ruth (2006) and Foster and Gifford (2005).

107. Travis and Visher 2005. Nationwide in 1997, almost 9,300 individuals who entered prison as juveniles exited prison (Foster and Gifford 2005).

108. Settersten, Furstenberg, and Rumbaut 2005.

109. Binswanger et al. 2007a; Wang et al. 2009; Howell et al. 2016; Baillargeon et al. 2009; Wildeman, Noonan, et al. 2016; Wildeman, Carson, et al. 2016; Schnittker, Massoglia, and Uggen 2012; Baćak, Andersen, and Schnittker 2018.

110. James and Glaze 2006.

111. Schnittker 2014.

112. Hammett, Roberts, and Kennedy 2001.

113. Mumola 1999.

114. Raphael 2007; Foster and Gifford 2005; Chung, Little, and Steinberg 2005.

115. Uggen and Wakefield 2006.

116. Langhan and Levin 2002; Travis and Visher 2005.

117. Bonczar 2003.

118. Visher and Travis 2003.

119. Western 2006.

120. Harding, Morenoff, and Wyse 2019.

CHAPTER 2: STUDYING THE TRANSITION TO ADULTHOOD AFTER PRISON

1. Pew Center on the States 2009; Sawyer and Wagner 2019.
2. Sampson and Laub 1992, 64.
3. Elder 1988.
4. Elder 1988; Hogan and Astone 1986, 110.
5. Sampson and Laub 1992, 1993.
6. Staff and Mortimer 2008.
7. Elder 1988.
8. Elder 1974.
9. Sampson and Laub 1992; Hogan and Astone 1986.
10. Hogan and Astone 1986.
11. Furstenberg 2010; Kerckhoff 1993; Elder 1988.
12. Laub and Sampson 2001; Osgood et al. 2006, 12.
13. Hogan and Astone 1986; Settersten 2005; Lee 2014.
14. DeLuca, Clampet-Lundquist, and Edin 2016a; Lee 2014.
15. Sampson and Laub 1993.
16. Sampson and Laub 1992, 1993.
17. Sampson and Laub 1993, 18.
18. Laub, Nagin, and Sampson 1998; Sampson, Laub, and Wimer 2006.
19. Warr 1993; Laub and Sampson 2001.
20. Maruna 2001b; see also Paternoster and Bushway 2009.
21. Braman 2004.
22. Hagan 1993; Pager 2003.
23. Desmond 2012; Waters et al. 2011; Western et al. 2015.
24. Settersten, Furstenberg, and Rumbaut 2005; Danziger and Rouse 2007; Waters et al. 2011; DeLuca, Clampet-Lundquist, and Edin 2016a; Buchmann and Kriesi 2011; Alexander, Entwisle, and Olson 2014.
25. Arnett 2000; Benson and Furstenberg 2006; Andrew et al. 2006; Waters et al. 2011; Eliason, Mortimer, and Vuolo 2015; DeLuca, Clampet-Lundquist, and Edin 2016a. Parenthood and marriage are also key markers of the transition to adulthood in the literature. Marriage during the age range covered by our study is now incredibly rare among those who are involved with the criminal justice system (Wyse, Harding, and Morenoff 2014). Our data allow us to capture cohabitation, but this is less clearly a marker of the transition to adulthood. With regard to parenthood, half of the young black men and one-third of the young white men we study were parents at prison entry (table 2.1), and few recently incarcerated young men leaving prison are financially capable of supporting children (Harding, Morenoff, and Wyse 2019), making this a poor marker of the transition to adulthood for this study.

26. Pettit and Western 2004.
27. Pettit and Western 2004; Weaver, Papachristos, and Zanger-Tishler 2019.
28. Comfort 2012; Seim 2016; Harding, Dobson, et al. 2016.
29. Bradley et al. 2001.
30. Lutze, Rosky, and Hamilton 2013.
31. Braman 2004.
32. On housing instability, see Herbert, Morenoff, and Harding (2015); on homelessness, see Metraux and Culhane (2004) and Roman and Travis (2006).
33. Settersten, Furstenberg, and Rumbaut 2005.
34. Fomby and Bosick 2013; Schoeni and Ross 2005.
35. Furstenberg 2008, 2010.
36. Schulenberg et al. 2005; see also Andrews and Westling 2014.
37. Granovetter 1973.
38. Merton 1938.
39. Wyse, Harding, and Morenoff 2014; Felson et al. 2012.
40. Morenoff, Sampson, and Raudenbush 2001a.
41. Cadora, Swartz, and Gordon 2003; Lynch and Sabol 2004; Solomon, Thomson, and Keegan 2004.
42. Hipp, Petersilia, and Turner 2010; Kubrin and Stewart 2006; Mears et al. 2008; Morenoff and Harding 2011.
43. Massoglia, Firebaugh, and Warner 2013.
44. Massoglia, Firebaugh, and Warner 2013; Lee, Harding, and Morenoff 2017.
45. Massoglia, Firebaugh, and Warner 2013; Warner 2016; on the greater residential instability of blacks, see Warner 2015.
46. Neighborhoods in this study are census tracts.
47. These scales measure different dimensions, as there are many neighborhoods that are low on both disadvantage and affluence; these tend to be white working-class neighborhoods.
48. Harris and Lee 2012.
49. Sampson, Morenoff, and Earls 1999; Sampson, Raudenbush, and Earls 1997.
50. Raphael and Weiman 2007; Sabol 2007.
51. Smith 2007; Wilson 1987; Young 2004.
52. Mouw 2000; Wilson 1987.
53. Hipp et al. 2009a, 2009b.
54. Cloward and Ohlin 1960.
55. Clear 2007; Freisthler et al. 2005; Hill and Angel 2005.
56. Bushway, Stoll, and Weiman 2007; Western 2002; Harding, Morenoff, and Wyse 2019.
57. Pager 2007.
58. Lageson 2017.
59. For example, Torche 2011.
60. Lareau and Cox 2011; Lareau 2000, 2011.

61. Rios 2011, 2017.
62. DeLuca, Clampet-Lundquist, and Edin 2016a; Holzer 2018.
63. Roksa and Velez 2012.
64. Bushway and Piehl 2007; Frase 2009; Petersilia and Turner 1993.
65. Kirk and Sampson 2013.
66. Hart 2013.
67. Desmond 2012; Waters et al. 2011; Western et al. 2015.
68. Hatzenbuehler and Link 2014.
69. Bozick et al. 2018; National Research Council 2014; Patterson 2010, 2013; Schnittker et al. 2015.
70. National Commission on Correctional Health Care 2002; Visher, LaVigne, and Travis 2004; Braman 2004; Massoglia 2008a, 2008b; Caputo-Levine 2013; Smith 2015.
71. Haney 2002; Guenther 2013.
72. Sharkey 2018b; Patterson 2010, 2013.
73. Comfort 2012.
74. Lattimore and Visher 2009.
75. Valentine, Mears, and Bales 2015.
76. Petersilia 2003; Feeley and Simon 1992.
77. Petersilia and Turner 1993.
78. Harding, Morenoff, and Herbert 2013; Harding, Siegel, and Morenoff 2017.
79. Harding, Morenoff, Nguyen, and Bushway 2017.
80. Sabol, West, and Cooper 2009; Carson 2014.
81. Pew Center on the States 2009. Parole is just one form of community correctional supervision. The other major category of community supervision is probation, which is usually a sentence that is an alternative to incarceration in prison or jail.
82. Petersilia 2003.
83. Note that we are not asking how the transition to adulthood is directly affected by imprisonment, since everyone in our data has been imprisoned. See Harding et al. (2018) for a study of the effect of imprisonment on employment among young adults.
84. Our data also include sixty-three female parolees ages eighteen to twenty-five at the time of their parole in 2003. We chose to exclude them from our analyses because the reentry experiences of women differ substantially from those of men (Leverentz 2014), and because the group is unfortunately too small to analyze separately.
85. Michigan is a low immigration state, so there are almost no Latinos or Asians in our data.
86. Settersten, Furstenberg, and Rumbaut 2005; see, for example, Danziger and Rouse 2007.

87. Waters et al. 2011; see, for example, DeLuca, Clampet-Lundquist, and Edin 2016a.
88. On the difficulty of survey-based methods, see Western, Braga, and Kohl 2017.
89. Pettit 2012. See Bushway, Briggs, et al. (2007) for other studies using state-specific administrative data.
90. Cadora, Swartz, and Gordon 2003; Rose and Clear 1998; Visher, LaVigne, and Travis 2004; Western 2018.
91. Kirk 2019.
92. Individuals were selected for the sample who had a parole date in 2003, but some individuals were released to the community prior to their parole (12 percent). Those individuals were released to what the MDOC termed "correctional centers" at the time, or were put on electronic monitoring. They had access to the community to look for work and visit family. Thus the years that start the post-prison observation period range from 2000 to 2003. Only one individual in the sample was released in 2000. Nine were released in 2001 and 83 in 2002.
93. This is an example of what methodologists call "endogenous selection" (Elwert and Winship 2014).
94. Lee and Staff 2007.
95. Steele 2008.
96. Nagin, Jones, and Lima Passos 2016.
97. National Association of Manufacturers 2019.
98. Farley 2018.
99. U.S. Bureau of Labor Statistics 2019.
100. Kalleberg and von Wachter 2017.
101. Wagner and Sawyer 2018.
102. University at Albany 2011.
103. Harding, Morenoff, Nguyen, and Bushway 2017.
104. Pew Center on the States 2012.
105. Kerson 2013.
106. Farley 2018; Massey and Denton 1993.
107. Farley 2018.
108. Farley 2018.

CHAPTER 3: EDUCATION, PART 1: THE GED

1. Wight et al. 2010; Zaff et al. 2014.
2. Rampey et al. 2016, 5.
3. Kirk and Sampson 2013.
4. Greenberg et al. 2007.
5. Greenberg et al. 2007, 48.

6. Entwisle, Alexander, and Olson 2005; Tyler and Lofstrom 2009; Kirk and Sampson 2013.

7. Entwisle, Alexander, and Olson 2005.

8. The GED test covers five subject areas and does not require individuals to complete all subject tests at one time. Therefore, individuals often attempt different subject tests at different times. For the purposes of our study, a GED is earned as of the date of the award, which is typically when the last subject test is passed.

9. We construct the following five categories for GED attainment: pre-prison GED in the community; pre-prison GED from previous custody spell; GED during focal prison sentence; post-prison GED in the community; and post-prison GED while in custody.

10. Rothstein 2015; Roscigno 1998.

11. Heckman, Humphries, and Kautz 2014.

12. U.S. Department of Education 2011.

13. Wayman 2001.

14. U.S. Department of Education 2011.

15. Cameron and Heckman 1993.

16. Tyler, Murnane, and Willett 2000.

17. Tyler, Murnane, and Willett 2000.

18. Jepsen, Mueser, and Troske 2017.

19. Tyler and Kling 2007; Cho and Tyler 2010.

20. Tyler and Kling 2007.

21. Nowotny, Masters, and Boardman 2016.

22. Esperian 2010; Davis et al. 2013.

23. Maralani 2011.

24. Hair et al. 2009; MaCurdy et al. 2014.

25. Becker 1962.

26. Quinn 2015.

27. Phillips and Chin 2004.

28. Roscigno 1998.

29. Hogan and Astone 1986, 121.

30. Hair et al. 2009.

31. Jencks and Mayer 1990; Owens 2010.

32. Reardon 2016.

33. Phillips and Chin 2004.

34. Owens 2010.

35. Coleman 1988.

36. Sampson, Sharkey, and Raudenbush 2008; Sharkey 2010.

37. Phillips and Chin 2004.

38. Phillips and Chin 2004.

39. For example, Morgan and Jung 2016.

40. Phillips and Chin 2004.
41. Sweeten 2006; Hirschfield 2009; Kirk and Sampson 2013.
42. Kirk and Sampson 2013.
43. Kirk and Sampson 2013, 37.
44. Michigan Code of Criminal Procedure, Act 175 of 1927 (section 771.3).
45. Sampson and Laub 1993.
46. Employment can also open future opportunities through on-the-job training and the acquisition of new skills. According to Gary Becker (1962), workers increase their productivity through learning new skills and perfecting previously learned skills while on the job.
47. Sampson and Laub 1995.
48. Sampson and Laub 1995, 141.
49. For example, Sampson, Laub, and Wimer 2006.
50. For example, Travis 2005.
51. Upchurch and McCarthy 1990.
52. Table 3.A4 displays bivariate comparisons for figure 3.3.
53. See, for example, Kirk and Sampson 2013.
54. For example, Mclanahan 2004.
55. Table 3.A5 displays bivariate comparisons for figure 3.4.
56. U.S. Department of Education 2011.
57. Table 3.A6 displays full model results for figure 3.5. We use a logistic regression model to estimate the probability of earning a GED in prison versus in the community before prison. The outcome variable includes all individuals who earned a GED while in prison and compares them to individuals who had earned a GED in the community before entering prison. The model includes age at prison entrance, race, the number of years in prison, in-prison management level, mental illness, whether ever married (widowed, divorced, or separated), whether ever employed, median household income, dependent(s), attempts to complete ninth grade or higher, pre-prison living situation (with older relatives, independent: alone, with spouse, with roommates, at a treatment center, at a criminal justice institution, homeless/unknown), the proportion of individuals in the neighborhood over age twenty-five with less than a high school education, K-12 income-adjusted math and reading score percentile, K-12 student-teacher ratio, K-12 student expenditures, in-prison misconduct (violent), in-prison misconduct (property), in-prison misconduct (drug), and the number of prior prison entries.
58. Table 3.A7 displays full model results for figure 3.6. We use a logistic regression model to predict the probability of earning a GED in prison among individuals who could have earned the degree. The outcome variable compares individuals who earned a GED in prison to those who could have earned the credential in prison but did not. The model includes age at

prison entry, race, the number of years in prison, in-prison management level, mental illness, whether ever married (widowed, divorced, or separated), whether ever employed, median household income, dependent(s), attempted to complete ninth grade or higher, pre-prison living situation (with older relatives, independent: alone, with spouse, with roommates, at a treatment center, at a criminal justice institution, homeless/unknown), the proportion of individuals in the neighborhood over age twenty-five with less than a high school education, K-12 income-adjusted math and reading score percentile, K-12 student-teacher ratio, K-12 student expenditures, in-prison misconduct (violent), in-prison misconduct (property), in-prison misconduct (drug), and the number of prior prison entries.

CHAPTER 4: EDUCATION, PART 2: POSTSECONDARY ENROLLMENT

1. National Center for Education Statistics 2014.
2. Donovan and Bradley 2018.
3. U.S. Bureau of Labor Statistics 2015.
4. Arnett 2000; Fitzpatrick and Turner 2007.
5. National Center for Education Statistics 2017b.
6. Beginning Postsecondary Students 2009.
7. National Center for Education Statistics 2017a. The increase in enrollments is not as notable for men as it is for women, but the gap between enrollments and degree completion is even larger for men. Not all NCES statistics presented here are readily disaggregated by gender, so we present estimates for the entire population for consistency.
8. Gale et al. 2014.
9. Pager 2003.
10. Foster and Hagan 2007.
11. Dynarski, Hemelt, and Hyman 2013.
12. Breen and Goldthorpe 1997.
13. These were students with NSC records prior to their 2003 release, and their enrollments may not have been for college-level credit.
14. National Center for Education Statistics 2012.
15. Cameron and Heckman 1993.
16. The number of "persisting" enrollments—the medium gray in each stacked bar—is equal to the difference between the total enrollments (the stacked bars above zero) and the enrollments ending in the preceding quarter. For example, an enrollment that began in August 2005 and ended in December 2006 would be represented as beginning in the third quarter of 2005, persisting in the first, second, third, and fourth quarters of 2006, and ending in the fourth quarter of 2006. Enrollments are considered "new" if they are

separated by more than a summer (or a month during the traditional academic year), meaning that the same individual may be represented in this figure multiple times. The intent here is to capture the presence of our sample cohort in postsecondary institutions in each quarter.

17. This figure is calculated for the Great Lakes region, which also includes Illinois, Indiana, Ohio, and Wisconsin. All BPS statistics reported were generated using NCES QuickStats or PowerStats.

18. Data on enrollment status is frequently missing from the NSC, particularly for the private four-year colleges. Of the 364 men with recorded "enrollments" from the NSC, 85 had no record of enrollment status. Figure 4.1 therefore utilizes imputed status where necessary. Twenty-four of the men are always withdrawn—the NSC never reports them as being enrolled either full- or part-time—and two additional men are imputed into this group. Withdrawn "enrollments" are especially common in the for-profit sector, where attrition may be high at the beginning of the instruction period, particularly for online courses.

19. Beginning Postsecondary Students 2009.

20. Deming, Goldin, and Katz 2011.

21. Bailey, Badway, and Gumport 2001.

22. Deming, Goldin, and Katz 2011.

23. Deming et al. 2016; Darolia et al. 2015.

24. Pager 2003.

25. Dynarski, Hemelt, and Hyman 2013.

26. Figure 4.3 represents only those enrollments that have at least part-time status.

27. Enrollment reporting became nearly universal (97 percent) for private four-year colleges in the fall of 2009, whereas fewer than half (44 percent) of private four-year colleges had reported in previous years. This aligns with the pattern of private four-year enrollments in our data, suggesting that there may be more enrollments in previous years that were not reported. On the other hand, although for-profit enrollments in our sample also increased significantly in the latter half of our observation period, NSC reporting by for-profit institutions was actually relatively consistent (and low) throughout our observation period. More specifically, for-profit institution reporting rates were steady at around 30 percent from 2003 to 2009 and actually dropped in 2010, to 25 percent (a year in which our for-profit enrollments increased), before rebounding to 41 percent in 2011 (when enrollments were very similar, but actually slightly lower than in 2010). Thus, there is no evidence that reporting practices are driving the patterns we observe in for-profit enrollments. Overall, we have reasonable confidence that enrollments were indeed increasing over our observation period, as suggested by figure 4.1.

28. Fry 2009.

29. Shapiro et al. 2014.

30. Separate graduation rates for male and female students are not available.

31. The BPS stipulates that the individual point estimates for AAs, BAs, and certificates should be interpreted with caution because standard errors are more than 30 percent of the estimate. Collectively, these graduation rates total to 20 percent, an overall rate that can be interpreted with confidence.

32. One possible explanation for the full-time enrollments in the for-profit sector is that enrollment registration happens in increments shorter than standard semesters or quarters, such that being enrolled at all (that is, in at least one course worth a regular course credit) would be considered a full-time load. There is some evidence that this occurs—individual for-profit enrollment records are shorter than public enrollments, and short enrollments are more likely to be full-time. However, the private four-year institutions in our data also tend to have short durations for their individual enrollment records, but still frequently enroll these students at part-time status.

33. Leigh and Gill 1997; Marcotte et al. 2005.

34. DeLuca, Clampet-Lundquist, and Edin 2016b.

35. DeLuca, Clampet-Lundquist, and Edin 2016b.

36. *Detroit Free Press* 2019.

37. Holzer, Raphael, and Stoll 2006; Pager, Western, and Bonikowski 2009; Pager 2003.

38. Although more black men enrolled and more whites earned a degree—fifteen versus five—these frequencies are too small to meaningfully test for significance. Among students who enrolled, blacks and whites enrolled for the same FTE duration on average.

39. See, for example, Hoynes, Miller, and Schaller 2012.

40. Betts and McFarland 1995; Hillman and Orians 2013.

41. Sampson and Laub 1997.

42. Alexander, Entwisle, and Olson 2014; Pager 2003; Royster 2003. On relative risk aversion, see Breen and Goldthorpe (1997).

43. During the period in which members of our sample were imprisoned, state funds could not be spent on college education for prisoners.

44. Attewell, Heil, and Reisel 2012. Note that this finding is based on a single cohort of students and a relatively short follow-up, so that even those who delayed entry began college by their early twenties. Effects may differ for students who begin college well into adulthood.

45. The first arrest is not necessarily the arrest that precipitated the focal incarceration.

46. The Michigan Department of Corrections aims to have each of its inmates earn a GED or an "Industry-Recognized Certification in Vocational Training" prior to release, and a GED is required for parole eligibility. See chapter 3 for more on incarceration and GED attainment.

47. Breen and Goldthorpe 1997.
48. Pager 2003.
49. Royster 2003; Alexander, Entwisle, and Olson 2014.
50. Oliver and Shapiro 2001.
51. The first question is addressed using logistic regression, and the second using event history analysis. In the analyses throughout this book, all models include controls for a set of covariates: criminal justice involvement, mental health and substance use history, earnings before and after the 2003 prison spell, living arrangements and neighborhood characteristics before and after 2003, and education before (and during) prison. Complete model results are available in the online appendix.
52. Because the young men in the sample were typically first arrested significantly earlier than the beginning of the focal incarceration spell, these variables do not produce a collinearity issue.
53. We acknowledge that interpretation of interaction effects is challenging with logistic regressions, but note that the logistic results presented here are essentially identical to estimates from the linear probability models in table 4.A1.
54. The bottom 50 percent of black men in our sample had no earnings in the first year after release. The twelve-percentage-point increase in the likelihood of enrollment pertains to a $500 increase in earnings and therefore reflects a jump to the sixty-seventh percentile from either the first or fiftieth percentile.
55. Eighty-five percent of men who returned in 2009 or later had zero or negative earnings growth compared to 65 percent of those who returned before 2009, for an average highest quarterly earnings difference of –$848 and $108, respectively. (The average difference for those who never enrolled is –$301.) This difference is driven by men with a zero earnings gap (zero earnings in both the year after release and in 2008): 40 percent of those who enrolled later had no earnings compared to 20 percent in the group that enrolled earlier. It is possible, however, that informal employment is masked in this "non-earning" group.
56. Those who enroll later probably differ in significant and substantively important, but unobservable, ways from those who enroll earlier, and identical factors could have different effects for these two groups. Special caution should be given to the interpretation of the black-only models, as the uptick in enrollments in later years is especially pronounced for this group. Despite these limitations, we consider the investigation of earlier enrollments empirically valuable.
57. This makes it simple to match our enrollment data to the employment data, which is also given in quarters, and is appropriate because academic sessions typically begin once per quarter. Although we do observe start

dates in continuous time (in days), we do not consider it to be of theoretical or practical importance whether an individual begins his fall semester in, for example, August or September.

58. The event history analysis uses multinomial logistic regressions in which imprisonment is a competing event. In other words, the men in our sample were only considered to be "at risk" of becoming enrolled in a given quarter if they were not in prison and if they were not currently enrolled. Jail terms generally last less than a calendar quarter and therefore do not completely disqualify men from the possibility of enrolling in postsecondary education. To account for this, we include a control for whether the individual began the given quarter in a criminal justice facility. Operationally, if the individual was in a facility on day one of the quarter, he received this indicator. This largely functions as a marker of whether the man spent time in the criminal justice system in the prior quarter.

59. In fact, the static measure of maximum quarterly earnings in the first year after release (shown in the full regression table in table 4.A2) remains significant in predicting any enrollment in a given quarter after release.

60. Living arrangements in our sample were likely to change within a quarter. Note that, because this is an indicator for residence at the beginning of the quarter, it essentially operates as an indicator of last residence during the prior quarter.

61. Shanahan 2000.

62. This is inclusive of control variables that, for the sake of brevity, are omitted from figures 4.6 and 4.7.

63. Foster and Hagan 2007.

64. DeLuca, Clampet-Lundquist, and Edin 2016b.

CHAPTER 5: HEALTH AND RISKY HEALTH BEHAVIORS

1. Centers for Disease Control and Prevention 2019.

2. Umberson and Montez 2010, S55.

3. Dobrin 2001; Jennings et al. 2010; Lauritsen, Heimer, and Lang 2018; Lauritsen, Sampson, and Laub 1991; Sherman and Harris 2013; Western 2015. Although this "victim offender overlap" is not perfect, even in studies that identify only victims or only offenders, the majority of individuals fall into both categories (see, for example, Schreck, Stewart, and Osgood 2008).

4. Violent crimes include abuse, assault, extortion and threats, homicide, kidnapping, motor vehicle with injury, rape and other sex crimes, robbery, stalking, and weapons offenses.

5. The Michigan Department of Corrections administers immunoassay and breathalyzer tests to prisoners and parolees randomly and when they are

suspected of using. Two-thirds of administered tests are immunoassay. Only about 10 percent of tests are administered under suspicion of use.

6. As in most criminal justice data, drug crimes range from possession to sales, delivery, and manufacturing, which are typically not reliably disentangled; they are not in our data.

7. Engel et al. 2019.

8. Morgan and Oudekerk 2019.

9. Scott et al. 2019.

10. Visher 1991.

11. National mortality data were sourced from the National Death Index (NDI) and cross-checked with MDOC data. One death was missing from the NDI but confirmed by MDOC with date and cause of death information.

12. The average unadjusted parolee mortality rate over the nine-year follow-up was 392 deaths per 100,000. To approximately adjust the mortality rate, we computed the standardized mortality ratio (SMR) from the number of actual deaths of twenty- to thirty-four-year-old males in Michigan. The SMR is 0.356, so the adjusted mortality rate among the Michigan parolees is 164 per 100,000.

13. Lattimore, Linster, and MacDonald 1997; Ramchand, Morral, and Becker 2009; Teplin et al. 2005.

14. Popovici et al. 2017.

15. These quarterly probabilities reflect "time at risk," meaning that only quarters when the young men could have been arrested for violence or tested for drug use factor into the denominator. For arrests, time in custody is excluded from the denominator. For drug tests, time in custody is included because testing takes place in prison, but time after parole discharge and between new arrests is not.

16. Visher 1991.

17. According to the 2003 National Study on Drug Use and Health, fewer than 1 percent of transitional-aged youth received residential treatment.

18. Cook and Alegría 2011.

19. Farabee, Prendergast, and Anglin 1998.

20. Abrams and Terry 2017; DeLuca, Clampet-Lundquist, and Edin 2016a; Alexander, Entwisle, and Olson 2014; Arnett 2000.

21. For example, Arnett 2005; Jackson and Sartor 2016; Schulenberg et al. 2005.

22. Sampson and Wilson 1995; Wolfgang and Ferracuti 1967.

23. Harris et al. 2006; Massoglia 2006.

24. Schnittker and McLeod 2005; Massey and Brodmann 2014.

25. Link and Phelan 1995.

26. Resources include material (wealth, income), cognitive (intelligence), emotional (self-control, grit), social (friends, networks), and "symbolic" (power, prestige) attributes that people can leverage (Massey and Brodmann 2014).

27. Hatzenbuehler, Phelan, and Link 2013.
28. Duncan and Kawachi 2018.
29. Ellen, Mijanovich, and Dillman 2001.
30. Friedson and Sharkey 2015; Lauritsen, Heimer, and Lang 2018; Krivo et al. 2018.
31. Western 2015.
32. Desmond 2012.
33. Desmond 2016.
34. Sampson, Raudenbush, and Earls 1997.
35. Winship and Krupnick 2015; Caulkins and Reuter 2017.
36. Rothstein 2017; Kubrin and Squires 2004; Galster and Sharkey 2017; Blanchflower, Levine, and Zimmerman 2003.
37. Boshara, Emmons, and Noeth 2015; Krivo and Kaufman 2004; Williams and Collins 2001.
38. Sampson and Wilson 1995; Peterson and Krivo 2010; Shaw and McKay 1942.
39. Sampson and Wilson 1995.
40. Western 2015.
41. Sampson and Wilson 1995.
42. Sampson and Wilson 1995.
43. Bursik and Grasmick 1993.
44. Kirk and Matsuda 2011.
45. Western 2015; Sampson and Wilson 1995.
46. Boardman et al. 2001; Karriker-Jaffe 2011.
47. Carter, Mohler, and Ray 2019; Visconti et al. 2015; Monnat et al. 2019; Des Jarlais et al. 2019.
48. Beckett, Nyrop, and Pfingst 2006; Pollack 2017; Ruhm 2018.
49. Hatzenbuehler 2016.
50. Harris and Edlund 2005.
51. Pollack 2017.
52. Dumont et al. 2012; Patterson 2010; Wildeman and Wang 2017.
53. Schnittker, Massoglia, and Uggen 2012; Turney, Schnittker, and Wildeman 2012; Wildeman, Turney, and Schnittker 2014.
54. Massoglia and Pridemore 2015.
55. Massoglia and Pridemore 2015; Wildeman and Wang 2017.
56. Pearlin et al. 2005.
57. Sykes 1965; Clemmer 1950; Western 2018.
58. Crewe 2007.
59. Schnittker and Massoglia 2015. Self-efficacy refers to an individual's belief in her ability to engage successfully in behaviors necessary for achieving a specific outcome (Bandura 1977).
60. Eliason, Mortimer, and Vuolo 2015; Lewis, Ross, and Mirowsky 1999; Arnett 2000.

61. Clemmer 1950; Western 2015.
62. Rocheleau 2013; Western 2015; Wildeman, Turney, and Schnittker 2014.
63. Bronson and Berzofsky 2017.
64. Rocheleau 2013.
65. Haney 2018b; Smith 2006.
66. Schnittker and John 2007, 117.
67. Evans, Blount-Hill, and Cubellis 2019; Schnittker and Massoglia 2015; Pager 2003; Schnittker, Massoglia, and Uggen 2012; Travis 2005; Wakefield and Uggen 2010; Western et al. 2015.
68. Schnittker and Massoglia 2015, 359.
69. Link et al. 1989.
70. Schnittker and Massoglia 2015.
71. Schnittker and Massoglia 2015.
72. Hatzenbuehler and Link 2014; Travis 2005.
73. Evans, Blount-Hill, and Cubellis 2019; Pager 2003; Western 2018.
74. Avery and Avery 2019.
75. Pascoe and Smart Richman 2009; Turney, Lee, and Comfort 2013.
76. LeBel 2012.
77. Benson et al. 2011, 389.
78. Mossakowski 2011,
79. Hatzenbuehler, Phelan, and Link 2013; Herda and McCarthy 2018; Priest and Williams 2017; Pascoe and Smart Richman 2009.
80. Felson et al. 2012; Mowen and Boman 2019; Agnew 1992.
81. Maruna 2001a.
82. Lewis, Ross, and Mirowsky 1999.
83. Thoits 2006.
84. Maruna 2001a; Mossakowski 2011; Thoits 2006.
85. Massoglia and Uggen 2010.
86. Umberson, Crosnoe, and Reczek 2010; Thoits 2010.
87. Mowen, Stansfield, and Boman 2019.
88. Western et al. 2015.
89. Western et al. 2015, 1538.
90. Umberson, Crosnoe, and Reczek 2010; Umberson and Montez 2010.
91. Felson et al. 2012.
92. Mowen and Visher 2015; Mowen, Stansfield, and Boman 2019; Mowen and Fisher 2019.
93. Lewis, Ross, and Mirowsky 1999; Schulenberg, Bryant, and O'Malley 2004.
94. Cloward and Ohlin 1960; MacCoun, Kilmer, and Reuter 2003.
95. Braveman et al. 2010; Farmer and Ferraro 2005.
96. Jensen and Lleras-Muney 2012.
97. Harris and Lee 2012, 189.
98. Uggen 2000.

99. Apel and Horney 2017.
100. Greenberg and Barling 1999; Hershcovis et al. 2007; Melzer 2002.
101. Larsen 1994; Moore et al. 2009.
102. Grattet, Lin, and Petersilia 2011; Petersilia and Turner 1993.
103. Grattet, Lin, and Petersilia 2011, 373.
104. Rucks-Ahidiana, Harding, and Harris (forthcoming).
105. In Michigan at the time the young men in our study were in prison and on parole, prisoners could be moved to correctional centers in the community before their minimum sentence was complete, in preparation for release. Truth-in-sentencing laws now prohibit this form of release.
106. Grattet, Lin, and Petersilia 2011; Petersilia and Turner 1993.
107. Pager 2003; Evans, Blount-Hill, and Cubellis 2019; Hatzenbuehler, Phelan, and Link 2013.
108. We examined the determinants of post-prison risky health behaviors using four discrete time-event history models that predict the quarterly post-prison probability of engaging in substance use and violence for black and white men. Specifically, we estimate whites-only violence, whites-only substance use, blacks-only violence, and blacks-only substance use models separately.

    In the substance use models, the base condition is a negative test. In other words, testing positive is conditional on being tested. Not being tested is treated as a competing risk. We do not report competing risks—meaning the alternative outcomes that preclude the risky health behavior outcomes. In the substance use models, additional competing risks include parole discharge, absconding, and death. MDOC does not drug-test men after they discharge from parole, abscond from parole, or die, but men can be drug-tested in prison. In the violence models, competing risks include incarceration and death because men cannot be arrested if they are incarcerated or die.

109. Output from the models is presented in tables 5.A1 and 5.A2. To ensure consistency in interpretation, we present average marginal effect (AME) estimates rather than logistic regression coefficients. An AME indicates the magnitude and direction of the association between a predictor variable and the outcome variable averaged over all quarters, with all other variables constrained to their mean values. For example, the AME of prior-quarter employment indicates that, all other things equal, being employed in the previous post-prison quarter is associated with a decrease of 1.8 percentage points in the likelihood that a young black man will be arrested for a violent offense in the current quarter. That is, his quarterly probability of being arrested for a violent offense decreases from his baseline of 6.9 percent to 4.1 percent. Importantly, despite the "effect" terminology, a causal interpretation does not necessarily apply to our AME estimates, so we discuss them as associations. In addition, the magnitude of the AME estimates for

young black men are not directly comparable to the magnitude of the AME estimates for young white men because we estimated the models separately for each (Mood 2010). To date, "the problem of comparing [non-linear probability model] coefficients across models fitted to different samples has no satisfactory solution" (Breen, Karlson, and Holm 2018, 51).

110. Sherman and Harris 2013, 2015.
111. Schnittker and John 2007; Schnittker and Massoglia 2015.
112. Caulkins and Reuter 2017, 105.
113. Pollack 2017, 162 (emphasis added).
114. Pollack 2017.
115. Becker and Murphy 1988.
116. Kirk 2012.
117. Western 2015.
118. Heckman, Humphries, and Mader 2011.
119. Farmer and Ferraro 2005.
120. Grattet, Lin, and Petersilia 2011; Petersilia and Turner 1993.
121. To examine how the post-prison social context contributes to risky health behaviors, we first examine how social context measured at the neighborhood and county levels influences our AME estimates. We measure quarterly neighborhood disadvantage at the census tract level using the index described in chapter 2. We then explore various aspects of the county context. Return county fixed effects account for static elements of the post-prison environment that affect substance use and violence, such as differences in parole regimes and policies. We also examine a dynamic aspect of the county context that is likely to impact post-prison risky health behaviors: the quarterly crime rate.
122. Results from the full specification can be seen in table 5.A3.
123. We tested both of these results to determine whether they are artifacts of the rescaling associated with logistic regression (Breen, Karlson, and Holm 2018). Neither is. The confounding percentage for the substance use model is 3.57 percent, with a rescaling factor of 1.0003. The confounding percentage for the violence model is 3.26 percent, with a rescaling factor of 0.9964.
124. Schnittker and John 2007.
125. LeBel 2012.
126. Western et al. 2015; Mowen, Stansfield, and Boman 2019.
127. Danziger and Rouse 2007; DeLuca, Clampet-Lundquist, and Edin 2016a; Siennick and Osgood 2008.
128. Eliason, Mortimer, and Vuolo 2015.
129. Apel and Horney 2017.
130. Warr 1998a.
131. Farmer and Ferraro 2005.

CHAPTER 6: EMPLOYMENT

1. Western 2008; City of New York 2017.
2. Baker and Elias 1991.
3. Toby 1957; Sampson and Laub 1993; Wilson 1996.
4. Warr 1998a; Crutchfield 2014.
5. Fagan and Freeman 1999.
6. Crutchfield and Pitchford 1997; Sampson and Laub 1993; Engelhardt 2010.
7. Petersilia 2003; Uggen 2000.
8. Maruna 2001a.
9. Harlow 2003.
10. National Research Council 2014.
11. Travis 2005.
12. Western 2006.
13. See, for example, Pager 2003.
14. Kalleberg 2013.
15. Danziger and Ratner 2010.
16. Sugie 2018.
17. Apel and Sweeten 2010.
18. Western 2018.
19. Our findings are qualitatively similar when defining stable employment using slightly shorter or longer spans of time.
20. Pager 2003; Bertrand and Mullainathan 2004.
21. Bendick, Jackson, and Reinoso 1994.
22. Pager 2003.
23. Eberhardt et al. 2004.
24. Hetey and Eberhardt 2014.
25. For example, Royster 2003.
26. Smith 2007.
27. Men who were incarcerated during the current quarter were not removed from any employment statistics in this section.
28. Kling 2006; Pettit and Lyons 2007; Sabol 2007; Tyler and Kling 2007.
29. Seim and Harding 2020.
30. Uggen 1999; LaBriola 2020.
31. Hirsch and Macpherson 2003.
32. Gottfredson and Hirschi 1990.
33. Uggen 2000.
34. Gottfredson 1985.
35. Cameron and Heckman 1993.
36. Rumberger 2011.
37. Frone 2011.

38. Jencks and Mayer 1990.
39. Pager 2003.
40. Visher et al. 2004; Braman 2004.
41. Schoeni and Ross 2005.
42. Warr 1998a.
43. See Harding, Morenoff, et al. 2016.
44. Osborn 1980; Kirk 2009.
45. Freeman and Rodgers 1999.
46. Table 6.A1 includes descriptive statistics for each of the variables listed here. There is a small amount of missingness on some variables; we use multiple imputation methods (see, for example, Rubin 1987) to include observations with missing variables in our analysis.
47. Our estimation of the ordinary least squares (OLS) model returns a set of coefficients for each potential determinant of stable employment, with each coefficient representing the magnitude of the association between the determinant and the probability of attaining stable employment, net of all other variables. The full model results can be found in table 6.A2.
48. These predicted probabilities rely on marginal effects generated using Daniel Klein's user-written Stata command "mimrgns" (Klein 2014), which produces marginal effects from models estimated on multiply-imputed data.
49. Visher, Debus, and Yahner 2008.
50. Seim and Harding 2020.
51. Sampson and Laub 1993; Warr 1998a; Nightingale and Wandner 2011.
52. Kornfeld and Bloom 1999.
53. Bureau of Labor Statistics 1997.
54. State of Michigan Department of Licensing and Regulatory Affairs 2014.
55. Kalleberg 2013.
56. Mueller-Smith and Schnepel 2019.

CHAPTER 7: RESIDENTIAL STABILITY

1. Lutze, Rosky, and Hamilton 2013.
2. Harding, Morenoff, and Herbert 2013; Herbert, Morenoff, and Harding 2015.
3. Lee, Harding, and Morenoff 2017.
4. Metraux and Culhane 2004.
5. Geller and Curtis 2011; Harding, Morenoff, and Herbert 2013.
6. Herbert, Morenoff, and Harding 2015. These frequent residential changes also imply that they stayed a relatively short time in one place, on average. The median length of stay in a private residence is 116 days—half of the residential stays in our sample were less than four months (table 7.A2).
7. There were 234 individuals in our sample who directly transferred to other correctional institutions or treatment facilities after prison. In these cases,

their private residence after leaving such institutions was treated as their first residence.

8. Massey and Denton 1993.
9. Bradley et al. 2001; Geller and Curtis 2011; Harding, Morenoff, and Herbert 2013.
10. Bradley et al. 2001.
11. Visher and Travis 2003; Nelson, Deess, and Allen 1999, 2011; Travis, Solomon, and Waul 2001.
12. Nelson, Deess, and Allen 1999.
13. Mears et al. 2008; La Vigne and Parthasarathy 2005.
14. Schoeni and Ross 2005. Of course, the expected positive influence of parents on residential stability may be conditioned by the characteristics of the parents. Many researchers have reported that a parent or guardian's history of incarceration or drug abuse increases their children's vulnerability to involvement in crime or drug abuse (Hagan and Palloni 1990; Johnson and Waldfogel 2004). Although our data do not directly measure parent qualities, relationship quality can be controlled, at least partially, by including information on pre-incarceration living arrangements in our models.
15. Sampson and Laub 1993; Warr 1998b.
16. Wyse, Harding, and Morenoff 2014.
17. Fleming, White, and Catalano 2010; McCarthy and Casey 2008.
18. Edin and Nelson 2013.
19. Wyse, Harding, and Morenoff 2014.
20. Harding, Siegel, and Morenoff 2017.
21. Harding, Morenoff, and Herbert 2013.
22. Glaze 2003.
23. Simon 1993.
24. Travis 2005.
25. The association between temporary detention in criminal justice facilities and residential instability is, of course, quite complex. Residential stability may also result in detention. At the same time, temporary detention may create residential instability. Or some confounding factors could cause both residential instability and frequent detention. In any case, the experience of temporary detention is tightly associated with residential insecurity and instability in important ways.
26. Lynch and Sabol 2001; Visher and Travis 2003; Solomon, Thomson, and Keegan 2004.
27. Lynch and Sabol 2001.
28. Rose et al. 1999; Anderson 1990.
29. Lerman and Weaver 2014b; Grattet, Lin, and Petersilia 2011.
30. In our analysis, four neighborhood variables were included that were drawn from the tract-level data from the U.S. Census Bureau: black percentage of

the population, percentage of households with income below the poverty line (poverty rate), percentage of population unemployed, and percentage of household in the same house as one year prior—the last variable being an indicator of neighborhood residential instability that is commonly thought of as a measure of capacity for informal social control (Morenoff, Sampson, and Raudenbush 2001b; Sampson, Raudenbush, and Earls 1997).

31. Sampson, Raudenbush, and Earls 1997.
32. Sampson, Raudenbush, and Earls 1997.
33. Sampson, Raudenbush, and Earls 1997; Hirschfield and Bowers 1997; Morenoff, Sampson, and Raudenbush 2001a; Bellair 2000.
34. Lerman and Weaver 2014b; Grattet, Lin, and Petersilia 2011.
35. Lerman and Weaver 2014b, 204.
36. Thacher 2010.
37. Smith 1986; Sun, Payne, and Wu 2008.
38. Pettit and Western 2004.
39. Bonczar and Beck 1997.
40. Harper, Coleman, and Devine 2003.
41. Mumola 2000.
42. Rose and Clear 1998.
43. Schachter 2004.
44. In our analysis, we include three life-course variables: gross earnings for the prior calendar quarter (ranging from zero for those unemployed to $25,812), college enrollment status in the prior month (1 for enrolled, 0 for not enrolled), and earning a GED in the prior month (1 for receiving a GED, 0 otherwise).
45. To estimate the timing of each moving event and gauge the influence of the associated factors on residential mobility, we created a data set in which each record corresponds to one week of residence for a specific person and residence. For example, if a person lived in two private residences during his parole period and stayed at those residences for twenty weeks and fifteen weeks, respectively, he would have thirty-five records in the data set. Residential mobility and stability only pertain to private residences; weeks in which an individual lived in a correctional or treatment facility, was homeless, or lived at an unknown residence were excluded from the analysis. The outcome variable in the person-week data set used for the residential move analysis is the typology of moving events that captured the type of residence to which that person moved or censoring events. There are six categories: not moving (the reference), moving to another private place, moving to a nonprivate place (such as jail or a treatment facility), being discharged from parole, absconding or moving out of the state of Michigan, and being sent to prison. The marginal effects of the main variables are reported in

table 7.A6 and full model results are in tables 7.A8 and 7.A9, including all control variables.

46. Residential stability was defined as staying in one place for more than a year; thus, the earliest residential stability could be achieved was in the fifty-third week. The outcome variables in this model were divided into four categories. (1) When an individual lived in one place for more than fifty-three weeks, we marked this residential episode at the fifty-third week as a "year-long residence." (2) If an individual was censored due to absconding, returning to prison, or moving out of the state of Michigan before reaching one year, the last week of that residence period was marked as "censored." (3) When an individual moved to another place before the reaching the fifty-third week in their current residence, the last week of the residence was coded as "moved." (4) When an individual was discharged from parole before fifty-three weeks in the same private residence, he was defined as "discharged." The reference category for the outcome was a move or censoring event in that week.

The statistical model predicts the probability that each residential episode will continue for more than one year before encountering a censoring, discharge, or moving event. We should also note that the time period covered in this analysis starts from the fifty-third week after the parolees' release from prison in 2003, instead of from the first week following their release, because the one-year-in-residence criterion for residential stability cannot occur before the fifty-third week. Thus, residences during the first year (that is, before the fifty-third week) were excluded from this analysis. For the same reason, individuals who experienced a censoring event before the fifty-third week after release were also excluded. Marginal effects of core variables are reported in table 7.A7. Full model results with all control variables and all outcome comparisons are presented in tables 7.A10 and 7.A11.

47. Although our data do not have detailed information about social relationships, where and with whom the men in our sample were living provides one indicator of social support. In particular, we relied on information about both the type of coresidents with whom they lived and the type of residence (for example, a private residence or an institutional or nonprivate facility). We constructed a time-varying measure of living arrangements with eight categories based on type of place and type of cohabitants. Within private residences, coresidents were divided into five types of relations: parents; older, nonparent adults; romantic partners; alone, with children, or with other young people; and unknown. Nonprivate residences were divided into four different types: criminal justice facilities, treatment or care institutions, homeless (living on the streets or in a shelter), and unknown. In the

models, living with parents is the reference group for both previous and current residence variables.

48. Differences between older relatives and parents are never statistically significant and consistently very small in magnitude.

49. These numbers are derived from the marginal effects of the living arrangement of the current residence reported in table 7.A6.

50. Unsurprisingly, unknown living arrangements are associated with higher residential mobility of both types, because the residence information is unknown to the parole officer and therefore likely to be highly unstable.

51. Harding, Morenoff, and Herbert 2013.

CHAPTER 8: TRANSITION-TO-ADULTHOOD TRAJECTORIES

1. Nagin 2005; Nagin, Jones, and Lima Passos 2016.
2. Laub and Sampson 2003; Paternoster and Bushway 2009.
3. Sweeten 2012.
4. Shanahan 2000.
5. Nagin 2005; Nagin, Jones, and Lima Passos 2016.
6. Nagin and Land 1993; Nagin 2005. These models combine features of latent class analysis and multilevel modeling to characterize variation in longitudinal outcomes and the processes that generate them.
7. Unlike GBTM, in which a single trajectory is modeled, GBMTM allows multiple measures of the same underlying construct to be modeled simultaneously (Nagin, Jones, and Lima Passos 2016). In contrast to dual-trajectory modeling, in which two coevolving processes are modeled, GBMTM models a single process for which multiple indicators exist. Thus, GBMTM models each of the indicators separately *and* in relation to each other, producing, in effect, multi-trajectory groups comprising domain-specific trajectory groups.
8. Owing to the noncomparability of logit model coefficients across models with different explanatory variables, we work with average marginal effects (Mood 2010).
9. Massoglia and Uggen 2010.
10. Because our data are drawn from law enforcement databases, they should include juvenile records that were sealed.
11. Haney 2003, 2018a; Smith 2006.
12. We implement GBMTM with the traj module in Stata. The odds of correct classification in the five-group model are 60.4 ("persisting"), 45.5 ("disconnected"), 36.5 ("unsettled"), 73.6 ("transitioning"), and 219.9 ("continuing education"). The average posterior probability of group assignment by group is 0.948, 0.922, 0.924, 0.957, and 0.950, respectively. These metrics are far above conventional thresholds. To determine the optimal number

of latent groups, we follow the conventional advice of considering a combination of measures of fit (the Bayesian Information Criterion [BIC] and appropriateness of functional form), classification (the average posterior probability of group assignment and the odds of correct classification [OCC]), group size and composition, and extant theory and evidence to determine whether the resultant groups "communicate the distinct features of the data" (Nagin 2005, 77). The last criterion, admittedly subjective, means that if an additional trajectory group has a substantively similar trajectory pattern as another group, then the model with fewer groups should be preferred. In our analysis, a model with four groups has a slightly higher BIC score (33,405) than the current model (32,834). However, we use the five-group model because it is in this model that the continuing education group emerges as a separate group with a unique trajectory involving increasing probability of college enrollment over time. We believe that this group is important on substantive and conceptual grounds.

13. The individuals profiled in this chapter and in the introduction were chosen at random from among the members of the five trajectory groups, stratifying by race.

14. Unfortunately, the unemployment insurance data contain no information on the industry of Jared's secondary employment during this period.

15. Alexander, Entwisle, and Olson 2014.

16. Seefeldt 2017.

17. Osgood et al. 2006.

18. See, for example, Baker, Metcalfe, and Piquero 2015; Metcalfe, Baker, and Brady 2019; Piquero 2004; Ouellet 2019; Loughran, Nagin, and Nguyen 2017.

19. It is also possible that some members of this group remain involved in criminal activity but that activity remains undetected by law enforcement and therefore does not result in arrest or custody. We believe that this is unlikely to be the case for more than a trivial number of individuals, given the intense scrutiny experienced by parolees.

20. For example, Harding et al. 2014.

21. Umberson and Montez 2010.

22. Given the relatively small number of young men in our sample who died, it appears to be coincidence that the two members of the disconnected group we randomly selected to profile in this chapter both died.

23. Harris and Harding 2019.

24. Petersilia 2003; Pager, Western, and Bonikowski 2009; Pager 2003; 2007; Uggen et al. 2014.

25. Pager 2003.

26. Pager, Western, and Bonikowski 2009.

27. Pager 2007.

28. Agan and Starr 2018.
29. See, for example, Ewens, Tomlin, and Wang 2014; Page 1995; Pager and Shepherd 2008.
30. Royster 2003.
31. Smith 2007.
32. Alexander, Entwisle, and Olson 2014.

CHAPTER 9: CONCLUSION

1. Shanahan 2000; Hogan and Astone 1986; Sampson and Laub 1992, 1993.
2. Sampson and Laub 1992, 1993.
3. Furstenberg 2010; Kerckhoff 1993.
4. Pettit and Western 2004.
5. Pettit and Western 2004; Western 2002; Schnittker et al. 2015; Schnittker and John 2007; Massoglia and Pridemore 2015.
6. Harding, Morenoff, and Wyse 2019.
7. Kirk and Sampson 2013.
8. Pettit and Lyons 2007; Tyler and Kling 2007.
9. Fomby and Bosick 2013; Schoeni and Ross 2005. Our primary measures of social support are the type and composition of the household in which a young man lived. Living in private housing with parents, grandparents, or romantic partners implies a greater level of social support than living in institutional housing or living alone or with roommates.
10. Sampson and Laub 1992, 1993.
11. Settersten, Furstenberg, and Rumbaut 2005.
12. Morenoff and Harding 2014.
13. Settersten 2005.
14. Alexander, Entwisle, and Olson 2014.
15. Settersten, Furstenberg, and Rumbaut 2005.
16. Piquero et al. 2002; Visher and Travis 2003.
17. Osgood et al. 2006.
18. Harding, Morenoff, and Wyse 2019; Visher and Travis 2003.
19. Fader 2013; Osgood et al. 2006; Pettit and Western 2004; Piquero et al. 2002.
20. See, for example, Apel and Horney 2017; Crutchfield 2014; Schnepel 2018; Uggen 1999.
21. See, for example, Edelman, Holzer, and Offner 2005; Mincy 2006.
22. Schoeni and Ross 2005.
23. Sharkey and Faber 2014.
24. Western 2018.
25. Hair et al. 2009; Roksa and Velez 2012.
26. Alexander, Entwisle, and Olson 2014; Waters et al. 2011; DeLuca, Clampet-Lundquist, and Edin 2016a.

27. Holzer 2009; Royster 2003.
28. See, for example, Kelly 1994.
29. Shanahan 2000.
30. Chung, Little, and Steinberg 2005.
31. Maruna 2001b; Copp et al. 2019.
32. Arnett 2006.
33. McDowell 2002.
34. Wald 2006; Schoeni and Ross 2005.
35. Wald 2006; Wimer and Bloom 2014.
36. Wald 2006, 614.
37. Holzer 2018.
38. Holzer 2018; Treskon 2016; Bohn, Jackson, and McConville 2019.
39. Edelman and Holzer 2013; Edelman, Holzer, and Offner 2005; Jackson, Cook, and Johnson 2019; Rodriguez, Mejia, and Johnson 2018.
40. Holzer 2018; Treskon 2016.
41. Holzer 2018; Edelman, Holzer, and Offner 2005; Edelman and Holzer 2013.
42. Bohn and McConville 2018.
43. Wimer and Bloom 2014.
44. Bozick et al. 2018.
45. Mooney, Kelley, and Bala 2016.
46. Government Accountability Office 2019.
47. Hair et al. 2009.
48. Edelman and Holzer 2013; Holzer 2018.
49. Treskon 2016.
50. Cameron and Heckman 1993; Maralani 2011; Tyler and Kling 2007; Cho and Tyler 2010; Tyler, Murnane, and Willett 2000.
51. See Comfort (2012) on the similarities between prison and college in the eyes of the formerly incarcerated.
52. Wald 2006.
53. Pager 2003, 2007; Pager, Western, and Bonikowski 2009; Western 2002.
54. Lundquist, Pager, and Strader 2018.
55. Aamodt 2015.
56. Agan and Starr 2018; Doleac and Hansen 2016.
57. Hager 2015.
58. Bushway and Apel 2012; Blumstein and Nakamura 2009; Bushway, Nieuwbeerta, and Blokland 2011.
59. Prescott and Starr 2019.
60. Denver, Siwach, and Bushway 2017.
61. Lageson 2020.
62. Royster 2003.
63. Schneider and Harknett 2019.
64. Redcross et al. 2012.

65. Edelman, Holzer, and Offner 2005; Edelman and Holzer 2013.
66. Edelman, Holzer, and Offner 2005; Edelman and Holzer 2013; Wimer and Bloom 2014.
67. Western 2018; Holzer and Martinson 2005.
68. Hunt et al. 2014.
69. Hunt et al. 2014, xi.
70. Pollack 2017.
71. Beronio et al. 2013.
72. Wexler, Falkin, and Lipton 1990; Stainbrook, Hanna, and Salomon 2017.
73. Lipsey, Landenberger, and Wilson 2007; Wimer and Bloom 2014.
74. Moore et al. 2019.
75. Wildeman and Wang 2017.
76. Xu et al. 2016.
77. Cook and Donohue 2017; Cook and Pollack 2017; Cook, Pollack, and White 2019.
78. Braga 2017; Collins et al. 2017; Alper and Glaze 2019.
79. Azrael et al. 2017.
80. Cook, Pollack, and White 2019.
81. Crifasi et al. 2017.
82. Brunson and Wade 2019.
83. Sharkey 2018a.
84. Krivo et al. 2018.
85. Cook and Pollack 2017; Lauritsen, Heimer, and Lang 2018.
86. Azrael et al. 2017; Spano, Pridemore, and Bolland 2012; Felson and Painter-Davis 2012; Felson and Pare 2010.
87. Western 2015.
88. Cook and Donohue 2017.
89. Edwards, Lee, and Esposito 2019.
90. Desmond, Papachristos, and Kirk 2016; Fagan and Ash 2017.
91. Brunson and Wade 2019.
92. Herbert, Morenoff, and Harding 2015; Travis 2005.
93. Comfort 2008.
94. Braman 2004.
95. Mears et al. 2013; Cochran 2019.
96. Mears et al. 2013; Mitchell et al. 2016.
97. Clark and Duwe 2016; Duwe 2018; Cochran 2019.
98. Duwe 2018; Duwe and Johnson 2016; Mowen, Stansfield, and Boman 2019.
99. Duwe 2018; Western et al. 2015.
100. Turney, Lee, and Comfort 2013; Massoglia 2008b; Sykes 1965; Clemmer 1950.
101. Binswanger et al. 2007b, 2013; Wang, Wang, and Krumholz 2013.
102. Schnittker and John 2007; Western 2018.
103. Tyler and Brockmann 2017.

104. Bronson et al. 2017; Maruschak, Berzofsky, and Unangst 2015.
105. Massoglia and Uggen 2010; Uggen 2000.
106. Lindquist et al. 2018; Willison 2019.
107. Doleac 2019.
108. Simon 1993; Petersilia 2009.
109. Harding et al. 2017.
110. Harding, Morenoff, and Herbert 2013; Harding, Siegel, and Morenoff 2017.
111. Simon 1993; Petersilia 2003; Burke and Tonry 2006.
112. Feeley and Simon 1992; Lynch 2000.
113. Ford and Harding 2019.
114. Western 2018.
115. Bronson and Carson 2019.
116. Clear 2011.
117. Lofstrom and Raphael 2016.
118. Austin et al. 2019.
119. Harding et al. 2019.

References

Aamodt, Michael G. 2015. "Using Background Checks in the Employee Selection Process." In *Practitioner's Guide to Legal Issues in Organizations*, edited by Chester Hanvey and Kayo Sady. Bonn: Springer.

Abrams, Laura S., and Diane Terry. 2017. *Everyday Desistance: The Transition to Adulthood among Formerly Incarcerated Youth*. New Brunswick, N.J.: Rutgers University Press.

Agan, Amanda, and Sonja Starr. 2018. "Ban the Box, Criminal Records, and Racial Discrimination: A Field Experiment." *Quarterly Journal of Economics* 133(1): 191–235. DOI: 10.1093/qje/qjx028.

Agnew, Robert. 1992. "Foundation for a General Strain Theory of Crime and Delinquency." *Criminology* 30(1): 47–87.

Alexander, Karl L., Doris R. Entwisle, and Linda S. Olson. 2014. *The Long Shadow: Family Background, Disadvantaged Urban Youth, and the Transition to Adulthood*. New York: Russell Sage Foundation.

Alexander, Michelle. 2010. *The New Jim Crow: Mass Incarceration in the Age of Colorblindness*. New York: New Press.

Alper, Mariel, and Lauren E. Glaze. 2019. "Source and Use of Firearms Involved in Crimes: Survey of Prison Inmates, 2016." *Special Report* (January). Washington, D.C.: Bureau of Justice Statistics. https://www.bjs.gov/content/pub/pdf/suficspi16.pdf.

Anderson, Elijah. 1990. *Streetwise*. Chicago: University of Chicago Press.

Andrew, Megan, Jennifer Eggerling-Boeck, Gary D. Sandefur, and Buffy Smith. 2006. "The 'Inner Side' of the Transition to Adulthood: How Young Adults See the Process of Becoming an Adult." *Advances in Life Course Research* 11(6): 225–51. DOI: 10.1016/S1040-2608(06)11009-6.

Andrews, Judy A., and Erika Westling. 2014. "Substance Use in Emerging Adulthood." In *The Oxford Handbook of Emerging Adulthood*, edited by Jeffrey Jensen Arnett. Oxford: Oxford University Press.

Apel, Robert, and Julie Horney. 2017. "How and Why Does Work Matter? Employment Conditions, Routine Activities, and Crime among Adult Male Offenders." *Criminology* 55(2): 307–43. DOI: 10.1111/1745-9125.12134.

Apel, Robert, and Kathleen Powell. 2019. "Level of Criminal Justice Contact and Early Adult Wage Inequality." *RSF: The Russell Sage Foundation Journal of the Social Sciences* 5(1): 198. DOI: 10.7758/rsf.2019.5.1.09.

Apel, Robert, and Gary Sweeten. 2010. "The Impact of Incarceration on Employment during the Transition to Adulthood." *Social Problems* 57(3): 448–79. DOI: 10.1525/sp.2010.57.3.448.

Arnett, Jeffrey Jensen. 2000. "Emerging Adulthood: A Theory of Development from the Late Teens through the Twenties." *American Psychologist* 5(5): 469–80. DOI: 10.1037/0003-066X.55.5.469.

———. 2004. *Emerging Adulthood: The Winding Road from the Late Teens through the Twenties.* New York: Oxford University Press.

———. 2005. "The Developmental Context of Substance Use in Emerging Adulthood." *Journal of Drug Issues* 35(2): 235–54. DOI: 10.1177/002204260503500202.

———. 2006. "Emerging Adulthood: Understanding the New Way of Coming of Age." In *Emerging Adults in America: Coming of Age in the 21st Century,* edited by Jeffrey Jensen Arnett and Jennifer Lynn Tanner. Washington, D.C.: American Psychological Association.

Attewell, Paul, Scott Heil, and Liza Reisel. 2012. "What Is Academic Momentum? And Does It Matter?" *Educational Evaluation and Policy Analysis* 34(1): 27–44. DOI: 10.3102/0162373711421958.

Austin, James F., Vincent Schirladi, Bruce Western, and Anamika Dwivedi. 2019. "Reconsidering the 'Violent Offender.'" New York: Square One Project (May). https://static1.squarespace.com/static/5b4cc00c710699c57a454b25/t/5d07b8d1ad75600001c270f2/1560787154096/Reconsidering-the-violent-offender-report-ONLINE_FINAL.pdf.

Avery, Jonathan D., and Joseph J. Avery. 2019. *The Stigma of Addiction: An Essential Guide.* Cham, Switzerlande: Springer.

Azrael, Deborah, Lisa Hepburn, David Hemenway, and Matthew Miller. 2017. "The Stock and Flow of U.S. Firearms: Results from the 2015 National Firearms Survey." *RSF: The Russell Sage Foundation Journal of the Social Sciences* 3(5): 38–57. DOI: 10.7758/rsf.2017.3.5.02.

Baćak, Valerio, Lars H. Andersen, and Jason Schnittker. 2018. "The Effect of Timing of Incarceration on Mental Health: Evidence from a Natural Experiment." *Social Forces* 98(1): 303–28. DOI: 10.1093/sf/soy102.

Bailey, Thomas, Norena Badway, and Patricia J. Gumport. 2001. "For-Profit Higher Education and Community Colleges." Stanford, Calif.: National Center for Postsecondary Improvement. https://eric.ed.gov/?id=ED463824.

Baillargeon, Jacques, Ingrid A. Binswanger, Joseph V. Penn, Brie A. Williams, and Owen J. Murray. 2009. "Psychiatric Disorders and Repeat Incarcerations:

The Revolving Prison Door." *American Journal of Psychiatry* 166(1): 103–9. DOI: 10.1176/appi.ajp.2008.08030416.

Baker, Meredith, and Peter Elias. 1991. "Youth Unemployment and Work Histories." In *Life and Work History Analyses: Qualitative and Quantitative Developments*, edited by Shirley Dex. London: Routledge.

Baker, Thomas, Christi Falco Metcalfe, and Alex R. Piquero. 2015. "Measuring the Intermittency of Criminal Careers." *Crime and Delinquency* 61(8): 1078–1103. DOI: 10.1177/0011128712466382.

Bandura, Albert. 1977. "Self-Efficacy: Toward a Unifying Theory of Behavioral Change." *Psychological Review* 84(2): 191–215.

Becker, Gary S. 1962. "Investment in Human Capital?: A Theoretical Analysis." *Journal of Political Economy* 70(5): 9–49. https://www.jstor.org/stable/1829103.

Becker, Gary S., and Kevin M. Murphy. 1988. "A Theory of Rational Addiction." *Journal of Political Economy* 96(4): 675–700. https://pdfs.semanticscholar.org/ebf3/f79cd5e3795db374d715206b83deee4057db.pdf.

Beckett, Katherine, and Steve Herbert. 2010. *Banished: The New Social Control in Urban America*. New York: Oxford University Press.

Beckett, Katherine, Kris Nyrop, and Lori Pfingst. 2006. "Race, Drugs, and Policing: Understanding Disparities in Drug Delivery Arrests." *Criminology* 44(1): 105–37.

Beginning Postsecondary Students Longitudinal Study (BPS). 2009. Computation by National Center for Education Statistics QuickStats. https://nces.ed.gov/datalab/index.aspx.

Bell, Lisa, Gary Burtless, Janet Gornick, and Timothy M. Smeeding. 2007. "Failure to Launch: Cross-National Trends in the Transition to Economic Independence." In *The Price of Independence: The Economics of Early Adulthood*, edited by Sheldon Danziger and Cecilia Elena Rouse. New York: Russell Sage Foundation.

Bellair, Paul E. 2000. "Informal Surveillance and Street Crime: A Complex Relationship." *Criminology* 38(1): 137–69.

Bendick, Marc, Charles Jackson, and Victor Reinoso. 1994. "Measuring Employment Discrimination through Controlled Experiments." *Review of Black Political Economy* 23(1): 25–48.

Benson, Janel E., and Frank F. Furstenberg Jr. 2006. "Entry into Adulthood: Are Adult Role Transitions Meaningful Markers of Adult Identity?" *Advances in Life Course Research* 11(January): 199–224. DOI: 10.1016/S1040-2608(06)11008-4.

Benson, Michael L., Leanne Fiftal Alarid, Velmer S. Burton, and Francis T. Cullen. 2011. "Reintegration or Stigmatization? Offenders' Expectations of Community Re-entry." *Journal of Criminal Justice* 39(5): 385–93. DOI: 10.1016/j.jcrimjus.2011.05.004.

Beronio, Kirsten, Rosa Po, Laura Skopec, and Sherry Glied. 2013. "Affordable Care Act Will Expand Mental Health and Substance Use Disorder Benefits and Parity Protections for 62 Million Americans." ASPE Research Brief. Washington: U.S. Department of Health and Human Services (February 20). https://aspe.hhs.gov/

report/affordable-care-act-expands-mental-health-and-substance-use-disorder-benefits-and-federal-parity-protections-62-million-americans.

Bertrand, Marianne, and Sendhil Mullainathan. 2004. "Are Emily and Greg More Employable than Lakisha and Jamal? A Field Experiment on Labor Market Discrimination." *American Economic Review* 94(4): 991–1013. http://datacolada.org/wp-content/uploads/2015/04/bertrand_mullanaithan-1.pdf.

Besharov, Douglas J. 1999. *America's Disconnected Youth: Toward a Preventive Strategy*. Washington, D.C.: American Enterprise Institute.

Betts, Julian R., and Laurel L. McFarland. 1995. "Safe Port in a Storm: The Impact of Labor Market Conditions on Community College Enrollments." *Journal of Human Resources* 30(4): 741–65.

Binswanger, Ingrid A., Patrick J. Blatchford, Shane R. Mueller, and Marc F. Stern. 2013. "Mortality after Prison Release: Opioid Overdose and Other Causes of Death, Risk Factors, and Time Trends from 1999 to 2009." *Annals of Internal Medicine* 159(9): 592–600. DOI: 10.7326/0003-4819-159-9-201311050-00005.

Binswanger, Ingrid A., Marc F. Stern, Richard A. Deyo, Patrick J. Heagerty, Allen Cheadle, Joann G. Elmore, and Thomas D. Koepsell. 2007a. "Release from Prison—A High Risk of Death for Former Inmates." *New England Journal of Medicine* 356(2): 157–65.

———. 2007b. "Release from Prison: A High Risk of Death for Former Inmates." *New England Journal of Medicine* 356(2): 157–65.

Blanchflower, David G., Phillip B. Levine, and David J. Zimmerman. 2003. "Discrimination in the Small-Business Credit Market." *Review of Economics and Statistics* 85(4): 930–43.

Blumstein, Alfred, and Kiminori Nakamura. 2009. "Redemption in the Presence of Widespread Criminal Background Checks." *Criminology* 47(2): 327–59.

Boardman, Jason D., Brian Karl Finch, Christopher G. Ellison, David R. Williams, and James S. Jackson. 2001. "Neighborhood Disadvantage, Stress, and Drug Use among Adults." *Journal of Health and Social Behavior* 42(2): 151–65. DOI: 10.2307/3090175.

Bohn, Sarah, Jacob Jackson, and Shannon McConville. 2019. "Career Pathways and Economic Mobility at California's Community Colleges." San Francisco: Public Policy Institute of California (June). https://www.ppic.org/wp-content/uploads/career-pathways-and-economic-mobility-at-californias-community-colleges.pdf.

Bohn, Sarah, and Shannon McConville. 2018. "Stackable Credentials in Career Education at California Community Colleges." San Francisco: Public Policy Institute of California (October). https://www.ppic.org/publication/stackable-credentials-in-career-education-at-california-community-colleges/.

Bonczar, Thomas P. 2003. "Prevalence of Imprisonment in the U.S. Population, 1974–2001." *Special Report* (August). Washington, D.C.: Bureau of Justice Statistics. https://www.bjs.gov/content/pub/pdf/piusp01.pdf.

Bonczar, Thomas P., and Allen J. Beck. 1997. "Lifetime Likelihood of Going to State or Federal Prison." *Special Report* (March). Washington, D.C.: Bureau of Justice Statistics. DOI: NCJ160092.

Boshara, Ray, William R. Emmons, and Bryan J. Noeth. 2015. "How Age, Education, and Race Separate Thrivers from Strugglers in Today's Economy: Race, Ethnicity and Wealth." In "Demographics of Wealth" series. St. Louis: Federal Reserve Bank of St. Louis (February). https://www.stlouisfed.org/~/media/files/pdfs/hfs/essays/hfs-essay-1-2015-race-ethnicity-and-wealth.pdf.

Bozick, Robert, Jennifer Steele, Lois Davis, and Susan Turner. 2018. "Does Providing Inmates with Education Improve Postrelease Outcomes? A Meta-Analysis of Correctional Education Programs in the United States." *Journal of Experimental Criminology* 14(3): 389–428.

Bradley, Katherine H., R. B. Michael Oliver, Noel C. Richardson, and Elspeth M. Slayter. 2001. "No Place Like Home: Housing and the Ex-Prisoner." Policy brief. Boston: Community Resources for Justice (November). https://b.3cdn.net/crjustice/a5b5d8fa98ed957505_hqm6b5qp2.pdf.

Braga, Anthony A. 2017. "Long-Term Trends in the Sources of Boston Crime Guns." *RSF: The Russell Sage Foundation Journal of the Social Sciences* 3(5): 76–95. DOI: 10.7758/rsf.2017.3.5.04.

Braman, Donald. 2004. *Doing Time on the Outside: Incarceration and Family Life in Urban America*. Ann Arbor: University of Michigan Press.

Brame, Robert, Michael G. Turner, Raymond Paternoster, and Shawn D. Bushway. 2012. "Cumulative Prevalence of Arrest from Ages 8 to 23 in a National Sample." *Pediatrics* 129(1): 21–27. http://pediatrics.aappublications.org/content/129/1/21.abstract.

Braveman, Paula A., Catherine Cubbin, Susan Egerter, David R. Williams, and Elsie Pamuk. 2010. "Socioeconomic Disparities in Health in the United States: What the Patterns Tell Us." *American Journal of Public Health* 100(suppl. 1): S186–96. DOI: 10.2105/AJPH.2009.166082.

Breen, Richard, and John H. Goldthorpe. 1997. "Explaining Educational Differentials: Towards a Formal Rational Action Theory." *Rationality and Society* 9(3): 275–305. DOI: 10.1177/104346397009003002.

Breen, Richard, Kristian Bernt Karlson, and Anders Holm. 2018. "Interpreting and Understanding Logits, Probits, and Other Nonlinear Probability Models." *Annual Review of Sociology* 44(1): 39–54. DOI: 10.1146/annurev-soc-073117-041429.

Bronson, Jennifer, and Marcus Berzofsky. 2017. "Indicators of Mental Health Problems Reported by Prisoners and Jail Inmates, 2011–12." *Special Report* (June). Washington, D.C.: Bureau of Justice Statistics. https://www.bjs.gov/content/pub/pdf/imhprpji1112.pdf.

Bronson, Jennifer, and E. Ann Carson. 2019. "Prisoners in 2017." *Bulletin* (April). Washington, D.C.: Bureau of Justice Statistics. https://www.bjs.gov/content/pub/pdf/p17.pdf.

Bronson, Jennifer, Jessica Stroop, Stephanie Zimmer, and Marcus Berzofsky. 2017. "Drug Use, Dependence, and Abuse." *Special Report* (June). Washington, D.C.: Bureau of Justice Statistics. https://www.bjs.gov/content/pub/pdf/dudaspji0709.pdf.

Brunson, Rod K., and Brian A. Wade. 2019. "'Oh Hell No, We Don't Talk to Police.'" *Criminology and Public Policy* 18(3): 623–48. DOI: 10.1111/1745-9133.12448.

Buchmann, Marlis C., and Irene Kriesi. 2011. "Transition to Adulthood in Europe." *Annual Review of Sociology* 37: 481–503. DOI: 10.1146/annurev-soc-081309-150212.

Bureau of Labor Statistics. 1997. "Chapter 5: Employment and Wages Covered by Unemployment Insurance." Washington: U.S. Department of Justice. https://www.bls.gov/opub/hom/pdf/cew-19970404.pdf.

Burke, Peggy, and Michael Tonry. 2006. "Successful Transition and Reentry for Safer Communities: A Call to Action for Parole." Silver Spring, Md.: Center for Effective Public Policy. https://cepp.com/wp-content/uploads/2015/12/Successful-Transition-and-reentry-for-safer-communities-a-call-to-action-for-parole.pdf.

Bursik, Robert J., and Harold G. Grasmick. 1993. *Neighborhoods and Crime: The Dimensions of Effective Community Control.* New York: Lexington Books.

Bushway, Shawn D., and Robert Apel. 2012. "A Signaling Perspective on Employment-Based Reentry Programming." *Criminology and Public Policy* 11(1): 21–50.

Bushway, Shawn, Shauna Briggs, Faye Taxman, Meredith Thanner, and Mischelle Van Brakle. 2007. "Private Providers of Criminal History Records: Do You Get What You Pay For?" In *Barriers to Reentry? The Labor Market for Released Prisoners in Post-Industrial America,* edited by Shawn Bushway, Michael Stoll, and David Weiman. New York: Russell Sage Foundation.

Bushway, Shawn D., Paul Nieuwbeerta, and Arjan Blokland. 2011. "The Predictive Value of Criminal Background Checks: Do Age and Criminal History Affect Time to Redemption?" *Criminology* 49(1): 27–60. DOI: 10.1111/j.1745-9125.2010.00217.x.

Bushway, Shawn D., and Anne Morrison Piehl. 2007. "Social Science Research and the Legal Threat to Presumptive Sentencing Guidelines." *Criminology and Public Policy* 6(3): 461–82. DOI: 10.1111/j.1745-9133.2007.00447.x.

Bushway, Shawn, Michael A. Stoll, and David F. Weiman, eds. 2007. *Barriers to Reentry? The Labor Market for Released Prisoners in Post-Industrial America.* New York: Russell Sage Foundation.

Cadora, Eric, Charles Swartz, and Mannix Gordon. 2003. "Criminal Justice and Health and Human Services: An Exploration of Overlapping Needs, Resources, and Interests in Brooklyn Neighborhoods." In *Prisoners Once Removed: The Impact of Incarceration and Reentry on Children, Families, and Communities,* edited by Jeremy Travis and Michelle Waul. Washington, D.C.: Urban Institute Press.

Cameron, Stephen, and James J. Heckman. 1993. "The Nonequivalence of High School Equivalents." *Journal of Labor Economics* 11(1): 1–47.

Caputo-Levine, Deirdre D. 2013. "The Yard Face: The Contributions of Inmate Interpersonal Violence to the Carceral Habitus." *Ethnography* 14(2): 165–85.

Carson, E. Ann. 2014. "Prisoners in 2013." *Bulletin* (September). Washington, D.C.: Bureau of Justice Statistics. https://www.bjs.gov/content/pub/pdf/p13.pdf.

Carter, Jeremy G., George Mohler, and Bradley Ray. 2019. "Spatial Concentration of Opioid Overdose Deaths in Indianapolis: An Application of the Law of Crime Concentration at Place to a Public Health Epidemic." *Journal of Contemporary Criminal Justice* 35(2): 161–85. DOI: 10.1177/1043986218803527.

Caulkins, Jonathan P., and Peter Reuter. 2017. "Dealing More Effectively and Humanely with Illegal Drugs." *Crime and Justice* 46(1): 95–158. DOI: 10.1086/688458.

Centers for Disease Control and Prevention. 2019. "Web-Based Injury Statistics Query and Reporting System (WISQARS)." Washington: U.S. Department of Health and Human Services (last updated September 18, 2019). www.cdc.gov/injury/wisqars.

Cho, Rosa Minhyo, and John H. Tyler. 2010. "Does Prison-Based Adult Basic Education Improve Postrelease Outcomes for Male Prisoners in Florida?" *Crime and Delinquency* 59(7): 975–1005. DOI: 10.1177/0011128710389588.

Chung, He Len, Michelle Little, and Laurence Steinberg. 2005. "The Transition to Adulthood for Adolescents in the Juvenile Justice System: A Developmental Perspective." In *On Your Own without a Net: The Transition to Adulthood for Vulnerable Populations*, edited by D. Wayne Osgood, E. Michael Foster, Constance Flanagan, and Gretchen R. Ruth. Chicago: University of Chicago.

City of New York. 2017. "Mayor de Blasio Announces Re-entry Services for Everyone in City Jails by End of This Year." March 29. https://www1.nyc.gov/office-of-the-mayor/news/187-17/mayor-de-blasio-re-entry-services-everyone-city-jails-end-this-year#/0.

Clark, Valerie A., and Grant Duwe. 2016. "Distance Matters: Examining the Factors That Impact Prisoner Visitation in Minnesota." *Criminal Justice and Behavior* 44(2): 184–204. DOI: 10.1177/0093854816667416.

Clear, Todd R. 2007. *Imprisoning Communities: How Mass Incarceration Makes Disadvantaged Neighborhoods Worse.* New York: Oxford University Press.

———. 2011. "A Private-Sector, Incentives-Based Model for Justice Reinvestment." *Criminology and Public Policy* 10(3): 585–608.

Clemmer, Donald. 1950. "Observations on Imprisonment as a Source of Criminality." *Journal of Criminal Law and Criminology (1931–1951)* 41(3): 311–19. DOI: 10.2307/1138066.

Cloward, Richard A., and Lloyd E. Ohlin. 1960. *Delinquency and Opportunity: A Theory of Delinquent Gangs.* New York: Free Press.

Cochran, Joshua C. 2019. "Inmate Social Ties, Recidivism, and Continuing Questions about Prison Visitation." In *The Palgrave Handbook of Prison and the Family*, edited by Marie Hutton and Dominique Moran. London: Palgrave Macmillan.

Coleman, James S. 1988. "Social Capital in the Creation of Human Capital." *American Journal of Sociology* 94(1988): S95–120.

Collins, Megan E., Susan T. Parker, Thomas L. Scott, and Charles F. Wellford. 2017. "A Comparative Analysis of Crime Guns." *RSF: The Russell Sage Foundation Journal of the Social Sciences* 3(5): 96–127. DOI: 10.7758/rsf.2017.3.5.05.

Comfort, Megan. 2008. *Doing Time Together: Love and Family in the Shadow of the Prison.* Chicago: University of Chicago Press.

———. 2012. "'It Was Basically College to Us': Poverty, Prison, and Emerging Adulthood." *Journal of Poverty* 16(3): 308–22.

Cook, Benjamin Lê, and Margarita Alegría. 2011. "Racial-Ethnic Disparities in Substance Abuse Treatment: The Role of Criminal History and Socioeconomic Status." *Psychiatric Services* 62(11): 1273–81. DOI: 10.1176/appi.ps.62.11.1273.

Cook, Philip J., and John J. Donohue. 2017. "Saving Lives by Regulating Guns: Evidence for Policy." *Science* 358(6368): 1259–61. DOI: 10.1126/science.aar3067.

Cook, Philip J., and Harold A. Pollack. 2017. "Reducing Access to Guns by Violent Offenders." *RSF: The Russell Sage Foundation Journal of the Social Sciences* 3(5): 2–36. DOI: 10.7758/rsf.2017.3.5.01.

Cook, Philip J., Harold A. Pollack, and Kailey White. 2019. "The Last Link: From Gun Acquisition to Criminal Use." *Journal of Urban Health* 96: 784–91. DOI: 10.1007/s11524-019-00358-0.

Copp, Jennifer E., Peggy C. Giordano, Monica A. Longmore, and Wendy D. Manning. 2019. "Desistance from Crime during the Transition to Adulthood: The Influence of Parents, Peers, and Shifts in Identity." *Journal of Research in Crime and Delinquency* (October 2): 1–39. DOI: 10.1177/0022427819878220.

Craig, Jessica, and Alex R. Piquero. 2014. "Crime and Punishment in Emerging Adulthood." In *The Oxford Handbook of Emerging Adulthood,* edited by Jeffrey Jensen Arnett. Oxford: Oxford University Press. DOI: 10.1093/oxfordhb/9780199795574.013.010.

Crewe, Ben. 2007. "Power, Adaptation, and Resistance in a Late-Modern Men's Prison." *British Journal of Criminology* 47(2): 256–75. DOI: 10.1093/bjc/azl044.

Crifasi, Cassandra K., Shani A. L. Buggs, Seema Choksy, and Daniel W. Webster. 2017. "The Initial Impact of Maryland's Firearm Safety Act of 2013 on the Supply of Crime Handguns in Baltimore." *RSF: The Russell Sage Foundation Journal of the Social Sciences* 3(5): 128–40. DOI: 10.7758/rsf.2017.3.5.06.

Crutchfield, Robert D. 2014. *Get a Job: Labor Markets, Economic Opportunity, and Crime.* New York: New York University Press.

Crutchfield, Robert D., and Susan R. Pitchford. 1997. "Work and Crime: The Effects of Labor Stratification on Criminality." *Social Forces* 76(1): 93–118.

Danziger, Sheldon, and David Ratner. 2010. "Labor Market Outcomes and the Transition to Adulthood." *The Future of Children* 20(1): 133–58.

Danziger, Sheldon, and Cecilia Elena Rouse. 2007. *The Price of Independence: The Economics of Early Adulthood*. New York: Russell Sage Foundation.

Darolia, Rajeev, Cory Koedel, Paco Martorell, Katie Wilson, and Francisco Perez-Arce. 2015. "Do Employers Prefer Workers Who Attend For-Profit Colleges? Evidence from a Field Experiment." *Journal of Policy Analysis and Management* 34(4): 881–903. DOI: 10.7249/WR1054.

Davis, Lois M., Robert Bozick, Jennifer L. Steele, Jessica Saunders, and Jeremy N. V. Miles. 2013. *Evaluating the Effectiveness of Correctional Education*. Santa Monica, Calif.: RAND Corporation.

DeLuca, Stefanie, Susan Clampet-Lundquist, and Kathryn Edin. 2016a. *Coming of Age in the Other America*. New York: Russell Sage Foundation.

———. 2016b. "In and Out Before You Know It: The Educational and Occupational Traps of Expedited Adulthood." In *Coming of Age in the Other America*, edited by Stefanie DeLuca, Susan Clampet-Lundquist, and Kathryn Edin. New York: Russell Sage Foundation.

Deming, David J., Claudia Goldin, and Lawrence F. Katz. 2011. "The For-Profit Postsecondary School Sector: Nimble Critters or Agile Predators?" Working Paper 17710. Cambridge, Mass.: National Bureau of Economic Research (December). https://www.nber.org/papers/w17710.

Deming, David J., Noam Yuchtman, Amira Abulafi, Claudia Goldin, and Lawrence F. Katz. 2016. "The Value of Postsecondary Credentials in the Labor Market: An Experimental Study." *American Economic Review* 106(3): 778–806. DOI: 10.1257/aer.20141757.

Denver, Megan, Garima Siwach, and Shawn D. Bushway. 2017. "A New Look at the Employment and Recidivism Relationship through the Lens of a Criminal Background Check." *Criminology* 55(1): 174–204. DOI: 10.1111/1745-9125.12130.

Des Jarlais, D. C., Courtney McKnight, Kamyar Arasteh, Jonathan Feelemyer, Zev Ross, and H. L. F. Cooper. 2019. "Geographic Distribution of Risk ('Hotspots') for HIV, HCV, and Drug Overdose among Persons Who Use Drugs in New York City: The Importance of Local History." *Harm Reduction Journal* 16(1): 1–12. DOI: 10.1186/s12954-019-0326-2.

Desmond, Matthew. 2012. "Disposable Ties and the Urban Poor." *American Journal of Sociology* 117(5): 1295–1335.

———. 2016. *Evicted: Poverty and Profit in the American City*. New York: Penguin Books.

Desmond, Matthew, Andrew V. Papachristos, and David S. Kirk. 2016. "Police Violence and Citizen Crime Reporting in the Black Community." *American Sociological Review* 81(5): 857–76. DOI: 10.1177/0003122416663494.

Detroit Free Press. 2019. "Baker College Plans to Close Some Michigan Campuses." *Detroit Free Press*, January 11.

Dobbie, Will, Jacob Goldin, and Crystal S. Yang. 2018. "The Effects of Pretrial Detention on Conviction, Future Crime, and Employment: Evidence from Randomly Assigned Judges." *American Economic Review* 108(2): 201–40. DOI: 10.1257/aer.20161503.

Dobrin, Adam. 2001. "The Risk of Offending on Homicide Victimization: A Case Control Study." *Journal of Research in Crime and Delinquency* 38(2): 154–73. DOI: 10.1177/0022427801038002003.

Doleac, Jennifer L. 2019. "Encouraging Desistance from Crime." Working Paper. College Station: Texas A&M University. http://jenniferdoleac.com/wp-content/uploads/2019/02/Doleac_Desistance_Feb2019.pdf.

Doleac, Jennifer L., and Benjamin Hansen. 2016. "Does 'Ban the Box' Help or Hurt Low-Skilled Workers? Statistical Discrimination and Employment Outcomes When Criminal Histories Are Hidden." Working paper 22469. Cambridge, Mass.: National Bureau of Economic Research.

Donovan, Sarah A., and David H. Bradley. 2018. "Real Wage Trends, 1979 to 2017." Congressional Research Service Report R45090. Washington, D.C.: Congressional Research Service (March 15).

Dumont, Dora M., Brad Brockmann, Samuel Dickman, Nicole Alexander, and Josiah D. Rich. 2012. "Public Health and the Epidemic of Incarceration." *Annual Review of Public Health* 33(1): 325–39. DOI: 10.1146/annurev-publhealth-031811-124614.

Duncan, Dustin T., and Ichiro Kawachi. 2018. *Neighborhoods and Health*, 2nd ed. New York: Oxford University Press.

Duwe, Grant. 2018. "The Importance of the Company You Keep." Washington, D.C.: American Enterprise Institute (October). https://www.aei.org/wp-content/uploads/2018/10/The-importance-of-the-company-you-keep.pdf.

Duwe, Grant, and Byron R. Johnson. 2016. "The Effects of Prison Visits from Community Volunteers on Offender Recidivism." *Prison Journal* 96(2): 279–303. DOI: 10.1177/0032885515618468.

Dynarski, Susan M., Steven W. Hemelt, and Joshua M. Hyman. 2013. "The Missing Manual: Using National Student Clearinghouse Data to Track Postsecondary Outcomes." Working Paper 19552. Cambridge, Mass.: National Bureau of Economic Research. https://www.nber.org/papers/w19552.

Eberhardt, Jennifer L., Phillip Atiba Goff, Valerie J. Purdie, and Paul G. Davies. 2004. "Seeing Black: Race, Crime, and Visual Processing." *Journal of Personality and Social Psychology* 87(6): 876–93. DOI: 10.1037/0022-3514.87.6.876.

Edelman, Peter B., and Harry J. Holzer. 2013. "Connecting the Disconnected: Improving Education and Employment Outcomes among Disadvantaged Youth." Policy Paper 56. Bonn: Institute for the Study of Labor (April). http://ftp.iza.org/pp56.pdf.

Edelman, Peter, Harry J. Holzer, and Paul Offner. 2005. *Reconnecting Disadvantaged Young Men*. Washington, D.C.: Urban Institute Press.

Edin, Kathryn, and Timothy J. Nelson. 2013. *Doing the Best I Can: Fatherhood in the Inner City*. Berkeley: University of California Press.

Edwards, Frank, Michael H. Esposito, and Hedwig Lee. 2018. "Risk of Police-Involved Death by Race/Ethnicity and Place, United States, 2012–2018." *American Journal of Public Health* 108(9): 1241–48. DOI: 10.2105/AJPH.2018.304559.

Edwards, Frank, Hedwig Lee, and Michael Esposito. 2019. "Risk of Being Killed by Police Use of Force in the United States by Age, Race-Ethnicity, and Sex." *Proceedings of the National Academy of Sciences* 116(34): 16793–98. DOI: 10.1073/pnas.1821204116.

Elder, Glen H. 1974. *Children of the Great Depression: Social Change in Life Experience*. Chicago: University of Chicago Press.

———. 1988. "The Life Course as Developmental Theory." *Child Development* 69: 1–12.

Eliason, Scott R., Jeylan T. Mortimer, and Mike Vuolo. 2015. "The Transition to Adulthood: Life Course Structures and Subjective Perceptions." *Social Psychology Quarterly* 78(3): 205–27. DOI: 10.1177/0190272515582002.

Ellen, Ingrid G., Tod Mijanovich, and Keri-Nicole Dillman. 2001. "Neighborhood Effects on Health: Exploring the Links and Assessing the Evidence." *Journal of Urban Affairs* 23(3/4): 391–408. DOI: 10.1111/0735-2166.00096.

Elwert, Felix, and Christopher Winship. 2014. "Endogenous Selection Bias: The Problem of Conditioning on a Collider Variable." *Annual Review of Sociology* 40: 31–53. DOI: 10.1146/annurev-soc-071913-043455.

Engel, Robin S., Robert E. Worden, Nicholas Corsaro, Hannah D. McManus, Danielle Reynolds, Hannah Cochran, Gabrielle T. Isaza, and Jennifer Calnon Cherkauskas. 2019. *The Power to Arrest: Lessons from Research*. Cham, Switzerland: Springer.

Engelhardt, Bryan. 2010. "The Effect of Employment Frictions on Crime." *Journal of Labor Economics* 28(3): 677–718.

Entwisle, Doris R., Karl L. Alexander, and Linda Steffel Olson. 2005. "First Grade and Educational Attainment by Age 22: A New Story." *American Journal of Sociology* 110(5): 1458–1502. DOI: 10.1086/428444.

Esperian, John H. 2010. "The Effect of Prison Education Programs on Recidivism." *Journal of Correctional Education* 61(4): 316–34.

Evans, Douglas N., Kwan-Lamar Blount-Hill, and Michelle A. Cubellis. 2019. "Examining Housing Discrimination across Race, Gender, and Felony History." *Housing Studies* 34(5): 761–78. DOI: 10.1080/02673037.2018.1478069.

Ewens, Michael, Bryan Tomlin, and Liang Choon Wang. 2014. "Statistical Discrimination or Prejudice? A Large Sample Field Experiment." *Review of Economics and Statistics* 96(1): 119–34.

Fader, Jamie J. 2013. *Falling Back: Incarceration and Transitions to Adulthood among Urban Youth*. New Brunswick, N.J.: Rutgers University Press.

Fagan, Jeffrey, and Elliott Ash. 2017. "New Policing, New Segregation: From Ferguson to New York." *Georgetown Law Journal* 106(1): 25–102. https://papers.ssrn.com/sol3/papers.cfm?abstract_id=3070479.

Fagan, Jeffrey, and Richard B. Freeman. 1999. "Crime and Work." *Crime and Justice* 25: 225–90.

Farabee, David, Michael Prendergast, and M. Douglas Anglin. 1998. "The Effectiveness of Coerced Treatment for Drug-Abusing Offenders." *Federal Probation* 62(1): 3–10.

Farber, Henry S. 2007. "Is the Company Man an Anachronism? Trends in Long-Term Employment in the United States, 1973 to 2006." In *The Price of Independence*, edited by Sheldon Danziger and Elena Rouse. New York: Russell Sage Foundation.

Farley, Reynolds. 2018. "Detroit Fifty Years after the Kerner Report: What Has Changed, What Has Not, and Why?" *RSF: The Russell Sage Foundation Journal of the Social Sciences* 4(6): 206. DOI: 10.7758/rsf.2018.4.6.10.

Farmer, Melissa M., and Kenneth F. Ferraro. 2005. "Are Racial Disparities in Health Conditional on Socioeconomic Status?" *Social Science and Medicine* 60(1): 191–204. DOI: 10.1016/j.socscimed.2004.04.026.

Feeley, Malcolm M., and Jonathon Simon. 1992. "The New Penology: Notes on the Emerging Strategy of Corrections and Its Implications." *Criminology* 30(4): 449–74.

Felson, Richard B., D. Wayne Osgood, Julie Horney, and Craig Wiernik. 2012. "Having a Bad Month: General Versus Specific Effects of Stress on Crime." *Journal of Quantitative Criminology* 28(2): 347–63. DOI: 10.1007/s10940-011-9138-6.

Felson, Richard B., and Noah Painter-Davis. 2012. "Another Cost of Being a Young Black Male: Race, Weaponry, and Lethal Outcomes in Assaults." *Social Science Research* 41(5): 1241–53. DOI: 10.1016/j.ssresearch.2012.04.006.

Felson, Richard B., and Paul-Philippe Pare. 2010. "Gun Cultures or Honor Cultures? Explaining Regional and Race Differences in Weapon Carrying." *Social Forces* 88(3): 1357–78. DOI: 10.1353/sof.0.0310.

Fernandes-Alcantara, Adrienne L. 2015. "Disconnected Youth: A Look at 16- to 24-Year Olds Who Are Not Working or in School." In *Youth in America: Transitions to Adulthood and Disconnected Youths.* Washington, D.C.: Nova Science Publishers. http://www.scopus.com/inward/record.url?eid=2-s2.0-84896180261&partnerID=tZOtx3y1.

Fitzpatrick, Maria D., and Sarah E. Turner. 2007. "Blurring the Boundary: Changes in Collegiate Participation and the Transition to Adulthood." In *The Price of Independence: The Economics of Early Adulthood*, edited by Sheldon Danziger and Cecilia Elena Rouse. New York: Russell Sage Foundation.

Fleming, Charles B., Helene R. White, and Richard F. Catalano. 2010. "Romantic Relationships and Substance Use in Early Adulthood: An Examination of the Influences of Relationship Type, Partner Substance Use, and Relationship

Quality." *Journal of Health and Social Behavior* 51(2): 153–67. DOI: 10.1177/ 0022146510368930.

Fomby, Paula, and Stacey J. Bosick. 2013. "Family Instability and the Transition to Adulthood." *Journal of Marriage and Family* 75(5): 1266–87. DOI: 10.1111/ jomf.12063.

Ford, Clarence, and David J. Harding. 2019. "Our Parole System Focuses on Control and Punishment. What about Reintegration?" *Sacramento Bee*, June 14. https://www.sacbee.com/opinion/op-ed/article230803154.html.

Foster, Holly, and John Hagan. 2007. "Incarceration and Intergenerational Social Exclusion." *Social Problems* 54(4): 399–433.

———. 2015. "Punishment Regimes and the Multilevel Effects of Parental Incarceration: Intergenerational, Intersectional, and Interinstitutional Models of Social Inequality and Systemic Exclusion." *Annual Review of Sociology* 41(1): 135–58. DOI: 10.1146/annurev-soc-073014-112437.

———. 2017. "Maternal Imprisonment, Economic Marginality, and Unmet Health Needs in Early Adulthood." *Preventive Medicine* 99: 43–48. DOI: 10.1016/ j.ypmed.2017.01.018.

Foster, Michael E., and Elizabeth J. Gifford. 2005. "The Transition to Adulthood for Youth Leaving Public Systems." In *On the Frontier of Adulthood: Theory, Research, and Public Policy*, edited by Richard A. Settersten Jr., Frank F. Furstenberg Jr., and Rubén G. Rumbaut. Chicago: University of Chicago Press.

Frase, Richard S. 2009. "What Explains Persistent Racial Disproportionality in Minnesota's Prison and Jail Populations?" *Crime and Justice* 38(1): 201–80. DOI: 10.1086/599199.

Freeman, Richard B., and William M. Rodgers. 1999. "Area Economic Conditions and the Labor Market Outcomes of Young Men in the 1990s Expansion." Working Paper 7073. Cambridge, Mass.: National Bureau of Economic Research (April). https://www.nber.org/papers/w7073.pdf.

Freisthler, Bridget, Elizabeth A. Lascala, Paul J. Gruenewald, and Andrew J. Treno. 2005. "An Examination of Drug Activity: Effects of Neighborhood Social Organization on the Development of Drug Distribution Systems." *Substance Use and Misuse* 40(5): 671–686.

Friedman, Brittany, and Mary Pattillo. 2019. "Statutory Inequality: The Logics of Monetary Sanctions in State Law." *RSF: The Russell Sage Foundation Journal of the Social Sciences* 5(1): 173. DOI: 10.7758/rsf.2019.5.1.08.

Friedson, Michael, and Patrick Sharkey. 2015. "Violence and Neighborhood Disadvantage after the Crime Decline." *Annals of the American Academy of Political and Social Science* 660(1): 341–58. DOI: 10.1177/0002716215579825.

Frone, Michael R. 2011. "Alcohol and Illicit Drug Use in the Workforce and Workplace." In *Handbook of Occupational Health Psychology*, 2nd ed., edited by James C. Quick and Lois E. Tetrick. Washington, D.C.: American Psychological Association.

Fry, Richard. 2009. "College Enrollment Hits All-Time High, Fueled by Community College Surge." Washington, D.C.: Pew Research Center (October 29). https://www.issuelab.org/resource/college-enrollment-hits-all-time-high-fueled-by-community-college-surge.html.

Furstenberg, Frank F. 2008. "The Intersections of Social Class and the Transition to Adulthood." In *Social Class and Transitions to Adulthood: New Directions for Child and Adolescent Development,* edited by Jeylan T. Mortimer and Lene Arnett Jense. San Francisco: Jossey-Bass.

——. 2010. "Diverging Development: The Not-So-Invisible Hand of Social Class in the United States." In *Families as They Really Are,* edited by Barbara J. Risman. New York: W. W. Norton & Co.

Gale, William, Benjamin Harris, Bryant Renaud, and Katherine Rodihan. 2014. "Student Loans Rising: An Overview of Causes, Consequences, and Policy Options." Washington, D.C.: Tax Policy Center of Brookings Institution and Urban Institute (May). https://www.brookings.edu/wp-content/uploads/2016/06/student_loans_rising_gale_harris_09052014.pdf.

Galster, George, and Patrick Sharkey. 2017. "Spatial Foundations of Inequality: A Conceptual Model and Empirical Overview." *RSF: The Russell Sage Foundation Journal of the Social Sciences* 3(2): 1–33. DOI: 10.7758/rsf.2017.3.2.01.

Garland, David. 2001. *The Culture of Control: Crime and Social Order in Contemporary Society.* Oxford: Oxford University Press.

Geller, Amanda. 2013. "Paternal Incarceration and Father-Child Contact in Fragile Families." *Journal of Marriage and Family* 75(5): 1288–1303. DOI: 10.1111/jomf.12056.

Geller, Amanda, and Marah A. Curtis. 2011. "A Sort of Homecoming: Incarceration and the Housing Security of Urban Men." *Social Science Research* 40(4): 1196–1213.

Geller, Amanda, and Jeffrey Fagan. 2019. "Police Contact and the Legal Socialization of Urban Teens." *RSF: The Russell Sage Foundation Journal of the Social Sciences* 5(1): 26. DOI: 10.7758/rsf.2019.5.1.02.

Glaze, Lauren E. 2003. "Probation and Parole in the United States, 2002." *Bulletin* (August). Washington, D.C.: Bureau of Justice Statistics. https://www.bjs.gov/content/pub/pdf/ppus02.pdf.

Goldscheider, Frances, and Calvin Goldscheider. 1999. *Understanding Families,* vol. 17, *The Changing Transition to Adulthood: Leaving and Returning Home.* Thousand Oaks, CA: Sage Publications.

Gottfredson, Linda. 1985. "Education as a Valid but Fallible Signal of Worker Quality: Reorienting an Old Debate about the Functional Basis of the Occupational Hierarchy." In *Research in Sociology of Education and Socialization,* vol. 5, edited by Alan C. Kerckhoff. Greenwich, Conn.: JAI Press.

Gottfredson, Michael R., and Travis Hirschi. 1990. *A General Theory of Crime.* Stanford, Calif.: Stanford University Press.

Gottschalk, Marie. 2016. *Caught: The Prison State and the Lockdown of American Politics*. Princeton, N.J.: Princeton University Press.

Government Accountability Office. 2019. "Actions Needed to Evaluate Pell Grant Pilot for Incarcerated Students Report." GAO-19-030. Washington: Government Accountability Office (March). https://www.gao.gov/assets/700/697248.pdf.

Granovetter, Mark S. 1973. "The Strength of Weak Ties." *American Journal of Sociology* 78: 1360–81.

Grattet, Ryken, Jeffrey Lin, and Joan Petersilia. 2011. "Supervision Regimes, Risk, and Official Reactions to Parolee Deviance." *Criminology* 49(2): 371–99.

Greenberg, Elizabeth, Eric Dunleavy, Mark Kutner, and Sheida White. 2007. "Literacy behind Bars: Results from the 2003 National Assessment of Adult Literacy Prison Survey." NCES 2007-473. Washington: U.S. Department of Education, National Center for Education Statistics (May). https://nces.ed.gov/pubs2007/2007473.pdf.

Greenberg, Liane, and Julian Barling. 1999. "Predicting Employee Aggression against Coworkers, Subordinates, and Supervisors: The Roles of Person Behaviors and Perceived Workplace Factors." *Journal of Organizational Behavior* 20(6): 897–913. DOI: 10.1002/(SICI)1099-1379(199911)20:6{897::AID-JOB975}3.0.CO;2-Z.

Grinstead, Olga, Bonnie Faigekes, Carrie Bancroft, and Barry Zack. 2001. "The Financial Cost of Maintaining Relationships with Incarcerated African-American Men: Results from a Survey of Women Prison Visitors." *Journal of African-American Men* 6(1): 59–70.

Guenther, Lisa. 2013. *Solitary Confinement: Social Death and Its Afterlives*. Minneapolis: University of Minnesota Press.

Hagan, John. 1993. "The Social Embeddedness of Crime and Unemployment." *Criminology* 31(4): 465–91.

Hagan, John, and Holly Foster. 2012. "Intergenerational Educational Effects of Mass Imprisonment in America." *Sociology of Education* 85(3): 259–86. DOI: 10.1177/0038040711431587.

———. 2017. "Mass Incarceration, Parental Imprisonment, and the Great Recession: Intergenerational Sources of Severe Deprivation in America." *RSF: The Russell Sage Foundation Journal of the Social Sciences* 1(2): 80. DOI: 10.7758/rsf.2015.1.2.05.

Hagan, John, and Alberto Palloni. 1990. "The Social Reproduction of a Criminal Class in Working-Class London, Circa 1950–1980." *American Journal of Sociology* 96(2): 265–99. http://www.jstor.org/stable/2781103.

Hager, Eli. 2015. "Forgiving vs. Forgetting." *The Marshall Project*, March 17. https://www.themarshallproject.org/2015/03/17/forgiving-vs-forgetting.

Hair, Elizabeth C., Kristin A. Moore, Thomson J. Ling, Cameron McPhee Baker, and Brett V. Brown. 2009. "Youth Who Are 'Disconnected' and Those Who Then Reconnect: Assessing the Influence of Family, Programs, Peers, and Communities." *Child Trends: Research Brief* (July). https://rhyclearinghouse.acf.hhs.gov/

sites/default/files/docs/18790-Youth_Who_Are_Disconnected_and_Those_Who_Then_Reconnect.pdf.

Hammett, Theodore M., Cheryl Roberts, and Sofia Kennedy. 2001. "Health-Related Issues in Prisoner Reentry." *Crime and Delinquency* 47(3): 390–409.

Haney, Craig. 2002. "The Psychological Impact of Incarceration: Implications for Post-Prison Adjustment." Paper prepared for the "From Prison to Home: The Effect of Incarceration and Reentry on Children, Families, and Communities" project (December). https://aspe.hhs.gov/basic-report/psychological-impact-incarceration-implications-post-prison-adjustment.

———. 2003. "The Psychological Impact of Incarceration: Implications for Post-Prison Adjustment." In *Prisoners Once Removed: The Impact of Incarceration and Reentry on Children, Families, and Communities*, edited by Jeremy Travis and Michelle Waul. Washington, D.C.: Urban Institute Press.

———. 2018a. "Restricting the Use of Solitary Confinement." *Annual Review of Criminology* 1(1): 285–310. DOI: 10.1146/annurev-criminol-032317-092326.

———. 2018b. "The Psychological Effects of Solitary Confinement: A Systematic Critique." *Crime and Justice* 47(1): 365–416. DOI: 10.1086/696041.

Harding, David J., Cheyney C. Dobson, Jessica J. B. Wyse, and Jeffrey D. Morenoff. 2016. "Narrative Change, Narrative Stability, and Structural Constraint: The Case of Prisoner Reentry Narratives." *American Journal of Cultural Sociology* 5(1/2): 261–304.

Harding, David J., Jeffrey D. Morenoff, Cheyney C. Dobson, Erin R. Lane, Kendra Opatovsky, Ed-Dee Williams, and Jessica J. B. Wyse. 2016. "Boys and Men in African American Families." In *Boys and Men in African American Families*, edited by Linda M Burton, Derrick Burton, Susan M McHale, Valerie King, and Jennifer Van Hook. New York: Springer.

Harding, David J., Jeffrey D. Morenoff, and Claire W. Herbert. 2013. "Home Is Hard to Find: Neighborhoods, Institutions, and the Residential Trajectories of Returning Prisoners." *Annals of the American Academy of Political and Social Science* 647(1): 214–36.

Harding, David J., Jeffrey D. Morenoff, Anh P. Nguyen, and Shawn D. Bushway. 2017. "Short- and Long-Term Effects of Imprisonment on Future Felony Convictions and Prison Admissions." *Proceedings of the National Academy of Sciences* 114(42): 11103–8. DOI: 10.1073/pnas.1701544114.

Harding, David J., Jeffrey D. Morenoff, Anh P. Nguyen, Shawn D. Bushway, and Ingrid A. Binswanger. 2019. "A Natural Experiment Study of the Effects of Imprisonment on Violence in the Community." *Nature Human Behaviour* 3(7): 671–77. DOI: 10.1038/s41562-019-0604-8.

Harding, David J., Jeffrey D. Morenoff, and Jessica J. B. Wyse. 2019. *On the Outside: Prisoner Reentry and Reintegration.* Chicago: University of Chicago Press.

Harding, David J., Anh P. Nguyen, Jeffrey D. Morenoff, and Shawn D. Bushway. 2018. "Effects of Incarceration on Labor Market Outcomes among Young Adults."

In *Youth, Jobs and the Future: Problems and Prospects,* edited by Lynn Chancer, Martin Sanchez-Jankowski, and Christine Trost. New York: Oxford University Press.

Harding, David J., Jonah A. Siegel, and Jeffrey D. Morenoff. 2017. "Custodial Parole Sanctions and Earnings after Release from Prison." *Social Forces* 96(2): 909–34. DOI: 10.1093/sf/sox047.

Harding, David J., Jessica J. B. Wyse, Cheyney C. Dobson, and Jeffrey D. Morenoff. 2014. "Making Ends Meet after Prison." *Journal of Policy Analysis and Management* 33(2): 440–70. https://onlinelibrary.wiley.com/doi/abs/10.1002/pam.21741.

Harlow, Caroline Wolf. 2003. "Education and Correctional Populations." *Special Report* (January). Washington, D.C.: Bureau of Justice Statistics. https://www.bjs.gov/content/pub/pdf/ecp.pdf.

Harper, Greg, Chuck Coleman, and Jason Devine. 2003. "Evaluation of 2000 Subcounty Population Estimates." Working Paper Series 70. Washington: U.S. Census Bureau, Population Division (May). https://www.census.gov/population/www/documentation/twps0070/twps0070.html.

Harris, Alexes. 2016. *A Pound of Flesh: Monetary Sanctions as a Permanent Punishment for Poor People.* New York: Russell Sage Foundation.

Harris, Heather M., and David J. Harding. 2019. "Racial Inequality in the Transition to Adulthood after Prison." *RSF: The Russell Sage Foundation Journal of the Social Sciences* 5(1): 223–54. DOI: 10.7758/RSF.2019.5.1.10.

Harris, Katherine M., and Mark J. Edlund. 2005. "Self-Medication of Mental Health Problems: New Evidence from a National Survey." *Health Services Research* 40(1): 117–34. DOI: 10.1111/j.1475-6773.2005.00345.x.

Harris, Kathleen Mullan, Penny Gordon-Laren, Kim Chantal, and Richard Udry. 2006. "Longitudinal Trends in Race/Ethnic Disparities in Leading Health Indicators from Adolescence to Young Adulthood." *Archives of Pediatric and Adolescent Medicine* 160(1): 74–81.

Harris, Kathleen Mullan, and Hedwig Lee. 2012. "Pathways of Social Disadvantage from Adolescence into Adulthood." In *Investing in Children,* edited by Ariel Kalil, Ron Haskins, and Jenny Chesters. Washington, D.C.: Brookings Institution Press.

Hart, Carl. 2013. *High Price: A Neuroscientist's Journey of Self-Discovery That Challenges Everything You Know about Drugs and Society.* New York: HarperCollins.

Haskins, Anna R. 2014. "Unintended Consequences: Effects of Paternal Incarceration on Child School Readiness and Later Special Education Placement." *Sociological Science* 1(1): 141–58.

———. 2015. "Paternal Incarceration and Child-Reported Behavioral Functioning at Age 9." *Social Science Research* 52: 18–33.

———. 2016. "Beyond Boys' Bad Behavior: Paternal Incarceration and Cognitive Development in Middle Childhood." *Social Forces* 95(2): 861–92. DOI: 10.1093/sf/sow066.

Hatzenbuehler, Mark L. 2016. "Structural Stigma and Health Inequalities: Research Evidence and Implications for Psychological Science." *American Psychologist* 71(8): 742–51. DOI: 10.1037/amp0000068.

Hatzenbuehler, Mark L., and Bruce G. Link. 2014. "Introduction to the Special Issue on Structural Stigma and Health." *Social Science and Medicine* 103: 1–6. DOI: 10.1016/j.socscimed.2013.12.017.

Hatzenbuehler, Mark L., Susan Nolen-Hoeksema, and John Dovidio. 2009. "How Does Stigma 'Get under the Skin'?" *Psychological Science* 20(10): 1282–89. DOI: 10.1111/j.1467-9280.2009.02441.x.

Hatzenbuehler, Mark L., Jo C. Phelan, and Bruce G. Link. 2013. "Stigma as a Fundamental Cause of Population Health Inequalities." *American Journal of Public Health* 103(5): 813–21. DOI: 10.2105/AJPH.2012.301069.

Heckman, James J., John E. Humphries, and Tim Kautz, eds. 2014. *The Myth of Achievement Tests: The GED and the Role of Character in American Life.* Chicago: University of Chicago Press.

Heckman, James J., John Eric Humphries, and Nicholas S. Mader. 2011. "The GED." In *Handbook of the Economics of Education,* edited by Eric A. Hanushek, Stephen Machin, and Ludger Woessmann, 3: 423–83. DOI: 10.1016/B978-0-444-53429-3.00009-0.

Herbert, Claire W., Jeffrey D. Morenoff, and David J. Harding. 2015. "Homelessness and Housing Insecurity among Former Prisoners." *RSF: The Russell Sage Foundation Journal of the Social Sciences* 1(2): 44–79. DOI: 10.7758/RSF.2015.1.2.04.

Herda, Daniel, and Bill McCarthy. 2018. "No Experience Required: Violent Crime and Anticipated, Vicarious, and Experienced Racial Discrimination." *Social Science Research* 70(November 2017): 115–30. DOI: 10.1016/j.ssresearch.2017.11.008.

Hershcovis, M. Sandy, Nick Turner, Julian Barling, Kara A. Arnold, Kathryne E. Durpe, Inness Michelle, Manon Mireille LeBlanc, and Niro Sivanathan. 2007. "Predicting Workplace Aggression: A Meta-Analysis." *Journal of Applied Psychology* 92(1): 228–38.

Hetey, Rebecca C., and Jennifer L. Eberhardt. 2014. "Racial Disparities in Incarceration Increase Acceptance of Punitive Policies." *Psychological Science* 25(10): 1949–54. DOI: 10.1177/0956797614540307.

Hill, Terrence D., and Ronald J. Angel. 2005. "Neighborhood Disorder, Psychological Distress, and Heavy Drinking." *Social Science and Medicine* 61(5): 965–75.

Hillman, Nicholas W., and Erica Lee Orians. 2013. "Community Colleges and Labor Market Conditions: How Does Enrollment Demand Change Relative to Local Unemployment Rates?" *Research in Higher Education* 54(7): 765–80. https://eric.ed.gov/?id=EJ1039157.

Hinton, Elizabeth. 2016. *From the War on Poverty to the War on Crime: The Making of Mass Incarceration in America.* Cambridge, Mass.: Harvard University Press.

Hipp, John R., Jesse Jannetta, Rita Shah, and Susan Turner. 2009a. "Parolees' Physical Closeness to Health Service Providers: A Study of California Parolees." *Health and Place* 15(3): 679–88.

———. 2009b. "Parolees' Physical Closeness to Social Services: A Study of California Parolees." *Crime and Delinquency* 57(1): 102–29.

Hipp, John R., Joan Petersilia, and Susan Turner. 2010. "Parolee Recidivism in California: The Effect of Neighborhood Context and Social Service Agency Characteristics." *Criminology* 48(4): 947–79.

Hirsch, Barry T., and David A. Macpherson. 2003. "Union Membership and Coverage Database from the Current Population Survey: Note." *Industrial and Labor Relations Review* 56(2): 349–54. http://www.jstor.org/stable/3590942.

Hirschfield, Alexander F., and Kate Bowers. 1997. "The Development of a Social, Demographic, and Land Use Profiler for Area of High Crime." *British Journal of Criminology* 37(1): 103–20. DOI: 10.1093/oxfordjournals.bjc.a014129.

Hirschfield, Paul. 2009. "Another Way Out: The Impact of Juvenile Arrests on High School Dropout." *Sociology of Education* 82(4): 368–93. DOI: 10.1177/003804070908200404.

Hogan, Dennis P., and Nan Marie Astone. 1986. "The Transition to Adulthood." *Annual Review of Sociology* 12: 109–30.

Holzer, Harry J. 2009. "The Labor Market and Young Black Men: Updating Moynihan's Perspective." *Annals of the American Academy of Political and Social Science* 621(1): 47–69.

———. 2018. "A 'Race to the Top' in Public Higher Education to Improve Education and Employment among the Poor." *RSF: The Russell Sage Foundation Journal of the Social Sciences* 4(3): 84. DOI: 10.7758/rsf.2018.4.3.05.

Holzer, Harry J., and Karin Martinson. 2005. "Can We Improve Job Retention and Advancement among Low-Income Working Parents?" Working Paper 05–10. Ann Arbor: University of Michigan, National Poverty Center (June). http://www.npc.umich.edu/publications/workingpaper05/paper10/HolzerMartinson paper62305.pdf.

Holzer, Harry, Paul Offner, and Elaine Sorensen. 2005. "Declining Employment among Young Black Less-Educated Men: The Role of Incarceration and Child Support." *Journal of Policy Analysis and Management* 24(2): 329–50.

Holzer, Harry J., Steven Raphael, and Michael A. Stoll. 2006. "Perceived Criminality, Criminal Background Checks, and the Racial Hiring Practices of Employers." *Journal of Law and Economics* 49(2): 451–80.

Howell, Benjamin A., Jessica B. Long, E. Jennifer Edelman, Kathleen A. McGinnis, David Rimland, David A. Fiellin, Amy C. Justice, and Emily A. Wang. 2016. "Incarceration History and Uncontrolled Blood Pressure in a Multi-Site Cohort." *Journal of General Internal Medicine* 31(12): 1496–1502. DOI: 10.1007/s11606-016-3857-1.

Hoxby, Caroline, and Christopher Avery. 2013. "Low-Income High-Achieving Students Miss Out on Attending Selective Colleges." In *Brookings Papers on Economic Activity* (April), edited by David H. Romer and Justin Wolfers. Washington, D.C.: Brookings Institution Press.

Hoxby, Caroline, and Sarah Turner. 2013. "Expanding College Opportunities: Intervention Yields Strong Returns for Low-Income High-Achievers." *Education Next* 13(4): 67–73.

Hoynes, Hilary, Douglas L. Miller, and Jessamyn Schaller. 2012. "Who Suffers During Recessions?" *Journal of Economic Perspectives* 26(3): 27–48.

Hunt, Dana, Meg Chapman, Sarah Jalbert, Ryan Kling, Yuli Almozlino, William Rhodes, Christopher Flygare, Kevin Neary, and Caroline Nobo. 2014. "Arrestee Drug Abuse Monitoring Program II: 2013 Annual Report." Washington: Executive Office of the President, Office of National Drug Control Policy (January). https://obamawhitehouse.archives.gov/sites/default/files/ondcp/policy-and-research/adam_ii_2013_annual_report.pdf.

Jackson, Jacob, Kevin Cook, and Hans Johnson. 2019. "Improving College Completion." San Francisco: Public Policy Institute of California, Higher Education Center (October). https://www.ppic.org/wp-content/uploads/higher-education-in-california-improving-college-completion-october-2019.pdf.

Jackson, Kristina M., and Carolyn E. Sartor. 2016. *The Natural Course of Substance Use and Dependence*, vol. 1, *The Oxford Handbook of Substance Use Disorders*, edited by Kenneth J. Sher. Oxford: Oxford University Press. DOI: 10.1093/oxfordhb/9780199381678.013.007.

James, Doris J., and Lauren E. Glaze. 2006. "Mental Health Problems of Prison and Jail Inmates." *Special Report* (September). Washington, D.C.: Bureau of Justice Statistics. https://www.bjs.gov/content/pub/pdf/mhppji.pdf.

Jencks, Christopher, and Susan E. Mayer. 1990. "The Social Consequences of Growing Up in a Poor Neighborhood." In *Inner-City Poverty in the United States*, edited by National Research Council. Washington, D.C.: National Academies Press.

Jennings, Wesley, George Higgins, Richard Tewksbury, Angela R. Gover, and Alex R. Piquero. 2010. "A Longitudinal Assessment of the Victim-Offender Overlap." *Journal of Interpersonal Violence* 25: 2147–74. DOI: 10.1177/0886260509354888.

Jensen, Robert, and Adriana Lleras-Muney. 2012. "Does Staying in School (and Not Working) Prevent Teen Smoking and Drinking?" *Journal of Health Economics* 31(4): 644–57. DOI: 10.1016/j.jhealeco.2012.05.004.

Jepsen, Christopher, Peter Mueser, and Kenneth Troske. 2017. "Second Chance for High School Dropouts? A Regression Discontinuity Analysis of Postsecondary Educational Returns to the GED." *Journal of Labor Economics* 3(S1): S273–304. DOI: 10.1086/691391.

Johnson, Elizabeth Inez, and Jane Waldfogel. 2004. "Children of Incarcerated Parents: Multiple Risks and Children's Living Arrangements." In *Imprisoning America: The Social Effects of Mass Incarceration*, edited by Mary E. Pattillo, Bruce Western, and David Weiman. New York: Russell Sage Foundation.

Kaeble, Danielle, and Mary Cowhig. 2018. "Correctional Populations in the United States, 2016." *Bulletin* (April). Washington, D.C.: Bureau of Justice Statistics. https://www.bjs.gov/content/pub/pdf/cpus16.pdf.

Kalleberg, Arne L. 2013. *Good Jobs, Bad Jobs: The Rise of Polarized and Precarious Employment Systems in the United States 1970s to 2000s.* New York: Russell Sage Foundation.

Kalleberg, Arne L., and Till M. von Wachter. 2017. "The U.S. Labor Market during and after the Great Recession: Continuities and Transformations." *RSF: The Russell Sage Foundation Journal of the Social Sciences* 3(3): 1. DOI: 10.7758/rsf.2017.3.3.01.

Karriker-Jaffe, Katherine J. 2011. "Areas of Disadvantage: A Systematic Review of Effects of Area-Level Socioeconomic Status on Substance Use Outcomes." *Drug and Alcohol Review* 30(1): 84–95. DOI: 10.1111/j.1465-3362.2010.00191.x.

Kelly, M. Patricia Fernández. 1994. "Towanda's Triumph: Social and Cultural Capital in the Transition to Adulthood in the Urban Ghetto." *International Journal of Urban and Regional Research* 18(1): 88–111. DOI: 10.1111/j.1468-2427.1994.tb00252.x.

Kerckhoff, Alan C. 1993. *Diverging Pathways: Social Structure and Career Deflections.* New York: Cambridge University Press.

Kerson, Sarah. 2013. "Michigan Prison Sentences, Longest in U.S., under Review." Michigan Radio Newsroom, NPR, August 13. https://www.michiganradio.org/post/michigan-prison-sentences-longest-us-under-review.

Kirk, David S. 2009. "A Natural Experiment on Residential Change and Recidivism: Lessons from Hurricane Katrina." *American Sociological Review* 74(3): 484–505.

———. 2012. "Residential Change as a Turning Point in the Life Course of Crime: Desistance or Temporary Cessation?" *Criminology* 50(2): 329–58.

———. 2019. "Where the Other 1 Percent Live: An Examination of Changes in the Spatial Concentration of the Formerly Incarcerated." *RSF: The Russell Sage Foundation Journal of the Social Sciences* 5(1): 255. DOI: 10.7758/rsf.2019.5.1.11.

Kirk, David S., and Mauri Matsuda. 2011. "Legal Cynicism, Collective Efficacy, and the Ecology of Arrest." *Criminology* 49(2): 443–72.

Kirk, David S., and Robert J. Sampson. 2013. "Juvenile Arrest and Collateral Educational Damage in the Transition to Adulthood." *Sociology of Education* 86(1): 36–62. DOI: 10.1177/0038040712448862.

Klein, Daniel. 2014. "MIMRGNS: Stata Module to Run Margins after Mi Estimate." *EconPapers* (March 3). http://econpapers.repec.org/software/bocbocode/s457795.htm.

Kling, Jeffrey R. 2006. "Incarceration Length, Employment, and Earnings." *American Economic Review* 96(3): 863–76. DOI: 10.1257/aer.96.3.863.

Kohler-Hausmann, Issa. 2018. *Misdemeanorland: Criminal Courts and Social Control in an Age of Broken Windows Policing.* Princeton, N.J.: Princeton University Press.

Kornfeld, Robert, and Howard S. Bloom. 1999. "Measuring Program Impacts on Earnings and Employment: Do Unemployment Insurance Wage Reports from

Employers Agree with Surveys of Individuals?" *Journal of Labor Economics* 17(1): 168–97. https://www.journals.uchicago.edu/doi/pdfplus/10.1086/209917.

Krivo, Lauren J., and Robert L. Kaufman. 2004. "Housing and Wealth Inequality: Racial-Ethnic Differences in Home Equity in the United States." *Demography* 41(3): 585–605. DOI: 10.1353/dem.2004.0023.

Krivo, Lauren J., María B. Vélez, Christopher J. Lyons, Jason B. Phillips, and Elizabeth Sabbath. 2018. "Race, Crime, and the Changing Fortunes of Urban Neighborhoods, 1999–2013." *Du Bois Review* 15(1): 47–68. DOI: 10.1017/S1742058X18000103.

Kubrin, Charis E., and Gregory D. Squires. 2004. "The Impact of Capital on Crime: Does Access to Home Mortgage Money Reduce Crime Rates?" Unpublished manuscript. Washington, D.C.: George Washington University.

Kubrin, Charis E., and Eric A. Stewart. 2006. "Predicting Who Reoffends: The Neglected Role of Neighborhood Context in Recidivism Studies." *Criminology* 44(1): 165–97.

LaBriola, Joe. 2020. "Post-prison Employment Quality and Future Criminal Justice Contact." *RSF: The Russell Sage Foundation Journal of the Social Sciences* 6(1): 154–72. DOI: 10.7758/rsf.2020.6.1.07.

Lageson, Sarah E. 2017. "Crime Data, the Internet, and Free Speech: An Evolving Legal Consciousness." *Law and Social Inquiry* 51(1): 8–41.

———. 2020. *Digital Punishment.* Oxford: Oxford University Press.

Langhan, Patrick A., and David J. Levin. 2002. "Recidivism of Prisoners Released in 1994." *Special Report* (June). Washington, D.C.: Bureau of Justice Statistics. https://www.bjs.gov/content/pub/pdf/rpr94.pdf.

Lareau, Annette. 2000. *Home Advantage: Social Class and Parental Intervention in Elementary Education.* Oxford: Rowman & Littlefield.

———. 2011. *Unequal Childhoods: Class, Race, and Family Life,* 2nd ed. Berkeley: University of California Press.

Lareau, Annette, and Amanda Cox. 2011. "Social Class and the Transition to Adulthood Differences in Parents' Interactions with Institutions." In *Social Class and Changing Families in an Unequal America,* edited by Marcy Carlson and Paula England. Stanford, Calif.: Stanford University Press.

Larsen, Svein. 1994. "Alcohol Use in the Service Industry." *Addiction* 89(6): 733–41. DOI: 10.1111/j.1360-0443.1994.tb00959.x.

Lattimore, Pamela K., Richard L. Linster, and John M. MacDonald. 1997. "Risk of Death among Serious Young Offenders." *Journal of Research in Crime and Delinquency* 34(2): 187–209. DOI: 10.1177/0022427897034002002.

Lattimore, Pamela K., and Christy A. Visher. 2009. *The Multi-Site Evaluation of SVORI: Summary and Synthesis.* Washington, D.C.: Multi-Site Evaluation of the Serious and Violent Offender Reentry Initiative (April). https://www.ncjrs.gov/pdffiles1/nij/grants/230421.pdf.

Laub, John, Daniel Nagin, and Robert J. Sampson. 1998. "Trajectories of Change in Criminal Offending: Good Marriages and the Desistance Process." *American Sociological Review* 63(2): 225–38.

Laub, John H., and Robert J. Sampson. 2001. "Understanding Desistance from Crime." *Crime and Justice* 28(1): 1–69.

———. 2003. *Shared Beginnings, Divergent Lives: Delinquent Boys to Age 70*. Cambridge, Mass.: Harvard University Press.

Lauritsen, Janet L., Karen Heimer, and Joseph B. Lang. 2018. "The Enduring Significance of Racial and Ethnic Disparities in Male Violent Victimization, 1973–2010." *Du Bois Review* 15(1): 69–87. DOI: 10.1017/S1742058X18000097.

Lauritsen, Janet L., Robert J. Sampson, and John H. Laub. 1991. "The Link between Offending and Victimization among Adolescents." *Criminology* 29(2): 265–92. DOI: 10.1111/j.1745-9125.1991.tb01067.x.

La Vigne, Nancy, and Barbara Parthasarathy. 2005. "Prisoner Reentry and Residential Mobility." Washington, D.C.: Urban Institute, Justice Policy Center.

Leasure, Peter, and Tara Martin. 2017. "Criminal Records and Housing: An Experimental Study." *Journal of Experimental Criminology* 13(4): 527–35. DOI: 10.1007/s11292-017-9289-z.

LeBel, Thomas P. 2012. "'If One Doesn't Get You Another One Will': Formerly Incarcerated Persons' Perceptions of Discrimination." *Prison Journal* 92(1): 63–87. DOI: 10.1177/0032885511429243.

Lee, Hedwig, Christopher Wildeman, Emily Wang, Niki Matusko, and James S. Jackson. 2014. "A Heavy Burden? The Health Consequences of Having a Family Member Incarcerated." *American Journal of Public Health* 104(3): 421–27.

Lee, Jennifer C., and Jeremy Staff. 2007. "When Work Matters: The Varying Impact of Work Intensity on High School Dropout." *Sociology of Education* 80(April): 158–78. DOI: 10.1177/003804070708000204.

Lee, JoAnn S. 2014. "An Institutional Framework for the Study of the Transition to Adulthood." *Youth and Society* 46(5): 706–30. DOI: 10.1177/0044118X12450643.

Lee, Keun Bok, David J. Harding, and Jeffrey D. Morenoff. 2017. "Neighborhood Attainment after Prison." *Social Science Research* 66: 211–33.

Lee, Rosalyn D., Xiangming Fang, and Feijun Luo. 2013. "The Impact of Parental Incarceration on the Physical and Mental Health of Young Adults." *Pediatrics* 131(4): e1188–95. DOI: 10.1542/peds.2012-0627.

Lei, Lei, and Scott South. 2016. "Racial and Ethnic Differences in Leaving and Returning to the Parental Home: The Role of Life Course Transitions, Socioeconomic Resources, and Family Connectivity." *Demographic Research* 34(4): 109–42. https://www.demographic-research.org/volumes/vol34/4/.

Leigh, Duane E., and Andrew M. Gill. 1997. "Labor Market Returns to Community Colleges: Evidence for Returning Adults." *Journal of Human Resources* 32(2): 334–53. DOI: 10.2307/146218.

Lerman, Amy E., and Velsa M. Weaver. 2014a. *Arresting Citizenship: The Democratic Consequences of American Crime Control*. Chicago: University of Chicago Press.

———. 2014b. "Staying Out of Sight? Concentrated Policing and Local Political Action." *Annals of the American Academy of Political and Social Science* 651(1): 202–19.

Leverentz, Andrea. 2014. *The Ex-Prisoner's Dilemma: How Women Negotiate Competing Narratives of Reentry and Desistance*. New Brunswick, N.J.: Rutgers University Press.

Lewis, Susan K., Catherine E. Ross, and John Mirowsky. 1999. "Establishing a Sense of Personal Control in the Transition to Adulthood." *Social Forces* 77(4): 1573–99. DOI: 10.1093/sf/77.4.1573.

Lindquist, Christine, Pamela Lattimore, Janeen Buck Willison, Danielle Steffey, Mindy Herman Stahl, Sam Scaggs, Jeremy Welsh-Loveman, Joshua Eisenstat. 2018. "Cross-Site Evaluation of the Bureau of Justice Assistance FY 2011 Second Chance Act Adult Offender Reentry Demonstration Projects: Final Report." Washington: National Institute of Justice, Office of Justice Programs, U.S. Department of Justice. https://www.ncjrs.gov/pdffiles1/nij/grants/251703.pdf.

Link, Bruce G., Francis T. Cullen, Elmer Struening, Patrick E. Shrout, and Bruce P. Dohrenwend. 1989. "A Modified Labeling Theory Approach to Mental Disorders: An Empirical Assessment." *American Sociological Review* 54(3): 400–423. DOI: 10.2307/2095613.

Link, Bruce G., and Jo Phelan. 1995. "Social Conditions as Fundamental Causes of Disease." *Journal of Health and Social Behavior* (extra issue): 80–94.

———. 2001. "Conceptualizing Stigma." *Annual Review of Sociology* 27(1): 363–85. DOI: 10.1146/annurev.soc.27.1.363.

Lipsey, Mark W., Nana A. Landenberger, and Sandra J. Wilson. 2007. "Effects of Cognitive-Behavioral Programs for Criminal Offenders." *Campbell Systematic Reviews* 3(1): 1–27.

Lofstrom, Magnus, and Steven Raphael. 2016. "Incarceration and Crime: Evidence from California's Public Safety Realignment Reform." *Annals of the American Academy of Political and Social Science* 664(1): 196–220. DOI: 10.1177/0002716215599732.

Loughran, Thomas A., Daniel S. Nagin, and Holly Nguyen. 2017. "Crime and Legal Work: A Markovian Model of the Desistance Process." *Social Problems* 64(1): 30–52. DOI: 10.1093/socpro/spw027.

Lundquist, Jennifer Hickes, Devah Pager, and Eiko Strader. 2018. "Does a Criminal Past Predict Worker Performance? Evidence from One of America's Largest Employers." *Social Forces* 96(3): 1039–68. DOI: 10.1093/sf/sox092.

Lutze, Faith E., Jeffrey W. Rosky, and Zachary K. Hamilton. 2013. "Homelessness and Reentry: A Multisite Outcome Evaluation of Washington State's Reentry Housing Program for High Risk Offenders." *Criminal Justice and Behavior* 41(4, December 19): 471–91.

Lynch, James P., and William J. Sabol. 2001. "Prisoner Reentry in Perspective." *Crime Policy Report* 3(September). Washington, D.C.: Urban Institute. https://www.urban.org/research/publication/prisoner-reentry-perspective/view/full_report.

———. 2004. "Assessing the Effects of Mass Incarceration on Informal Social Control in Communities." *Criminology and Public Policy* 3(2): 267–94.

Lynch, Mona. 2000. "Rehabilitation as Rhetoric." *Punishment and Society* 2(1): 40–65.

MacCoun, Robert, Beau Kilmer, and Peter Reuter. 2003. "Research on Drugs-Crime Linkages: The Next Generation." In *Toward a Drugs and Crime Research Agenda for the 21st Century*. Washington, D.C.: National Institute of Justice. https://law.stanford.edu/publications/research-on-drugs-crime-linkages-the-next-generation/.

MaCurdy, Thomas, Bryan Keating, Sriniketh Nagavarapu, and David Glick. 2014. "Profiling the Plight of Disconnected Youth in America." https://www.brown.edu/academics/economics/candidates/sites/brown.edu.academics.economics.candidates/files/Disconnected_Youth_9_2014_0.pdf.

Manza, Jeff, and Christopher Uggen. 2006. *Locked Out: Felon Disenfranchisement and American Democracy*. New York: Oxford University Press.

Maralani, Vida. 2011. "From GED to College: Age Trajectories of Nontraditional Educational Paths." *American Educational Research Journal* 48(5): 1058–90. DOI: 10.3102/0002831211405836.

Marcotte, Dave E., Thomas Bailey, Carey Borkoski, and Greg S. Kienzl. 2005. "The Returns of a Community College Education: Evidence from the National Education Longitudinal Survey." *Educational Evaluation and Policy Analysis* 27(2): 157–75. DOI: 10.3102/01623737027002157.

Maruna, Shadd. 2001a. *Making Good: How Ex-Convicts Reform and Rebuild Their Lives*. Washington, D.C.: American Psychological Association.

———. 2001b. *Making Good: How Ex-Offenders Reform and Reclaim Their Lives*. Washington, D.C.: American Psychological Association.

Maruschak, Laura M., Marcus Berzofsky, and Jennifer Unangst. 2015. "Medical Problems of State and Federal Prisoners and Jail Inmates, 2011–12." *Special Report* (February). Washington, D.C.: Bureau of Justice Statistics. https://www.bjs.gov/content/pub/pdf/mpsfpji1112.pdf.

Massey, Douglas S., and Stefanie Brodmann. 2014. *Spheres of Influence: The Social Ecology of Racial and Class Inequality*. Russell Sage Foundation.

Massey, Douglas S., and Nancy A. Denton. 1993. *American Apartheid: Segregation and the Making of the Underclass*. Cambridge, Mass.: Harvard University Press.

Massoglia, Michael. 2006. "Desistance or Displacement? The Changing Patterns of Offending from Adolescence to Young Adulthood." *Journal of Quantitative Criminology* 22(3): 215–39.

———. 2008a. "Incarceration, Health, and Racial Disparities in Health." *Law and Society Review* 42(2): 275–306.

———. 2008b. "Incarceration as Exposure: The Prison, Infectious Disease, and Other Stress-Related Illnesses." *Journal of Health and Social Behavior* 49(March): 56–71.

Massoglia, Michael, Glenn Firebaugh, and Cody Warner. 2013. "Racial Variation in the Effect of Incarceration on Neighborhood Attainment." *American Sociological Review* 78(1): 142–65.

Massoglia, Michael, and William Alex Pridemore. 2015. "Incarceration and Health." *Annual Review of Sociology* 41(1): 291–310. DOI: 10.1146/annurev-soc-073014-112326.

Massoglia, Michael, and Christopher Uggen. 2010. "Settling Down and Aging Out." *American Journal of Sociology* 116(2): 543–82.

McCarthy, Bill, and Teresa Casey. 2008. "Love, Sex, and Crime: Adolescent Romantic Relationships and Offending." *American Sociological Review* 73: 944–69.

McDowell, Linda. 2002. "Transitions to Work: Masculine Identities, Youth Inequality, and Labour Market Change." *Gender, Place, and Culture* 9(1): 39–59. DOI: 10.1080/09663690120115038.

Mclanahan, Sara. 2004. "Diverging Destinies: How Children Are Faring under the Second Demographic Transition." *Demography* 41(4): 607–27. DOI: 10.1353/dem.2004.0033.

Mears, Daniel P., Eric A. Stewart, Sonja E. Siennick, and Ronald L. Simons. 2013. "The Code of the Street and Inmate Violence: Investigating the Salience of Imported Belief Systems." *Criminology* 51(3): 695–728. DOI: 10.1111/1745-9125.12017.

Mears, Daniel P., Xia Wang, Carter Hay, and William D. Bales. 2008. "Social Ecology and Recidivism: Implications for Prisoner Reentry." *Criminology* 46(2): 301–40.

Melzer, Scott A. 2002. "Gender, Work, and Intimate Violence: Men's Occupational Violence Spillover and Compensatory Violence." *Journal of Marriage and Family* 64(4): 820–32. DOI: 10.1111/j.1741-3737.2002.00820.x.

Merton, Robert K. 1938. "Social Structure and Anomie." *American Sociological Review* 3(5): 672–82. DOI: 10.2307/2084686.

Metcalfe, Christi, Thomas Baker, and Caitlin M. Brady. 2019. "Exploring the Relationship between Lasting, Quality Social Bonds and Intermittency in Offending." *American Journal of Criminal Justice* 44: 892–912. DOI: 10.1007/s12103-019-09486-4.

Metraux, Stephen, and Dennis P. Culhane. 2004. "Homeless Shelter Use and Reincarceration Following Prison Release." *Criminology and Public Policy* 3(2): 139–60.

Mincy, Ronald B. 2006. *Black Males Left Behind*. Washington, D.C.: Urban Institute Press.

Mitchell, Meghan M., Kallee Spooner, Di Jia, and Yan Zhang. 2016. "The Effect of Prison Visitation on Reentry Success: A Meta-Analysis." *Journal of Criminal Justice* 46: 74–83.

Monnat, Shannon M., David J. Peters, Mark T. Berg, and Andrew Hochstetler. 2019. "Using Census Data to Understand County-Level Differences in Overall Drug

Mortality and Opioid-Related Mortality by Opioid Type." *American Journal of Public Health* 109(8): 1084–91. DOI: 10.2105/AJPH.2019.305136.

Mood, Carina. 2010. "Logistic Regression: Why We Cannot Do What We Think We Can Do, and What We Can Do about It." *European Sociological Review* 26(1): 67–82. DOI: 10.1093/esr/jcp006.

Mooney, Emily, Jesse Kelley, and Nila Bala. 2016. "Postsecondary Education in Michigan Prisons." R Street Shorts 65. Washington, D.C.: R Street Institute (January). https://www.rstreet.org/wp-content/uploads/2019/01/Final-Short-No.-65.pdf.

Moore, Kelly E., Walter Roberts, Holly H. Reid, Kathryn M. Z. Smith, Lindsay M. S. Oberleitner, and Sherry A. McKee. 2019. "Effectiveness of Medication Assisted Treatment for Opioid Use in Prison and Jail Settings: A Meta-Analysis and Systematic Review." *Journal of Substance Abuse Treatment* 99: 32–43. DOI: 10.1016/j.jsat.2018.12.003.

Moore, Roland S., Carol B. Cunradi, Michael R. Duke, and Genevieve M. Ames. 2009. "Dimensions of Problem Drinking among Young Adult Restaurant Workers." *American Journal of Drug and Alcohol Abuse* 35(5): 329–33. DOI: 10.1080/00952990903075042.

Morenoff, Jeffrey D., and David J. Harding. 2011. "Final Technical Report: Neighborhoods, Recidivism, and Employment among Returning Prisoners." Report submitted to the National Institute of Justice, grant award 2008-IJ-CX-0018.

———. 2014. "Incarceration, Prisoner Reentry, and Communities." *Annual Review of Sociology* 40: 411–29.

Morenoff, Jeffrey D., Robert J. Sampson, and Stephen W. Raudenbush. 2001a. "Neighborhood Inequality, Collective Efficacy, and the Spatial Dynamics of Urban Violence." *Criminology* 3(3): 517–59.

———. 2001b. "Neighborhood Inequality, Collective Efficacy, and the Spatial Dynamics of Urban Violence." *Criminology* 39(3): 517–59.

Morgan, Rachel E., and Barbara A. Oudekerk. 2019. "Criminal Victimization, 2018." *Bulletin* (September). Washington, D.C.: Bureau of Justice Statistics. https://www.bjs.gov/content/pub/pdf/cv18.pdf.

Morgan, Stephen L., and Sol Bee Jung. 2016. "Still No Effect of Resources, Even in the New Gilded Age?" *RSF: The Russell Sage Foundation Journal of the Social Sciences* 2(5): 83–116. DOI: 10.7758/rsf.2016.2.5.05.

Mossakowski, Krysia N. 2011. "Unfulfilled Expectations and Symptoms of Depression among Young Adults." *Social Science and Medicine* 73(5): 729–36. DOI: 10.1016/j.socscimed.2011.06.021.

Mouw, Ted. 2000. "Job Relocation and the Racial Gap in Unemployment in Detroit and Chicago, 1980 to 1990." *American Sociological Review* 65(5): 730–53.

Mowen, Thomas J., and John H. Boman. 2019. "Do We Have It All Wrong? The Protective Roles of Peers and Criminogenic Risks from Family during Prison Reentry." *Crime and Delinquency* 65(5): 681–704. DOI: 10.1177/0011128718800286.

Mowen, Thomas J., and Benjamin W. Fisher. 2019. "Youth Reentry from Prison and Family Violence Perpetration: The Salience of Family Dynamics." *Journal of Family Violence* (September 12). DOI: 10.1007/s10896-019-00098-4.

Mowen, Thomas J., Richard Stansfield, and John H. Boman. 2019. "Family Matters: Moving beyond 'If' Family Support Matters to 'Why' Family Support Matters during Reentry from Prison." *Journal of Research in Crime and Delinquency* 56(4): 483–523. DOI: 10.1177/0022427818820902.

Mowen, Thomas J., and Christy A. Visher. 2015. "Drug Use and Crime after Incarceration: The Role of Family Support and Family Conflict." *Justice Quarterly* 32(2): 337–59. DOI: 10.1080/07418825.2013.771207.

Mueller-Smith, Michael, and Kevin T. Schnepel. 2019. "Diversion in the Criminal Justice System." January 17. https://sites.lsa.umich.edu/mgms/wp-content/uploads/sites/283/2019/01/Diversion.pdf.

Mumola, Christopher. 1999. "Substance Abuse and Treatment State and Federal Prisoners, 1997." *Special Report* (January). Washington, D.C.: Bureau of Justice Statistics. https://www.bjs.gov/content/pub/pdf/satsfp97.pdf.

———. 2000. "Incarcerated Parents and Their Children." *Special Report* (August). Washington D.C.: Bureau of Justice Statistics. https://www.bjs.gov/content/pub/pdf/iptc.pdf.

Nagin, Daniel S. 2005. *Group-Based Modeling of Development.* Cambridge, Mass.: Harvard University Press.

Nagin, Daniel S., Bobby L. Jones, and Valeria Lima Passos. 2016. "Group-Based Multi-Trajectory Modeling." *Statistical Methods in Medical Research* 27(7): 2015–23.

Nagin, Daniel S., and Kenneth C. Land. 1993. "Age, Criminal Careers, and Population Heterogeneity: Specification and Estimation of a Nonparametric, Mixed Poisson Model." *Criminology* 31(3): 327–62.

National Association of Manufacturers. 2019. "Manufacturing Employment by State" (Bureau of Economic Analysis). https://www.nam.org/wp-content/uploads/2019/05/MFG_Employment_2018103.pdf.

National Center for Education Statistics. 2012. "Table 219.40: Public High School Graduates and Averaged Freshman Graduation Rate, by Race/Ethnicity and State or Jurisdiction: 2009–2010." *Digest of Education Statistics.* Washington: U.S. Department of Education, National Center for Education Statistics. https://nces.ed.gov/programs/digest/d13/tables/dt13_219.40.asp.

———. 2014. "Table 302.60: Percentage of 18- to 24-Year-Olds Enrolled in Degree-Granting Institutions, by Level of Institution and Sex and Race/Ethnicity of Student: 1967 through 2013." *Digest of Education Statistics.* Washington: U.S. Department of Education, National Center for Education Statistics. https://nces.ed.gov/programs/digest/d14/tables/dt14_302.60.asp.

———. 2017a. "Table 104.20: Percentage of Persons 15 to 29 Years Old with Selected Levels of Educational Attainment, by Race/Ethnicity and Sex: Selected Years,

1920 through 2017." *Digest of Education Statistics*. Washington: U.S. Department of Education, National Center for Education Statistics. https://nces.ed.gov/programs/digest/d17/tables/dt17_104.20.asp.

———. 2017b. "Table 302.30: Percentage of Recent High School Completers Enrolled in College, by Income Level: 1975 through 2016." *Digest of Education Statistics*. Washington: U.S. Department of Education, National Center for Education Statistics. https://nces.ed.gov/programs/digest/d17/tables/dt17_302.30.asp.

———. 2019. *The Condition of Education 2019*. Washington: U.S. Department of Education (May). https://nces.ed.gov/pubs2019/2019144.pdf.

National Commission on Correctional Health Care. 2002. *The Health Status of Soon-to-Be-Released Inmates: A Report to Congress*, vol. 1. Washington, D.C.: National Commission on Correctional Health Care (March). https://www.ncchc.org/filebin/Health_Status_vol_1.pdf.

National Research Council. 2007. *Parole, Desistance from Crime, and Community Integration*. Washington, D.C.: National Academies Press.

———. 2014. *The Growth of Incarceration in the United States: Exploring Causes and Consequences*. Washington, D.C.: National Academies Press.

Neal, Derek, and Armin Rick. 2014. "The Prison Boom and the Lack of Black Progress after Smith and Welch." Working Paper 20283. Cambridge, Mass.: National Bureau of Economic Research. DOI: 10.3386/w20283.

Nelson, Marta, Perry Deess, and Charlotte Allen. 1999. "The First Month Out: Post-Incarceration Experiences in New York City." New York: Vera Institute of Justice.

———. 2011. "The First Month Out: Post-Incarceration Experiences in New York City." *Federal Sentencing Reporter* 24(1): 72–75. DOI: 10.1525/fsr.2011.24.1.72.

Newman, Katherine S., and Sofia Aptekar. 2007. "Sticking Around: Delayed Departure from the Parental Nest in Western Europe." In *The Price of Independence*, edited by Sheldon Danziger and Elena Rouse. New York: Russell Sage Foundation.

Nightingale, Demetra Smith, and Stephen A. Wandner. 2011. "Informal and Non-standard Employment in the United States: Implications for Low-Income Working Families." Brief 20. Washington, D.C.: Urban Institute (August). https://www.urban.org/sites/default/files/publication/32791/412372-informal-and-nonstandard-employment-in-the-united-states.pdf.

Nowotny, Kathryn M., Ryan K. Masters, and Jason D. Boardman. 2016. "The Relationship between Education and Health among Incarcerated Men and Women in the United States." *BMC Public Health* 16(1): 916. DOI: 10.1186/s12889-016-3555-2.

Oliver, Melvin L., and Thomas M. Shapiro. 2001. "Wealth and Racial Stratification." In *America Becoming: Racial Trends and Their Consequences*, vol. 2, edited by Neil Smelser, William Julius Wilson, and Faith Mitchell. Washington, D.C.: National Academies Press.

Osborn, Steven G. 1980. "Moving Home, Leaving London, and Delinquent Trends." *British Journal of Criminology* 20(1): 54–61. DOI: 10.1093/oxfordjournals.bjc. a047132.

Osgood, D. Wayne, E. Michael Foster, Constance Flanigan, and Gretchen R. Ruth, eds. 2006. *On Your Own without a Net: The Transition to Adulthood for Vulnerable Populations.* Chicago: University of Chicago Press.

Ouellet, Frédéric. 2019. "Stop and Go: Explaining the Timing of Intermittency in Criminal Careers." *Crime and Delinquency* 65(5): 630–56. DOI: 10.1177/0011128717753114.

Owens, Ann. 2010. "Neighborhoods and Schools as Competing and Reinforcing Contexts for Educational Attainment." *Sociology of Education* 83(4): 287–311. DOI: 10.1177/0038040710383519.

Page, Joshua, Victoria Piehowski, and Joe Soss. 2019. "A Debt of Care: Commercial Bail and the Gendered Logic of Criminal Justice Predation." *RSF: The Russell Sage Foundation Journal of the Social Sciences* 5(1): 150. DOI: 10.7758/rsf.2019.5.1.07.

Page, Marianne. 1995. "Racial and Ethnic Discrimination in Urban Housing Markets: Evidence from a Recent Audit Study." *Journal of Urban Economics* 38(2): 183–206.

Pager, Devah. 2003. "The Mark of a Criminal Record." *American Journal of Sociology* 108(5): 937–75.

———. 2007. *Marked: Race, Crime, and Finding Work in an Era of Mass Incarceration.* Chicago: University of Chicago Press.

Pager, Devah, and Hana Shepherd. 2008. "The Sociology of Discrimination: Racial Discrimination in Employment, Housing, Credit, and Consumer Markets." *Annual Review of Sociology* 34: 181–209.

Pager, Devah, Bruce Western, and Bart Bonikowski. 2009. "Discrimination in a Low-Wage Labor Market: A Field Experiment." *American Sociological Review* 74(5): 777–99.

Pascoe, Elizabeth A., and Laura Smart Richman. 2009. "Perceived Discrimination and Health: A Meta-Analytic Review." *Psychological Bulletin* 135(4): 531–54. DOI: 10.1037/a0016059.

Paternoster, Ray, and Shawn Bushway. 2009. "Desistance and the 'Feared Self': Toward an Identity Theory of Criminal Desistance." *Journal of Criminal Law and Criminology* 99(4): 1103–56.

Patterson, Evelyn J. 2010. "Incarcerating Death: Mortality in U.S. State Correctional Facilities." *Demography* 47(3): 587–607.

———. 2013. "The Dose-Response of Time Served in Prison on Mortality: New York State, 1989–2003." *American Journal of Public Health* 103: 523–28.

Pearlin, Leonard I., Scott Schieman, Elena M. Fazio, and Stephen C. Meersman. 2005. "Stress, Health, and the Life Course: Some Conceptual Perspectives." *Journal of Health and Social Behavior* 46(2): 205–19.

Perkins, Kristin L., and Robert J. Sampson. 2017. "Compounded Deprivation in the Transition to Adulthood: The Intersection of Racial and Economic Inequality among Chicagoans, 1995–2013." *RSF: The Russell Sage Foundation Journal of the Social Sciences* 1(1): 35. DOI: 10.7758/rsf.2015.1.1.03.

Petersilia, Joan. 2003. *When Prisoners Come Home: Parole and Prisoner Reentry.* Oxford: Oxford University Press.

———. 2009. *When Prisoners Come Home: Parole and Prisoner Reentry,* with a new afterword. Oxford: Oxford University Press.

Petersilia, Joan, and Susan Turner. 1993. "Intensive Probation and Parole." *Crime and Justice* 17(1993): 281–335. DOI: 10.1086/449215.

Peterson, Ruth D., and Lauren J. Krivo. 2010. *Divergent Social Worlds: Neighborhood Crime and the Racial-Spatial Divide.* New York: Russell Sage Foundation.

Pettit, Becky. 2012. *Invisible Men: Mass Incarceration and the Myth of Black Progress.* New York: Russell Sage Foundation.

Pettit, Becky, and Christopher J. Lyons. 2007. "Status and Stigma of Incarceration: The Labor-Market Effects of Incarceration, by Race, Class, and Criminal Involvement." In *Barriers to Reentry? The Labor Market for Released Prisoners in Post-Industrial America,* edited by Shawn Bushway, Michael A. Stoll, and David F. Weiman. New York: Russell Sage Foundation.

Pettit, Becky, and Bruce Western. 2004. "Mass Imprisonment and the Life Course: Race and Class Inequality in U.S. Incarceration." *American Sociological Review* 69(2): 151–69.

Pew Center on the States. 2009. "One in 31: The Long Reach of American Corrections." Washington, D.C.: Pew Charitable Trusts (March 2).

———. 2012. "Time Served: The High Cost, Low Return of Longer Prison Terms." Washington, D.C.: Pew Charitable Trusts (June).https://www.pewtrusts.org/-/media/assets/2012/06/06/time_served_report.pdf.

Pew Charitable Trusts. 2014. "Max Out: The Rise in Prison Inmates Released without Supervision." Washington, D.C.: Pew Charitable Trusts (June).

Pfaff, John. 2017. *Locked In: The True Causes of Mass Incarceration—and How to Achieve Real Reform.* New York: Basic Books.

Phelps, Michelle S. 2016. "Mass Probation: Toward a More Robust Theory of State Variation in Punishment." *Punishment and Society* 19(1): 53–73. DOI: 10.1177/1462474516649174.

Phillips, Meredith, and Tiffani Chin. 2004. "School Inequality: What Do We Know?" In *Social Inequality,* edited by Kathryn M. Neckerman. New York: Russell Sage Foundation.

Piquero, Alex R. 2004. "Somewhere between Persistence and Desistance: The Intermittency of Criminal Careers." In *After Crime and Punishment: Pathways to Offender Reintegration,* edited by Shadd Maruna and Russ Immarigeon. Portland, OR: Willan Publishing.

Piquero, Alex R., Robert Brame, Paul Mazerolle, and Rudy Haapanen. 2002. "Crime in Emerging Adulthood." *Criminology* 40(1): 137–70. DOI: 10.1111/j.1745-9125.2002.tb00952.x.

Pollack, Harold A. 2017. "Dealing More Effectively with Problematic Substance Use and Crime." *Crime and Justice* 46(1): 159–200. DOI: 10.1086/688459.

Popovici, Ioana, Johanna Catherine Maclean, Michael T. French, Colleen Barry, Susan Busch, Gulcin Gumus, Rosalie Pacula, and Jonathan Woodruff. 2017. "Health Insurance and Traffic Fatalities: The Effects of Substance Use Disorder Parity Laws." Working Paper 23388. Cambridge, Mass.: National Bureau of Economic Research (May). http://www.nber.org/papers/w23388.

Prescott, J. J., and Sonja B. Starr. 2019. "Expungement of Criminal Convictions: An Empirical Study." Law and Economics Research Paper Series. Ann Arbor: University of Michigan Law School.

Priest, Naomi, and David R. Williams. 2017. "Racial Discrimination and Racial Disparities in Health." In *The Oxford Handbook of Stigma, Discrimination, and Health,* edited by Brenda Major, John F. Dovidio, and Bruce G. Link. Oxford: Oxford University Press. DOI: 10.1093/oxfordhb/9780190243470.001.0001.

Quinn, David M. 2015. "Kindergarten Black-White Test Score Gaps: Re-examining the Roles of Socioeconomic Status and School Quality with New Data." *Sociology of Education* 88(2): 120–39. DOI: 10.1177/0038040715573027.

Ramchand, Rajeev, Andrew R. Morral, and Kirsten Becker. 2009. "Seven-Year Life Outcomes of Adolescent Offenders in Los Angeles." *American Journal of Public Health* 99(5): 863–70. DOI: 10.2105/AJPH.2008.142281.

Rampey, Bobby D., Shelley Keiper, Leyla Mohadjer, Tom Krenzke, Jianzhu Li, Nina Thornton, Jacquie Hogan, Holly Xie, and Stephen Provasnik. 2016. "Highlights from the U.S. PIAAC Survey of Incarcerated Adults: Their Skills, Work Experience, Education, and Training: Program for the International Assessment of Adult Competencies: 2014." NCES 2016-040. Washington: U.S. Department of Education, National Center for Education Statistics (November). https://nces.ed.gov/pubs2016/2016040.pdf.

Raphael, Steven. 2007. "Early Incarceration Spells and the Transition to Adulthood." In *The Price of Independence: The Economics of Early Adulthood,* edited by Sheldon Danziger and Cecilia Rouse. New York: Russell Sage Foundation.

Raphael, Stephen, and Michael A. Stoll. 2013. *Why Are So Many Americans in Prison?* New York: Russell Sage Foundation.

Raphael, Steven, and David F. Weiman. 2007. "The Impact of Local Labor-Market Conditions on the Likelihood That Parolees Are Returned to Custody." In *Barriers to Reentry? The Labor Market for Released Prisoners in Post-Industrial America,* edited by Shawn Bushway, Michael A. Stoll, and David F. Weiman. New York: Russell Sage Foundation

Reardon, Sean F. 2016. "School Segregation and Racial Academic Achievement Gaps." *RSF: The Russell Sage Foundation Journal of the Social Sciences* 2(5): 34–57.

Redcross, Cindy, Megan Millenky, Timothy Rudd, and Valerie Levshin. 2012. "More than a Job: Final Results from the Evaluation of the Center for Employment Opportunities (CEO) Transitional Jobs Program." OPRE Report 2011-18. Washington: U.S. Department of Health and Human Services, Office of Planning, Research, and Evaluation. DOI: 10.2139/ssrn.2010208.

Rios, Victor M. 2011. *Punished: Policing the Lives of Black and Latino Boys.* New York: New York University Press.

———. 2017. *Human Targets: Schools, Police, and the Criminalization of Latino Youth.* Chicago: University of Chicago Press.

Rocheleau, Ann Marie. 2013. "An Empirical Exploration of the 'Pains of Imprisonment' and the Level of Prison Misconduct and Violence." *Criminal Justice Review* 38(3): 354–74. DOI: 10.1177/0734016813494764.

Rodriguez, Olga, Marison Cuellar Mejia, and Hans Johnson. 2018. "Remedial Education Reforms at California's Community Colleges: Early Evidence on Placement and Curricular Reforms." San Francisco: Public Policy Institute of California (August).

Roksa, Josipa, and Melissa Velez. 2012. "A Late Start: Delayed Entry, Life Course Transitions and Bachelor's Degree Completion." *Social Forces* 90(3): 769–94. DOI: 10.1093/sf/sor018.

Roman, Caterina Gouvis, and Jeremy Travis. 2006. "Where Will I Sleep Tomorrow? Housing, Homelessness, and the Returning Prisoner." *Housing Policy Debate* 17(2): 389–418. http://dx.doi.org/10.1080/10511482.2006.9521574.

Roscigno, Vincent J. 1998. "Race and the Reproduction of Educational Disadvantage." *Social Forces* 76(3): 1033–61.

Rose, Dina R., and Todd R. Clear. 1998. "Incarceration, Social Capital, and Crime: Implications for Social Disorganization Theory." *Criminology* 36(3): 441–80.

Rose, Jennifer S., Laurie Chassin, Clark C. Presson, and Steven J. Sherman. 1999. "Peer Influences on Adolescent Cigarette Smoking: A Prospective Sibling Analysis." *Merrill-Palmer Quarterly* 45(1): 62–84.

Rothstein, Richard. 2015. "The Racial Achievement Gap, Segregated Schools, and Segregated Neighborhoods: A Constitutional Insult." *Race and Social Problems* 7(1): 21–30. DOI: 10.1007/s12552-014-9134-1.

———. 2017. *The Color of Law: A Forgotten History of How Our Government Segregated America.* New York: Liveright.

Royster, Deidre. 2003. *Race and the Invisible Hand: How White Networks Exclude Black Men from Blue-Collar Jobs.* Berkeley: University of California Press.

Rubin, Donald B. 1987. *Multiple Imputation for Non-Response in Surveys.* New York: John Wiley & Sons.

Rucks-Ahidiana, Zawadi, David J. Harding, and Heather M. Harris. Forthcoming. "Race and the Geography of Opportunity in the Post-Prison Labor Market." *Social Problems.*

Ruhm, Christopher J. 2018. "Drivers of the Fatal Drug Epidemic." Seminar at Columbia Population Research Center, Columbia School of Social Work, New York (October 18).

Rumberger, Russell W. 2011. *Dropping Out: Why Students Drop Out of High School and What Can Be Done about It*. Cambridge, Mass.: Harvard University Press.

Sabol, William J. 2007. "Local Labor Market Conditions and Post-Prison Employment Experiences of Offenders Released from Ohio State Prisons." In *Barriers to Reentry? The Labor Market for Released Prisoners in Post-Industrial America*, edited by Shawn Bushway, Michael S. Stoll, and David F. Weiman. New York: Russell Sage Foundation.

Sabol, William J., Heather C. West, and Matthew Cooper. 2009. "Prisoners in 2008." *Bulletin* (December). Washington, D.C.: Bureau of Justice Statistics. https://www.bjs.gov/content/pub/pdf/p08.pdf.

Sampson, Robert J., and John H. Laub. 1992. "Crime and Deviance in the Life Course." *Annual Review of Sociology* 18: 63–84.

———. 1993. *Crime in the Making: Pathways and Turning Points through Life*. Cambridge, Mass.: Harvard University Press.

———. 1995. *Crime in the Making: Pathways and Turning Points through Life* (Revised Edition). Cambridge, MA: Harvard University Press.

———. 1997. "A Life-Course Theory of Cumulative Disadvantage and the Stability of Delinquency." In *Developmental Theories of Crime and Delinquency*, edited by Terence P. Thornberry. New Brunswick, N.J.: Transaction Publishers.

Sampson, Robert J., John H. Laub, and Christopher Wimer. 2006. "Does Marriage Reduce Crime? A Counterfactual Approach to Within-Individual Causal Effects." *Criminology* 44(3): 465–508.

Sampson, Robert J., Jeffrey D. Morenoff, and Felton Earls. 1999. "Beyond Social Capital: Spatial Dynamics of Collective Efficacy for Children." *American Sociological Review* 64(5): 633–60.

Sampson, Robert J., Stephen W. Raudenbush, and Felton Earls. 1997. "Neighborhoods and Violent Crime: A Multilevel Study of Collective Efficacy." *Science* 277(5328): 918–24.

Sampson, Robert J., Patrick Sharkey, and Stephen W. Raudenbush. 2008. "Durable Effects of Concentrated Disadvantage on Verbal Ability among African-American Children." *Proceedings of the National Academy of Sciences* 105: 845–52.

Sampson, Robert J., and William Julius Wilson. 1995. "Toward a Theory of Race, Crime, and Urban Inequality." In *Crime and Inequality*, edited by John Hagan and Ruth D. Peterson. Stanford, Calif.: Stanford University Press.

Sandefur, Gary D., Jennifer Eggerling-Boeck, and Hyunjoon Park. 2005. "Off to a Good Start? Postsecondary Education and Early Adult Life." In *On the Frontier of Adulthood: Theory, Research, and Public Policy*, edited by Richard A. Settersten Jr., Frank F. Furstenberg Jr., and Rubén G. Rumbaut. Chicago: University of Chicago Press.

Sawyer, Wendy, and Peter Wagner. 2019. "Mass Incarceration: The Whole Pie 2019." Northampton, Mass.: Prison Policy Initiative (March 19). https://www. prisonpolicy.org/reports/pie2019.html.

Schachter, Jason P. 2004. "Geographic Mobility: 2002 to 2003: Population Characteristics." *Current Population Reports.* Washington, D.C.: U.S. Census Bureau (March). https://www.census.gov/prod/2004pubs/p20-549.pdf.

Schneider, Daniel, and Kristen Harknett. 2019. "Consequences of Routine Work-Schedule Instability for Worker Health and Well-being." *American Sociological Review* 84(1): 82–114. DOI: 10.1177/0003122418823184.

Schnepel, Kevin. 2018. "Good Jobs and Recidivism." *Economic Journal* 128(608): 447–69.

Schnittker, Jason. 2014. "The Psychological Dimensions and the Social Consequences of Incarceration." *Annals of the American Academy of Political and Social Science* 651(1): 122–38.

Schnittker, Jason, and Andrea John. 2007. "Enduring Stigma: The Long-Term Effects of Incarceration on Health." *Journal of Health and Social Behavior* 48(2): 115–30. DOI: 10.1177/002214650704800202.

Schnittker, Jason, and Michael Massoglia. 2015. "A Sociocognitive Approach to Studying the Effects of Incarceration." *Wisconsin Law Review* 2015(2): 349–74.

Schnittker, Jason, Michael Massoglia, and Christopher Uggen. 2012. "Out and Down: Incarceration and Psychiatric Disorders." *Journal of Health and Social Behavior* 53(4): 448–64.

Schnittker, Jason, and Jane D. McLeod. 2005. "The Social Psychology of Health Disparities." *Annual Review of Sociology* 31(1): 75–103. DOI: 10.1146/annurev. soc.30.012703.110622.

Schnittker, Jason, Christopher Uggen, Sarah Shannon, and Suzy McElrath. 2015. "The Institutional Effects of Incarceration: Spillovers from Criminal Justice to Health Care." *Milbank Quarterly* 93(3): 516–60.

Schoeni, Robert, and Karen Ross. 2005. "Material Assistance Received from Families during the Transition to Adulthood." In *On the Frontier of Adulthood: Theory, Research, and Public Policy,* edited by Richard A. Settersten Jr., Frank F. Furstenberg Jr., and Rubén G. Rumbaut. Chicago: University of Chicago Press.

Schoon, Ingrid. 2015. "Diverse Pathways: Rethinking the Transition to Adulthood." In *Families in an Era of Increasing Inequality: Diverging Destinies,* edited by Paul R. Amato, Alan Booth, Susan M. McHale, and Jennifer Van Hook. London: Springer.

Schreck, Christopher J., Eric A. Stewart, and D. Wayne Osgood. 2008. "A Reappraisal of the Overlap of Violent Offenders and Victims." *Criminology* 46(4): 871–906. DOI: 10.1111/j.1745-9125.2008.00127.x.

Schulenberg, John E., Alison L. Bryant, and Patrick M. O'Malley. 2004. "Taking Hold of Some Kind of Life: How Developmental Tasks Relate to Trajectories of Well-being during the Transition to Adulthood." *Development and Psychopathology* 16(4): 1119–40. DOI: 10.1017/S0954579404040167.

Schulenberg, John, Patrick O'Malley, Jerald Bachman, and Lloyd Johnston. 2005. "Early Adult Transitions and Their Relation to Well-being and Substance Use." In *Frontier of Adulthood: Theory, Research, and Public Policy*, edited by Richard A. Settersten, Frank F. Furstenberg, and Rubén G. Rumbaut. Chicago: University of Chicago Press.

Schulenberg, John, and Ingrid Schoon. 2013. "The Transition to Adulthood across Time and Space: Overview of Special Section." *Longitudinal and Life Course Studies* 3(2): 164–72. DOI: 10.14301/llcs.v3i2.194.

Scott, Thomas L., Charles Wellford, Cynthia Lum, and Heather Vovak. 2019. "Variability of Crime Clearance among Police Agencies." *Police Quarterly* 22(1): 82–111. DOI: 10.1177/1098611118796597.

Seefeldt, Kristin S. 2017. "Serving No One Well: TANF Nearly Twenty Years Later." *Journal of Sociology and Social Welfare* 44(2): 3–28. https://heinonline.org/HOL/LandingPage?handle=hein.journals/jrlsasw44&div=20&id=&page=.

Seim, Josh. 2016. "Short-Timing: The Carceral Experience of Soon-to-Be-Released Prisoners." *Punishment and Society* 18(4): 442–58.

Seim, Josh, and David J. Harding. 2020. "Parolefare: Post-prison Supervision and Low Wage Work." *RSF: The Russell Sage Foundation Journal of the Social Sciences* 6(1): 173–95. DOI: 10.7758/rsf.2020.6.1.08.

Settersten, Richard A. 2005. "Social Policy and the Transition to Adulthood: Toward Stronger Institutions and Individual Capacities." In *On the Frontier of Adulthood: Theory, Research, and Public Policy*, edited by Richard A. Settersten Jr., Frank F. Furstenberg Jr., and Rubén G. Rumbaut. Chicago: University of Chicago Press.

Settersten, Richard A., Frank F. Furstenberg, and Rubén Rumbaut Jr. 2005. "On the Frontier of Adulthood: Emerging Themes and New Directions." In *On the Frontier of Adulthood: Theory, Research, and Public Policy*, edited by Richard A. Settersten Jr., Frank F. Furstenberg Jr., and Rubén Rumbaut. Chicago: University of Chicago Press.

Settersten, Richard A., Timothy M. Ottusch, and Barbara Schneider. 2015. "Becoming Adult: Meanings of Markers to Adulthood." In *Emerging Trends in the Social and Behavioral Sciences*, edited by Robert Scott and Stephan Kosslyn. New York: John Wiley & Sons. DOI: 10.1002/9781118900772.etrds0021.

Settersten, Richard A., and Barbara Ray. 2010. *Not Quite Adults: Why 20-Somethings Are Choosing a Slower Path to Adulthood, and Why It's Good for Everyone*. New York: Penguin Books.

Shanahan, Michael J. 2000. "Pathways to Adulthood in Changing Societies: Variability and Mechanisms in Life Course Perspective." *Annual Review of Sociology* 26: 667–92. DOI: 10.1146/annurev.soc.26.1.667.

Shapiro, Doug, Afet Dundar, Faye Huie, Phoebe Khasiala Wakhungu, Ayesha Bhimdiwala, and Sean Eric Wilson. 2018. "Completing College: A National View of Student Completion Rates—Fall 2012 Cohort." Signature Report 16. Herndon, Va.: National Student Clearinghouse (December).

Shapiro, Doug, Afet Dundar, Xin Yuan, Autumn T. Harrel, and Phoebe Khasiala Wakhungu. 2014. "Completing College: A National View of Student Attainment Rates—Fall 2008 Cohort." Herndon, Va.: National Student Clearinghouse Research Center (November). https://eric.ed.gov/?id=ED556471.

Sharkey, Patrick. 2010. "The Acute Effect of Local Homicides on Children's Cognitive Performance." *Proceedings of the National Academy of Sciences* 107(26): 11733–38. DOI: 10.1073/pnas.1000690107.

———. 2013. *Stuck in Place: Urban Neighborhoods and the End of Progress toward Racial Equality.* Chicago: University of Chicago Press.

———. 2018a. *Uneasy Peace: The Great Crime Decline, the Renewal of City Life, and the Next War on Violence.* New York: W. W. Norton.

———. 2018b. "The Long Reach of Violence: A Broader Perspective on Data, Theory, and Evidence on the Prevalence and Consequences of Exposure to Violence." *Annual Review of Criminology* 1(1): 85–102. DOI: 10.1146/annurev-criminol-032317-092316.

Sharkey, Patrick, and Jacob W. Faber. 2014. "Where, When, Why, and for Whom Do Residential Contexts Matter? Moving Away from the Dichotomous Understanding of Neighborhood Effects." *Annual Review of Sociology* 40(1): 559–79. DOI: 10.1146/annurev-soc-071913-043350.

Shaw, Clifford R., and Henry D. McKay. 1942. *Juvenile Delinquency and Urban Areas.* Chicago: University of Chicago Press.

Sherman, Lawrence W., and Heather M. Harris. 2013. "Increased Homicide Victimization of Suspects Arrested for Domestic Assault: A 23-Year Follow-up of the Milwaukee Domestic Violence Experiment (MilDVE)." *Journal of Experimental Criminology* 9(4): 491–514. DOI: 10.1007/s11292-013-9193-0.

———. 2015. "Increased Death Rates of Domestic Violence Victims from Arresting vs. Warning Suspects in the Milwaukee Domestic Violence Experiment (MilDVE)." *Journal of Experimental Criminology* 11(1): 1–20. DOI: 10.1007/s11292-014-9203-x.

Siennick, Sonja E., and D. Wayne Osgood. 2008. "A Review of Research on the Impact on Crime of Transitions to Adult Roles." In *The Long View of Crime: A Synthesis of Longitudinal Research,* edited by Akiva M. Liberman. New York: Springer-Verlag.

Silva, Jennifer M. 2013. *Coming Up Short: Working-Class Adulthood in an Age of Uncertainty.* New York: Oxford University Press.

Simon, Jonathan. 1993. *Poor Discipline: Parole and the Social Control of the Underclass, 1890–1990.* Chicago: University of Chicago Press.

———. 2007. *Governing through Crime: How the War on Crime Transformed American Democracy and Created a Culture of Fear.* Oxford: Oxford University Press.

Smeeding, Timothy M. 2017. "Multiple Barriers to Economic Opportunity for the 'Truly' Disadvantaged and Vulnerable." *RSF: The Russell Sage Foundation Journal of the Social Sciences* 2(2): 98. DOI: 10.7758/rsf.2016.2.2.04.

Smith, Douglas A. 1986. "The Neighborhood Context of Police Behavior." *Crime and Justice* 8: 313–41.

Smith, Peter Scharff. 2006. "The Effects of Solitary Confinement on Prison Inmates: A Brief History and Review of the Literature." *Crime and Justice: A Review of Research* 34: 441–528.

Smith, Sandra. 2007. *Lone Pursuit: Distrust and Defensive Individualism among the Black Poor*. New York: Russell Sage Foundation.

——. 2015. "Job-Finding among the Poor: Do Social Ties Matter?" In *Oxford Handbook of Poverty and Society*, edited by Linda M. Burton and David Brady. New York: Oxford University Press.

Solomon, Amy L., and Gillian L. Thomson, with Sinead Keegan. 2004. "Prisoner Reentry in Michigan." Research Report (October). Washington, D.C.: Urban Institute, Justice Policy Center. https://www.urban.org/sites/default/files/publication/58241/411172-Prisoner-Reentry-in-Michigan.PDF.

Soss, Joe, and Vesla Weaver. 2017. "Police Are Our Government: Politics, Political Science, and the Policing of Race-Class Subjugated Communities." *Annual Review of Political Science* 20(1): 565–91. DOI: 10.1146/annurev-polisci-060415-093825.

Spano, Richard, William Alex Pridemore, and John Bolland. 2012. "Specifying the Role of Exposure to Violence and Violent Behavior on Initiation of Gun Carrying: A Longitudinal Test of Three Models of Youth Gun Carrying." *Journal of Interpersonal Violence* 27(1): 158–76. DOI: 10.1177/0886260511416471.

Staff, Jeremy, and Jeylan T. Mortimer. 2008. "Social Class Background and the School-to-Work Transition." *New Directions for Child and Adolescent Development* 119: 55–69.

Stainbrook, Kristin, Jeanine Hanna, and Amy Salomon. 2017. *The Residential Substance Abuse Treatment (RSAT) Study: The Characteristics and Components of RSAT Funded Treatment and Aftercare Services: Final Report*. New York: Advocates for Human Potential. https://www.ncjrs.gov/pdffiles1/nij/grants/250715.pdf.

State of Michigan Department of Licensing and Regulatory Affairs. 2014. "Employer Handbook." Lansing: State of Michigan, Unemployment Insurance Agency (November). https://www.michigan.gov/documents/uia/Employer_Handbook1-14_455893_7.pdf.

Steele, Fiona. 2008. "Multilevel Model for Longitudinal Data." *Journal of the Royal Statistical Society*, series A-1 (1): 5–19.

Sugie, Naomi F. 2018. "Work as Foraging: A Smartphone Study of Job Search and Employment after Prison." *American Journal of Sociology* 123(5): 1453–91. DOI: 10.1086/696209.

Sugie, Naomi F., and Kristin Turney. 2017. "Beyond Incarceration: Criminal Justice Contact and Mental Health." *American Sociological Review* 82(4): 719–43. DOI: 10.1177/0003122417713188.

Sun, Ivan Y., Brian K. Payne, and Yuning Wu. 2008. "The Impact of Situational Factors, Officer Characteristics, and Neighborhood Context on Police Behavior: A Multilevel Analysis." *Journal of Criminal Justice* 36(1): 22–32.

Swartz, Teresa Toguchi, Minzee Kim, Mayumi Uno, Jeylan Mortimer, and Kirsten Bengtson O'Brien. 2011. "Safety Nets and Scaffolds: Parental Support in the Transition to Adulthood." *Journal of Marriage and Family* 73(2): 414–29. DOI: 10.1111/j.1741-3737.2010.00815.x.

Sweeten, Gary. 2006. "Who Will Graduate? Disruption of High School Education by Arrest and Court Involvement." *Justice Quarterly* 23(4): 462–80. DOI: 10.1080/07418820600985313.

———. 2012. "Scaling Criminal Offending." *Journal of Quantitative Criminology* 28(3): 533–57. DOI: 10.1007/s10940-011-9160-8.

Swisher, Raymond R., and Maureen R. Waller. 2008. "Confining Fatherhood." *Journal of Family Issues* 29(8): 1067–88. DOI: 10.1177/0192513x08316273.

Sykes, Bryan L., and Michelle Maroto. 2016. "A Wealth of Inequalities: Mass Incarceration, Employment, and Racial Disparities in U.S. Household Wealth, 1996 to 2011." *RSF: The Russell Sage Foundation Journal of the Social Sciences* 2(6): 129. DOI: 10.7758/rsf.2016.2.6.07.

Sykes, Gresham M. 1965. *The Society of Captives*. New York: Atheneum.

Teplin, Linda A., Gary M. McClelland, Karen M. Abram, and Darinka Mileusnic. 2005. "Early Violent Death among Delinquent Youth: A Prospective Longitudinal Study." *Pediatrics* 115(6): 1586–93. DOI: 10.1542/peds.2004-1459.

Thacher, David. 2010. "The Distribution of Police Protection." *Journal of Quantitative Criminology* 27(3): 275–98.

Thoits, Peggy A. 2006. "Personal Agency in the Stress Process." *Journal of Health and Social Behavior* 47(4): 309–23. DOI: 10.1177/002214650604700401.

———. 2010. "Stress and Health: Major Findings and Policy Implications." *Journal of Health and Social Behavior* 51(suppl. 1): S41–53. DOI: 10.1177/0022146510383499.

Toby, Jackson. 1957. "Social Disorganization and Stake in Conformity: Complementary Factors in the Predatory Behavior of Hoodlums." *Journal of Criminal Law and Criminology* 48(1): 12–17. https://scholarlycommons.law.northwestern.edu/cgi/viewcontent.cgi?article=4566&context=jclc.

Tonry, Michael. 1996. *Sentencing Matters*. New York: Oxford University Press.

Torche, Florencia. 2011. "Is a College Degree Still the Great Equalizer? Intergenerational Mobility across Levels of Schooling in the United States." *American Journal of Sociology* 117(3): 763–807. DOI: 10.1086/661904.

Travis, Jeremy. 2005. *But They All Come Back: Facing the Challenges of Prisoner Reentry*. Washington, D.C.: Urban Institute Press.

Travis, Jeremy, Amy L. Solomon, and Michelle Waul. 2001. *From Prison to Home: The Dimensions and Consequences of Prisoner Reentry*. Washington, D.C.: Urban Institute.

Travis, Jeremy, and Christy Visher. 2005. *Prisoner Reentry and Crime in America.* New York: Cambridge University Press.

Treskon, Louisa. 2016. "What Works for Disconnected Young People: A Scan of the Evidence." New York: MDRC (February). https://eric.ed.gov/?id=ED564456.

Turney, Kristin. 2015. "Liminal Men: Incarceration and Relationship Dissolution." *Social Problems* 62(4): 499–528. DOI: 10.1093/socpro/spv015.

Turney, Kristin, and Anna R. Haskins. 2014. "Falling Behind? Children's Early Grade Retention after Paternal Incarceration." *Sociology of Education* 87(4): 241–58. DOI: 10.1177/0038040714547086.

Turney, Kristin, Hedwig Lee, and Megan Comfort. 2013. "Discrimination and Psychological Distress among Recently Released Male Prisoners." *American Journal of Men's Health* 7(6): 482–93. DOI: 10.1177/1557988313484056.

Turney, Kristin, Jason Schnittker, and Christopher Wildeman. 2012. "Those They Leave Behind: Paternal Incarceration and Maternal Instrumental Support." *Journal of Marriage and Family* 74(5): 1149–65. DOI: 10.1111/j.1741-3737.2012.00998.x.

Turney, Kristin, and Sara Wakefield. 2019. "Criminal Justice Contact and Inequality." *RSF: The Russell Sage Foundation Journal of the Social Sciences* 5(1): 1. DOI: 10.7758/rsf.2019.5.1.01.

Turney, Kristin, and Christopher Wildeman. 2013. "Redefining Relationships: Explaining the Countervailing Consequences of Paternal Incarceration for Parenting." *American Sociological Review* 78. DOI: 10.1177/0003122413505589.

——. 2018. "Maternal Incarceration and the Transformation of Urban Family Life." *Social Forces* 96(3): 1155–82. DOI: 10.1093/sf/sox070.

Tyler, Elizabeth Tobin, and Bradley Brockmann. 2017. "Returning Home: Incarceration, Reentry, Stigma, and the Perpetuation of Racial and Socioeconomic Health Inequity." *Journal of Law, Medicine, and Ethics* 45(4): 545–57. DOI: 10.1177/1073110517750595.

Tyler, John H., and Jeffrey R. Kling. 2007. "Prison-Based Education and Reentry into the Mainstream Labor Market." In *Barriers to Reentry? The Labor Market for Released Prisoners in Post-Industrial America,* edited by Shawn Bushway, Michael Stoll, and David Weiman. New York: Russell Sage Foundation.

Tyler, John H., and Magnus Lofstrom. 2009. "Finishing High School: Alternative Pathways and Dropout Recovery." *Future of Children* 19(1): 77–103. https://eric.ed.gov/?id=EJ842053.

Tyler, John H., Richard J. Murnane, and John B. Willett. 2000. "Estimating the Labor Market Signaling Value of the GED." *Quarterly Journal of Economics* 115(2): 431–68. DOI: 10.1162/003355300554818.

Uggen, Christopher. 1999. "Ex-Offenders and the Conformist Alternative: A Job Quality Model of Work and Crime." *Social Problems* 46(1): 127–51.

——. 2000. "Work as a Turning Point in the Life Course of Criminals: A Duration Model of Age, Employment, and Recidivism." *American Sociological Review* 65(4): 529–46.

Uggen, Christopher, Mike Vuolo, Sarah Lageson, Ebony Ruhland, and Hilary Whitham. 2014. "The Edge of Stigma: An Experimental Audit of the Effects of Low-Level Criminal Records on Employment." *Criminology* 52(4): 627–54.

Uggen, Christopher, and Sara Wakefield. 2006. "Young Adults Reentering the Community from the Criminal Justice System: The Challenge of Becoming an Adult." In *On Your Own without a Net: The Transition to Adulthood for Vulnerable Populations*, edited by D. Wayne Osgood, E. Michael Foster, Constance Flanagan, and Gretchen R. Ruth. Chicago: University of Chicago Press.

Umberson, Debra, Robert Crosnoe, and Corinne Reczek. 2010. "Social Relationships and Health Behavior across the Life Course." *Annual Review of Sociology* 36: 139–57.

Umberson, Debra, and Jennifer Karas Montez. 2010. "Social Relationships and Health: A Flashpoint for Health Policy." *Journal of Health and Social Behavior* 51(suppl. 1): S54–66. DOI: 10.1177/0022146510383501.

University at Albany, Hindelang Criminal Justice Research Center. 2011. *Sourcebook of Criminal Justice Statistics*, table 6.66.

Upchurch, Dawn M., and James McCarthy. 1990. "The Timing of a First Birth and High School Completion." *American Sociological Review* 55(2): 224–34. https://eric.ed.gov/?id=EJ411312.

U.S. Bureau of Labor Statistics. 2015. "Projections of Industry Employment, 2014–24." *Career Outlook* (December). Washington: U.S. Bureau of Labor Statistics. https://www.bls.gov/careeroutlook/2015/article/projections-industry.htm.

——. 2019. "Unemployment Rate in Michigan [MIUR]." Retrieved from FRED Economic Data, Federal Reserve Bank of St. Louis, https://fred.stlouisfed.org/series/MIUR.

U.S. Department of Education. 2011. "Characteristics of GED Recipients in High School: 2002–06." NCES 2012-025. Washington: U.S. Department of Education, National Center for Education Statistics (November). https://nces.ed.gov/pubs2012/2012025.pdf.

Valentine, Colby L., Daniel P. Mears, and William D. Bales. 2015. "Unpacking the Relationship between Age and Prison Misconduct." *Journal of Criminal Justice* 43(5): 418–27. DOI: 10.1016/j.jcrimjus.2015.05.001.

Visconti, Adam J., Glenn Milo Santos, Nikolas P. Lemos, Catherine Burke, and Phillip O. Coffin. 2015. "Opioid Overdose Deaths in the City and County of San Francisco: Prevalence, Distribution, and Disparities." *Journal of Urban Health* 92(4): 758–72. DOI: 10.1007/s11524-015-9967-y.

Visher, Christy A. 1991. *A Comparison of Urinalysis Technologies for Drug Testing in Criminal Justice*. Washington: U.S. Department of Justice, Office of Justice Programs, National Institute of Justice.

Visher, Christy, Sara Debus, and Jennifer Yahner. 2008. "Employment after Prison: A Longitudinal Study of Releasees in Three States." Washington, D.C.: Urban Institute (October). https://www.urban.org/sites/default/files/

publication/32106/411778-Employment-after-Prison-A-Longitudinal-Study-of-Releasees-in-Three-States.PDF.

Visher, Christy, Vera Kachnowski, Nancy La Vigne, and Jeremy Travis. 2004. "Baltimore Prisoners' Experiences Returning Home." Washington, D.C.: Urban Institute (March). https://www.opensocietyfoundations.org/sites/default/files/baltimore_prisoners.pdf.

Visher, Christy, Nancy G. La Vigne, and Jeremy Travis. 2004. *Returning Home: Understanding the Challenges of Prisoner Reentry Maryland Pilot Study: Findings from Baltimore*. Washington, D.C.: Urban Institute, Justice Policy Center (January). https://www.urban.org/sites/default/files/publication/42841/410974-Returning-Home-Understanding-the-Challenges-of-Prisoner-Reentry.PDF.

Visher, Christy A., and Jeremy Travis. 2003. "Transitions from Prison to Community: Understanding Individual Pathways." *Annual Review of Sociology* 29: 89–113.

Wacquant, Loïc. 2001. "Deadly Symbiosis: When Ghetto and Prison Meet and Mesh." *Punishment and Society* 3(1): 95–133.

———. 2009. *Prisons of Poverty*. Minneapolis: University of Minnesota Press.

Wagner, Peter. 2012. "Incarceration Is Not an Equal Opportunity Punishment." Northampton, Mass.: Prison Policy Initiative (August 28). https://www.prison policy.org/articles/notequal.html.

Wagner, Peter, and Wendy Sawyer. 2018. "States of Incarceration: The Global Context 2018." Northampton, Mass.: Prison Policy Initiative (June). https://www.prisonpolicy.org/global/2018.html.

Wakefield, Sara, and Christopher Uggen. 2010. "Incarceration and Stratification." *Annual Review of Sociology* 36: 387–406.

Wakefield, Sara, and Christopher Wildeman. 2013. *Children of the Prison Boom: Mass Incarceration and the Future of American Inequality*. New York: Oxford University Press.

Wald, Michael S. 2006. "Where Do We Go from Here? Using Knowledge to Improve Policy and Practice for Disconnected Youth." *Temple Law Review* 79(1): 607–16.

Wang, Emily A., Mark Pletcher, Feng Lin, Eric Vittinghoff, Stefan Kertesz, Catarina I. Kiefe, and Kirsten Bibbins-Domingo. 2009. "Incarceration, Incident Hypertension, and Access to Health Care: Findings from the Coronary Artery Risk Development in Young Adults (CARDIA) Study." *Archives of Internal Medicine* 169(7): 687–93.

Wang, Emily A., Yongfei Wang, and Harlan M. Krumholz. 2013. "A High Risk of Hospitalization Following Release from Correctional Facilities in Medicare Beneficiaries: A Retrospective Matched Cohort Study, 2002 to 2010." *JAMA Internal Medicine* 173(17): 1621–28. DOI: 10.1001/jamainternmed.2013.9008.

Warner, Cody. 2015. "On the Move: Incarceration, Race, and Residential Mobility." *Social Science Research* 52: 451–64. DOI: 10.1016/j.ssresearch.2015.03.009.

——. 2016. "The Effect of Incarceration on Residential Mobility between Poor and Nonpoor Neighborhoods." *City and Community* 15(4): 423–43. DOI: 10.1111/cico.12207.

Warr, Mark. 1993. "Parents, Peers, and Delinquency." *Social Forces* 72(1): 247–64.

——. 1998a. "Life-Course Transitions and Desistance from Crime." *Criminology* 36(2): 183–216.

——. 1998b. "Life-Course Transitions and Desistance from Crime." *Criminology* 36(2): 183–216.

Waters, Mary C., Patrick Joseph Carr, Maria Kefalas, and Jennifer Ann Holdaway. 2011. *Coming of Age in America: The Transition to Adulthood in the Twenty-First Century.* Berkeley: University of California Press.

Wayman, Jeffrey. 2001. "Factors Influencing GED and Diploma Attainment of High School Dropout." *Education Policy Analysis Archives* 9(4): 1–19.

Weaver, Velsa M. 2007. "Frontlash: Race and the Development of Punitive Crime Policy." *Studies in American Political Development* 21(2): 230–65.

Weaver, Velsa M., and Amy E. Lerman. 2010. "Political Consequences of the Carceral State." *American Political Science Review* 104(4): 817–33.

Weaver, Vesla M., Andrew Papachristos, and Michael Zanger-Tishler. 2019. "The Great Decoupling: The Disconnection between Criminal Offending and Experience of Arrest across Two Cohorts." *RSF: The Russell Sage Foundation Journal of the Social Sciences* 5(1): 89. DOI: 10.7758/rsf.2019.5.1.05.

Western, Bruce. 2002. "The Impact of Incarceration on Wage Mobility and Inequality." *American Sociological Review* 67(4): 526–46.

——. 2006. *Punishment and Inequality in America.* New York: Russell Sage Foundation.

——. 2008. "From Prison to Work: A Proposal for a National Prisoner Reentry Program." Washington, D.C.: Brookings Institution (December). https://www.brookings.edu/wp-content/uploads/2016/06/12_prison_to_work_western.pdf.

——. 2015. "Lifetimes of Violence in a Sample of Released Prisoners." *RSF: The Russell Sage Foundation Journal of the Social Sciences* 1(2): 14–30. DOI: 10.7758/rsf.2015.1.2.02.

——. 2018. *Homeward: Life in the Year after Prison.* New York: Russell Sage Foundation.

Western, Bruce, Anthony A. Braga, Jaclyn Davis, and Catherine Sirois. 2015. "Stress and Hardship after Prison." *American Journal of Sociology* 120(5): 1512–47. DOI: 10.1086/681301.

Western, Bruce, Anthony Braga, and Rhiana Kohl. 2017. "A Longitudinal Survey of Newly-Released Prisoners: Methods and Design of the Boston Reentry Study." *Federal Probation* 81(1): 32–40.

Western, Bruce, and Sara McLanahan. 2001. "Fathers behind Bars: The Impact of Incarceration on Family Formation." *Contemporary Perspectives in Family Research* 2: 309–24.

Wexler, Harry K., Gregory P. Falkin, and Douglas S. Lipton. 1990. "Outcome Evaluation of a Prison Therapeutic Community for Substance Abuse Treatment." *Criminal Justice and Behavior* 17(1): 71–92.

Wight, Vanessa R., Michelle Chau, Yumiko Aratani, Susan Wile Schwarz, and Kalyani Thampi. 2010. "A Profile of Disconnected Young Adults in 2010." New York: Columbia University, National Center for Children in Poverty (December). http://nccp.org/publications/pdf/text_979.pdf.

Wildeman, Christopher, E. Ann Carson, Daniela Golinelli, Margaret E. Noonan, and Natalia Emanuel. 2016. "Mortality among White, Black, and Hispanic Male and Female State Prisoners, 2001–2009." *SSM—Population Health* 2: 10–13. DOI: 10.1016/j.ssmph.2015.12.002.

Wildeman, Christopher, Jacob S. Hacker, Vesler M. Weaver, and Trace R. Burch. 2014. "Effects of Imprisonment and Community Supervision on Neighborhood Political Participation in North Carolina." *Annals of the American Academy of Political and Social Science* 651(1): 184–201. DOI: 10.1177/0002716213503093.

Wildeman, Christopher, and Christopher Muller. 2012. "Mass Imprisonment and Inequality in Health and Family Life." *Annual Review of Law and Social Science* 8: 11–30.

Wildeman, Christopher, Margaret E. Noonan, Daniela Golinelli, E. Ann Carson, and Natalia Emanuel. 2016. "State-Level Variation in the Imprisonment-Mortality Relationship, 2001–2010." *Demographic Research* 34(1): 359–72. DOI: 10.4054/DemRes.2016.34.12.

Wildeman, Christopher, Jason Schnittker, and Kristin Turney. 2012. "Despair by Association? The Mental Health of Mothers with Children by Recently Incarcerated Fathers." *American Sociological Review* 77(2): 216–43. DOI: 10.1177/0003122411436234.

Wildeman, Christopher, Kristin Turney, and Jason Schnittker. 2014. "The Hedonic Consequences of Punishment Revisited." *Journal of Criminal Law and Criminology* 104(1): 133–63.

Wildeman, Christopher, and Emily A. Wang. 2017. "Mass Incarceration, Public Health, and Widening Inequality in the USA." *Lancet* 389(10077): 1464–74. DOI: 10.1016/S0140-6736(17)30259-3.

Williams, David R., and Chiquita Collins. 2001. "Racial Residential Segregation: A Fundamental Cause of Racial Disparities in Health." *Public Health Reports* 116(5): 404–16. http://www.ncbi.nlm.nih.gov/entrez/query.fcgi?cmd=Retrieve&db=PubMed&dopt=Citation&list_uids=12042604.

Willison, Janeen Buck. 2019. "Response to 'Wrap-Around Services Don't Improve Prisoner Reentry Outcomes.'" *Journal of Policy Analysis and Management* 38(2): 514–16.

Wilson, William Julius. 1987. *The Truly Disadvantaged: The Inner City, the Underclass, and Public Policy.* Chicago: University of Chicago Press.

———. 1996. *When Work Disappears: The World of the New Urban Poor.* New York: Alfred A. Knopf.

Wimer, Christopher, and Dan Bloom. 2014. "Boosting the Life Chances of Young Men of Color: Evidence from Promising Programs." New York: MDRC (June). https://eric.ed.gov/?id=ED545310.

Winship, Christopher, and Joe Krupnick. 2015. "Keeping Up the Front: How Young Black Men Avoid Street Violence in the Inner City." In *Bringing Culture Back In: New Approaches to the Problems of Disadvantaged Black Youth,* edited by Orlando Patterson and Ethan Fosse. Cambridge, Mass.: Harvard University Press.

Wolfgang, Marvin E., and Franco Ferracuti. 1967. *The Subculture of Violence: Towards an Integrated Theory in Criminology.* London: Tavistock Publications.

Wyse, Jessica J. B., David J. Harding, and Jeffrey D. Morenoff. 2014. "Romantic Relationships and Criminal Desistance: Pathways and Processes." *Sociological Forum* 29(2): 365–85. DOI: 10.1111/socf.12088.

Xu, Jiaquan, Sherry L. Murphy, Kenneth D. Kochanek, and Elizabeth Arias. 2016. "Mortality in the United States, 2015." NCHS Data Brief 267. Washington: U.S. Department of Health and Human Services, National Center for Health Statistics (December). https://www.cdc.gov/nchs/data/databriefs/db267.pdf.

Yi, Youngmin. 2019. "Leaving Home, Entering Institutions: Implications for Home-Leaving in the Transition to Adulthood." *Journal of Marriage and Family* (October 25). DOI: 10.1111/jomf.12616.

Young, Alford. 2004. *The Minds of Marginalized Black Men: Making Sense of Mobility, Opportunity, and Future Life Chances.* Princeton, N.J.: Princeton University Press.

Zaff, Jonathan F., Kei Kawashima Ginsberg, Michelle J. Boyd, and Zenub Kakli. 2014. "Reconnecting Disconnected Youth: Examining the Development of Productive Engagement." *Journal of Research on Adolescence* 24(3): 526–40. DOI: 10.1111/jora.12109.

Index

Boldface numbers refer to figures and tables.